THE RUSSIAN SHORES OF THE BLACK SEA

LAURENCE OLIPHANT

THE RUSSIAN SHORES
OF THE BLACK SEA

AND

A JOURNEY TO KATMANDU

KÖNEMANN

© 1998 for this edition
Könemann Verlagsgesellschaft mbH
Bonner Straße 126, D–50968 Köln

Series and volume editor: Michael Hulse
Cover design: Peter Feierabend
Layout and typesetting: Birgit Beyer
Printed in Hungary
ISBN 3-8290-0894-5
10 9 8 7 6 5 4 3 2 1

CONTENTS

THE RUSSIAN SHORES OF THE BLACK SEA

CHAPTER X

CHAPTER XI

CHAPTER XII

CHAPTER XIII

CHAPTER XIV

CHAPTER XV

A JOURNEY TO KATMANDU

THE RUSSIAN SHORES
OF THE BLACK SEA

IN THE AUTUMN OF 1852
WITH A VOYAGE DOWN THE VOLGA,
AND A TOUR THROUGH THE COUNTRY
OF THE DON COSSACKS

PREFACE TO THE SECOND EDITION

The Eastern Question has now assumed so serious an aspect, that facts connected with the Russian Shores of the Black Sea, which at the period of my visit in 1852 were devoid of any special political interest, are invested with the utmost importance, for it is possible that the southern portion of the Empire may shortly become the theatre of war, and considerations, the value of which I scarcely appreciated a few months ago, have since occurred to me as possessing strong claims upon our attention. Some of these I have now endeavoured to embody in an additional chapter; and while the publication of a Second Edition enables me to do this, I gladly avail myself of the opportunity which it also affords, of gratefully acknowledging the very favourable reception which the public has accorded to this work.

December 1853.

PREFACE TO THE FIRST EDITION

It may seem singular that there is no country in Europe about which so little has been written, and about which, consequently, so little is known, as that vast empire of Russia, which absorbs in itself half the Continent, and which, from its extent and position, would seem to demand a principal share of the attention of those nations whose destinies it may one day control; and yet it is not very difficult to account for this, when the great difficulty of obtaining authentic information is considered.

The system of government renders it impossible that any light should be thrown upon the present condition of the Empire from internal sources, while few strangers are tempted to extend their travels beyond St. Petersburg or Moscow. It is not an inviting country to the dilettante tourist, for the accommodation is execrable—the means of locomotion barbarous—the obstacles thrown in the way by Government annoying—and the results, with respect to fine arts, literature, and social life, comparatively unworthy of his attention. Nor does Russia possess those charms for the more enterprising traveller which a new and unexplored country offers.

Since, then, the scanty information which the public already possesses has been of such a nature as to create an indifference towards acquiring more, I should have felt it necessary to offer some apology for publishing this volume, had not the events which have agitated Europe for the last six months induced me to suppose that an excuse is no longer needed for giving some account of those more remote provinces of the Empire of the Autocrat through which my travels led me. Upon my arrival at St. Petersburg, circumstances induced me to change the plans I had originally entertained of visiting the rivers which run into the White Sea, for the purpose of salmon-fishing, and I have found no reason to regret the alteration in my route, since it furnished me with objects of interest of a more useful and solid description.

At a time when the power of Russia seems about to be tested, and its vast resources called into requisition, the shores of the Volga are invested with an increased importance, for Russian Tartary is the granary of the Empire.—If the Imperial forces are again to be matched with the armies of the West, the country of the Don Cossacks possesses an especial claim upon our attention, for the soldiers which are levied from its boundless steppes occupy the most prominent position among Muscovite troops.—So long as the independence of Turkey is menaced by its insatiate neighbour, associations of the deepest significance attach to those provinces bordering upon the Black Sea which Russia has appropriated to herself within the last sixty years, and which compose a territory as extensive as all that remains in Europe of the ill-fated empire from which they have been plundered.

But though the prominence of a topic so engrossing as Russian aggression, at the present crisis, lends an immediate interest to everything which seems to have reference to it, there can be no doubt that any information upon the internal economy of the Empire is deserving of more general attention than has been hitherto accorded to it, since its importance must increase with the growing influence of Russia over the rest of Europe. Yet, while strongly impressed that a desire for a more extended knowledge of the subject would produce most beneficial effects, I am fully conscious of my own inability to create it. This must be my excuse for not venturing more frequently beyond the simple course of my narrative.

The claims which the once celebrated kingdom of Crim Tartary has upon our notice, however, rest upon other grounds than its political associations. I trust, therefore, that they may be more easily recognised; and if I can succeed in giving some idea, however inadequate, of the magnificent scenery, romantic cities, and interesting inhabitants of the Crimea, I shall feel, at least, that I have offered the only tribute in my power to those charms which seem to have imposed this obligation upon me.

October 1853.

CHAPTER I

Our first ordeal—The Izak's church—Sham fight at Krasna Selo—Leave St. Petersburg—A Russian railway—Railroads: their extension, and political influences—Arrival at Moscow—The Church of St. Basil—The Ryädi—Journey to Nijni Novgorod— First view of the Fair—Our quarters

St. Petersburg will amply repay the traveller for the expenditure of temper which, except in the case of a favoured few, will be the consequence of a visit to the Russian capital. Let him, therefore, cheerfully endure the delay of two hours at Cronstadt, just when the gilded domes and cupolas, which glitter at his journey's end, look most inviting—let him unhesitatingly plunge into the smoky cabin of the little steamer, where a dozen mustached officials, seated in an atmosphere of stale tobacco, and overpowered by a sense of their own importance, are busily engaged in recording the private history of himself and his fellow-passengers; nor should he grudge them an exaggerated estimate of the authority with which they are vested, or sneer at the pomposity with which they put their questions, or deem those inquiries impertinent, which are simply the result of a most laudable curiosity on the part of the government. He may be less disposed to make allowances for the severe torture to which he will be subjected at the custom-house; but the consciousness of being in St. Petersburg at last must compensate for this; and after a few hours' delay, by dint of wholesale bribery, he will probably be released with half his baggage; and then, if his stay in the metropolis is not to be a very long one, he should commence taking the steps necessary for his departure, almost before he can be said fairly to have entered the city; for, having once put the government to so much trouble by coming there at all, he thenceforward becomes an object of its most tender care and solicitude—not that he ought ever to get tired of wandering along the spacious

21

quays, or admiring the architectural beauties of St. Petersburg while he rattles furiously over the execrable pavement, clinging to a frail drosky. Everything is new but the pavement and the droskies; and if locomotion by the latter be not enjoyable, it has the merit of being, in the first place, singular, from the manner in which the passenger seats himself across a cushion behind the driver; and, secondly, exciting from the extreme difficulty he finds in retaining his seat there, which is considerably increased when a wheel comes off—an incident of not unfrequent occurrence.

I found it impossible to see the lions of St. Petersburg with any sort of composure; the consciousness of Moscow being attainable in twenty-two hours by railway ever disturbed me; and thus it happened that I strolled discontentedly through the sumptuous halls of the Winter Palace, looked upon the Hermitage as a necessary evil, and was glad to find that one visit sufficed for the Izak's church. I can, perhaps, hardly be excused for this. Modern art has reared few edifices comparable with this cathedral, which no doubt owes some of its charm to a kind of barbaric character with which it is invested. Those lofty monoliths carry one back to a period of architecture long anterior to that of the Corinthian capitals with which they are crowned, when nations loved to perpetuate their greatness by monuments of a more lasting nature than do their more civilised posterity. To convey these gigantic masses of stone from the morasses of Finland, required a power almost as vast as that of which the evidences remain to this day in Egypt and Assyria. The rest of the building is Byzantine; and the barbaric tinge thus given to it, only renders it all the more in keeping with the religion to which it is consecrated.

But even those visions of the Kremlin which had hitherto haunted me, vanished before the excitement of a grand field-day at Krasna Selo. Nearly a hundred thousand men were here reviewed by the Emperor. The enormous camp extended for many miles; and on the vast plain beyond it, took place the sham fight which was to close the evolutions. From the heights above the plain we had a most magnificent view of the various manœuvres. Half of the army, consisting of upwards of forty thousand men, under General Count Rüdiger, engaged the other half under the Emperor, whose forces occupied the plain. Like a long silver thread, immense bodies of Circassian cavalry, their steel helmets and cuirasses glittering in the morning sun, came winding into the field. Soon after, the horse-artillery dashed over the heights, and we were nearly carried away by a charge of hussars, while vainly endeavouring to understand what was going on. The result was, that the Emperor's army retired behind the trenches near their camp, when a heavy cannonading ensued. The whole was rendered more interesting by the fact of each general being wholly ignorant of the tactics of his opponent; and, though I understood afterwards that the board of umpires had given their verdict in favour of the Emperor, as an impartial spectator, and wholly unlearned in military matters, seeing his forces in full retreat, I naturally concluded that he had lost the day; and so, perhaps, did Count Rüdiger.

I had an opportunity in the evening of meeting at dinner some of the officers at the "English club," which, with the exception of three or four Englishmen, is composed entirely of Russians. Here they refreshed themselves, after the labours of the day, with porter and champagne mixed in large jugs; or played skittles—a most aristocratic game in the Muscovite capital, and one upon which immense sums are lost and won.

I was glad to find that my friend, to whose agreeable companionship throughout our travels I owe the beguilement of many a tedious hour, was as prepared as I to bid adieu to St. Petersburg. We accordingly proceeded, bag and baggage, to the station of the Moscow Railway. Only one train starts daily; and the hour at which this most important event takes place is, or ought to be, 11 A.M. Travellers are commanded by the government to be at the station at 10 precisely; and even then they are liable to be told that the train is full—as it is quite an unheard-of thing to put on an extra carriage for any number of passengers. Having arrived, therefore, at ten minutes before 10, to be quite sure of being in time, our luggage was seized by a soldier, policeman, or railway porter (for they all wear somewhat the same uniform), and carried in one direction, while we rushed in another to show our passport for Moscow, to procure which we had been to three different offices the day before. Here the description of our persons and our reasons for travelling, which it contained, being copied at full length, we were hurried to another counter, where we got it stamped; whence, catching sight of our baggage *en passant*, we sped on to the ticket office, and then, returning to our portmanteaux, went through a few formalities, which ended in receiving a ticket to add to the number of those with which our pockets were now pretty well filled. The anxiety of mind which such a variety of documents causes is not to be wondered at, when the consequences which the loss of any of them would entail are considered. Ladies in Russia do not think of trying to carry their tickets in their gloves. We now betook ourselves to the waiting-room, which we should have thought handsome had we not been detained in it so long that we got tired of admiring it.

For an hour did the destined occupants of the train sit patiently on the benches, every man with head uncovered—for even a skull-cap is an abomination to a Russian under a roof. Everyone in military garb seemed to have the *entrée* to the platform, while the doors were rigorously shut against us unhappy civilians. At a quarter before 11, however, they are opened—a general rush follows, and we are hurried through a barrier, the doors of which close behind us. Soon the whole barrier becomes thronged with people, waving their adieux as ardently as if we were booked for Australia. A bell, a whistle, and a sort of dull attempt at a scream, are, as in more civilised parts of the world, the signals for starting; we leave the weeping eyes and waving pocket-handkerchiefs behind us, and, in the course of ten minutes, find, to our satisfaction, that we have increased our speed to fifteen miles an hour. We have hardly done so ere we arrive at a station. Everybody rushes out and lights a cigarette. We are to stop here ten minutes, and the people during that time walk up and down the platform and smoke; then we huddle into our old places, and have time to look about us. The carriages are large. Nobody seems to go in the first class. A second-class carriage accommodates about fifty people. They are built as in Austria and America, with a passage in the centre, perambulated by a man in uniform, who occasionally asks people for their tickets. He seems to make the inquiry the first time to satisfy himself that you have got one, and afterwards merely as an amusement, which he apparently enjoys the more if he fancies you are going to sleep. The men are bearded and dirty, and relate stories in a loud tone of voice, for the benefit of the whole company, most of whom have evidently never been in a railway before. At every station the same scene ensues. The unsmoked ends of the last station's cigars, having been carefully preserved, are lighted afresh, and vehemently smoked on the platform during five or ten minutes, as the case may be.

The stations are all very spacious and uniformly constructed, with an immense domed building for engines, attached to each. Though there is only one passenger-train daily, there are three goods-trains, always well loaded with inland produce, tallow, fur, tea, &c., or with cotton from St. Petersburg to the interior. I should hardly think the line could possibly pay; but as it is a government concern, nobody has any means of ascertaining this fact. Whether it pays or not, the railway traveller in Russia soon discovers that the requirements of trade are as little regarded by government as his own personal convenience; for the restrictive policy of the empire must ever neutralise, in a great measure, the beneficial effects of rapid internal communication, while the difficulties which have always been placed in the way of free mercantile intercourse exist in full force, though the physical obstacles by which it has hitherto been encompassed are overcome. In fact, though the public cannot but be benefited by the formation of railroads throughout a country, it is hardly for the public benefit that railroads are constructed here. Russian railroads seem to be meant for Russian soldiers; and it is the facility thus afforded of moving large bodies of men, that invests this mode of communication in Russia with an importance which does not attach to it in Great Britain, or perhaps any other country in Europe, to an equal extent.

When St. Petersburg, Moscow, Odessa, and Warsaw become connected, Russia assumes an entirely new position with regard to the rest of Europe. A few days, instead of many months, will then suffice to concentrate the armies of the north and south upon the Austrian or Prussian frontiers. Through this same quarter of the world, many hundred years ago, poured those barbaric hordes which overran civilised Europe;—it would, indeed, be a singular testimony to the spirit of the age, if the next invaders made their descent by means of railroads.

It is not to be supposed, however, that railways in Russia are to effect no change whatever upon the commercial relations of the empire. It is certain not only that the civilising tendencies of railways will be felt here, but that the results will be all the more marked that the country which they intersect is rude and barbarous. At present, one of the most striking proofs of the primitive condition of trade in Russia is to be found in the existence of those numerous fairs which are annually celebrated all over the empire, and which are incidental to a country of such vast extent, such a scattered population, and so totally devoid of adequate means of internal communication.

That fairs in Russia perform the functions of large towns in other countries, seems apparent from the fact that the whole urban population of the empire is not more than five millions—only about double that of London. The ultimate result of an extensive system of railway communication would be the abolition of such remnants of barbarism; as, with greater facilities of intercourse, trade would increase, and towns spring up; markets would be in existence all the year round; and roads not now thought of would become necessary, as lateral means of communication to and from the line. At the same time, it is to be remarked that the absence of these very roads at present is a serious drawback to the success of railways in Russia.

It has undoubtedly been the traditionary policy of the empire to consider the commercial prosperity of the country as second in importance to the extension of its political influence. It is interesting to compare the probable results of this policy with that of England under somewhat similar circumstances, and to observe how different may be the effects produced by the introduction of railways in one country, from those which characterise their existence in another. The railways that traverse England in every direction, have not altered her political aspect with regard to the rest of Europe, except as they have affected and extended her commercial relations; while the prosperity of the nation has increased to an unparalleled extent, by reason of the entire change which railway communication has wrought upon the mercantile transactions of the country. In Russia, on the other hand, the only important railway which has recently been completed, invests the empire with an interest which it never before possessed in the eyes of Europe; and the formation of others now in progress, will mark the period at which the other Continental nations were first compelled to measure the political influence of this mighty empire by an altogether new standard. How long it will be ere Russia exerts an indirect influence upon the commercial relations of other countries by means of her railways, or even works that great change upon her own social system already predicted, is a problem somewhat difficult of solution.

We completed our journey of four hundred and fifty miles in twenty-two hours.

The country throughout is tame and uninteresting. Now and then a picturesque wooden village is seen, but generally a sort of fir-scrub lines the railway. There are no tunnels, but some large rivers are crossed by bridges of considerable elevation. On arriving at Moscow, we were nearly torn to pieces by the Isvoschiks or drosky boys, who afterwards did their best to jolt us together again before arriving at Mr. Pickersgill's hotel. After renovating ourselves there, we were in a condition to commence a survey of the town, and sallied forth to delight our eyes with the lovely and unique views from the Kremlin, and to explore the wonders of its far-famed precincts.

I was puzzled to decide which was the most striking—the prospect stretching before us as we stood upon the terrace under the shadow of the great bell, in which green roofs and tapering steeples, or gilded domes and star-spangled cupolas, met the eye on every side—while the river, spanned by two picturesque bridges, and covered with boats from distant provinces, flowed smoothly at our feet: or whether, whilst leaning against the parapet of the wooden bridge beneath, and gazing upwards at the confused mass of buildings enclosed by the quaint old turreted wall, I was not still more fascinated with that vast assemblage of cathedrals and palaces. Here were the remnants of a barbaric age, which had escaped an almost universal destruction, mingled with the elaborate productions of modern art still unfinished, in style and architecture so strangely dissimilar, yet here placed side by side, while seeming to bear as much affinity to one another as the Taj and the Tuileries; the whole, nevertheless, so happily grouped, that the combination, far from leaving any painful impression on the mind from its singularity, seemed absolutely necessary to the composition of a picture altogether unrivalled in its novelty.

Outside the walls, and forming a foreground, stands the Church of St. Basil, well worthy its prominent position. If the buildings in the Kremlin be like Eastern temples and modern palaces, this is an edifice which can certainly lay claim to being unlike anything ever before produced in any part of the world. Its grotesque appearance and brilliant colouring at first sight would have rendered me insensible to that charm which I could not ultimately fail to perceive in the quaint irregularity of its buildings, while a certain solemnity of position and character pervaded the whole; and at last it became my greatest favourite among the buildings which stand near, and seem in vain to rival it.

The Church of St. Basil, Moscow

The interior of the Kremlin is worthy of attention no less than the exterior. The Church of the Assumption is one of the most fantastically ornamented even of Greek churches; while the gorgeous state-rooms in the palace, only completed within the last year, may safely be pronounced the handsomest in Europe. Passing with uncovered head through the Stass Vorota, or Gate of the Redeemer, where sentries are stationed to enforce the usual mark of respect due to the picture suspended in the archway, the traveller will soon become involved in an inextricable maze of streets; but he will wander on, quite content to lose himself amid objects of such novel and varied interest.

One rainy day we took refuge in the covered passages of the Ryädi, an Eastern-looking bazaar, where the owners of gay open shops vociferously entreated us to inspect the strange assortment of wares thus ostentatiously exhibited, and seemed quite surprised at our resisting their pressing invitations to become purchasers of coloured wax-lights, glittering wedding crowns, or huge gaudy pictures of hard-favoured saints. Wearied with the incessant cry of Paschaltz, and finding that we ran a great chance of being drenched by the shower-baths which in places deluged these galleries, we adjourned to a famous tea-shop, where we were waited upon by the cleanest of waiters, soothed by fragrant tobacco, and regaled by the most delicious tea, in company with an immense number of bearded devotees of that beverage for which Russia is so justly famed. Here we were first initiated into the orthodox way of drinking it with a slice of lemon as a substitute for milk.

Though the droskies and pavements of Moscow are, if possible, more execrable than those of St. Petersburg, and the streets far less handsome, the city itself is much more interesting than the modern metropolis. We determined, therefore, after visiting the great fair at Nijni Novgorod, to return here and explore at our leisure those attractive scenes in which we had already revelled; a design which the facilities offered by steam of descending the Volga induced us afterwards to abandon.

The journey from Moscow to Nijni occupies two days and two nights, and is performed in a comfortable roomy diligence. The road is a *chaussée* macadamized, evidently warranted to last for ever. Notwithstanding its general excellence, it proved treacherous in one or two places. I say *it* in order to avoid accusing the government of having left sundry sloughs with apparently the express intention of disturbing the slumbers of unfortunate travellers. Upon our becoming firmly imbedded in one of these about two in the morning, we felt our indignation rise with every vain attempt to extricate the large vehicle. Nor was it much appeased by the midnight tramp through the mud which our mishap entailed. Fortunately some return post-horses came up, on which we laid violent hands; and by dint of expending an amount of caresses and oaths which a Russian driver could alone lavish, and which Russian horses could alone appreciate, we succeeded in dragging our ponderous conveyance out of the hole. We were too sleepy on the following night to care about a wheel coming off, which delayed us for two hours. The country all the way is undulating, and the road, upon the old Roman principle, preserves an undeviating course, utterly regardless of hills and ravines. We passed through whole seas of oats and buckwheat—then over tracts of pasture, on which were scattered large herds of cattle, and through which meandered considerable streams—and finally plunged into a vast expanse of pine forest, thence again to emerge upon fresh fields, arrive at fresh post-houses, and get fresh horses. The process of changing horses generally lasts about half an hour, which, when one considers the complexity of the arrangement by which they are attached to the carriage, does not seem an immoderately long time. In the post-house excellent tea is always to be procured, and a strong flavour of garlic must generally be endured while drinking it.

During the continuance of the great fair of Nijni Novgorod there is no lack of traffic along this road; and at one station I counted no fewer than seven carriages, each having four horses: these, which look more like large rats, are harnessed four abreast, and hunted along by loud cries from the bearded Yamschik. They have extraordinary powers of endurance, and one team took us twenty-six miles in four hours, without appearing distressed.

Every eight or ten miles we rattled through a wooden village, the houses all standing detached at some little distance from the road, and highly ornamented—the picturesque church with its green cupolas occupying the centre. Still there is a little to vary the monotony of the road; and it was with no small satisfaction that, on the forty-seventh hour after leaving Moscow, we saw the white walls of Nijni on a distant hill, while its golden domes glittered brightly in the first ray of sunshine we had rejoiced in for nearly a week. Shortly afterwards we were galloping over the sandy island on which the annual fair takes place, desolate for the greater part of the year, but now teeming with a vast and varied population, inhabiting the temporary dwellings which our heavy vehicle seemed to shake as it rumbled past.

We were set down at an office, in the midst of a confused mass of merchandise, people, and droskies.

Our first object was to disentangle ourselves from the crowd; our next, to find some sort of accommodation. Securing three droskies, we dashed up and down the winding streets, looking in vain for some place that was not a shop or warehouse. At least half of the dense multitude through which we passed must have lived nowhere; they were certainly dirty enough to warrant the suspicion that the lanes and alleys formed their only resting-place. Being unable to speak a word of the language, our Isvoschiks did not in the least seem to understand the object of our search. It was to them a most unusual thing that anybody who came to Nijni should wish to go to an inn, and they probably expected us to pull up at some unoccupied corner, and, spreading out the contents of our portmanteaux, extemporise a shop in the mud, with a view to the immediate realisation of profit.

At last we found a kind German merchant, who directed us to a more substantial part of the town, where we obtained possession of a small dirty room, in which, worn out with fatigue, we were glad to spread ourselves and our baggage. Here our ears were dinned by three of the loudest bells that ever called pious worshippers to church, our noses assailed by the foulest odours that ever a Russian even could imagine, and our skins tortured by more innumerable hosts of fleas than the combined experiences of Eastern travellers ever recounted; but yet, as we afterwards discovered, few could boast of better quarters than ourselves at the grand fair of Nijni Novgorod.

CHAPTER II

There are so many different meanings attached to the word
fair, and the purposes for which people assemble together at
what they designate by this term are occasionally so very
different, that those who have only visited the fairs of their
own country can have no just conception of the divers means
which other nations employ in their celebration; and,
therefore, before beginning to describe the sensations which,
as an Englishman, I experienced at a Russian fair, it seems right
to speculate upon what the probable feelings of a Russian
would be on visiting what have been called fairs in our own
country.

Let us suppose, for instance, that, on a rumour reaching
Nijni, in the early part of the year 1851, of the preparations
being made for the celebration of the World's Fair in Hyde
Park, an inhabitant of that town, considering himself rather a
judge of fairs, had intimated to the government his desire to
visit England;—let us further suppose that, having obtained the
necessary permission, he has reached London about the
beginning of May; he would there observe a large proportion
of a certain class of the population transferring themselves, by
means of steamboat and railway, to a steep grassy hill on the
banks of the Thames; and if, impelled by a stranger's curiosity
to become acquainted with the manners and customs of the
people among whom he is, he followed in the wake of this
extensive emigration, upon arriving at the aforesaid hill, he
would find himself struggling with a crowd of a very
miscellaneous description. At one moment he is jostled by a

respectable middle-aged couple, who are straining every nerve to reach a distant platform, allured thither by a brass band and some young ladies in tights, who flutter before the crowd for a few moments, and then disappear, followed by a multitude eager to see the show, a representation of which waves gracefully over the brass band. At another, he is requested to take a penny peep at the sun through a telescope, or wearied with pressing solicitations to take shots with sticks at distant toys, disposed in the form of a druidical circle, for the small charge of a halfpenny each. In short, wandering, stunned and stupified, amid shows, tents, and booths, he gazes with bewilderment at the noisy excited throng and their various occupations, apparently so insane, wondering if these are the evidences of English civilisation; and as he sees gentlemen deliberately engage partners for the purpose of rolling down the hill, he may perhaps regret that the barbarism of his education prevents his duly appreciating this amusement. He will perceive, by the peculiar costume and dialect of many of the men, that they belong to distinct tribes; and he may afterwards discover that the Cockney is a native of the city of London; while the swell-mob are a nomadic race, living a careless life, with indistinct ideas as to the rights of property, like the Calmucks of his own country. Proof of this, more personal than pleasant, will not be wanting; and he will hurry back to London, crushed, bewildered, and robbed, there to be told that his misfortunes are a necessary consequence of an inexperienced visit to Greenwich Fair; and so, when soon afterwards he hears that the World's Fair—for the purpose of seeing which he has undertaken so long a journey—is to commence, he congratulates himself upon his recently acquired experience; and, with a firm resolve of braving British eccentricities to the utmost, he buttons up his empty pockets, with the air of a man prepared for the worst, and fights his way to the Crystal Palace. But a very different scene from what he expected awaits him there; for as he enters the fairy-like structure, and, surrounded by the noblest of the land, is an eyewitness of a ceremony rendered as imposing as the pomp of royalty could make it, he is overcome by a display which owes much of its effect to the circumstances under which it takes place; for never before has he seen collected under one roof, and that a glass one, the representatives of every country, as well as specimens of their arts and manufactures.

When at last he bids adieu to the wonders of the Exhibition, and, while journeying back to the steppes of Russia, contrasts these different scenes, the English seem to him a people more and more incomprehensible; and he wonders which, in his own country, would be esteemed the most unnatural—that the great fair of his native town should be opened by the Emperor and nobility in *propriis personis*, or that those tribes who had come from distant lands should occupy themselves with throwing sticks at toys, or rolling in pairs down the steep hill that overhangs the Volga.

But when he reaches his destination, and forms one of the busy throng at this the third fair he has witnessed in as many months, all these varied scenes will rise up in review before him; and he may moralise, perchance, on the pervading spirit of each,—may recognise, in the noisy multitude at Greenwich, the love of pleasure as the prevailing object; in the vast European assemblage at the Crystal Palace, the nobler desire for instruction predominant; while the more engrossing pursuit of gain is all-powerful to attract from distant quarters the motley groups at Nijni.

To us, as strangers, the earnest, business-like appearance of the people was especially striking. There was evidently no time to be lost in merry-go-rounds or penny shows. Here fortunes were to be lost or won in a few short weeks. The rich merchant had brought valuable wares from distant lands at an enormous expense; the poor pedlar had trudged many a weary mile with his heavy pack: both had staked their all on the results of their transactions in the allotted time, and were in no humour to trifle with it. It had evidently never struck them that Nijni fair was a place to which people would resort either for pleasure or instruction, or for anything but gold; and certainly, interesting though it was, some such motive as the last would be required to induce a second visit. The fair is held on a low sandy spot of land, formed by the junction of the Oka and the Volga, and which is subject to constant inundation in winter. The substantial part of it, inhabited by the wealthy merchants, is arranged in twelve parallel streets, composed of neat two-storeyed brick houses, the lower part forming the shops and warehouses, which are protected by covered verandahs. Each street terminates at one end in a pagoda, indicating the Chinese quarter; while at the other it is connected with a square, where the governor's house and public offices are situated.

This respectable nucleus is encompassed by a deep border of temporary wooden huts, inhabited by an indescribable swarm of ragged Tartars, Tchouvasses, Kirghees, and Calmucks, besides the peasantry of the neighbourhood, who frequent the fair with provisions, fruit, and all sorts of farm and country produce. A long bridge of boats across the Oka connects this busy peninsula with the hill on which is situated the town of Nijni, commanding an extensive view of the whole scene. Both rivers are covered with every conceivable shape and description of boat and barge; some from the distant Caspian, laden with raw or spun cotton, Persian shawls, Georgian carpets, and Bukharian skins, or dried fruits: these vessels, of square unwieldy construction, are elaborately painted and ornamented, and on their decks are erected curious wooden habitations, from the peaked roofs of which flutter gaudy flags, while out of the carved windows peep Eastern maidens. Others, rude and strongly built, have come down the Kama with Siberian iron or tea; while the more civilised appearance of a few denotes their Western origin, and these have threaded their way from the shores of the Baltic, laden with the manufactured goods of Europe. On board this singular mixture of craft is found as singular a mixture of inhabitants, whole families coming from their distant homes to take some share in what—now that the Exhibition exists no longer in that capacity—may resume its old title of the World's Fair.

Our abode was situated in a suburb on the opposite side of the river, so that it was necessary to cross the bridge of boats every time we wished to visit the fair; and here the confusion was always the greatest. We were obliged to struggle our way, if on foot, amidst sheepskins, greasy enough to scent us for the rest of our lives, thereby adding to the store of fleas with which we had started from our lodging. Women, with waists immediately under their throats, and petticoats tucked up to their knees, tramped it gallantly through the mud, and made better progress than we could. A Cossack on horseback rode up and down the bridge for the purpose of keeping order amid the droskies, which, heedless of the rules of the road, dashed in every direction, apparently bent upon splashing those they did not run over. Drunken men continually stumbled against us; and when at last we reached the slough on the opposite side, the confusion and hubbub were greater than ever. The mud in the shallowest parts was at least two feet in depth, and nearly everybody waded about in it with Russian leather jack-boots. Numbers of small shops surrounded the bespattered populace, while a few miserable attempts at shows only proved how little they were appreciated. At the corners of the streets running into this delectable hole were stationed Cossacks, who showered blows upon offending Mujiks or

peasants with their heavy-lashed whips, without regard to the nature of the offence or the size of the victim. Turning up one of these streets, and penetrating further into the fair, other scenes and pleasanter forms meet the eye. The gay dress of the Georgian forms a pleasing contrast to the everlasting sheepskin; and, as we enter the shop of the Tiflis merchant, beautifully embroidered slippers, rich table-covers, and the finest silks are spread out temptingly before us; and it is fortunate for our pockets that we have a steppe journey in prospect, and the vision of sundry custom-houses afterwards. In the next shop are handsome furs and skins piled in every available corner, and the owner of the valuable collection stands at the door, his flowing robe and dignified demeanour betokening his Eastern origin. Aaron was, in fact, a Bukharian Jew, who delighted to show us his costly wares, even though there was no chance of our becoming purchasers; and, finally, regaled us with almonds, split peas, and raisins—flattered, perhaps, by the admiration we expressed at the belt he wore, the buckle of which, composed of solid silver, was set with turquoises. But it would be hopeless to attempt a description of the costumes of the different merchants and shopkeepers, or to enumerate the variety of articles exposed for sale.

The Bukharians, Persians, and Georgians inhabit one quarter, which is likely to prove the most interesting to the stranger; and I recognised in the countenances of many of the representatives of these nations, a strong resemblance to some old Affghan and Persian horse-dealing friends. It is a convenient arrangement, no less for the sight-seer than the merchant, that the fair is divided into quarters, devoted to the sale of different merchandise. The Ketaiski Red, or Chinese division, is at once distinguishable by the rows of square leather boxes which contain the tea. No Chinaman, however, displayed his pigtail in the crowd, much to our dis-appointment, the transfer being made at Kiahta, whence the tea comes overland to the Kama, down which river it is conveyed to the Volga. In the cutlers' quarter I was surprised to find so great a preponderance of Russian ware; still Sheffield maintains its own, and the prices are much lower than in St. Petersburg; indeed this is the case with all English or foreign goods, which, though subject to a most exorbitant duty on entering Russia, may be procured more cheaply here, on account of the comparative facility with which they can be exposed for sale. The guild dues at St. Petersburg are so high, that the merchant, after paying 2000 rubles (*assignation*) for his position in the first Guild, and 2000 or 3000 rubles more for his shop on the Nevski Prospect, has but little margin left for his profits.

The whole system seems most elaborately devised to destroy all enterprise, and to depress as much as possible the spirit of trade, in a country which naturally possesses it in but a very limited degree; and it must be long ere the resources of the country can be properly developed while the government seeks its own aggrandisement regardless of the prosperity of the community, since the protection it affords to home manufactures, by the duty on foreign goods, is effectually neutralised by the expenses attendant upon the sale and manufacture of the home produce itself. At Nijni, however, these difficulties do not exist; the only expense is house rent; and thus it happens that foreign goods are to be procured more cheaply here than they can be at a seaport seven hundred miles nearer the country from whence they come; and, in some instances, the manufactured articles of a Russian town some hundreds of miles distant, are to be found here exposed for sale at lower prices than in the very town where they have been produced—an anomaly which is quite in accordance with the political economy of the country. The palpable result of all this is, that the variety of goods brought to Nijni for sale far exceeds what it would be, were there not so many attendant advantages to counterbalance the expense of transport; and the traveller has only to wander along the narrow, insignificant-looking streets of the fair, to find articles which he would be unable to obtain in the handsomest shops of St. Petersburg and Moscow. He, therefore, owes the Russian government at least one debt of gratitude for procuring him a more extensive assortment of goods than he would find collected anywhere else in the same space.

The greatest quantity of raw produce comes from the East, either down the Kama or up the Volga. Besides tea from China, the barges down the former river bring quantities of Siberian iron, furs, and skins, together with curious-looking wooden boxes, covered with lacquered tin, which seemed to be in great request; while madder, hides, dried fruits, Caucasian wines, and fish, are among a few of the articles which come from the countries bordering on the Caspian. It was an endless source of interest to us Westerns to explore the Eastern quarter; while, no doubt, our Western manufactures prove still more attractive to the ragged-looking Kirghees, or half-tamed Tartars. It is generally the case, where much business is done, that the most important transactions are negotiated in a quiet way; and so at Nijni, a dirty little Frankfort Jew may be seen in the back shop of some dignified aristocratic-looking Armenian, true to his vocation and calling, driving his bargain as keenly as if he had one of his own persuasion to haggle with. All distinctions of rank are forgotten in that more engrossing pursuit which attracts people so many thousands of miles, and through so many difficulties. Here persons of the most opposite persuasions fraternise with the greatest harmony, and form pleasing contrasts to the eye of him who comes only to be a passive spectator of the novel scene; should he even venture on a purchase, he is comforted by the consideration that he is being cheated by a dealer, perhaps, from the frontiers of China. As there is little or no duty on Asiatic produce, it can be procured here at a proportionably lower rate than any Western manufactures, and therefore doubles in extent the total amount of the importations from European countries.

Those articles of commerce to which most attention seemed directed—and which form, indeed, the main features of the fair to a stranger's eye—were teas and furs from the East, and silk and cotton goods from the West. England supplies the great quantity of indigo which is annually sold here, and used extensively as a dye throughout Russia. The governor's house, to which is attached the police-office, is a large well-built edifice: the whole of the lower storey is devoted to commercial purposes, and forms a most Eastern-looking bazaar, quite in keeping with the shawls and carpets here tastefully arranged for sale. These handsome shops, a fashionable coffeehouse, and a military band every afternoon, always drew together a large concourse of idlers, who found the covered piazza an agreeable lounge. To this coffeehouse we were obliged daily to resort, since no Russian inn is expected to provide food for its inmates; and here, surrounded by merchants and traders from almost every country under heaven, we made sundry nondescript repasts, our ears regaled the while by two harps and a fiddle. Once we tried a purely Armenian eating-house; but though both the company and dishes were national, and unlike anything we had seen or eaten before, we were not tempted to repeat the visit.

When evening came, and, worn out with the fatigue and excitement of the day, we would bestride a rickety drosky, and rattle towards the bridge we had traversed in the morning, a somewhat similar scene to that then displayed was enacted. Now we were buried in mud, splashed from neighbouring droskies—now almost jostled from our precarious perch—or so jammed amid other vehicles, that I frequently found a horse's head resting on my shoulder. We were, therefore, thankful at last to reach our gaunt comfortless-looking mansion, and take what rest therein the fleas would allow us. The windows of our small ill-furnished bedroom looked out upon the bustling street which connected the fair with the town, and the want of comfort indoors was in some measure compensated for by the street scenes which we occasionally witnessed. Now and then a grandee with a lumbering vehicle, to which six or eight horses were attached, rolled heavily past; or the light private drosky conveyed the business man to his mercantile avocations.

Just opposite to us, in a small niche near a chapel, hung a picture of the Virgin, and it was amusing to watch the amount of devotion which each passer-by thought it necessary to bestow. The most devout passengers were old women, who never failed to make long and repeated reverences before the holy picture. The next most scrupulous class were the Mujiks, who, with beards as greasy and ragged as their sheepskins, blocked up the way for a quarter of an hour at a time, bowing reverentially to the ground, throwing back their long tangled locks every time they crossed themselves, and evidently feeling deeply the necessity and importance of the ceremonies they were performing. After them came the young women, who seldom passed without a sort of nod, either as an acknowledgment of the respect due, or because they thought it wiser to be on the safe side in case of accidents; at any rate, they did not feel called upon to linger among Mujiks or old women, to go through a ceremony by no means becoming. Next in order came the priests, who paid as little veneration to the picture as decency would permit—perhaps because they had better at home. Of the remaining crowds that daily passed the chapel, few did more than take off their hats, and the more respectable part of the population took no notice of it whatever.

The terrace on the summit of the hill overhanging the Volga, on which the town of Nijni is situated, commands a most singular and interesting view of the fair and the two rivers, upon which a swarm of human beings seems to have hived, whose dwellings, aquatic and terrestrial, cover both land and water for a considerable distance. Immediately below us was the crowded bridge of boats; while from the tops of hundreds of masts, on each side of it, fluttered vanes, and often gay-coloured flags. At the junction of the Oka and Volga were warehouses and primitive-looking temporary wharves, near which, however, were six or eight business-like steamers and loaded barges; on the low flat beyond, one hundred and fifty thousand people, crowded into the smallest possible space, ply their avocations. This human hive is only in existence six weeks in the year, during which time it is visited by upwards of three hundred thousand people.

The town of Nijni is interesting, chiefly from its position on the brow of an abrupt hill, in a country where hills of any sort are scarce, and from its containing a genuine old Kremlin, and a few handsome churches. The hill is composed of soft clay soil, which has been run into gullies and ravines, rugged and abrupt enough to give a wild character to the scene; while the thick wood which clothes the steep banks, and from which pretty cottages peep out, softens it into one of great beauty.

As the sun set warmly upon it, and cast a pleasant genial glow over the hillside, we were glad to have our backs turned upon the noise and turmoil of the fair, to which the calm still scene before us formed so strong a contrast; and we thought that peaceful Nijni could surely have nothing in common with the bustling scene below, and must long for the day when the unsightly excrescence should disappear, and leave it to enjoy its quiet beauty undisturbed.

CHAPTER III

Laying in stores—Getting under weigh—A collision—A narrow escape—Russian steam companies—Dishonesty practised by employés—The "Samson," and her crew—Mackarief—Maza— Sketching under difficulties—A sudden apparition— Rechievahs—Corn trade on the Volga—Horse-machines— Intricate navigation—Pericartes—Mysterious visitors—The Tchouvasses: their manners and customs—Curious shields

We had spent five days at Nijni, had learnt the fair by heart, and explored the old town with its romantic cliffs and wooded dells; and it was, therefore, with no small satisfaction, that we embarked on board the Volga Steam Navigation Company's steam-tug "Samson," bound for Astrakhan, which ought to have left some days before, but had never managed to effect a start. The passenger-boats down the Volga do not go farther than Kazan, and the steamers going beyond that place are mere tugs, not carrying cargo themselves, but generally towing two or three heavily-laden barges down the river, and starting as soon as possible after these are ready. As their departure is entirely dependent upon the police, it is impossible to say when the officials in that department may think fit to give up the necessary papers. None of these gentry receive more pay than is sufficient to keep them in cigars, and their subsistence in a great measure depends upon what they can levy from the public by direct taxation; consequently, as nobody can predict the exact day on which all the clerks will consider themselves adequately bribed, there can be no fixed time for the departure of the steamers.

In consequence of the purely commercial character of the traffic of these boats, passengers are obliged to lay in their own stock of provisions for the voyage—a most arduous under-taking for people who could not speak a word of the language. We found it impossible to procure a servant at Nijni who knew any other language than Russian, and were, therefore, obliged to make our purchases of the necessaries of life by signs. Finally, we became very expert in driving a bargain, by means of wooden beads strung upon parallel wires, and fastened into a square frame. With these originally-constructed tables a Russian shopkeeper performs the most elaborate calculations with the greatest rapidity; and though rather perplexing at first, we found them very useful and convenient indicators of sums, which it would have been hopeless to attempt expressing in any other way.

As Nijni shopkeepers do not send articles purchased to the dwelling of the buyer, we were employed for the greater part of the day preceding our embarkation in rushing through the muddy streets in droskies, with packages of bread, meat, and potatoes under our arms; for a drosky is not meant to carry anything but a man, and would certainly not be considered capable of doing that anywhere but in Russia. These we finally stowed away in a sumptuous cabin; for, being the only passengers, we were put in exclusive possession of the afterpart of the ship, and took up our quarters on board, as being more comfortable than those we had vacated on shore. It was a pleasant change, and we enjoyed the soft evening as we lay surrounded by hosts of quaint shipping. We had not calculated, however, upon spending it in the dark, and were much dismayed on being told that no lights were allowed on board the craft in the river. As we had put off our dinner until a fashionable hour, we were guided chiefly by instinct during that meal, and afterwards were fain to wrap ourselves in our plaids, and, stretched on a capacious mattress, soon became independent of light or darkness.

Our delays seemed never ending; for though, upon the following day, the papers arrived, we were obliged to wait until the barges had floated themselves over the first shallows—a feat we had no sooner seen them accomplish in safety, than it was rumoured that the second engineer was nowhere to be found, but that he was probably locked up in the station-house. However, the anchor was weighed without further delay, and we glided gently past Nijni, which looked more beautiful than ever. After rounding the peninsula on which it is situated, we came upon a lovely nook, where the monastery of Pietcherskie, almost hidden in a thickly-wooded glen, appeared an enviable retreat from the cares of the world. A straggling village, picturesquely built of rough logs, nestled along the base of the cliffs, here about 200 feet high, and completed a more charming prospect than I had supposed the Volga capable of affording.

Here the first barge awaited us, heavily laden with Siberian iron and Western manufactures for the Astrakhan and Persian markets. Having taken her in tow, we proceeded prosperously, till a sudden jerk startled us; and scarcely had we discovered that our vessel was hard and fast on a sand-bank, before the barge, which had considerable way on her from the speed at which we had been going, scraped rapidly past, and the tow-rope, getting foul, swept over our deck, carrying away some of the funnel-stays, and creating much confusion. There is great danger to unwary loungers on deck when such occurrences take place. A mere touch from the end of the tow-rope as it sweeps along would certainly break a leg, if it did no greater damage; and the whole thing is so sudden, that occasionally there is great difficulty in getting out of the way. Upon the last voyage a man had been knocked overboard and drowned, under similar circumstances. Immediately on the steamer touching the ground, those on board the barge should have let go the anchor. Through some clumsiness this was not done, and the consequences might have been serious. As it was, another detention for two or three hours was the only annoyance which resulted from the accident.

This was a fitting time and place to become enlightened upon the subject of *pericartes*, a word I had never heard before I experienced this practical demonstration of its meaning. During the next three weeks, pericartes formed the most engrossing topics of conversation, while they afforded us admirable opportunities of exercising all our spare philosophy. Of all the navigable rivers of Europe, there is probably none so uncertain and difficult of navigation as the Volga. Seldom very deep, the channel is in many places devious, and, as the bed is composed of loose sand, is ever changing. These shallows are called pericartes; and as they occur very frequently, either the barges or the steamer were constantly running aground. Those immediately below Nijni are esteemed some of the worst on the river, and numerous craft are generally to be seen hopelessly imbedded in them.

At last our boat floated off, but it was only to drop anchor once more, and wait for the missing engineer. While gazing wistfully down the stream, in the direction we seemed destined never to go, I was once more aroused by a sudden crash, and found that another barge had fairly run into us, toppling over and staving in a quantity of casks she had on board, and very nearly breaking our rudder. I was standing near the tiller chains at the time, and as they suddenly jerked round, my leg was caught, and jammed against the side of the vessel, thus affording me personal experience of the risk attendant upon this sort of concussion. Fortunately the buttons of my boot gave way, and I had the satisfaction of seeing it severely crushed instead of my foot, which was just pulled out in time—not, however, without receiving a warning squeeze. The barge had suffered more than we had, and all hands were employed stuffing tow into a large hole in her side. After having progressed only fourteen versts, we anchored for the night, as (the channels being so intricate) it is always out of the question to proceed after dark.

Notwithstanding the difficulties attendant upon the navigation of the Volga, there are upwards of thirty steamers plying upon it. The two principal companies are—the Volga Steam Navigation Company, of which the managers and many of the shareholders are English; and the Mercury, a purely Russian company, which is managed, or rather very much mismanaged, by Russians.

Perhaps the most serious impediment to the successful

prosecution of commercial enterprise in Russia, is the impossibility of finding *employés* upon whose honesty any reliance can be placed. All Russians are so much in the habit of cheating their government, that they are unable to divest themselves of this propensity where the pockets of private individuals are concerned. Nor do rank or station offer any guarantee, since greater responsibilities only afford greater facilities for successful peculation. The experiences of the Volga Steam Company amusingly illustrate the truth of this. It was found that while the affairs of the company were managed by some Russian gentlemen resident at Nijni, there was a heavy annual loss; and, notwithstanding the certain prospect of remuneration which the speculation had originally held out, it became apparent that, unless an entire change took place in the circumstances of the Volga Steam Company, that respectable association would soon be inevitably bankrupt. Some Englishmen were consequently deputed to inquire into a state of matters so extremely unsatisfactory. They at once discovered that a system of wholesale robbery had been practised by the agents, to such an extent that the deficiencies were easily accounted for. Among other ingenious contrivances resorted to for appropriating the company's funds, the most highly approved was that of sharing the demurrage obtained by the owners of cargo upon those barges which were detained beyond a certain time upon their voyage. It was easily arranged between the merchants, the captains of the steam-tugs, and the managers at Nijni, that these delays should frequently occur; and as the amount of demurrage was regulated by the length of their duration, the company was mulcted of large sums, and these worthy associates divided the spoil. Since then the affairs of the company are managed by Englishmen, who are rapidly making up the losses sustained under the Russian administration.

During the months of May and June, boats ply between Astrakhan and Rhybinski, beyond Yaroslaf, and barges then make their way on to Tver, whence the goods can either be forwarded by water to St. Petersburg, or transferred to the railway, and conveyed by it to that city or to Moscow. The navigation of the river generally closes about the end of October; and, during the winter, the whole river as far as the Caspian is frozen over. The boats, meanwhile, are laid up at Kriusky, near Simbirsk, and other convenient places.

The Volga Company owns twelve or fifteen steamers, all employed as tugs, and none drawing more than five feet of water. The "Samson" was a powerful boat, with excellent accommodation; our cabin being most comfortably fitted up, and measuring twenty feet by twelve. In fact, the only doubtful point which can arise, as regards the passengers, is on the question of provisions. As much as possible should be laid in before starting, few articles being procurable at the wood stations. However, with the exercise of a little judicious domestic arrangement, we managed to fare very well. The traveller will probably have become accustomed to Russian diet before he gets as far as the Volga, and consequently will not be very particular.

On the following morning we made fast our second barge, on the deck of which were erected a number of cabins, occupied by sixty or seventy merchants and travellers returning from the fair; and, with these two cumbrous attendants, we pursued our course down the river, under a brighter sun, and more favourable auspices altogether, than we had started with from Nijni the day before. The late incidents had so fully occupied our thoughts, that hitherto I had found time to make but few observations on the company with whom the next two or three weeks were to be spent. The captain was the primary consideration, a most good-natured, warm-hearted Dutchman—presenting an agreeable contrast to the boors by whom he was surrounded. Secondly, there was a loquacious mate, who said he had been to Kamschatka, and gave me a great deal of interesting information upon Russian North America; but the captain slily hinted that his voyages had been limited to the Mediterranean and the Baltic. There were four stalwart pilots, with large red beards, round fur caps, and sheepskin coats, between whom and the captain differences of opinion were not unfrequent; and there were the crew, with loose trousers tucked into huge jack-boots, and red shirts fluttering outside—thus reversing the usual arrangement of those garments. This is, indeed, the costume of the Mujik generally. Lastly, there was a shrivelled old woman, who acted as a sort of housekeeper to the captain, and cook to the passengers.

The right bank of the river, with the exception of a few miles before arriving at Vasil Soursk, varies in height from one hundred to three hundred feet; in some places it almost seems to overhang the river, while steep ravines intersect it in every direction; but more frequently it swells gently back, clothed to the summit with fine trees; while up some picturesque glen the wooden houses cluster, and the green cupolas of the village church peep forth, contrasting agreeably with the opposite shore, as it stretches away, tame, flat, and uninteresting. The river itself varies from one to two miles in breadth, and occasionally the stream is very rapid. About ninety versts from Nijni, and almost upon the water's edge, stands the monastery of Mackarief, facing a noble reach of the river. It is shaded by some beautiful trees, and, as seen from the steamer, appears a spacious pile. A wall, flanked by four round towers, encloses two churches and some smaller buildings. At the town of the same name, not far distant, the fair used to be held, which was afterwards transferred to Nijni.

On the opposite bank, a large wooden village seems to adhere to the side of the steep hill. Long flights of wooden stairs descend from the houses to the water's edge, where quantities of boats are lying. Higher up, the white stems of the birch trees shine amongst the others, with a singular and pleasing effect.

A few versts after leaving Mackarief, we arrived at our first wood station, and made fast under a steep bank, on which were piled large stacks of birch logs. Loading with wood is an operation which usually occupies six or seven hours. If the annoyance of coal-dust is unbearable, the noise involved in the process of *wooding* is no less so. It is, moreover, of such frequent occurrence, that it proves almost as serious a source of delay as do the pericartes. Every two days our hold was filled, and all the available corners above deck, as well as below, were piled with wood. In forty-eight hours, every stick had vanished in the most marvellous manner; and it was always a matter of wonder to me how the furnaces had managed to consume so vast a store in so short a time.

A verst or so from the river bank, and situated in a pine wood, lay the secluded little village of Maza. We astonished the unsophisticated inhabitants by our sudden appearance among them, and forthwith numbers of girls trooped down to the steamer with long sticks, on which to carry the wood they were to put on board. Passing up the little street, I watched the process of construction of one of the log-houses I had so frequently admired, and observed the peasants stuff moss into the interstices, which, while it no doubt added materially to the comfort of the dwelling, gave it a rough, unfinished look, to which the extremely elaborate carving on the overhanging gable-end formed an odd contrast. Altogether, these are not unlike Tyrolese houses; and the one which, to judge from its highly decorated state, I concluded to be the residence of the village chief, or "Starista," might fairly challenge a comparison with the picturesque habitation of Andreas Hofer.

Strolling along the outskirts of the village, armed with our sketch-books, we came upon a charming view, which only required a distant peep of the Volga to make it perfect. This desirable object would have been easily attained, had some friendly hillock or tree been near to afford us the requisite altitude. For lack of such convenience, my friend and I determined to mount an outhouse, most temptingly situated; and by means of a high paling we easily reached the thatched roof, up which we scrambled, at the risk of falling through upon the cows, or whatever else our shed might have contained. Having attained the ridge-pole, we were rewarded by the prospect of a fine bend of the river, stretching away bright and glistening. While thus engrossed, I was aroused by voices, and on looking down, we found ourselves, not unnaturally, the objects of interest to a small group of men, who seemed engaged in discussing the wonderful phenomenon above them, of two human-looking beings, attired in unknown costumes, destitute alike of sheepskins and of beards, most mysteriously employed. To judge from the deferential manner in which one, bolder than the others, addressed us, he supposed at least that we were spirits in shooting-jackets, who, descending from some brighter world to visit oppressed serfs, had found their first resting-place on the roof of the little shed they were so unconcernedly bestriding. We answered an unintelligible inquiry he addressed to us, by pointing to the river, and enunciating the word "Volga," as being the only one common to us both, thereby meaning him to infer what our real purpose had been, but probably only inducing the belief that we had been summoned from the vasty deep, rather than from the clouds above, to take notes of what was transpiring in "Maza." After some consultation among themselves, and ineffectual attempts at communication, they gradually dispersed, leaving us to ascribe their forbearance to a superstition which forbade them to do more than gaze reverentially, or to their confirmed habits of submission, which prevented them from taking the summary measures that our unceremonious intrusion would doubtless have provoked in any other part of the civilised world.

In walking back to the steamer, we put up a double snipe, a bird peculiar to this part of the world, and which only makes its appearance during a month in autumn, if the frost does not set in too early. It was a lovely evening. A reach of the river, ten miles long and nearly two broad, stretched away before us, brightly reflecting the setting sun, which threw a ruddy glow upon the steep-wooded bank opposite, and tinged the white sails of two or three country craft that were working their way gently up the stream. The melodious chant of the boatmen floated to us across the waters, as with measured tramp they warped them to their anchors, mingled with shouts of shrill laughter that proceeded from many bare-legged maidens, who were noisily engaged carrying the wood on board our steamer, a task which seemed to afford them no little amusement. Each peal that burst from that youthful throng, as it rang through the clear, still air, told of a happy unconsciousness of that state of servitude by which they were depressed, and which had evidently produced its effect upon those whose monotonous strains were so full of mournful meaning.

As I watched the progress of the singular-looking barques, thus almost insensibly propelled up the stream, it seemed a wonder how they could ever reach their destination; or how it should be possible, considering the number of men required, and the length of the voyage, that there could ever be any remuneration upon so bulky a cargo as wheat. The following information, which I obtained respecting these very boats, in some measure solved the difficulty; they were carrying wheat from Samara to Rhybinski, and the voyage between these two places, under the most favourable circumstances, occupies at least two months. The season would then be too far advanced to admit of any farther progress, and consequently the wheat remains stored at Rhybinski until the spring. As soon as the water communication is again open, it is re-shipped, and probably reaches St. Petersburg towards the end of summer. Sometimes an early winter and contrary winds will retard the boats for a whole season, thus making the wheat two years old ere it arrives at its destination. A large "Rechievah"—for this is the native name of the vessel—contains 20,000 poods, or about 320 tons. The complement is in the proportion of four men to a thousand poods. No less than eighty would therefore be employed in a rechievah of this size, and the pay of each man is ten silver rubles, or thirty-three shillings and sixpence a month. The price of wheat per pood at Samara is thirty-five copeks—at St. Petersburg, sixty.

Occasionally horses are employed instead of men, and then seven or eight boats are lashed, one behind the other, to the immense barge which contains the horses; and the whole looks like some gigantic river monster working its way up the stream. On the deck of the leading barge a covered stage is erected, which serves as a stable sometimes to as many as a hundred and fifty horses. These may be observed working the huge capstan by which the boat is warped, and round which they perambulate, as in a threshing-machine. As many men as horses inhabit this floating establishment, and boats are continually employed carrying anchors ahead, and sounding the channels. With this cumbersome and expensive contrivance, however, not more than fifteen or twenty versts are made in a day, and the voyage to Rhybinski occupies about six months. The amount of cargo which such a train of barges would convey, is about 300,000 poods, or about 4700 tons. On one occasion we calculated the whole length of the train must have been at least half a mile. Some idea of the size of these boats nay be formed from the fact of our passenger-barge being 320 feet long, and capable of containing 200 passengers. They are of a construction totally different from rechievahs, and are called "Pashaliks."

We passed the scene of a recent catastrophe which had happened to one of these horse-machines, in which four barges and all the horses had been burnt. It is ridiculous to suppose that these barbarously contrived horse-machines can much longer compete with the steamers, when the advantages which these latter afford are considered. At a very small increase of freight, one steamer can convey 200,000 poods of wheat to Rhybinski in twenty-three days, where the cargo is at once transhipped for St. Petersburg, and arrives there in three weeks.

Not being a party interested, a rechievah was to me always a pleasing object, with its elaborately-carved triangular stern, and spacious deck that projected like a stage over each bow, on which a sort of wooden pedestal, also painted, and sometimes decorated with flags, was erected. Here, six or eight feet above the deck, stood a booted and sheepskinned figure leaning upon the long tiller, and able, from his elevation, to see how he could most easily run into everything that came in his way, much to the detriment of a pair of huge eyes that were often painted on the square bow, and probably proved of as much use as those of anybody else on board. One enormous square sail, together with the eighty men, were the propelling forces of the more than usually ornamented rechievah I was inspecting.

The weather continued lovely, and the scenery on the right bank was often beautiful. Where, however, the banks are low on both sides, the want of beauty is generally compensated for by some highly interesting pericarte which is to be traversed, and the excitement becomes considerable as we approach the shallows with our long unwieldy train. Two men with long poles are engaged in melodiously sounding, and "piatt polovinai" (five and a half), "schiest" (six), are ominous words to the ears of the captain, who instantly seizes a red speaking-trumpet nearly as long as himself, alternately waving it and speaking through it to the barges, on board of which everybody seems frantically engaged in doing something, which probably ends in the largest barge leaving the right channel, and suddenly grounding. Upon this a great bustle ensues on board the steamer, and the tow-rope creaks and jams in every possible direction, always seeming bent upon doing somebody damage, in which it very nearly succeeded two or three times. The steamer goes half-speed, stops, backs, stops again, and allows the pilot an opportunity of crossing himself vehemently. To all this bustle a perfect lull succeeds. The barge that is not aground leaves her companion to her fate, and drops composedly down the stream. We wait for an hour to think about the position of matters in general, and then turn our head, and anchor just above the barge in distress. The captain goes on board, while we contemplate her for another hour, without doing anything in particular, during which time she becomes more firmly imbedded than ever. Then follow a series of most complicated manœuvres, the result of which is, that after eight or ten hours of continual tugging at all quarters, we get her off, and, picking up the other barge, proceed on our way to the next pericarte, where the same scene occurs, with variations. On one occasion the tow-rope broke, and the end of it striking our cabin window on deck, stove it in bodily, the smashed glass flying in every direction. I had fortunately just quitted my chair close to it; but my friend, who was a little farther off, was slightly cut.

Upon the evening of the fourth day after leaving Nijni—during which we experienced a delay of eight hours on a pericarte—we arrived at our second wood station. The bank of the river on which it stood was low and marshy, and the night air struck cold and aguish; so we remained below, grumbling at the incessant thumping overhead, as the wood was thrown heavily on the deck with a violence that rendered any attempt at sleep out of the question. In despair I abandoned the cabin, and at once found reason to be thankful for the annoyance which had driven me on deck to witness one of the most singular scenes imaginable; it was some moments before I could really believe myself not only awake, but in Russia.

Men and women, whose dress and features were totally unlike any I had before seen in the country, were engaged in carrying wood on board. If the captain had rubbed some magic ring, he could not have conjured from the nether regions more orthodox-looking slaves; and had we been on the shores of the Tigris, such an event would have been most natural; but whence these beings had sprung, on that bleak desolate bank of the Volga, was indeed mysterious. The dress of men and women was the same. A white tunic, fitting close at the neck and wrists, reached to the knees. The legs were swathed in black cloth and felt, and their shoes made of the bark of trees matted together. The men wore high black hats, tapering to the middle, but wide at the top and bottom, like an hour-glass. The dark locks of the women hung in tangled masses over their shoulders, or in a long plait behind, among which glittered gold coins; while from their necks were suspended large silver breastplates, about eight inches long and six broad, also formed of coins. Half a dozen huge fires of birch logs threw a bright glare upon their wild costumes and swarthy countenances, as they sped swiftly up and down with their loads.

Tchouvasse Peasants at a Wood Station

The Tchouvasses (for to that tribe belonged these strange-looking beings) are said to be a mixture of the Mongolian and Finnish races; and certainly the result fully evidences the singular compound. I thought, however, that the Tartar blood predominated in their composition, and did not see, in any one instance, the flaxen hair and blue eyes of the Finlander. Some Finnish words are said to exist still in their language, however. I could gain but little information concerning them at the time; but in looking over old John Bell of Antermony, I find he says—"The Tchouvasses have a tradition among them that, in former times, they had a book of religion, but, as nobody could read it, a cow came and swallowed it. They pay great veneration to a bull. From whence they come is unknown; but, from their complexion, it is probable they are from Asia. They live by agriculture, and seem to be an inoffensive kind of people. Their huntsmen offer in sacrifice, to some deity, the first creature they catch: hence some curious men have imagined these people part of the ten tribes of the Jews expelled by Shalmanezer. I advance this only as a conjecture, which every reader may follow or not as he pleases." I have since obtained additional information concerning some of their religious opinions and ceremonies. When a Tchouvasse wishes to marry, he commissions a friend to bargain for a wife. They are to be met with of all prices, from fifty to two hundred and fifty rubles; but most of them bring a portion nearly equal to the purchase-money. When the bride is conducted to her husband's house, she remains for a short time concealed behind a partition; she then makes her appearance, and, in a modest, serious manner, walks three times round the company. At the last turn, the husband snatches off her veil and salutes her. From that moment she becomes his wife, and receives the cap, which is the distinctive dignity of a married woman. When bedtime approaches, she is obliged to draw off her husband's boots. Her servitude then commences.

The Tchouvasses have no idols. Thor is the name of the supreme being, and Thor Amysch, the mother of the gods, is his wife. Their priests are called Zemmas. They are nearly allied in manners and customs to the Scheremisses, another tribe of Finnish and Tartar origin, and inhabiting the same part of the country. These differ from the Tchouvasses in the names of their divinities, but seem to agree with them in thinking that there is a father and mother of gods, and a devil, whom they call by the Arabic name of "Chaitan." Besides these, there are the Mordvin and Votiak tribes, all more or less allied to one another, but widely differing in language and religion. While subject to the Tartar, these were wandering tribes; but since their annexation to Russia, they have given up their nomadic habits, and settled down quietly in the government of Kazan.

It was scarcely a matter of regret to me that I only obtained a midnight glimpse of the Tchouvasses. To have beheld them dwelling like ordinary mortals in a village, or sharing the common destiny of mankind by tilling the ground, would have been a dreadful shock to one's romantic system. I wished much to obtain one of those mysterious shields worn by the women, as a memento of this singular race; but the attempt which I made to inspect one was so vehemently resented by the fair damsel whose bosom it adorned, that I was obliged to relinquish all hope of being able to do more than carry away the vivid recollection, which long after haunted me, of that moonlit scene.

CHAPTER IV

Approach to Kazan—A drive in a telèga—First impressions of Kazan—Silent streets—View at sunrise—Muscovite deception— Dulness of Russian towns—Magnificent horses—Tartar village—Origin of the Kazan Tartars: their history—Sterlet fishing—Inland navigation

We were now in the once famous Tartar kingdom of Kazan. The Sura, a small river flowing into the Volga from the southward, was formerly the eastern boundary of the Russian empire, and now it separates the province of Kazan from that of Nijni Novgorod. At the confluence of the two rivers, the town of Vasil Soursk is picturesquely situated, where the remains of a fortress, erected by the celebrated Prince Ivan Vasiley, are said still to be visible, reminding the Tartars of their former independence, which had called it into existence. As we approached Kazan, the banks gradually lost their thickly-wooded character, and assumed the appearance of well-cultivated gently swelling knolls, the villages succeeding more frequently. Our voyage was on the whole prosperous, although upon one occasion we again remained for nine hours on a pericarte. The disappointment occasioned by this delay was in some measure compensated by the magnificent view of the reach, which we had thus time to admire at our leisure. I could have supposed this vast expanse of water to be a lake, had not the curling eddies betrayed its real character. The water of the Volga looks muddy, but its appearance belies it, and we found it clear and delicious. The last few days had been very hot, while the nights were cold, the thermometer frequently standing at 52° in our cabin before breakfast, and rising at midday to 72°.

We were within 25 versts (20 miles) of Kazan, when a doubt seemed to arise in the mind of the captain as to the expediency of stopping there at all, and I began to fear that our arguments to induce him to allow us a few hours to visit that interesting city would prove unavailing, when a friendly pericarte settled the matter, and he most good-naturedly gave us his boat, enabling us thereby to take advantage of a fair wind, and the few hours yet remaining of a glorious day. Leaving the old Samson tugging hopelessly at her barges, we glided swiftly in our tiny craft past gorgeous rechievahs and unwieldy horse-machines, now overshadowed by lofty trees or wooded banks, now skimming near some sandy islet, while our sailors beguiled the way with Russian ditties.

The town of Kazan, which, as we approached, seemed built upon the water's edge, is really situated at a distance of seven versts from the river; and as the whole intervening country is flooded for a great part of the year, the road thither is a mere temporary track across a marshy irregular piece of ground, and the drosky-drivers, who are their own engineers, naturally choose the most impracticable line.

Upon arriving at the few huts which serve as the summer port, we found that the only vehicles to be procured were some telègas, or native carts—decidedly the most primitive of all modes of conveyance extant, consisting simply of a flat framework of bark placed between four wheels. The mate mounted with us on one of these, our legs dangling over the sides; and we hoped that our number would in some measure insure our safety, as we might in any case of emergency cling to one another. Where rapidity and wholesome exercise are the objects desired, I should decidedly prefer a telèga to all other modes of conveyance; as, by means of a few admonitory taps on the back of the Tartar driver, the speed may be increased to any amount; while the jolting is so excessive, that a walk of double the distance would be far less fatiguing. Wherever the horse can go, the telèga is bound to follow, and does so in the most matter-of-fact manner.

As we approached the town, and crossed a piece of smooth ground, I was enabled to let go my hold, and bestow upon it some of the attention I had hitherto been devoting exclusively to my vehicle; and certainly the scene which now presented itself was well worthy of undivided admiration.

Situated on a gentle eminence, in the midst of an extensive plain, its many-coloured roofs rising one above another to the walls of the Kremlin, which crowns the hill to the extreme left, tall spires and domes appearing in every direction, and betokening the magnitude of the city, while adding to its beauty, Kazan presented a more imposing aspect than any town I had seen in Russia, and seemed to vie with Moscow as to exhibiting, in the most favourable manner, the characteristic buildings of the country. Twilight was just failing us as we entered the broad deserted streets, and reached the principal hotel, where we secured rooms, and then sallied forth to see as much as we could by lamp-light. Had we known a little more of Russian civilisation, we might have spared ourselves the trouble; but I innocently supposed that, in a town containing fifty thousand inhabitants, the streets would be lighted up, and could hardly believe, on finding myself in the principal thoroughfare, that we were in a city of the living. As we walked its whole length, not a gleam from a window, far less a street lamp, cheered us. Three or four foot-passengers, and one or two droskies—the only moving things—seemed hurrying noiselessly home along the wooden pavement, as if ashamed of being out after dark; so we disconsolately did the same, and returned to our dismal rambling hotel, which was quite in character with everything else. Though this was the principal place of the sort in the city, sheets were a luxury unknown, and I was glad to stretch myself on a hard wooden frame, which harboured every species of irritating insect. For this pallet, and the dirty room in which it stood, the charge was a ruble-three shillings and fourpence!

We had determined not to leave Kazan without exploring it; and as the captain had warned us to be at the port at an early hour on the following morning, we were up at daybreak, and on our way to the Kremlin by four o'clock. We passed a number of houses which had been recently burnt down; indeed, the town seemed to have suffered from fire in all directions. The Kazansky, or main street, traverses the entire ridge of the hill; and from the corners of the various intersecting streets, good views are obtained over the town upon each side. Following along it, past handsome well-built mansions, and through the colonnade of a large bazaar, or Gastinni Dvor, we reached the Kremlin, and, from the terrace in front of the governor's house, revelled in a most glorious prospect. Stretching away to the north, the eye ranged over a vast expanse of country, thinly dotted with villages and church spires; whilst our position commanded a panoramic view of the town, which in no way belied my impressions of the previous evening. To the south, the Volga, with its steep banks, bounded the prospect, while the Tartar villages in the foreground, with their singularly built mosques, seemed to

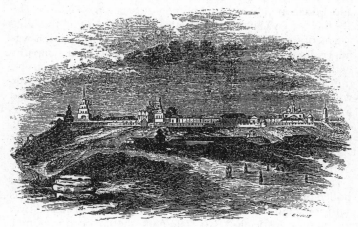

Kremlin of Kazan

invite a visit. The effect of the scene was completed by the sun most opportunely rising, as it were, out of the steppe, tipping spire and dome, until we ourselves felt its genial influence.

The Kremlin contains three churches, each with the usual complement of green cupolas, two towers containing bells, and two more containing windows only. In one of these towers is a curious archway which has a striking effect when seen from the plain beneath, but seems to be built for no discoverable object beyond that of ornament or singularity. Altogether the Kremlin looks better from without than from within; and the sooner an immense range of yellow government-buildings which it contains is burnt down, the better. The exteriors of many of the churches are handsome; and I observed, for the first time in Russia, numerous fresco-paintings on the walls. There is a large university at the end of the Kazansky; and parallel to it are some gardens, which would afford a pleasant promenade to the inhabitants if they ever walked; but, to judge from the weedy beds, they are not much patronised. In fact, nothing could be more solemnly dreary, and, consequently, more genuinely Russian, than Kazan. The absence of vivacity in the street, characteristic of all the large towns of the country, was here painfully apparent; and it was impossible not to feel depressed, were it only from sympathy with everything else. Comfort seemed sacrificed for effect, and the desolate aspect of the interior of the city contrasted harshly with the gorgeousness of its brightly coloured roofs and innumerable churches, as seen from a distance. Kazan was to me the first of a series of disappointments, and I gradually learned to avoid entering those cities whose brilliant exteriors promised most, if I wished to preserve a favourable impression of them.

Nothing bears looking into in Russia, from a metropolis to a police-office: in either case, a slight acquaintanceship is sufficient; and first impressions should never be dispelled by a too minute inspection. No statement should be questioned, however preposterous, where the credit of the country is involved; and no assertion relied upon, even though it be a gratuitous piece of information—such as, that there is a diligence to the next town, or an inn in the next street. There is a singular difficulty in getting at the truth, probably originating with subordinate officials, whose duty it seems to be to deceive you, and whose support is derived from bribes which you give them for their information. Whatever may be the cause, the effect certainly is, that a most mysterious secresy pervades everything; and an anxious desire is always visible to produce an impression totally at variance with the real state of the case: and so it happened that, not having been long enough in Russia to have learned this, I was disappointed with Kazan.

But looking less theoretically at those handsome churches and silent streets, and regarding them rather as tangible bricks and mortar than as emblems of the state of Russia, their air of dulness may easily be accounted for, by the plan of concentrating all the shops in the town into one market-place, or Gastinni Dvor, which, while it may be more convenient for those making purchases, detracts most materially from the life and bustle of the place. A main street devoid of a single shop, or any side pavement, must necessarily have a dull appearance; and the gaunt houses, with all the shutters closed to keep out the glare, contribute to its melancholy. Yet Kazan has advantages which few other inland towns possess. The capital of an ancient kingdom, it is not the mere creation of government, kept alive, as it were, by law, and tenanted by compulsion; it rests upon foundations long since laid, and owes its present prosperity to its position on the great highway from Siberia to Moscow and Nijni. It thus becomes an emporium for the productions of that distant part of the

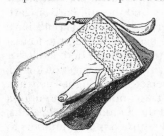

empire which pass through it. It boasts, moreover, manufactures peculiar to itself. The inhabitants are well known to excel in leather embroidery—for workmanship of this sort Kazan is celebrated all over eastern Europe. It is therefore too highly favoured to be a fair specimen of a Russian town; and I appreciated it more

Leather Gloves, of Kazan manufacture, and Wooden Spoon

correctly after visiting some of the other provincial towns on the Volga. The magnificence of the horses which stand harnessed in every common drosky, bear testimony to that skill in the science of horse-flesh, which formed a great national characteristic of their former possessors, but to which the Russian can lay no claim. Most of the Isvoschiks, or drosky-drivers, were Tartars; and it was quite a pleasure to dash along the streets in their well-appointed vehicles. The Kazanese are very proud of their wood pavement, and are most earnest in pointing out this mark of their civilisation. It certainly is a luxury, where the only alternative is the execrable chaussée of Russian cities generally.

Our former experience of the road to the port decided us to trust to our own legs, as a less expeditious, but safer and more agreeable mode of traversing it. Moreover, we could not resist a Tartar village, and a sketch or two *en route*; and we found the fresh morning air most invigorating. Tall Tartar maidens, in graceful costumes, with gay-coloured shawls drawn over their heads, and partly concealing their feces, passed us on the road, carrying water or driving cows to pasture. As we approached, they considerately disclosed the charms which their headdress was intended to conceal, thus affording an opportunity of observing how far superior they are in personal attractions to the damsels of the country. The Oriental attire and stately bearing of the men, contrasted still more favourably with their sheepskin-clad Russian conquerors; and the comparison gave rise to regrets that this old eastern principality should have vanished from off the face of the earth. However, the tourist may esteem himself fortunate in finding them here at all; for when the kingdom of Kazan became the conquest of Russia, the Tartars who composed it dispersed, and sought safety at a distance from their conquerors. It was not, therefore, until a tranquil possession had disarmed the hatred of the Russians, that the families of the conquered returned in any numbers to the spots which were dear to them as the places of their nativity, and as containing the sepulchres of their ancestors.

They are scattered over all the country now called the government of Kazan, which is considerably more extensive than that of which they were the former masters.

On some low ground near the village stood a most curiously-fashioned little mosque, in construction totally unlike any other building of the sort I had ever seen; and in close proximity to it, a Greek monastery peeped out through some large trees, its white walls running along the gentle slope. Two or three other churches, not far distant, while they proved valuable additions to the view, seemed to overawe the unpretending Tartar edifice; and it was striking to remark the insignificant character here of a religion, whose usual feature is, that, where it exists at all, it generally preponderates. The pretensions of Mahomedanism are estimated more correctly in Russia than in many other countries; and we were not sorry to see the arrogant pride of the faithful humbled. Though professing Mahomedan tenets, these Tartars did not seem to be very orthodox followers of the Prophet; and the open manner in which the women exposed their countenances to view, would have scandalised true believers.

I might perhaps have ventured to enter one of their wooden houses, but that there was nothing tempting in their appearance; or have satisfied my curiosity by looking in at the windows, had they not been composed of parchment. The Tartars of Kazan differ in every respect from the surrounding tribes, possessing neither the flat noses nor wide eyes which mark the Kirghees, Calmuck, and other Mongolian races, nor the flaxen hair and fair complexion of the Sclave. According to Heberstein, the Russian notion is, that they are of Moabitish origin; and certainly the classic mould of their features would appear to suggest a southern extraction. In the account which this celebrated diplomatist gives of these races, we find that King Bathi, in the year 1237, completely routed the Russian army, slew the Grand-Duke George, and laid the provinces of Vladimir and Muscovy under tribute. Bathi was succeeded by sundry princes who periodically overran the neighbouring countries; and it was not till the early part of the fourteenth century that any successful resistance was offered to their arms by the famous Duke Ivan Vasiley, who not only threw off the Tartar yoke, but in 1352 laid siege to the city of Kazan. He was opposed by King Scheale, who, in his turn, invaded the Russian

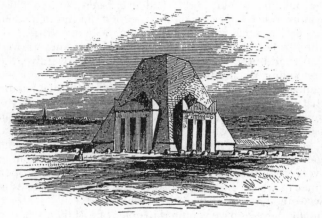

Tartar Mosque near Kazan

provinces. The Tartar power was not, however, wholly crushed till Ivan the Terrible ascended the throne; and about the middle of the sixteenth century this great Eastern kingdom was, to use a modern phrase, annexed to the Empire of Russia.

We had lingered too long over Kazan and its environs, and arrived at the port just in time to see the three funnels of the Samson disappear behind a hill; so, seating ourselves in our little skiff, surrounded by loaves of black bread and legs of mutton, we went in chase, with a fair wind and a strong current in our favour, trusting to some pericarte to befriend us. Of course the steamer, with most unusual good fortune, had escaped all such obstacles; and not until we had perseveringly followed for five hours did we overtake her, anchored in mid-stream, helplessly looking at one of the barges aground on a sand-bank.

On our way, we had been occupied in admiring the fiery autumnal tints on the wooded hillsides, and the many and bright hues with which the stunted copsewood was variegated; in some places the banks were steep and scarped, a few dwarf oaks or wild rose-bushes being all that could find holding ground, and large blocks of sandstone were strewn along the river's edge at the foot of the cliffs, which were often wild and romantic.

Nothing could exceed the magnificence of the Volga, as it stretched away like some inland sea, which the strong breeze, as it hurried us down its mighty stream, rippled into tiny waves. Numbers of little boats, each containing one man, were anchored in the river, the occupants engaged in fishing for sterlet. This delicate fish, peculiar to the rivers of the south of Russia, is much prized; and deservedly so, for I thought it undoubtedly the best freshwater fish I had ever eaten. The mode of fishing is simply with a cork attached to the line near the hook, which is suddenly jerked as the fish is playing near the cork.

We had now reached the Kama, the largest tributary to the Volga, into which it falls about fifty versts below Kazan. Until within a recent period, nothing more civilised than huge pine-rafts floated on its broad bosom; now, active little steamers ply diligently between Perm, Nijni, and Astrakhan, loaded with Siberian and Chinese produce. The voyage to Perm from Kazan occupies a week or ten days. The former place has, since the introduction of steamers, proved a formidable rival to Kazan as an Eastern emporium, and is reported to be a rapidly increasing city. Its proximity to the gold mines has long rendered it a place of some importance.

It is much to be regretted that the difficulties attendant upon the formation of private steam companies are so formidable, and the risk of interference so great, that a country possessing the most extensive capabilities in the world of inland navigation is in great measure deprived of the advantages which could not fail to accrue to it, were a more enlightened system introduced. There is no doubt that a change has already taken place, in this respect, on the Volga—I understood that an Englishman, who is engaged at Nijni in putting together steamers, brought thither in separate pieces for the purpose, had launched four in the summer of 1851, and five the following year, for one company alone.

When we look at Perm on the map, and consider that there are steamers plying on the rivers of that distant province, we should, indeed, be almost American in our notions of progress did we require more; and we ought rather, perhaps, to congratulate Russia on having accomplished so much.

CHAPTER V

A poverty-stricken village—Serfs: their spiritual destitution—
System of agriculture—Haxthausen on serfdom—Evils of the
system—"Obrok"—Scarcity of villages—Absence of an urban
population—Evils resulting from it—Russian political economy

On the following day, as we were nearing the numerous stacks of birch-logs that betokened a wood station, we fell in with one of the company's steamers from Astrakhan. We were soon moored side by side under the sandy bank, and the captains retired to discuss grog and pericartes till the news of our arrival should bring the country people down to load.

Meantime we went on shore to explore, and had not gone far before we met all the inhabitants of the nearest village hastening to the scene of action. It was a grand holiday, and so the population had turned out *en masse*, which was rather fortunate, considering that two steamers were dependent on their exertions.

The country was flat, and covered with a rich alluvial soil, of which, for a wonder, some advantage was taken. The village, which was about two miles from the river, was situated upon the banks of a small lake, and was as wild and uncouth as the inhabitants that issued from it.

It was a large irregular place, with the gable-ends, instead of the sides of the houses, facing the street, in true Russian fashion. There was an unwonted air of poverty pervading everything. The telègas at the cottage-doors seemed more rickety than usual. No elaborate carving indicated the residence of the Starista; no green-domed church was there, to make up in spiritual for what the inhabitants evidently lacked in temporal things. Squalid children dabbled in the muddy water of the lake, in much the same condition as the wheat which was growing on its opposite margin—the one as little likely to be cared for or properly cultivated as the other.

71

Here, in a country which boasts of the rapid advances it has recently made in civilisation, we saw a large and populous village in a state of utter heathenism, and apparently destined to remain so; though it is a question whether it might not be considered fortunate in having escaped the infliction of some profligate priest.

Even if the plea of being unable to cope with an immoral and debased priesthood could excuse the neglect which the absence of any place of worship implies on the part of the government, this very incapacity ought at least to act as a stimulus to the improvement of the intellectual condition of the people by means of secular instruction, thus enabling them to acquire for themselves that information in spiritual as well as temporal concerns, of which they must otherwise remain destitute.

A very different view, however, is entertained by those in authority, all schools being positively prohibited, except in a few large towns; a state of things which must seriously retard the due development of the resources of the country, composed as they are in an equal degree of moral and physical elements. Of the near relationship subsisting between these influences, we had a most convincing proof before us, when, on leaving the mudlarking little serfs to live and die in the state of ignorance provided for them, we crossed over to consider the no less hard case of the wheat, which was the more forcibly brought to our notice by a splendid bank of manure in close proximity, used for the purpose of forming a dam at the bottom of the lake. It is not often that manure is so well employed. As a general rule, it is all carried to the banks of the nearest river, and left to be washed away by the first flood; but here it was turned to some account; and not ten yards distant, some wheat waved sadly towards it, as if resigned to its fate in being the produce of a barbarous country. On the whole, however, the wheat promised to turn out better than the children; for, depending on a rich soil, and genial summer weather, not upon an exacting master and unsympathising government, it was more highly favoured than they, although the manure was so tantalisingly near.

Here, as elsewhere in Russia, owing to the great extent of arable land, the system of cultivating fields in alternate years prevails—it is only the most magnificent soil which could produce such fine crops. The whole cultivation consists in a slight scratching previous to sowing; and probably in no other part of the world are people so well rewarded by nature, considering their small acquaintance with, or study of her requirements.

It is a merciful provision that this is the case; for in no other country do the peasantry labour under similar disadvantages, and nowhere is less stimulus offered to the enterprise of the labouring man to induce him to overcome them. Notwithstanding the theory strenuously maintained by all Russians, that the system of serfdom is conducive to the improvement of agriculture, it appeared to me to act as a most effectual clog to any efforts that might otherwise be made by the poorer class towards the introduction of a better mode of cultivation. Their argument, in a condensed form, amounts to this, that in order to promote the progress of agriculture, there should exist, as at the present time, large properties in the hands of a wealthy aristocracy, possessing funds adequate for the development of the agricultural resources of the country. On this subject Haxthausen says[1]—"If the existence of these large properties is absolutely necessary for the progress of agriculture and of the national welfare, it follows, as a natural consequence, that serfdom cannot, at the present moment, be abolished." But it is difficult to see how this result should so naturally follow upon the existence of the large properties spoken of, seeing that, if the wages of the labourer were to come out of the proceeds of the estate, the probability is, that the proprietor would be far more careful to have it properly cultivated, than when, as under the present system, he is

[1] Studien über die inneren Zustände das Volksleben, und inbesondere die ländlichen Einrichtungen Russlands.

certain of being put to no expense regarding it; whilst also, as a general rule, forced labour is far more slovenly than paid work. The result of the prevailing state of things is indifference, not only on the part of the lord, but on the part of the serf, to whom is allotted a portion of land near the village, upon which he is expected to support himself by the crops which he rears when not working for his master.

As this land does not really belong to him, and has only fallen to his share in the usual course of allotment, he does not naturally feel the same interest in it as if it appertained to him and his heirs for ever; while the amount of labour frequently exacted by his master, precludes the possibility of his devoting adequate attention to it.

It thus happens that the lands of noble and peasant are equally ill cultivated, and likely to remain so, until a stern necessity shall force the one, and a prospect of remuneration shall entice the other, to adopt the more enlightened systems of other countries. Perhaps these hardships seem to press more heavily upon the inhabitants of the fertile districts watered by the Volga, than in other more remote and inaccessible parts of the country, where it is said that the peasant pays his lord more satisfactorily to himself by his work than in money—that being an article more than ordinarily unprocurable; while the soil is too barren to cover the expense of farming it.

If the excuses offered by Russians for the servitude which obtains throughout their country, were, the barren nature, the inaccessible position, and scanty population of many parts of it, the more favoured and civilised countries of Europe might be disposed to pity rather than condemn them. When, however, we see, in some of the richest provinces of the empire, serfdom grinding the poor, and hear it, nevertheless, supported as a liberal and enlightened institution, we find it difficult to reconcile such a state of things with our English notions of what is requisite for the prosperity of a nation, and feel almost disposed to suspect that the nobility of Russia are only coercing their government into retarding the well-being of the state itself. It is said that the Emperor is most desirous for the emancipation of the serfs; and recent measures have indicated that attempts are making to render the condition of the private serf more tolerable. Those who are the property of the crown have, indeed, comparatively little to complain of. Paying a tax of fifteen rubles for every male, they are only subject to the extortion of the tax-gatherers, who usually double the amount for their own benefit.

Occasionally the services of the crown peasant are required by the state, and, in compensation for these, they receive orders upon the treasury, which are never cashed by the nobility who officiate as clerks in that department; but, in remote districts, the peasants are not often called upon for this purpose, and seek to enrich themselves by obtaining employment in the towns, or vegetate upon plots of buck-wheat, in ignorant barbarism and bliss.

Yet it must be said, in extenuation of the present condition of the inhabitants bordering on the Volga, that many of those who are owned by noblemen are under the system of "Obrok", which consists in the payment by the serf, of a certain rent, for the privilege of working all the week on his own account.

As considerable traffic is springing up in many of the towns upon the banks of the river, the process of making money is becoming more common, and there is an unusual motive supplied for the exercise of the intellectual faculties; still the pursuit of gain is not followed so keenly as might be, those peasants to whom noblemen have accorded their liberty being subject to an augmentation of their "Obrok" proportionate to their prosperity—a consideration which must materially damp the ardour of speculation, and subdue any tendency to self-gratulation upon the successful issue of an adventure.

From the fact of the peasantry so readily deserting agri-culture for more congenial modes of gaining their livelihood, it has been said that a wholesale liberation would be ruinous to the large proprietors; and as land is less valuable than labour in Russia, this would probably be the case to some extent in very remote districts.

Agriculture would pay, however, under any circumstances in the Volga provinces; and whatever may be its prospects in the more distant parts, here the richness of the soil, and the facility of water communication, will always secure the proprietor; and the only effect of such a liberation would probably be an improved method of farming. At present, while so few attractions are offered to the farm-labourer, his choosing a more profitable occupation is not to be wondered at. Hitherto he has cultivated, on his own account, a number of scattered little plots of ground, which have been allotted to him according to the quality of the soil. Sometimes he owns a patch at a distance of ten versts from his house, another at five versts, and a third at one verst; all the soils differing in quality, and the allotments subject to re-division amongst his family, who, like himself, will be destitute of sufficient capital to cultivate them properly.

The rare occurrence of villages is particularly noticeable in the government we had now entered, the population of the province of Simbirsk being small, and the villages very far apart. Even on the river banks, where they had hitherto generally appeared within short distances of one another, an interval of many miles now occasionally occurred without a trace of human habitation; indeed, I do not remember ever having noticed even one *small* village. Not only do the Russian peasants positively object to living alone, but they prefer large communities, and a village seldom contains less than a thousand inhabitants; the consequence of which is, that at harvest and seed-time the greater part of the population is obliged to move in a body to the more distant portion of the lands under cultivation, and bivouac there until their labours are terminated. For this most inconvenient mode of proceeding, the following remedy has been proposed. It being admitted that, once in every thirty years, the greater part of a Russian village is burnt down, it is suggested by the same writer (Haxthausen), that the government "should command all those inhabitants whose houses have been consumed, to rebuild their dwellings in a totally different situation, so that, in thirty years, the number of villages would thus be doubled or trebled." Whether this ingenious device would effect the desired end, is rather problematical; at any rate, there seems to me to be a much more natural and self-evident remedy, which, by improving the present agricultural system of the country, would render it necessary for the population to distribute themselves more advantageously. It is clear that, if there were more large towns scattered throughout the country, agricultural produce would rise in value. Russia is almost devoid of an urban population; St. Petersburg, Moscow, and Odessa are the only cities whose populations exceed a hundred thousand; indeed, there is some doubt whether that of Odessa reaches this figure. There are only four towns containing more than fifty thousand inhabitants each, and eighteen or twenty with populations exceeding twenty-five thousand. In fact, it has been computed, from the official reports, that there is only one town with an average population of seven thousand, in an area of a hundred and thirty square miles. Now, the result of this is obvious. The absence of any market renders it unnecessary for the proprietor, who has no facilities for transporting his grain to a seaport, to grow more than is sufficient for his own consumption; and the peasant only cultivates land enough to yield the produce required to support his family.

It may be said that, with so thin a population, it is unwise to congregate the inhabitants into towns, and leave large tracts of country uncultivated. In support of this theory, the Russian political economist points to those towns founded by the Empress Catharine, for the purpose of trying the remedy above mentioned, and complains that, with very few exceptions, they are in precisely the same condition as on the day when they were founded.

This fact proves, says one of them, that, "since the days of Peter the Great, it is the government which has taken the lead in the progress of civilisation, and *it* is obliged to slacken its steps, in order not to advance too rapidly the wants, the ideas, and the manners of the people." A most ingenious way of solving the problem, truly! Whatever else may be laid to the charge of the Russian government, to accuse it of being too rapidly progressive is, I think, basely to traduce its strictly conservative character. The peasantry have at present nothing to fear from go-ahead tendencies, and are perfectly able to keep pace with their rulers in the march of civilisation; and we have only to compare the condition of the more remote states of North America with these provinces, to perceive that the failure in the establishment of towns does not proceed from the inaptitude of the *peasant* for a town life, but of the *serf*. There is a considerable difference between a population of slaves, on the one hand, obliged to live in a town, devoid of any natural advantage of position, and dependent for its continued existence, as for its original creation, upon the whim of the government alone—and a population of free men, on the other, who collect together of their own accord, in a spot possessing all the requisites essential to their prosperity, and who, though small in numbers at first, go on increasing as external circumstances combine with their own industry to promote such augmentation. Of course the existence of any foreign market, which could be made available by means of increased facilities of internal communication, would be the most valuable stimulus to agricultural operations, and would render the improvement of transit a primary and imperative duty upon the government; but where the sea-coast is altogether unattainable, the more judicious distribution of the population seems to be that now proposed, as tending to promote both the civilisation and prosperity of the country.

It is hopeless to expect skilful artisans when a man is obliged to pay an annual rent proportionate to his earnings for permission to work at a trade. He naturally does not feel bound to perfect himself in a craft for the benefit of his owner, and would rather lead a comparatively independent life of promiscuous labour in the country, than be bound as a workman in the town.

Thus it happens that those who supply the inhabitants of the towns are the shoemakers, the blacksmiths, and the carpenters of the villages; and, as may be imagined, their productions are of the roughest description.[1] Of course, so long as such a state of things exists, just so long will the towns of Russia maintain the cold lifeless aspect which distinguishes them at the present time. In contemplating their condition, a Privy-Councillor of the empire observes, that "if the industry of the villages is not favourable to the prosperity of the towns, it has, on the other hand, the advantage of preserving us for a long time from the Proletariat, that scourge of modern society, which contains within itself the seed of its own dissolution."—One of the most imaginary evils this, as applied to his own country, that ever harrowed, in anticipation, the benevolent feelings of a Russian statesman.

[1] The proportion of artisans to the rest of the population, by the statistical papers, is one in a hundred.

CHAPTER VI

*Arrival at Simbirsk—Statue to Karamsin—The Jigoulee—
Samara—The government of Orenburg—Turbulent votaries of
vodka—Retributive justice—Government spirit-monopoly—
Grace before meat—Hills of Saratov*

A little fleet of rechievahs, some pashaliks and horse-machines,
are lying under the steep bank, along the base of which
wooden cottages and storehouses are plentifully scattered.
There seems absolutely to be some business going forward;
enough, at any rate, to suggest the proximity of a large town.
From this commercial little village a broad track is visible
straight up the hillside; and so precipitous is the ascent, that
the carts and people who traverse it appear to cling to the
mountain as they climb up it. This original-looking road leads
to Simbirsk, and the craft lying at its port are probably loading
with potash, the most considerable article of export in this
province. I found it difficult to keep my seat on the plank,
which, placed upon four wheels, was the mode of conveyance
used to effect the difficult ascent. The wiry little Cossack horse,
however—and he was the party principally concerned—
seemed to think nothing of attaining an altitude of four
hundred feet in about as many yards.

We entered the main street immediately on reaching
Simbirsk. The mate of the steamer, who accompanied me, not
thinking our vehicle sufficiently respectable, dismounted,
whilst I joined my friend, who had preferred walking up, and
we proceeded together to explore the town. For a place which
is said to contain nearly twenty thousand inhabitants, Simbirsk
wears a mean and insignificant appearance—its situation,
indeed, being its only recommendation. From the terrace, near
the governor's house, a magnificent and expansive view is
obtained over the basin of the river, which here spreads itself
in narrow channels over the low land, beyond which the high
hills of the Jigoulee bound the prospect to the south, while in

every other direction the steppes seem illimitable. Immediately at our feet were cottages and gardens, and on the opposite bank of the river some large villages. The white sails of many pashaliks glistened on the broad surface of the stream, and completed a charming picture.

Near this terrace, and in the centre of a square from which the principal streets diverge, stands a statue of Karamsin, the celebrated Russian historian. There is an annual horse-fair held at Simbirsk; but the town is not in so prosperous a condition as many others on the Volga from which corn is more largely exported. The suburbs seemed more than usually wretched, and the principal street more than usually dull. I found two or three German tradesmen, however, who seemed to be making the most of their superior intelligence, and gave a thriving account of themselves.

About twenty versts below Simbirsk we passed Kriusky, the winter station for the steamers of this company—possessing the advantage of an excellent harbour, in which vessels are safe from the melting ice in spring. Not far from the village rises Hadwallee, a picturesque hill, seven or eight hundred feet high, the greatest altitude which the banks have attained since leaving Nijni. Near Simbirsk they are bare, and covered with a short seared grass; but as we entered the Jigoulee they became more thickly wooded, and we observed, for the first time,

The "Samson" passing through the Jigoulee

some dark-green pines intermingled with the autumn-tinted foliage, with which they pleasingly contrasted.

The Jigoulee is the opening—for it can hardly be called the gorge—by which the Volga forces its way through a range of considerable altitude. The river, which here takes a bend to the eastward a hundred and seventy versts long, encloses a mountainous peninsula, forming an isthmus only twelve versts across. As this divergence afforded us the finest scenery which is to be met with on the Volga, we did not grudge the time spent in making it. For once, too, we had occasion to congratulate ourselves upon our captain's prudence, which never hazarded a stroke of the paddle-wheels after dark, and which now secured to us noble scenery for the morrow. He was no less satisfied with our successful run of a hundred and sixty versts from Simbirsk since the morning, together with the absence of all pericartes. Indeed, since the Kama had added its important contribution to the waters of the Volga, navigation had been comparatively free from difficulty.

At an early hour we were dashing, with a strong current, towards Samara. The stream, though nearly two miles broad, is here rapid and deep, and, for the first time, the left bank has totally changed its character: rising to a height of seven or eight hundred feet, its beetling crags overhang the river, and give an unusual boldness to the scene.

The opposite hills, though of equal if not greater height, swell gently back from the water's edge, or occasionally recede and form amphitheatres, in which villages, picturesquely situated, look as if they were completely cut off from the rest of the world. Not far from one of these, we observed a neat-looking boat moored, and near it a small white tent, close to which a curling wreath of blue smoke suggested the idea of a picnic, if the Russians are ever guilty of thus profaning the beauties of their river.

I discovered that these signs of comfort and civilisation proceeded from a party of soldiers, who constitute some of the river-guard. Until quite recently, robberies of boats were frequent in this romantic spot; and three or four "highrivermen" have been known to batten down the hatches of a rechievah, containing a hundred and twenty men, rifle the cabin, and make their escape, before the astonished occupants could collect the senses or pluck up the courage they possessed.

Emerging from the Jigoulee, which had for a distance of seventy versts displayed its beauties, the better appreciated from being in some measure unexpected, we shortly after reached Samara, situated on a sloping bank, to which were moored numerous barges and rechievahs.

Samara is the busiest port on the Volga. Backed by an immense corn-growing country, it supplies a great part of the interior of Russia with wheat. No less than nine million poods are shipped here annually, and carried either down to Astrakhan, and so across the Caspian, or, on the backs of camels, from Orenburg to the adjacent countries; or conveyed by water to St. Petersburg.

It is evident that the introduction of steam must soon work its usual miracles even on these distant rivers. Samara was already beginning to feel its magical effects; and what between a recent fire and the increasing trade, the streets seemed filled with scaffolds and ladders, while the chink of hammer and chisel resounded in all quarters. Large, substantial, and often handsome-looking brick edifices were springing up everywhere. Whole streets were being laid out; while along the water's edge numbers of wooden houses and sheds served as dwellings and stores for the nonce.

Samara contains from fifteen to twenty thousand inhabitants; but it is too matter-of-fact and business-like a place to be at all attractive to the tourist; and its unpicturesque appearance, as we approached, quite harmonised with its purely commercial character. This proves, notwithstanding, its redeeming feature for the short period during which the great annual fair is held here, when the numerous races assembled at it are said to be even more diversified than at Nijni. Only three hundred versts from the Asiatic frontier, a large trade is carried on with the inhabitants of those distant steppes, who flock hither in great numbers, the representatives of each tribe wearing a different costume. The rapid increase of the population of this town is but in accordance with the prospering condition of the government to which it mainly owes its existence. There is not a more highly favoured province in the empire of Russia than Orenburg; and those inhabitants of the neighbouring districts who, belonging to the crown, have been allowed to migrate to this land of plenty, have done so to such an extent that the population has doubled itself within the last few years, and now exceeds a million and a half. Its boundary extends to within a few versts of the left bank of the Volga; and where that river, more capricious than usual, reaches the most easterly point of its whole course, Samara has sprung up; and, forming a sort of port for the town of Orenburg, which is situated on the Tartar frontier, it helps to connect the distant regions beyond with the Cis-Volgan countries, and thus, as it were, completes the last link of the chain of European civilisation in this direction.

But apart from any topographical importance that Orenburg may possess, it is to the fertility of its soil that it chiefly owes its prosperity; and of the cheapness of every article of food we had most satisfactory proof. We laid in a small stock of beef at three copeks, or a penny-farthing a pound, while a hundred eggs only cost us twenty copeks, or eightpence. The Vodka, or corn-brandy of the country, is here procured in great perfection, as we discovered by the condition of our pilots when we were ready to proceed on our voyage. Both these indispensable personages were lying thoroughly intoxicated in the forepart of the ship, and thus we were again to be delayed. Each day hitherto, since we left Nijni, had furnished some fresh excuse for our tardy progress; and what the cause of the next stoppage was to be, became quite an interesting subject of speculation with us. We owed our detention at Simbirsk to the captain's wife, resident there, who was far too pretty for us to grudge it to her; and now—however unsentimental the cause of our delay-we felt that there was no alternative but to smother our indignation and resign ourselves to our fate. My companion and myself were in the act of deriving some little consolation from an excellent dinner, to which our hospitable but somewhat peppery captain had invited us, when our feelings of animosity towards the pilots were most unexpectedly gratified. Suddenly, and in the midst of a warm recommendation of some elaborate Armenian dish, our worthy host sprang up and rushed upon deck. We heard a scuffle, and shortly afterwards saw the end of a very thick rope, flourished by the captain's sturdy arm, descend with no small force upon the shoulders of the pilot, whose turn it now was to smother his indignation, while he dexterously avoided the blows. Quite out of breath, our skipper returned, and informing us that his excitement had banished all remains of an appetite, he left us to finish our meal alone, which was only disturbed once again by a heavy, dull sound, caused, we discovered, by the body of the pilot, who had just been hurled from the upper deck by the still irate captain.

Congratulating ourselves, in the first place, upon being in a country where such proceedings are considered as matters of course; and, in the second, on there being no more pericartes in prospect, which might enable a vindictive pilot to wreak his vengeance upon us, we soon had the further satisfaction of seeing Samara disappear behind the hills. I found out afterwards, by the way, that it was a little premature in us to imagine that, because we were in Russia, the captain could handle our drunken pilots thus roughly; it seems, on the contrary, that men, while in a state of intoxication, have, in this country, an especial claim upon the protection of the government, since the sums drawn from the monopoly of Vodka form an important item of the revenue. That there was a due appreciation of the obligation conferred by either party, I learned from a Russian gentleman, who told me that the police had strict orders not to take up any person found drunk in the streets. The numbers of tipsy men who reeled unnoticed about the large towns seemed living testimonies to the accuracy of this statement.

In excuse of these regulations, it may indeed be urged that the Russian peasant is so degraded, at any rate, that it amounts to much the same thing whether he be in a state of cultivated intoxication or natural incapacity.

But while every encouragement is given to an extensive and public consumption of the juice of the grape, the fragrant weed enjoys no such immunity; far from it—a most determined war is waged against all smokers. A policeman will regard with complacency the besotted mujik, stumbling up against every passenger he meets; but if perchance he detect the aroma of tobacco, or see the end of a cigar lighting up some dark dismal street, he pounces down upon the luckless wayfarer, who has trusted to the shadows of night to conceal his unlawful act, and barbarously demands from him the sum of three rubles.

The mujiks certainly show themselves sensible of the consideration which prompts this exception in favour of their besetting vice, by behaving in a most inoffensive manner while under the influence of their potations; nor, after they become sober, do they seem possessed with any other feelings than those of gratitude and self-satisfaction.

Our pilots, on the following day, were evidently amused at any hazy reminiscences which their bruises might suggest of

Pilots

the scenes at Samara, and the captain said that they never left the ship without a similar occurrence taking place. His invariable rule, therefore, was to prohibit their going on shore at all during the whole voyage; but they had contrived on this occasion to elude his vigilance.

The other sailors seemed to be more steady and manageable; and whatever might be their habits on shore, they certainly lived most abstemiously on board ship. About 5 in the evening they used to assemble round two enormous basins full of boiled millet-seed and linseed oil, while to each mess was also assigned a large loaf of black bread, junks of which they dipped into this delectable compound, and very soon lapped it all up. Both before and after the meal, a very elaborate ceremony of saying grace was gone through, which occupied nearly five minutes, and consisted of an infinite number of bowings and crossings to every point of the compass. Indeed this invariable manifestation of gratitude, even for the most trifling gift, is a remarkable characteristic of the poorer classes.

About half-way between Syzran and Kvaliensk, we entered the government of Saratov, and here the hills had subsided to their old elevation, seldom rising above three hundred feet; but they had again changed in character, and now receded some distance from the river. To judge also from the numerous herds of cattle grazing over them, they seemed to afford good pasture. The left bank was occasionally strewn for hundreds of yards with melons waiting to be conveyed away to those who should be imprudent enough to eat them.

CHAPTER VII

Singular misapplication of steam—Volsk—Sheep from steppes of Caspian—A merchant noble—Serfs: their intrinsic value—Saratov: its mercantile importance—Emancipation of serfs—The Czar and Ayuka Khan—Volga fever and ague—German colonies—Stinkorosin the robber—Leave the Samson—The Volga: its merits, and attractions to the tourist

It is difficult to conceive that so magnificent a river as the Volga should be so desecrated, or so noble a power as steam so abused, as by the astonishing contrivance which passed us the day before we arrived at Saratov, and which could only have emanated from the brain of some semi-civilised Russian. So long as steam was unknown, or its application thought to be impracticable here, from the difficulty of navigation, the clumsy horse-machine might be tolerated as an original, and perhaps a somewhat ingenious method of effecting the desired end; but after such notions had been exploded, and steamers were plying regularly from Astrakhan to Rhybinski, that any man should have been found so devoid of common sense as to construct an apparatus in which steam was to

Horse-Machine and Barges

supply the place of horses in the way it did in the one before us, was certainly most amazing.

First of all, we observed approaching us a small steamer, towing a boat, in which were a huge anchor and a quantity of men. At a distance of little more than half a mile appeared another funnel, planted in the midst of an unwieldy square-looking barge, on each side of which were very diminutive wheels, and on the deck sundry Chinese-looking habitations, some sticks with flags flying, and a mast. Behind this grotesque monster was a strong of gay-coloured barges; and the whole turn-out would have been very picturesque, had not the aforesaid funnel vomited forth black jets of smoke. Presently we saw the anchor hove over the side of the boat, which then returned with the steamer, bringing with it the hawser; upon arriving at the machine, another anchor was lowered into the boat, and both started again on the same errand. Meantime the engine on the square barge was employed in warping itself and suite to the anchor first laid down; having accomplished which, it found the second prepared for it half a mile farther on; and so it dragged its weary length along, making from twenty to thirty versts a day.

The ingenious inventor had evidently found it impossible to disabuse his mind of the excellence of this warping system; and, by this wondrous misapplication of steam, he was just six times as long, used twice as many steamers, and about twenty times as much fuel, as if he had employed a common tug-boat to convey the same amount of cargo.

An immense raft of pines from Perm and the Ural Mountains, on which were two or three cottages, was a more sensible-looking, as well as interesting object; and the wood in those regions is so cheap, that it pays to float timber from the head waters of the Kama down to the Caspian.

Before we approached our next wood station, Volsk, the downs had become more extensive. Hitherto the banks had been generally stratified, consisting of layers of yellowish sand, sometimes so soft as to be perforated by swallows, while in other parts it seemed to be undergoing a process of petrifaction. Now the cliffs were formed entirely of a cretaceous marl frequently composed of pure chalk, but often of a clayey colour. Here and there we passed a nobleman's house, situated near some miserable village, and in a very windy locality; but Volsk itself was charming. Snugly situated between two hills, one of which attains a height of nearly four hundred feet, its new green-domed churches and substantial-looking houses gave it a thriving appearance; while the valleys running inland were well cultivated and picturesque—the houses and fields, in some places, rising in terraces along the hillside.

Since leaving Nijni, we had not seen anything half so pretty; and we doubted, indeed, whether we did not give the preference to the less elevated but more sheltered position of Volsk. From the hills above it we had some extensive views—the Volga always forming the most prominent and interesting feature. As we strolled along a shady dell, in which the dwarf almond, linden, and stunted white poplar seemed to predominate, we heard a very unmelodious singing, and found it proceeded from a number of barefooted girls occupied in walking through wheat spread out on a barbecue, apparently for the purpose of turning it over. The song of each maiden was different, and pitched in a very high key. It was evidently considered a part of the performance; for our unwonted appearance even scarcely diverted them—it certainly could not make them forget their tunes.

Volsk contains about ten thousand inhabitants, and its principal trade is in tallow. We passed an immense herd of sheep, which seemed, from their conformation in certain quarters, to have been created expressly for the purpose of being melted into tallow, as their wool—of a very inferior description—was of little value. What added to the grotesqueness of their appearance, was their perfect innocence of anything like tails. Nature seemed to have compromised this absence with a fleecy bustle, which sat upon them in the most ridiculous and undignified manner. However, to these bustles does Volsk owe its prosperity; large herds of sheep, graced by this peculiarity, being driven up annually from the steppes of the Caspian to the towns on the Volga.

Sheep from the Steppes of the Caspian

The consignee of the flock we were then contemplating was said to be the richest merchant on the river—the countless millions of rubles which he was reputed to possess throwing Rothschild far into the shade. We were rather astonished when a heavy-looking man, clad in a shirt and loose drawers, who came reeling on board in a state of extreme intoxication, proved to be the millionaire in question; and it was highly disgusting to find that he, and a friend in no better condition, were to occupy the cabin adjoining ours. Everybody paid great deference to this personage, chiefly, as it appeared, because he was a noble, though of the lowest grade, and could afford to get drunk on English bottled stout, at five shillings a bottle. Porter certainly seemed a very odd thing for a man at Saratov to select as a beverage for this purpose; but the secret of the choice was, that it required an expenditure of about two pounds daily to enable him to effect the desired end—a circumstance that raised him immensely in the estimation of his fellows. How the pilots envied him! A few miserable copeks spent with a similar design, subjected them to the harshest treatment. Not so, however, the more fortunate passengers in the barge. Profiting by the example of the wealthy nobleman, rich with the spoils at Nijni, and responsible to no one, they one and all indulged most copiously; and the scenes of drunkenness and immorality which went on at every station would not bear description, if, indeed, words could convey any adequate notion of them.

Whatever may be the morals of the peasantry in remote districts, those living in the towns and villages on the Volga are more degraded in their habits than any other people amongst whom I have travelled; and they can hardly be said to disregard, since they have never been acquainted with, the ordinary decencies of life. What better result can indeed be expected from a system by which the upper classes are wealthy in proportion to the number of serfs possessed by each proprietor? The rapid increase of the population is no less an object with the private serf-owner, than the extensive consumption of ardent spirits is desired by the government. Thus each vice is privileged with especial patronage. Marriages, in the Russian sense of the term, are consummated at an early age, and are arranged by the steward, without consulting the parties—the lord's approval alone being necessary. The price of a family ranges from £25 to £40. Our captain had taken his wife on a lease of five years, the rent for that term amounting to fifty rubles, with the privilege of renewal at the expiration of it.

Our new fellow-passengers had no other luggage than some dozens of porter, upon which they regaled themselves during the night, until, overcome by their potations, they sunk on the floor of the cabin, and snored stertorously, till our arrival at Saratov roused them into the state of semi-consciousness which they had manifested on the previous day. We were indeed thankful to hear that Saratov was the destination of this merchant prince—a consideration which alone would have made our first view of the place delightful, had nature not asserted her own claims to our admiration. I thought the town, as we approached it, and saw its numerous domes and spires reflected in the glassy surface of the water, certainly entitled to the distinction of being called "Queen of the Volga." The high range of hills which form its background—the rugged cliffs on the right—and the river, nearly three miles broad, which washes its walls, seem to have induced the inhabitants to adorn their city with more bright-coloured roofs and tapering steeples than is usual even in Russia, as if to do justice to the scenery amid which it is situated. We were unwise enough to land and disenchant ourselves, amid dust and desolation. Though some of the houses are handsome, the streets are deserted, the shops poor, and the *tout ensemble* most uninviting. Yet Saratov is said to contain forty thousand inhabitants, and is, after Samara, the most prosperous town on the river. The capital of a district containing nearly two millions of inhabitants, its revenue, in proportion to its size, exceeds that of any other city in the empire, and places it high in the scale of Russian towns.

The smaller towns of the government are not behind their capital, and present a marked contrast to those in the Simbirsk district. From the want of commercial or manufacturing enterprise, and other causes referred to in a former chapter, the revenues of all Russian towns are remarkably small; and the only places which yield at all an adequate return, are those situated on the Volga, or the shores of the Black Sea, where the facility of transport at their doors, and the wonderfully prolific soil with which they are blessed, form an irresistible combination—compelling the inhabitants to take advantage of their favoured position, and to become rich in spite of themselves.

Thus it happens that the government of Saratov exports annually nearly as much grain as Orenburg; while some idea of its extent may be formed from the fact that, were it equally apportioned, each member of its population of two millions would possess a larger share of productive soil than could be awarded in any other district, except, perhaps, that of the Don Cossacks. It is difficult to account for the deficiency in the revenue of the towns of the neighbouring district of Simbirsk.

The soil there is doubtless inferior, and the population considerably larger in proportion to its extent; nor is there so much land under cultivation; but that would hardly explain the marked difference which exists between it and the provinces of Saratov, and particularly Orenburg. A more easy solution of the problem seems to be in the fact, that in Orenburg, which also contains a population of nearly two millions, not above thirteen in every hundred of the males are serfs. Those people having been originally the property of the crown, and made partially free, in accordance with the more enlightened system which the government is now pursuing, have turned their freedom to good account, and are enriching themselves and their country by an industry which, for the first time in their lives, they find to be profitable.

A more convincing proof could scarcely be obtained of the beneficial results of this liberation, than to find that the provinces in which it has taken place most largely, have already far outstripped any others in the empire. Well would it be for the country if the serfs of private individuals could be treated in like manner. The small serf-owners, in particular, prove the most invincible opponents to wholesale liberation, since those owning twenty serfs and under, by far outnumber the more extensive proprietors. Were the proportion of freemen to serfs the same in Saratov that it is in Orenburg, there can be no doubt that, with its superior advantages of position (being intersected by the Volga and its tributaries for a distance of three hundred and fifty miles), its prosperity would surpass that of the latter. Saratov exports large quantities of tobacco annually, the quality of which is considered superior to that grown in other provinces.

Bell gives an amusing account of an interview, at which he was present here in 1722, between Peter the Great and Ayuka Khan, who, accompanied by his wife, "fifty years old, of a decent and cheerful deportment," dined with the Emperor. In the course of conversation, His Majesty intimated to the Khan that he meditated an expedition into Persia, and required a contribution of ten thousand men. The Khan replied that they were quite at the Czar's disposal; but as he thought five thousand would be sufficient, he would give orders that this number should join the imperial army; with which reply the Emperor parted from him perfectly contented.

Congratulating ourselves on being rid of our late passenger, we returned on board, and found the deck-cabin, in which we had been accustomed to spend the day, occupied by a party of Armenians, whose imperturbable countenances, and the firm position they had taken up on the floor, with their legs doubled under them, forbade any attempt at expulsion, if we had thought such a measure justified by circumstances. They were harmless individuals, picturesquely attired, with long beards and flowing robes, who occupied themselves in quarrelling with one another, sleeping, smoking chibouks, drinking tea, and eating melons. They were so excessively in the way that I was almost tempted to wish that this fruit might disagree with them, knowing, as I did, from experience, the unpleasant results of such indulgence. Tempted at Samara by piles of magnificent melons exhibited for sale, we laid in a store wherewith to refresh ourselves during the sultry days, and had just finished our first dessert when the captain informed us that no stranger ever eats Volga melons without getting Volga fever. I hardly believed that anything half so disagreeable could be the attribute either of so noble a river, or of such delicious fruit, but that night our united pulses amounted to two hundred and thirty-eight, which, with an ague accompaniment, sufficiently proved the correctness of the captain's assertion. Fortunately, we had neither doctors nor medicine on board, still we suffered rather severely, as, after leaving Saratov, the heat gradually increased. The thermometer in the cabin seldom stood below seventy-two degrees. A week before there had been a sharp frost. To add to the effect of this sudden change of temperature, a scorching south wind set in, accompanied with clouds of dust, which made the deck a less agreeable lounge than we had hitherto found it. The banks, too, were parched and barren, and a hundred miles below Saratov, they might have been those of some burning African river.

Under such circumstances, we no longer hailed the wood station as a pleasant change, even had we been in a condition to profit by our stay. But what was most to be regretted was the impossibility of seeing anything of the German colonies, which commence upon the right bank a little below Saratov, and extend southward as far as Sarepta.

The inhabitants are, for the most part, of the Lutheran or Moravian persuasions. The villages amount in number to upwards of a hundred, each containing an average population of about a thousand souls. The first colonists settled here under the auspices of the Empress Catharine.

Kamichin is a large town on the right bank, where, as long ago as the beginning of the last century, an Englishman (Capt. Perry) began to cut a canal to the Ilovla, a tributary of the Don, the distance not exceeding twenty versts. The formation of the country, and the difference of level, presented difficulties which were then deemed almost insuperable. Had he succeeded, it is questionable whether a connection with so small a stream as the Ilovla would have been of much use.

One night we anchored under a precipitous cliff, on the edge of which, it is said, was once perched the castle of the famous robber, Stinkorosin. As I could obtain no further information respecting this celebrated personage, I have been particular in recording his euphonious name, with the hope that some future traveller may immortalise one who—if there be anything in a name—must be entitled to be so honoured. The winds had freshened into a gale, and the night was as black as the rocks that frowned above us. The waves, high enough to dash into our ports and drench our beds, forthwith inspired us with some little respect for a storm on the Volga. A small evil this, when we considered what delightful weather it would have been esteemed by Stinkorosin and his gallant band, who, descending from their stronghold by subterranean passages and other mysterious avenues, would doubtless have boarded the Samson under cover of the darkness, and immured its occupants for ever in the dungeons of the fortress. Originally these banks were inhabited by the Cossacks of the Volga, who, having been transported to the lines of the Caucasus, when the empire, about the year 1780, was extended in that direction, have been replaced by the less warlike peasantry of Pensa, Tambov, and the neighbouring provinces.

On the following day we passed upon the left a miserable village, with an unpronounceable name, which merits notice only from its exporting annually no less than nine million poods of salt, brought hither from a marsh sixty versts inland. A great part of the village was composed of tents; and that portion of the population which inhabited them consisted, probably, of Calmuck Tartars, who wander over these vast steppes. Numbers of bullocks, tethered near their carts, seemed to imply a recent arrival of the great article of export.

Notwithstanding the hurricane of the night before, which ought to have cleared the atmosphere, the weather was closer than ever, and at six in the evening the hot damp air increased the languor that always accompanies fever, so that our spirits appeared to be depressed, in sympathy with the smoke which hung over our track in a long low black streak, corresponding with the windings of the river. To add to our miseries, we stuck, most unexpectedly, on a sandbank, and when, having now been sixteen days upon the river, it was not unreasonable that we should be impatient to leave it.

It was satisfactory to hear that Astrakhan was not worth seeing, after we had decided not to go there; as, whatever may have been my inclination, I was now at least delighted to find that the irregularity of the steamers from Astrakhan, and the amount of additional time it would occupy to make the proposed tour from that city, warranted our disembarking at Dubovka; while the fever and ague with which we were both prostrated, rendered it advisable that we should quit the river without loss of time.

At Dubovka, then, on the morning of the 19th September, we

bade adieu to the Samson and its hospitable captain, whose kindness and attention had done much to make our voyage agreeable; and, however relieved I might have been once more to have a different mode of travelling in prospect, it was yet with a feeling of regret that I looked round our cabin for the last time, to see that nothing was left behind save sundry remains of stores, considered to be the perquisites of the old lady who had waited upon us. Had we been obliged to trust entirely to the said stores, we should have fared badly; but the captain took compassion on our inexperience, and, finding that our attempts at catering had proved unsuccessful, insisted upon our dining with him every evening during the voyage.

Until passenger-steamboats are established on the Volga, the length of time which the voyage occupies in a tug, and the difficulty of procuring provisions, prove serious obstacles to those who wish to see the river. The traveller would hardly complain of the delays to which he might be subject, in a boat with a light draught, and unhampered by barges. The wood stations afford pleasant walks, with the probability of a sketch; but, from being almost invariably situated on the left bank, it was often necessary to make interest with the captain to be sent to the opposite side. In a good boat, and under ordinary circumstances, the voyage from Nijni to Astrakhan ought not to occupy more than eight days, and the variety and novelty of the scenes through which he passes would suffice to keep the traveller amused for that period; while, at the same time, he would hardly consider that the beauties of the river compensated for a residence of three weeks on its bosom. Still, to those with plenty of time at their disposal, the life on board may be made to pass agreeably; and the personal comfort of the voyager will depend entirely upon the arrangements he makes before starting—and in securing a good cook and servants of his own.

Few towns in Russia are better worth a visit than Kazan, while the Jigoulee offers the finest scenery I had as yet seen in the country. Saratov vies with Nijni in beauty—the latter owing, perhaps, all to its lofty position—the former to its gay and handsome churches and buildings; but the cities on its banks, or those banks themselves—rocky or wooded—fail to inspire feelings equal to those suggested by this monarch of European rivers itself.

A sense of its grandeur and magnificence seemed to grow upon one daily; and now, though our experience had extended over more than a thousand miles of its winding course, I gazed with unabated wonder and admiration on its broad, rapid current, which swept away from us the Samson and its barges, and a feeling of desolation was induced, which reminded us that, our recent home having departed from us, it was time to seek another.

CHAPTER VIII

*Dubovka—The tram-road to the Don—Exception to Russian
dishonesty—Excessive politeness—Calmuck Tartars: their
history—An exodus—Religion and manners—A bad road—
Tzaritzin—Courier to the Caucasus—Sarepta—Moravian
missionaries—Sarepta: its manufactures and trade—
A pleasing picture*

Dubovka, formerly the capital of the country of the Volga
Cossacks, is prettily situated on the right bank, but is a place of
little importance, consisting chiefly of wooden houses, among
which are sprinkled a few built of red brick, and these give a
more unfinished look to the streets than if they were
composed entirely of wood. The population does not exceed
six or eight thousand. Its chief ornament—and one, indeed, of
which the inhabitants may be deservedly proud—is their
beautiful church, near which, unfortunately, we lodged, and
found the incessant tolling of the ponderous unmusical bells
distracting. Of course there was no inn to be found, but we
were very kindly lodged in one of the best houses of the town,
belonging to Mr. Vodalaken, the agent of the steam company;
and had it not been for the hardness of the bed, the heat of the
weather, the quantities of vermin, the barking of dogs, and my
own indisposition, I might have found our quarters more than
ordinarily comfortable. We had some difficulty in finding a
"tarantasse," or travelling-carriage, which it was necessary to
buy here before entering on the long steppe journey before us
to Taganrog; and this task was not rendered more easy by our
utter ignorance of the language. Fortunately, from the
proximity of the German colonies, most of the respectable
people hereabouts were either Germans or spoke German,
and most kindly afforded us every aid in their power.

Our host united in his person the two offices of steam
company's agent and manager of the tramroad across to the
Don. Unluckily he was absent from home, and I had scarcely

any opportunity of gaining information regarding the amount and nature of the traffic which passes through Dubovka on its way from the Volga to the Black Sea. By far the most important item is iron; and Siberian produce generally, timber from the northern provinces, and all manufactured goods intended for consumption throughout the greater part of Southern Russia, are also transported by means of the Don to Rostof and Taganrog; while some of the products from the shores of the Caspian are landed at Tzaritzin, a town fifty versts farther south, from whence they are conveyed to the same river. By the route of Dubovka is brought all the produce of Turkey and the south of Europe, necessary to supply the wants of the inhabitants on the Volga; which, finding its way as far north as the fair at Nijni, circulates from thence throughout the empire.

It is inconceivable how the country can rest satisfied with the wretched tram-road which now connects two such important rivers as the Volga and the Don. So far from their being any natural impediment to the formation of a canal across the isthmus which separates them, it is a perfectly simple undertaking, the distance not exceeding sixty versts, and the difference of level being comparatively trifling. The advantages to be gained by the completion of such a work must be apparent. A mere glance at the map will show that a canal forty miles long at this point would connect the Black Sea with the Baltic and the Caspian, and thus perfect a most elaborate system of inland communication. Nature has certainly done all that could be expected of her in this respect, and it seems hard that a government should not enable the inhabitants to avail themselves of the natural advantages which their country so eminently possesses.

If water-carriage excels land-carriage in proportion to the bulk of the produce to be conveyed, surely where iron or timber form the articles of transport, there can be no doubt of the superior merits of the former, even were the additional expenses incurred by the present system out of the question, or supposing that a railway had superseded the tram-road. At this particular juncture, when more wheat is exported from the ports in the south of Russia in one year than formerly left them during ten years, a connection between these rivers becomes of the highest importance; and did the wheat of Saratov and Orenburg find free access to the rising ports in the Sea of Azov, the increased facilities of communication with the sea-board would exert an influence which would be sensibly felt over the whole of the southeast of Russia. At present it is no wonder that the tram-road is not duly appreciated, since it does not descend to the water's edge; and in order to save the expense and trouble incurred by transferring the cargo into carts, conveying it in them to the tramroad, and there loading the cars, many of the merchants adhere to the old system of transporting both the goods and the barges, in which they have descended the Volga, across the isthmus in bullock-carts. These barges are flat-bottomed, and only draw two or three feet of water. They are taken to pieces at Dubovka, laid in the carts, and in eight or ten days reach Kakalinskaia on the Don, where they are put together again with bolts, and float down to Rostof. Upon arriving here they are broken up and converted into firewood.

We remained two days at Dubovka preparing for the coming journey, and trying to shake off Volga reminiscences under the motherly treatment of Madame Vodalaken. We here met that remarkable exception, which proved that dishonesty is the rule in Russia. A doctor with whom we vainly attempted to communicate in Latin, but who supplied his deficiency in the dead languages by his intelligent appreciation of the expressive signs which we used to convey to him some notions of our symptoms, positively refused to take a fee. This was so incomprehensible, that I was not in the least surprised at being cured by his prescription. A very short walk sufficed to show us Dubovka. The most striking peculiarity of the inhabitants appeared to be their excessive politeness: every respectable-looking man took off his hat to every other respectable-looking man. At first it seemed natural that people in so small a place should all know one another; but when we found that to cross the street involved, in our case, at least six acknowledgments of these salutations, it became necessary to do violence to our feelings of modesty, and attribute to our decency of deportment their frequent occurrence; and so I concluded the origin of this custom to be a desire on everybody's part to congratulate each other on looking so respectable in such an out-of-the-way part of the world as Dubovka. Against this mark of polished manners and good breeding, might be set off the indiscriminate way in which persons of both sexes bathed in the river, betraying a woeful lack of refinement, since it was evidently deemed a piece of unmitigated prudery to wear any covering whatever. Rather an apt illustration this of the spirit which pervades Russian society generally, where so much attention is paid to the most hollow conventionalities, and so little to those principles of honour and morality essential to the well-being of a community.

After a great deal of bargaining, carried on through the medium of a delightful little apothecary, we ultimately succeeded in buying a tarantasse, on so enlightened a construction that I doubted whether the C springs were not too far in advance of the age to be safe; while a pole, instead of the high yoke generally used, seemed not unlikely to puzzle the Don Cossack post-boys. However, we thought ourselves fortunate in obtaining anything half so civilised, and were rejoiced to see it appear at the door with three very tolerable horses.

We managed to get away by midday, and soon had the satisfaction of seeing the broad, bare, undulating steppe stretching interminably before us. As we left the town, a few small conical huts afforded fresh evidence of the Calmuck Tartars, who, quitting the deserts of Astrakhan, or crossing over the vast tracks of pasture-land which extend from the eastern shore of the Volga into Asia, occasionally travel to the northward, and pitch their tents near the towns on the western bank, when a fair or market-day attracts them. These "kybitkas" or tents consist simply of a framework of wood, over which felt is stretched, while a circular aperture at the top gives egress to the smoke.

I should have stopped and paid a visit to these wanderers in their own habitations, had I not already inspected a party of them in Dubovka, and nothing could be more interesting than their whole appearance. Of all the inhabitants of the Russian

Calmuck Tartars

empire, the Calmucks are the most distinguished by peculiarity of features and manners; and certainly their ragged flowing robes, bound round the waist with a coarse dirty scarf, and exposing to view a copper-coloured chest, together with their red boots and flat yellow caps trimmed with fur, completed a wild costume, unlike anything to be met with in less remote parts of the country. Their long black hair hung in thick braids on each side of their faces, which were of true Mongolian type; and it was difficult to look on the low wide noses, high cheek-bones, and long narrow eyes of these men, and yet believe that they were inhabitants of Europe. I felt transported again to the borders of Chinese Tartary, where I had already visited a race sprung from the same origin, adherents of the same faith, and probably, to some extent, speaking the same language.

It is singular how little we know of those nomadic hordes inhabiting the vast steppes of Tartary and Thibet, whose only real allegiance consists in a religious veneration for the sovereign pontiff at H'Lassa. Wandering over the deserts which form the boundary of Russia and China, they are a sort of connecting link between the two greatest empires in the world, as they become at pleasure the subjects of one or the other.

Once already from those regions have barbarian hosts poured forth, who, sweeping across the steppes which extend from the base of the Ural Mountains to the shores of the Caspian, spread themselves far and wide over the world of that day. We had crossed the very track of these invaders; and as we looked upon their successors, encamping in miserable tents, roving over arid plains, a scattered and degraded race, it was difficult to conceive that they could be the precursors of more barbarians, destined again to overrun the enlightened part of the world; and yet it is not long since the first Calmuck invasion took place. In the latter part of the seventeenth century, the Torgot and Derbet divisions of this tribe descended to the banks of the Volga, extending their wanderings over the country of the Don Cossacks to the shores of the Sea of Azov. About this time Ayuka Khan, of whom mention has already been made, ruled over the whole nation.

Shortly after his death, and while weakened by internal dissensions, the Calmucks fell an easy prey to the designs of the Russian government, and remained subject to the imperial sceptre, until, in the winter of 1770–71, offended by the despotic measures of the Empress Catharine II., half a million of the tribe wandered rather farther than usual, and ended by pitching their tents in the dominions of his Celestial Majesty— a warning this to despotic governments not to trouble their nomadic subjects with the arrangements of the Home Department.

It was, indeed, as remarkable an emigration as the revenge that prompted it was signal; and we are irresistibly reminded by it of the only parallel instance which history records, of those wanderings in the desert of Sinai, undertaken under somewhat similar circumstances; and if the sojourning in the wilderness was of much longer duration in the one case, the distance travelled in the other was immeasurably greater. Unfortunately a large portion of the Calmucks were left behind, having been prevented by an unusually late winter from crossing the Volga. Those who reached China, after a journey of eight months, were most cordially welcomed by the Emperor, who allotted for their occupation the Ily country in the province of Soongary, and granted them many privileges, in consideration of their voluntary submission to his rule.

To judge from the condition of the Calmucks I saw, their brethren in China have probably made an exchange for the better; and doubtless those who remained, suffered for the independent conduct of this portion of the tribe. They are in a great measure confined to the province of Astrakhan, and those who are immediately subject to the crown pay a tax amounting to seventy-five rubles a family. There is a committee for the administration of Calmuck affairs at Astrakhan, the president and some of the members of which are Russians.

Besides those who are under the dominion of the crown, there are several divisions of the tribe, each governed by separate princes. One of the most celebrated of these has built a palace on the shores of the Volga, not far from Astrakhan. This appears to be the nearest approach to a settled habitation that any of these restless beings have attained to; and so great is their dread of a more composed life and industrious habits, that when they are angry with a person, they wish "he may live in one place and work like a Russian." They live chiefly upon horseflesh and koumiss, or churned mare's milk, from which a kind of spirit is distilled. I did not observe any camels as we passed their tents; but these animals are the indispensable attendants of their wanderings. They pay the greatest respect and veneration to their Llamas, who, like their Russian neighbours, take every advantage of the supposed character for sanctity with which they are invested, to impose upon a barbarous and superstitious people; and there are now engrafted on their original Bhuddhistic faith a number of mystic rites and ceremonies, which are by no means orthodox additions.

The Calmucks and Nogays are the only nomad tribes which inhabit the country to the west of the Volga. They share, to some extent, the steppes to the eastward of that river with the Kirghees, some of whom I saw at the fair of Nijni, and who profess Mahomedanism. Though a smaller tribe, they occupy the territory allotted to them upon more independent conditions than do the Calmucks.

We did not make very rapid progress, though our horses were good and our carriage light. The yamschik or driver was deaf to threats affecting his vodka (drink-money); and the road was occasionally execrable. Following the bank of the Volga, it was continually intersected by rugged and precipitous ravines, not unlike those in the Campagna at Rome, except that they were steeper and narrower. It was left to the taste of the driver to take any one he chose of the numerous tracks that led to the bottom; and, indeed, it seemed of little consequence, as they were all equally bad, and full of fearful ruts.

We frequently found the remains of an imposing wooden bridge, which bore testimony to the fierce winter character of the present rivulet; and the government had apparently long since given up all idea of establishing permanent means of transit. Occasionally we passed long strings of bullock-waggons returning from market, where their owners had probably been vending water-melons—the staple article of consumption among the country people. I certainly never saw so many water-melons in my life, as in one day on these steppes. For hundreds of yards were they piled in heaps, and the entire population live upon them. A whole one is quite sufficient to constitute a sumptuous breakfast; while a peasant's dinner seldom consists of anything else.

It is fifty versts (thirty-four miles) from Dubovka to Tzaritzin; and the sun was just setting as we entered the town, descending the steep pitch down to the river at a break-neck pace. From these eights we had a lovely view of the Volga, as the last rays of a most brilliant sunset shed a warm glow over the vast basin, beautifully tinting the wooded islands in the distance.

Tzaritzin presents a very similar appearance to Dubovka. It contains about an equal population; and although it cannot boast of so handsome a church, it perhaps exceeds the latter in the number of substantially-built houses. The inhabitants carry on a considerable trade with the Calmucks and Kirghees, who resort hither in great numbers on festive occasions; and the country in the immediate vicinity is extremely fertile. It was so late when we arrived, that I had only time to take a cursory glance at the town; and I did that in no very amiable mood, our delay being compulsory, as no horses were to be procured at the post-station.

The fortress is situated on a cliff about a hundred feet above the river, but is, I believe, no longer garrisoned. Long ago, this town suffered much from frequent attacks of the lawless Cossack bands which infested the neighbourhood; and it was with a view of protecting the frontier that the liens of Tzaritzin were thrown up, consisting merely of a wall of earth defended by palisades, which extended across to the Don. Had we been wise, we should have disembarked here instead of at Dubovka, and thus have saved ourselves a rough drive along the bank of the Volga; for there is no post-road, as we imagined there was, directly across from Dubovka to the Don.

A dashing courier, with despatches for the Caucasus, started from the post-house just after we arrived, thus depriving us of the only available horses. He was dressed in true Circassian costume, and armed to the teeth. Screwing up his long twisted mustache, he scowled at us for daring to express a wish to proceed, and looked altogether so formidable, that it was a relief to see him rattle out of the courtyard, as he laughed contemptuously at our despair. I half envied him the journey on which he was bound. In thirty-six hours he would arrive at Astrakhan, and, crossing the steppes of the Caspian—if not murdered on the way—would, in a few days more, reach the seat of war. Fortunately the post-house was a clean-looking place, and we had a good room given us, with rather a comfortable floor, on which I spread a highly-scented sheepskin, and passed the night very tolerably. While vainly attempting to induce the post-master to give us horses, by dint of a vehement repetition of the word "vodka," a man in the costume of a mujik or peasant came up, and addressed me in German. He was the first genuine colonist of this class that I had seen; and there was something very singular in hearing good German from the lips of one with an exterior so uncultivated. He proved useful as an interpreter, and offered to drive us to Sarepta, the settlement to which he belonged, and which is situated about twenty miles to the south. Unluckily our route lay in an opposite direction, and I regretted that I could not accept his invitation.

As described to me by those who had visited it, Sarepta must be a perfect curiosity. Surrounded by tribes of barbarous Calmucks, and visited only by scarcely less barbarous Russians, its inhabitants maintain the genuine old Saxon character- adhere to their native tongue, and to the simple manners of their Fatherland. Uncontaminated by the indolent and vicious habits of those amongst whom they are situated, they are a prosperous community, reaping the rich harvest of that industry and frugality which are the characteristics of their race.

The colony was established in 1769, during the reign of the Empress Catharine, and consisted of but thirty individuals of both sexes. This little band belonged to the Moravian persuasion, and was under the guidance of some worthy missionaries, whose chief object in choosing so remote a locality was the conversion of the Calmucks.

No sooner had some symptoms of success, however, attended the efforts of these noble-minded men, than the Greek clergy interposed, and insisted that the converts should be admitted into their Church. Thinking, perhaps, that the

Calmuck was as enlightened an individual while a Bhuddhist, as he would be after he joined the Greek Church, the Moravian missionaries did not persist in their efforts at evangelisation. The government, as in duty bound, supported the priests in their opposition, and may thus be congratulated on having aided and abetted a Christian Church in its successful attempt to deprive a whole nation of the blessings of the Gospel.

No effort is made to atone for this wanton bigotry, by the establishment of missions by the Greek Church among these wandering tribes. Denying to them the means of acquiring a knowledge of those important truths which the Moravians so earnestly desired to impart, it yet supplies no substitute for them,—an omission which is tantamount to positively prohibiting the Calmucks from attempting to reach heaven at all.

Let the Moravian missionary but extend his efforts to those territories which own the spiritual jurisdiction of the Dalai Llama, and seek to convert the Calmucks there; he would certainly find more toleration in the headquarters of Bhuddhism than he has met with hitherto amongst the followers of the Greek Patriarch. Meanwhile, this little colony prospers under the wholesome influences of its faith, and by reason of the industry and integrity of its inhabitants. Unable more directly to benefit the surrounding savages, these honest Germans are living examples of the practical power of their religious principles, and form a striking contrast to the Russians of the neighbouring towns.

The population has now increased to eight hundred souls, who are chiefly employed in the cultivation of mustard, and the manufacture of the oil extracted from it. I could not ascertain the exact value of the exports in this article alone, but it is a product in such universal use all over Russia, that it must be very considerable.

The cotton and silk fabrics of Sarepta are extensively circulated throughout the empire; while calico and the coarser stuffs, of the nature of Manchester goods, find great favour with the surrounding tribes, who look to Sarepta for the fashions of the season. In this enlightened community, it is not to be supposed that the more refined trades are neglected. Here excellent watchmakers, opticians, bookbinders, and goldsmiths, follow their avocations, and are much resorted to by the inhabitants of the large Volga towns. Agriculture, too, obtains its due share of attention from the colonists, and the soil is made to yield of its abundance, under a more improved system of cultivation than that pursued by the Russians generally; while at the neighbouring little German village of Schönbrun, the rearing of cattle and sheep is successfully carried on. Such prosperity would be incompatible with the existence of the colony under the Russian government, did it not enjoy privileges and immunities which secure for it an exemption from the hardships which elsewhere press so heavily upon native enterprise. Sarepta pays a merely nominal rent to the crown, and the inhabitants possess the right, without restriction, of carrying on commercial transactions, not only throughout the Empire, but in other countries, as merchants of the first guild; consequently, in all the large towns of Russia there are agencies, or shops devoted exclusively to the sale of their merchandise. They enjoy, moreover, a species of constitution, regulate their own affairs, and adjudicate in criminal as well as civil matters. The ministers and the judges are identical—to wit, the mayor, and two members elected by the community.

Sarepta maintains intimate relations with the German colonies of the Saratov district, and in cases of a serious nature, an appeal is made to the general committee of these colonies. The town is neatly laid out, and beautifully supplied with clear water. The church, the school, and a few of the most important buildings, are of stone, the rest of wood. Avenues of trees line the streets; and here, under their grateful shade, we can imagine the patriarchs of the community seated during the afternoon, enjoying tobacco of their own growing, moistening it with beer of their own brewing, and regarding the members of the happy little society as children of their own rearing.

111

Had I known, before it was too late to alter our plans and secure another padaroshna, that such scenes as these were to be witnessed by making a detour of a few miles, I should not have hesitated to turn aside, and see the wonderful phenomenon of a community, prosperous, thriving, and happy, existing in a country, and under a government, which I had supposed incapable of affording the elements conducive to such a state of well-being.

CHAPTER IX

*Parting sensations—First discoverers of the Volga—Trade in the
thirteenth century—Early English commercial company—
Prohibitive policy of Russia—Steamers on the Caspian—The
shores of the Caspian—Arid desert of Astrakhan*

Shortly after daybreak we were again *en route*, and I gazed
somewhat wistfully at the post-house and wooden cottages
which surrounded it, as we turned our backs upon the last
signs of civilised life we should see for some time. No friendly
German colonist would meet us at any future station. The
people spoke an execrable *patois*,—an annoyance, by the way,
which did not affect us, as the purest Russian would have been
equally unintelligible to our unpractised ears. The Don
Cossacks have rather an evil reputation amongst their
neighbours; but I found that although but one opinion existed
regarding their honesty, they were not accused of habitually
resorting to acts of violence. Under these circumstances we
were likely to be as well off among Don Cossacks as among
any other of his Imperial Majesty's subjects; and so,
determined to put any losses we might sustain in the list of
incidental expenses, and to speak in the language of rubles
and copeks, we set out upon a five days' journey across the
Don Cossack steppes.

At first our way led up a steep ravine: in a short time we had
gained an elevation of four or five hundred feet. From this
point we looked back, for the last time, upon our old friend
with whom we had travelled in company for so many days;
and, forgetting the fever of its banks and the ague of its mists,
I remembered only that I should probably never again gaze on
this noblest of rivers, and endeavoured to stereotype upon my
mind the view which lay stretched before me, as one which,
while calculated to be a source of pleasant recollections
hereafter, was entitled, from its peculiar character, to a leaf in
the portfolio of my imagination also.

Is it not the case that, in proportion as the traveller extends his wanderings, they become invested with greater attractions,—not so much from the novelty of what he sees, as from the extreme improbability of his ever again beholding those objects which most deeply interest him? How many landscapes, churches, and pictures are coldly stored away in the memory, and occupy no prominent position there, simply because they may be revisited at pleasure. But how differently are those regarded, which may possess scarcely equal intrinsic merit, when the thought is associated with them that they are looked upon for the last time.

There are feelings engendered by the words "farewell for ever," which invest the objects from which we are about to part with an indescribable charm, when the imagination seems to have the power of causing the world to reflect our most intimate sensations. This, however, can only be the case when we know them as old friends; hence it is, that though first impressions may be more faithful, they are always accompanied by the harsh business-like tone of mere ordinary sight-seeing. The mind is entirely occupied in examining the details, and appreciating the general effect, and wants that familiarity with, or, if I may so call it, affection for, those well—known features, which springs from a longer and closer acquaintanceship.

Such, at least, I took to be the result of my experience, as I bade adieu to the Volga; and these feelings suggested themselves the more forcibly at this moment, when I remembered the different aspects under which this noble river had been presented to me. At Nijni, I saw it crowded with shipping from the seas of Europe and Asia, bearing to distant lands the productions of the two continents, serving for a highway from one to the other, and traversing the whole length of the mightiest empire in the world;—wonder and admiration then engrossed all my faculties. When, shortly afterwards, I was gliding down its rapid current, and living in the daily contemplation of its beauteous banks, the sensations were those of calm serenity and a placid appreciation of its various charms. And now, though the landscape at our feet was beautiful—for the river, which here trended sharply to the eastward, divided itself into so many channels that the wooded islands thus formed looked as if they studded some large lake—yet it was not so much the general view of the Volga which engaged my attention, but rather the many associations connected with it which crowded into my mind, as I watched its windings until they were lost in the deserts of Calmuck Tartary, and regretted that the mysterious course which the stream had taken, obliged us now to bid adieu to it for ever.

It was probably from this spot that the Volga first burst upon the gaze of the monks who, in the thirteenth century, explored these distant regions, and who, confirming the wonderfully accurate description of the Caspian given by Herodotus, upset the theory entertained by sceptics of that great geographer, that the Caspian and Frozen Ocean were connected by a channel, when they returned with the discovery that the largest river in Europe poured its waters into that remote eastern lake, the existence of which, without an outlet, has since puzzled so many successive generations. It is due to Ptolemy, however, to say, that his notions upon the subject of the Volga were correct, many centuries before the holy fathers reached this stream, though not substantially confirmed at the time, nor adhered to afterwards; and it can hardly be supposed that the Greek colonists in the Crimea could have been altogether ignorant of its existence. We have every reason to believe, at all events, that the first portion of the river which was ever navigated was that which extends from this last bend to the shores of the Caspian.

Towards the end of the thirteenth century the Genoese established factories in the Crimea, and on the Sea of Azov; and the position of Tana, at the mouth of the Tanais, or Don, goes far to show that communications were carried on by means of this river and the Volga. Monopolising the whole of the carrying trade between Europe and Asia, the traffic passed exclusively through the ports of these enterprising Italians, and continued to do so until the close of the fifteenth century, when they fell under the sway of the Ottoman Empire; and thus it was, either by way of the Phasis and the Cur, or across this narrow isthmus, that, nearly six hundred years ago, all those Eastern productions which delighted and amazed our ancestors were conveyed. Then, richly-freighted caravans passed along the dreary track, laden with the merchandise which was to supply a continent; while now, in the nineteenth century, and in this *civilised* empire, nothing is to be seen but an occasional creaking bullock-cart carrying timber or iron, the produce of the bleak north.

But there is an association, fraught with a still deeper significance, attached to this neck of land, which has served at the same time as a highway for the inroads of barbarian hordes, and as a barrier to that commercial enterprise in the East, upon the extension of which the civilisation of two continents in a great measure formerly depended. Here, some centuries ago, in an attempt made by the Porte to improve its commercial relations with Central Asia—which had been much impaired by the diversion of Eastern trade from the overland route to that round the Cape—the Ottoman troops *first* encountered Muscovite barbarians, who then succeeded in obstructing the formation of a canal, designed by Selim the Second. That enlightened enterprise, undertaken under Mahomedan auspices, has never been carried out by a Christian power, while the blighting influence which was then exercised upon the cause of civilisation still characterises the Russian sway; and a defeat of the Ottoman arms, by the Muscovite aggressors of the present day, will be no less disastrous to that cause than was the savage onslaught first made upon the Turks by the untamed subjects of Ivan the Terrible.

About the middle of the last century, an English company was formed for the purpose of carrying on an Oriental commerce through Russia; but the ignorance and jealousy of the Muscovite government remained unchanged, though manifested in a more civilised form, and the enterprise proved a total failure.[1]

The Eastern traffic which in these days passes through Tzaritzin is scarcely worth consideration. The only solution of the problem which involves this anomalous state of things, ought to be in the fact of some much better way having been discovered by the government, for the transit of Eastern goods, than that adopted by the Genoese; and considering that, for five hundred miles, the trans-Caucasian-Russian provinces are conterminous with Persia and Turkey, this would not seem an improbable conjecture to anyone not acquainted with the commercial policy of the country. Not that it is very easy to say what that policy is; but one effect of it, in this instance, is certain, that scarcely any use whatever is made of the route which does there exist. To explain this, it is necessary to discover the real principle upon which the government acts; for it is absurd to suppose that it can be so infatuated as to believe that the protective system which it now pursues can ever advance the commercial interests of the country. Projecting into the heart of Asia, while it monopolises more than half the continent of Europe—possessing means of communication with the East by way of the Caspian, denied to any other European power—intersected by rivers expressly adapted to connect the ports upon the four seas between which she is situated—Russia might become the highway of nations. The wealth of Europe and Asia would thus pour into the coffers of the country through the various channels which it alone could so advantageously offer for the commerce of the world; and the only reason why this result has not long since taken place, is the virtual prohibition by the government of the existence of such a state of things, by its denying to all foreign goods the right of transit through the Russian dominions. As a necessary consequence, the produce of the East passes

1 An interesting account of its proceedings was published by that remarkable man, Mr. Jonas Hanway, its principal agent in Persia.

through Smyrna and Trebisond, instead of through Tiflis to Redout Kalè on the Black Sea; or—if there were a canal between the Volga and the Don—by water all the way from Astrabad and the intermediate ports to Taganrog, *via* Astrakhan and Tzaritzin, or to St. Petersburg direct. Thus have those brilliant commercial designs cherished by Peter the Great, and founded upon an anticipated extension of his Eastern frontier, been destroyed by a policy unworthy the successors of so enlightened a monarch; and those ports on the Caspian, in attempts to acquire which he sacrificed his political reputation, are sinking under influences utterly blasting to their prosperity.

From a consideration of these circumstances, and in spite of the anxiety of government to induce an opposite belief, we are constrained to suppose that it is only solicitous for the prosperity of the nation, so long as this prosperity can coexist with the permanent state of gross ignorance and barbarism in which the people are kept; for it is evident that an extensive intercourse with European nations would open the eyes of this enslaved population, and introduce those principles of freedom which would soon prove utterly subversive to the imperial power as it at present exists. In order, therefore, that the traveller may duly appreciate the system of political economy practised by the government, it is necessary he should remember that its interests and those of the people are diametrically opposed to one another. He will then cease to wonder that men-of-war, instead of merchant steamers, regularly navigate the Caspian. The most wretched craft are freighted with the rich fabrics of Persia, while iron steamers are appropriated to the transport of precious soldiers. These steamers are also employed in blockading the eastern shores of Circassia; and are ready, in case of a war with Persia, to convey troops to that kingdom. At present, they ply twice a month between Astrakhan, Bakou, Lenkeran, Enzeli, and Astrabad. I was informed, moreover, that two iron steamers had been recently launched upon the Sea of Aral, with a view, it was said, of carrying out some commercial projects. These may some day prove to be of rather a questionable nature. There is a line of Cossacks extending across the Kirghees deserts to the Sea of Aral, established, no doubt, for the purpose of protecting these so-called mercantile arrangements.

I do not see, however, how it could compromise the selfish policy of the government to improve the navigation of the Volga; for, although it is at present used almost entirely for purposes of trade, it might, in case of a war in these parts, be found a most useful auxiliary in the transport of troops. The experience of those who have been navigating this river for any length of time, goes far to show that the volume of water is rapidly diminishing; and our captain referred to the increasing difficulties of navigation as a practical demonstration of the correctness of this conclusion. The numerous channels by means of which the Volga finds its way into the Caspian—percolating, as it were, through the Delta upon which Astrakhan is situated—are yearly becoming shallower, and the Caspian itself is said to be decreasing. Humboldt, however, most distinctly denies this to be the case; and though the inhabitants of Astrakhan insist that they are farther off from the sea now than they used to be, they have probably no better ground for the supposition than a vague tradition to that effect.

A most interesting series of observations has recently been made by Messrs Englehardt and Parrot, by which they have established the fact, that the level of the Caspian is about eighteen toises below that of the Black Sea; but as the Don flows with greater rapidity than the Volga, the difference of level of the two rivers at the point where they most nearly approximate is undoubtedly far greater than this. Professor Pallas has been at some pains to prove that this elevated plateau formed at some previous period the northern shore of the Caspian. Adopting Tournefort's theory, that, previous to the Deucalionian flood, the Black Sea was separated from the Mediterranean by the mountains of the Thracian Bosphorus,

119

he maintains that the Caspian and the Sea of Aral, being then united, were connected with the Black Sea by a channel flowing round the northern point of the Caucasus.

Whether this view be correct or not—and, in accordance with more modern notions, we should at any rate throw back the date to a pre-Adamite era—there can be little doubt that, at some period, the Caspian extended over the basin of the Volga, upon which we were now looking. The whole configuration of the country supports such a hypothesis. Near this point the steppe follows the course of the Sarpa to the southward, rising precipitously from the deserts through which the Volga meanders. These deserts are impregnated with salt, and shells exactly resembling those found in the Caspian are plentifully scattered over the surface, while the steppe, upon which we travelled to the Don, was composed of a fine rich black loam, devoid of any marine deposits. It seemed singular that, while crossing one of the most fertile districts in Russia, we should actually be looking down upon the most sterile; but there can be no more satisfactory way of accounting for so sudden a change in the surface of the country, than by supposing that a great portion of it was formerly submerged. We congratulated ourselves that it was our lot to traverse the more elevated line of country; and as we turned our backs upon the vast sandy deserts which extend to the Chinese frontier, and hurried away from the salt swamps of Astrakhan, the dull tame steppe looked quite pleasant, and a journey through the country of the Don Cossacks seemed invested with new and unexpected charms.

CHAPTER X

Don Cossack steppes—Wild travelling—Posting experiences—An unpleasant discovery—Somovars: their merits—Costume of peasants—A Don Cossack highway—The Donetz—Meeting a traveller—Novo Tcherkask

We entered the country of the Don Cossacks at Jablonsky, our first stage from Tzaritzin. Nothing could be more dreary than the aspect of the country between the Volga and the Don, except, perhaps, that through which we travelled after crossing the latter river. The undulating prairie, covered with a short dry grass, interspersed with quantities of wild thyme and lilac crocuses, stretched away illimitably, and looked like an ocean regaining its tranquillity after a three days' storm.

For miles we did not meet a soul; occasionally we saw a few bullock-carts carrying timber across to the Don, or a wild-looking Cossack galloped past on a wilder-looking horse. The road seemed carefully to avoid all villages, and the few we discovered at a distance consisted chiefly of round huts, so exactly like the haystacks amid which they were placed as to be scarcely distinguishable from them: but though I saw carts carrying straw, as well as these haystack villages, I do not remember passing a rood of cultivation until we reached the Don.

The weather having been fine for some weeks past, the road was pretty good, though a mere track; but the delays at the huts—dignified with the name of post-stations—were most annoying. However, after a ten hours' journey we reached the river, a placid and unpretending stream. Its banks had much the same character as those of the Volga—the high steppe on the west rising abruptly from the water's edge, intersected in every direction by ravines. We were ferried across, about sunset, to the pleasant little village of Piatisbanskaia, where, for the third time since leaving Tzaritzin, we changed horses.

And now, for the following night and day, our journey

presents one unwearied monotony; one undulation is as like another as are the post-stations: generally, on arriving at one of these, not a soul is to be seen—a solitary chicken, perched on the wheel of a broken-down cart, is the only visible sign of life. At length, after sundry ineffectual attempts to open the door of the wooden cabin, a slovenly woman looks out, followed by three or four ragged brats. One of the children immediately disappears upon the steppe, returning in about half an hour with a bearded sullen-looking man, who, without deigning a remark, mounts one of the last team, and gallops away as if he never meant to come back: presently, however, half-a-dozen horses are seen rattling at full speed down a distant slope, followed by two men—our sullen friend and his sullen friend, whom he seems to have picked up somewhere with the horses. By this time our yamschik, or driver, from the last place has succeeded in loosening the rope, which serves as a pole-strap, and which has hitherto been continually breaking on the side of every hill just when it was most wanted; upon the last occasion, however, he has apparently succeeded in getting it into a most permanent knot. Meantime three horses are selected from those which have just been driven into a sort of kraal—the work of harnessing begins, and occupies another half-hour. Notwithstanding all the experience which the driver brings to bear upon the subject of the pole-ropes, they prove a dreadful puzzle, and are evidently quite a modern and hitherto unseen invention.

At length everything is ready. The last driver is thrown into ecstasies at receiving a vodka of fourpence, after having driven us fifteen miles; the new driver is no less enchanted at the prospect of a similar magnificent remuneration; while the original sullen-looking man, who has been engaged inspecting and writing on our padaroshna, emerges with a grim smile on his countenance, and charges a ruble, by way of a good round sum, for the next fifteen miles, instead of the proper price, which is only eighty copeks (2s. 8d.). The yamschik then mounts the box in high spirits, and after having thus wasted an hour or two we are off again *ventre à terre*, down one pitch and up another, regardless of the ditch at the bottom, over which the carriage and horses take a sort of flying leap, much to our discomfiture. Our delays, however, are too long and numerous to admit of any remonstrance affecting our speed, and the yamschik continues to earn his vodka by undergoing the most tremendous exertion. He shouts, and curses, and applauds, and whistles, and yells without ceasing, flourishing his whip over his head, by way of a hint that the lash may come down, which, however, it very seldom does; for the horses, being without blinkers, invariably take the hint, and seem not to require much pressing. He is a picturesque figure altogether, this Don Cossack yamschik, with his huge red mustache, the ends of which are visible protruding on both sides of his head, as we sit behind him. He wears a grey fur cap, and a blue tunic reaching half-way to the knee, bound round the waist with a red sash. A huge pair of jack-boots, into which his loose trousers are thrust, complete a costume which, though not altogether unlike that of the ordinary Russian peasant, somehow invests the wearer with a greater degree of independence. In an hour and a half he has jolted us to the end of our stage, where the same delay occurs, and the same scene is reenacted.

At night, however, the routine is varied: the horses are sometimes at home, but the delay is not much less; we have to rattle at the door and wake the children, who cry and wake the woman, who wakes the husband, who, to be saved all further trouble, immediately says there are no horses. We repeat incessantly *loshedye* (horses) and *vodka*; and when at last we show him twenty-five copeks, he produces three nags. We pat him on the back, and try to be friends, but our advances are very coldly received; and he fumbles and scribbles on our padaroshna, by the dim flickering light, for a most interminable time.

The yamschiks are more mystified in the dark than ever, and lose all the nuts in attempting to grease the wheels. At last, when we are off, it begins to rain, and we discover, for the first time, that our carriage leaks like a shower-bath. We are vainly endeavouring to avoid the deluge, when, after a violent jolt, we hear a rattle; upon investigating the cause of which, we find that the wheel will probably come off before our arrival at the next station, in which case we shall be obliged to pass the black stormy night in a wet carriage on a dreary steppe, miles from any habitation or means of obtaining assistance.

It may be imagined with what intense anxiety—as we slackened our speed into a cautious walk—we watched the loosening of all the spokes of one of our fore-wheels on such a night—the third we had spent on the road; and it was with feelings of no less satisfaction that we at last hailed our arrival at an unusually substantial cabin, where we determined to stay until morning should bring us fine weather, and some person to repair the wheel. It fortunately contained a wooden stretcher, on which a sheepskin that I had bought was made to serve the purpose of a mattress, and, as such, proved very comfortable; its demerits chiefly consisting in a most unpleasant and overpowering odour, and a great capacity for retaining fleas, so that by the time we arrived at Taganrog my importations from Don Cossack post-huts were considerable.

Somovar

But if a Russian sheepskin may occasionally be regarded as a luxury, a Russian somovar is absolutely essential to one's existence. At its appearance all dreary reminiscences of shattered wheels and windy steppes vanish—the post-hut assumes a most cosy, comfortable aspect—the little animals hopping about one's legs are forgotten— you become utterly careless as to the existence of horses, overwhelm the sulky postmaster with politeness, confound the Don Cossack maidens with signs and gestures expressive of extreme satisfaction, and, finally, turn in upon the said sheepskin under the influence of feelings which nothing else could have inspired. The most pleasant sight that meets the traveller's eye, as he journeys through these vast plains, is the bright, burnished copper somovar—the most cheerful sound that falls upon his ear is the grateful hissing and bubbling that issues from it. It is an object upon which the affections of the noble, no less than of the peasant, deservedly centre, and a source of the only sentiment, probably, which these two classes possess in common. The noble values his somovar as highly as he does his serf; and the serf values his somovar, no doubt, more highly than he does his lord. If an imperial ukase were to issue tomorrow, abolishing somovars, I verily believe it would terminate the existence of Russia as an empire.

No doubt it betokens a scarcity in the comforts of life that a tea-urn should be thus highly esteemed; and the pleasures of existence must be few and far between, when tea-drinking is looked upon as the source of the highest enjoyment; but all as human joys are dependent for their intensity on the circumstances by which they are controlled, so tea can never be so highly appreciated as during a journey on the steppes. We had bought some at Nijni, which had just arrived overland from China, and our provision for the steppes consisted entirely of flowery Pekoe, sugar, and rusks. As nothing but black bread was to be procured, we confined ourselves to this invalid fare at every meal, occasionally indulging in a few eggs when they were obtainable. Living upon such simple diet, and undergoing, at the same time, great fatigue, tea acted as a most refreshing stimulant, while the peculiar construction of the somovar insured an excellent brew. Deriving its name from two Russian words, signifying "boil," "itself," the somovar is nothing more than a large brass urn, in the middle of which is a cylinder containing a quantity of live charcoal. The top is shaped like a funnel, and open. This is the correct place for the pot—the fire at the bottom keeping the tea hot, and boiling the water at the same time. A slice of lemon is always used as a substitute for milk, and I soon thought it a much more agreeable addition.

The following morning, after getting our wheel clumsily patched up, we started under the bright auspices of a most glorious rising sun. The steppe was not so rough, and presented a more varied aspect. We passed through a few villages occasionally, consisting of small one-storeyed houses, surrounded by balconies, and more substantially built than those we had hitherto seen; while a wooden mill, situated on a sluggish-looking stream, fringed with willows, once enlivened the prospect; but, with the exception of these few willows, I saw not a single tree during the whole journey. We had numerous and extensive views over the winding Don, and the interminable steppe which stretched uninterruptedly to the Caspian, and appeared to be on a level of about two hundred feet lower than ourselves. Moreover, we observed numerous large herds of cattle, sheep, and horses, and passed more bullock-carts than usual, loaded with every conceivable species of gourd. They were accompanied by rough, surly men, and most unprepossessing females—though perhaps some allowance should be made for the ladies, regard being had to their unbecoming costume, which was entirely composed of a coarse white nightgown and Wellington boots. The men were somewhat similarly attired, except that the nightgown was shortened into a tunic, and their loose trousers were tucked into their boots. The more respectable wore a sort of cavalry foraging-cap with a red band.

The country of the Don Cossacks is much more thickly peopled than the traveller who follows the line of white posts across the turf which mark the *post-road* has any reason to suppose; indeed, it seems an established principle that the post-hut should be in the most solitary position, where it is impossible to obtain the assistance requisite for the constant repairs which are rendered necessary by the rough nature of the country traversed. Upon obtaining our padaroshna at

Dubovka, we were furnished with a list of the post-stations, which, however, was only forthcoming after a great deal of delay, as the postmaster seemed never to have heard of the route we proposed taking. He must ultimately have invented the names and distances, which were carefully marked on the list, for, with the exception of the first, not a single station named existed in reality; and had it not been that occasional glimpses of the Don satisfied us that we were following our intended course, no possible means existed of knowing whether we were journeying in the right direction or not.

The chief characteristic of the Don Cossack postmasters—and they probably are good specimens of the race—is a sullen apathy and dogged imperturbability, excessively irritating to wayworn travellers, whose efforts to the understood were, in our case, absurdly futile,—threats, rubles, and supplications proved alike unavailing. We pointed to our feeble wheel, and to the setting sun; the postmaster exhibited no surprise, no sympathy—nothing but a pot of grease as a remedy for a worn-out tire. Once only my earnest entreaties elicited an abrupt inquiry as to whether I was a Christian. I knew enough Russian to understand the question, and answer in the affirmative; and was instantly desired to make the sign of the cross as a proof of the orthodoxy of my profession. As the cross is made in a peculiar manner, and varies in some of the sects of the Greek Church, I declined compromising myself by an unsuccessful attempt; upon which the Cossack shrugged his shoulders with a sneer, and reserved his aid and his sympathies for Christian travellers.

We were ferried across the Donetz, a noble stream rivalling the Don in magnitude; and from the heights above we had a good view of the confluence of the two rivers. The steppes to the westward of the Donetz are a vast carboniferous deposit; and the most important mines are situated at Bakmout, in the government of Iekaterinoslav. At certain seasons a steamer is employed—of course by government—in towing barges loaded with anthracite from these mines. The word Donetz is

127

supposed by Clarke and others to have been the origin of the name given by the Greeks to the Don; and the transition from Donetz, or Danaetz, to Tanais does not seem a very violent one.

Numerous vineyards line the banks of the Don the whole way to Tcherkask, which produce a great quantity of sparkling wines, somewhat similar to those of the Crimea. According to the last official reports, the exportations from these vineyards alone amount to three hundred and seventy-five thousand rubles. As we approached the capital of the province, we were startled by the unexpected vision of a traveller, the first we had met for more than three hundred miles. With curiosity something akin to that which is experienced on inspecting an unknown sail at sea, I gazed through the cloud of dust at the dirty vehicle and its still dirtier occupant as they rattled past, and was enabled to form some idea of the appearance we must ourselves have presented, though in no respect enlightened as to the rank or station of the individual. Indeed, there is nothing to guide one in estimating the condition of a Russian on a journey; horses, carriage, driver, traveller—all look equally ragged and unkempt, and are covered with one uniform coat of dust. The traveller and the carriage are neither of them washed until the end of the journey. This might therefore be a prince going to assume the government of a province, or the nineteenth clerk in a police-office, for any outward indications to the contrary.

The night was far advanced when we at last distinguished the picturesque outline of Novo Tcherkask by the clear light of a full moon. Crossing a small tributary of the Don, we toiled slowly up the base of the hill on which the town is situated, and passed under a grand triumphal arch erected in honour of Alexander, which looked all the more imposing and mysterious at that hour, from our being totally unprepared for any such architectural display. This being the first town we had seen since leaving the banks of the Volga, there was an excitement in the change from the dreary lifeless steppe; and although the tramp of the sentinel was the only sound that rung through the now deserted streets, it was a pleasure to rattle over them, and feel we were at length in the capital of the country of the Don Cossacks.

Girl of Tcherkask

Don Cossacks: their origin—Don Cossacks as soldiers, as agriculturists—Extent of arable land—Don Cossack statistics—A bad road—Delays—An aide-de-camp from the Caucasus—The posting system, and a Russian's notions of it

The town of Novo Tcherkask was founded by the Hetman Platoff in 1806, the inundations to which the former capital was exposed having rendered it necessary to remove the seat of government to a more elevated position. In his anxiety to avoid the floods of the Don, the Hetman has fallen into the opposite extreme, and perched the new capital on a most unfavourable site. Eight miles distant from the river, it is unable to benefit by the increasing traffic which passes along its stream, and the approaches are steep and inaccessible in almost every direction. The only advantage which is afforded by its lofty situation is an extensive view to the southward, and in clear weather the snowy peaks of the Caucasus are said to be distinctly visible. The population amounts to about ten thousand. The streets are broad, but the houses mean; and it is remarkable that the practice of raising them, as it were, upon stilts, like corn-stalks in a farmer's haggard, which was no doubt necessary in the old inundated town, has been continued by the working classes in the new; altogether it is a straggling, ill-laid-out place, in no degree calculated to realise the expectation raised by its approach through an ostentatious archway.

The creation of the last few years, Novo Tcherkask is in a great measure devoid of that national character which rendered the old capital so interesting, and which is so graphically described by Clarke. Since the Don has ceased to be the boundary of Europe and Asia, the inhabitants of this district have become to some extent occidentalised, and I saw none of those striking costumes described by earlier travellers. With the manners and customs by which they were once distinguished, the Cossacks are losing all traces of their former independence, and, as they become gradually absorbed into the Russian empire, their identity as a race must soon cease.

Nothing can be more convenient for Russia than the position of this province, and the martial character of its inhabitants. Situated in the remote corner of an empire whose extensive frontiers are continually threatened by neighbouring tribes, the Cossacks are regarded as its natural protectors, and, as such, are posted in one continuous line from Siberia to the Black Sea. They also compose a great proportion of the army engaged in the Caucasus, and which is being constantly reinforced by levies from the adjoining province. The ceremony of raising a regiment consists in the simple process of ordering a certain number of men to meet at a given point, whence they are marched incontinently to the scene of action; so that every Cossack may be looked upon as destined to become a soldier from his birth; indeed, Russians seem to consider that they are brought into the world for the express purpose of fighting their battles.

Don Cossacks are the most compound beings in the universe. According to Clarke, they are a mixture of Circassians, Malo-Russians, Russians, Tartars, Poles, Greeks, Turks, Calmucks, and Armenians; others contend that they are almost of a purely Sclavonic origin, and this seems to me the probable conjecture, as I could trace nothing whatever in their physiognomy to warrant the supposition of a Mongolian descent;—they are, moreover, bigoted adherents of the Greek Church, and have been Christians from the date of the first records we have of their existence. But if ethnologists have been at variance in accounting for their origin, etymologists have been no less at a loss in deciding on the derivation of their name, and have ended by leaving it an open question whether Cossacks are so called from the resemblance of that word to those in other languages, which signify respectively, an armed man, a sabre, a rover, a goat, a promontory, a coat, a cassock, and a district in Circassia.

The subjects of all this speculation can of course throw no light on the matter themselves, and so the derivation of the race and of the name will probably remain for ever an interesting subject of investigation. One thing is certain, that, whether springing from the same stock or not, the Cossacks cherish a most unmitigated hatred towards the Russians. They have been insidiously deprived of almost every privilege which they once possessed, and from being a free republic, responsible to no one but their own Hetman or President, they have sunk into the same condition of slavery as the inhabitants of the neighbouring provinces. In former days the distinction of rank was unknown—now, there is a Don Cossack aristocracy; then, there was a community in landed property—now, the whole district has been divided into estates, and serfdom established; and those who, as crown peasants, would be comparatively free in other districts, are here subject at any moment to be pressed into the army, Indeed, it is a most unfortunate thing for these poor Don Cossacks that they have obtained that character for bravery which the Russians are at the greatest pains to attribute to them. In the course of my later travels I fell in with a Hungarian officer who had been present at many of the skirmishes in the Caucasus, and who assured me that the valour of the Don Cossacks was one of those popular delusions which the government is most anxious to encourage; for it answers the double purpose of flattering the vanity of a discontented race, who are thereby rendered more easily subservient to their designs, and of inspiring a wholesome dread into other nations, who have hitherto been accustomed to regard them with a mysterious awe, and to conjure up monsters of appalling ferocity, and of a terrific aspect, as representatives of the high-sounding title by which they are distinguished. The Circassians have, by dint of frequent contact, learnt to estimate these formidable warriors at their true value, and hold them in almost as great contempt as they do the ordinary Russian soldier. It must be remembered that, in those campaigns in which the Cossacks have distinguished themselves, it was only by contrast with other Russian troops; and it is rather for their barbarity and cruelty in harassing a retreating army that they are celebrated, than for any satisfactory displays of real valour.

If, instead of draining the country of a vast proportion of its able-bodied population, the government were to encourage the inhabitants to pursue agricultural or mercantile occupations, there can be no doubt that the superior advantages which this district possesses, in respect both of its soil and its position, would offer additional incentives to their industry. The following statistics, as derived from the official reports, will, I think, not only prove that these advantages do exist, but that the Don Cossacks are highly endowed with that enterprising spirit in which Russians generally are so deplorably deficient, and which seems to be one of the few remaining indications of an independence long since extinguished.

We find that the population of the whole province amounts to seven hundred thousand, spread over an extent of three thousand square German miles, thus allowing an exceedingly low average of about two hundred and forty inhabitants to the square mile, and which gives forty acres of excellent pasture-land to each individual. When we divide the soil under cultivation by the population, it appears that each inhabitant cultivates about eight acres, or an extent of nearly two acres more than the inhabitants of any other province. Indeed, so low is the average of land under cultivation, in seventeen out of the fifty-one provinces of which the empire is composed, that the quantity of grain produced is insufficient for the support of the people. When we consider the interruptions to their labours, caused by their liability to serve as soldiers, and the decrease of the population by the absence of nearly a hundred thousand already so engaged, we are fairly entitled to conclude that the Don Cossacks are among the most energetic and enterprising of his Imperial Majesty's subjects.

It is only consistent with the general system of government that, as such, they should be employed chiefly as targets for Circassian riflemen, or exposed to the onslaughts of Kirghees robbers upon the Thibet frontier; and we may imagine a Don Cossack, keeping guard in these dreary deserts, congratulating himself upon being a native of the most highly-favoured province in Russia, and wondering how his wife and children are carrying on the cultivation of the eight acres of land he is never likely to see again. It is not to be supposed, however, that by these eight acres under cultivation is meant soil actually producing every year. The great extent of arable land renders it unnecessary to take any more than one crop out of the same ground every ten or fifteen years. It is said that the arable land is equal to about one-third of that in pasture; this our former calculation has shown to be considerably above the mark, although there can be no doubt that, in point of fact, almost the whole district is susceptible in the highest degree of cultivation. It consists of a fine rich black loam, peculiar to the steppe, and known under the Russian name of "tcherno-zième." The base throughout the greater part of the Don Cossack country consists of chalk. Besides corn of every variety, linseed is extensively cultivated for the sake of its oil. Mulberry-trees thrive wonderfully wherever they have been tried; and there can be no doubt that, if the manufacture of silk were encouraged, it would prove a most profitable article of export.

Upon the fine grazing-land which this province affords, cattle thrive amazingly, and at scarcely any expense to their owners, who so little appreciate their value that they frequently kill them for the sake of the tallow. It has been sagely suggested that the meat, instead of being buried, should be exported, and that some use should be made of the milk. I tasted some excellent cheese, but could not discover that it was an article of commerce. Horses are abundant, and highly esteemed throughout the empire: they were originally imported by the Tartars, and are a small wiry race, varying in price from thirty to fifty shillings each. Obliged, when young, to endure severe winters, they are capable afterwards of undergoing any hardship: should they escape the epidemics and droughts of their own country, they are probably destined to be exposed elsewhere to the fortunes of war, as they are drafted in large quantities into cavalry regiments.

As these details are extracted entirely from government reports, very little reliance can be placed upon them, containing, as they do, so many discrepancies and contradictions. Their general tendency is to err, by giving a too favourable view of matters; but they serve, nevertheless, officially to prove that the country of the Don Cossacks is the most ill-used province in the empire, since it is prevented from deriving any benefit from the advantages which its fertile soil, its hardy peasantry, and its countless herds of cattle would insure.

Notwithstanding our being in the capital of a province celebrated for its horses, we found great difficulty in procuring any at the post-station, and were only consoled for the delay by looking upon it as an additional evidence of our approach to civilisation. At last we quitted the town at full gallop, dashing with frightful rapidity to the bottom of the ravine upon the edge of which it is situated, and whirling over the steppe along a road so execrably rough that I at once perceived we were on the principal post-road in the country.

There was an end of rolling over smooth grassy turf, as we had hitherto done, guided only by the fancy of the yamschik, and a line of white posts. Now we were retained within proper limits by two ditches, and jolted in anguish over what had once been a marsh, and in which the deep tracks of winter traffic had been dried by the sun into hard ruts and furrows, and the caked unyielding clay threatened at once to break the springs of the carriage and to dislocate the joints of its occupants. We found it necessary to jam ourselves as firmly as possible into our seats, to prevent being struck against the sides; and as we hurried down the precipitous banks of the ravines by which the road was continually intersected, it required an additional exertion to prevent being jerked out altogether. It was a great relief at last to find that our light carriage had hopped rather than rolled over fifteen versts, and that we had arrived, though in a somewhat bruised condition, at the next station.

Here our road was crossed by one which connects St. Petersburg and Moscow with Stavropol, the headquarters of the Russian army in the Caucasus. We were at this point about two days' and nights' journey distant from the seat of war; and consequently we half expected, in answer to our inquiries for horses, to be told that they were all engaged by officers carrying despatches. It was useless, on hearing this, to point to a stableful doing nothing;—our padaroshna only bore one royal stamp instead of two, which indicate express government service, and as strangers and civilians we were considered by no means entitled to be forwarded on our journey; so we took up our abode, with philosophical resignation, in a room devoid of all furniture and swarming with vermin, and watched successive arrivals and departures;—officers hurrying in one direction, and ladies, with large families, journeying placidly in another, all producing the same padaroshna which intimated to the obedient station-master that the interests of the government were vitally concerned in the promptitude with which he supplied horses.

It was useless to expect any favourable result from a bribe. The station-master, who seemed to be a person of considerable importance, with a gold band round his cap, and attired in the costume of a government official, pocketed our rubles with great relish, but was immovable in his conscientious retention of the horses for the service of his imperial master, and would not trust our honesty so far as to harness them first and wait for the bribe until we were prepared to start. At length I accosted, in French, a dashing young aide-de-camp, whose appearance at the station operated like magic on this official yamschik, and who, on finding that we were English, ordered horses to be put at once into our carriage. His excessive politeness, evincing an evident readiness to die upon the spot if such a sacrifice would advance us one stage upon our journey, contrasted singularly with the incivility of the station-master—they were both perfect specimens of Russian honesty! I must say, however, that they were devoted servants of the crown, and I can conceive no severer test of the loyalty and obedience of a soldier than to order him off at an hour's notice on a ten days' journey in a Russian post telèga. It was with mingled feelings of wonder and respect that I saw the polite young officer seat himself upon a bundle of straw in an open springless cart, such as is commonly used by the peasants of the country, and, in defiance of wind and weather, proceed upon a dreary journey of eight consecutive days and nights to Moscow. Every two hours he would be aroused from slumbers, denied to any but a Russian under such circumstances, in order to change his vehicle—for the cart, like the horses, is the peculiar property of the last station. As he gracefully bid us adieu, and wrapt his white military cloak about him, I thought that the blood of his Scythian ancestors most surely still flowed in the veins beneath that polished exterior.

Our experiences at this station may serve to illustrate what we were doomed to undergo at every post-house between it and Taganrog. Sometimes we succeeded in bribing the yamschiks into exertion in our behalf; once we hired a private team, and paid for government horses into the bargain; once we were indebted to the kind offices of the little German wife of a surgeon of a Cossack regiment, who stood security for the due payment of a bribe upon our being ready to start; and once, upon the steppe, a sulky yamschik refused to accelerate his pace, and would have deserted us upon that dreary track, had I not presented a six-barrelled revolver at his head, and threatened him with immediate destruction if he quitted the box. Such, in the case of strangers, is the practical working of the much-vaunted system of Russian posting; and indeed no other result can be expected, when we consider the purely military purposes for which it has ever been organised.

Those crown peasants who belong to the postal administration are bound to furnish a certain number of carts, horses, and yamschiks, in consideration of which they are released from all pecuniary obligations for the land which they occupy, and are, moreover, entitled to a certain fixed charge per post. This is in some provinces an absurdly small sum: in none, probably, is it lower than in the country of the Don Cossacks. The average of our whole expenses, of posting with three horses, since leaving Dubovka, *including our living*, repairing the carriage, greasing the wheels, and all the bribes and vodkas we had found it necessary to lavish, only amounted to fourpence-halfpenny a mile. It is but fair to the sullen unsophisticated station-keepers on the other side of Tcherkask to say, that they rarely expected a bribe at all, or if they did, were easily moved by a gentle *douceur*. These men are appointed by government, and are bound to have horses always in readiness for couriers with despatches. There is a book kept at each station, in which the number of horses that belong to it is marked; and if the keeper cannot satisfactorily account for an empty stable, the complaint of the traveller is entered in the book. This is of course not attended to unless the person making it is in government employ. The impropriety of this arrangement throughout, lies in the fact of its being entirely a crown speculation; the whole object is to convey despatches to distant parts of the enormous empire in the most speedy and economical method possible. To effect this, the convenience of the rest of the community is completely sacrificed, when, at a very slight additional expense, the two things might be rendered quite compatible with one another. A few more horses should be furnished to each station, and the postmaster obliged to supply every traveller who could pay, without the necessity of his producing a padaroshna; and if, instead of charging the ridiculously low prices which are at present imposed, a higher rate were introduced, in order to cover the expenses incurred by a superabundance of idle horses, there can be no doubt that travellers would willingly pay for it, for the comfort of being able at once to proceed on their journey.

It is singular that, notwithstanding the detestable way in which the posting arrangements of the country are managed, there is no point upon which Russians pride themselves more highly than upon the facilities which they allege to exist for travelling. I have seldom been in the company of a Russian more than a few minutes without his asking me whether I did not consider that posting in Russia was unequalled in the world, since it combined at the same time comfort with economy, and safety with rapidity. Upon which I reply, that "I can discover no comfort in a room in a post-hut, with a mud floor, no window, and no furniture." "What!" says he, amazed, "you surely don't get out at the post-houses!"

Well, I admit the economy of the system, but demur to the idea of its being safe travelling, as sundry visions of broken-down wheels and steep ravines rise before me. My Russian friend triumphantly informs me that "he has just accomplished twelve thousand versts in three months without an accident."

"Or getting out at a post-house?"

"Of course not; why should I get out at a post-station when I have got a comfortable carriage to sleep in?"

"Well, at any rate you will allow that the delays for horses are most annoying, and the station-masters very insolent—the travelling is only rapid when absolutely *en route*."

"Ah! for you strangers it is impossible to get horses—if you don't speak the language, you will be both cheated and insulted; but it is very different with us, who know that, to manage such *canaille*, blows, and not rubles, ought to be abundantly bestowed."

And so my opponent walks proudly off, satisfied that, because he has journeyed twelve thousand versts in three months—during which time he has thrashed on an average twelve station-keepers a day, lived entirely on black bread, slept every night in his carriage, and never changed his clothes—the comforts of travelling in his country are unequalled in the world.

Tarantasse

CHAPTER XII

Colonies–Nackchivan–Rostof: its commerce–Obstacles to its prosperity–Quit the country of the Don Cossacks–Taganrog: its historical associations–The wool trade–Merinos– A dilemma

The most striking evidence of the indolence and incapacity of Russians generally, in mercantile affairs, is to be found in the prosperity of those colonies which have been established for the most part by the Empress Catharine the Second, at whose invitation bands of foreigners have immigrated from distant lands to reap the rich reward of their industry and enterprise, in a country where the inhabitants themselves have proved incompetent to take advantage of those sources of wealth which it affords. These colonists consist chiefly of Germans and Armenians; and the traveller who journeys from Sarepta for some hundreds of miles in a westerly direction, and arrives at last in the Armenian settlement of Nackchivan, might almost feel persuaded that his route had lain in a diametrically opposite direction, and that he had travelled from Germany into Turkey, rather than that he had passed only from one Russian province into another. Clarke, who descended the Don some fifty years ago, was much struck by the diversity of races which he observed upon its banks, particularly below Tcherkask, and gives the following graphic description of his approach to this colony:—

"We here beheld Tartars, Turks, Greeks, Cossacks, Russians, Italians, Calmucks, and Armenians: these, together with our English party, formed a representation of the costume of nine different nations, within the compass of a quarter of an English mile. The Tartars were fishing in the river, or driving cattle towards the town; the Turks were smoking in their coffee-houses; the Greeks, a bustling race, were walking about, telling lies, and bartering merchandise; the Cossacks were scampering in all directions on horseback; the Russians, as police-officers, were scratching their heads; the Italians appeared as Venetian and Neapolitan sailors; the Calmucks jabbering with each other; the Armenians, both men and women, airing in droskies; and the English staring at them all." And when, afterwards, these wondering English stroll through the Turkish bazaars, and bargain with merchants turbaned and bearded—or meet veiled waddling women in the crowd, visions purely Eastern rise to their imagination; and while listening to the voice of the muezzin calling true believers to prayer, they will forget that the pious invitation rings upon the ear of many an infidel Don Cossack, and finally dies away upon the boundless steppe. It is a pleasant delusion while it lasts. As long as you are in one of these Oriental colonies, you feel that you have quitted Russia, without the preliminary annoyances of innumerable police-offices, and advertisements of your intended departure in the newspapers.

Nackchivan is a name borrowed from that of the ancient town near the foot of Mount Ararat, which the Armenians believe to have been founded by Noah, after the Flood, and to contain his grave. The town contains about six thousand inhabitants; a most thriving, wealthy population, who carry on a brisk trade with the Caucasus, and are not averse to a sly stroke of business with Circassia. They enjoy an exemption from the poll-tax, and possess other privileges, and settled in the dreary steppe about the year 1780, having, according to Pallas, immigrated hither from Karassu Bazaar, in the Crimea. Its position, near the mouth of the Don, is eminently adapted for commercial purposes, and an important fair is held here annually. The Armenian merchants are noted for their enterprise, and the courage with which they undertake journeys into Tartary and Thibet, returning hither with the spoils of those distant lands.

After leaving Nackchivan, the road followed the ridge of the steppe overhanging the Don, and we obtained some extensive views towards the Caucasus. Soon the gay churches of the new and important town of Rostof glittered in the distance, and we rattled up to the post-house amid clouds of dust and hosts of other travellers.

Rostof proved the pleasantest interruption to our journey we had experienced since leaving the Volga. It would be an interesting town to visit in any country; it is doubly so to the traveller who has been accustomed for days to simple earth and sky. Whether he be romantic or utilitarian in his tastes, he will be delighted with Rostof. The steppe, which is here intersected by a precipitous ravine, projects boldly into the Don, forming an elevated promontory upon which the town is perched; the steep streets, often divided from one another by dangerous gullies, but united in the one common object of converging to the noble river which winds below the town, and which here suddenly becomes broad and deep enough to admit of a fleet of small craft anchoring in its stream; the picturesque houses, irregularly built, with their many-coloured roofs and varied styles of architecture; the mixed population, whose costumes differ no less than their pursuits; the gaudy churches crowning the heights, and the view from those heights themselves—all combine to form attractions which commend themselves to the attention of the traveller in search of the picturesque; while, on the other hand, the smoke from the little steamer puffing up the stream, the clang of iron as it is thrown into the holds of the vessels, the creaking of cranes as the work of loading and unloading goes busily forward, are sights and sounds no less congenial to him who is interested in the commercial prospects of the country through which he is travelling.

It does not require a very keen observer in such matters to discover in Rostof a town endowed with such great natural advantages that it has been compelled to assume a position of commercial importance in spite of those obstructions which are incidental to its existence under a Russian government. When the Greeks, sailing across the Palus Meotis, founded Tanais, at the mouth of the Don, they as highly appreciated the importance of the position as did the Venetians and Genoese, by whom they were succeeded, and who established factories at Tana, nearly opposite Rostof.

In modern times, Peter the Great was the first to discover that the resources of the country demanded an outlet, and so he built Taganrog in its present unfavourable position. Not long after the Turks evacuated the left bank of the river, Rostof sprung up—a testimony to the accurate judgment of those maritime nations who had placed their factories upon the river rather than on the sea-coast.

The importance of Rostof was in no degree diminished by its proximity to Taganrog; on the contrary, it has now become almost essential to the existence of that very port, which is the chief barrier to its prosperity. This is an apparent paradox, not very difficult to explain. All the commerce of the interior of the empire with the ports on the Black Sea, which comes by the way of the Volga and Dubovka, necessarily passes through Rostof; upon arriving here, the produce is transhipped from the shallow boats in which it has descended the Don, into lighters, and is conveyed to Taganrog. If the mouth of the river, which is now too shallow to admit anything larger than mere coasting craft, were deepened, there would be no necessity for this expensive proceeding. The merchants of Taganrog, instead of having branch establishments at Rostof, would remove thither; and Taganrog, which now prospers only because Rostof is unapproachable, would cease to retain its commercial importance.

Under the present system, the public pay heavily to support two ports instead of one. I was informed that there would be no great difficulty in removing the bar at the mouth of the Don; but this is not the only obstacle to the progress of Rostof. At present there are only certain seasons of the year when the river is navigable, even for flat boats, above Tcherkask; and although there is more traffic on the Don than on any other river in the south of Russia, no effort is made to remedy this evil by a judicious application of engineering skill, which would render the river available throughout the year. As I wandered along the quays, I observed great quantities of pig and wrought iron, timber, birch-bark, and firewood; and when I considered that these bulky articles had been brought down a distance of two thousand miles by means of two rivers alone, and that the expense of crossing the isthmus, forty miles broad, which separated them, probably exceeded the cost of the freight for the rest of the way, I did not so much wonder that the river remained shallow, as that Rostof should prosper in spite of every hindrance that the indifference of the government neglects to obviate or remove.

The present population of the town amounts to about twelve thousand. The river is crossed by a curiously constructed bridge, which has somewhat the appearance of a permanent raft. The opposite bank is low, marshy, and frequently flooded to a great distance. It is a vast plain, rising imperceptibly to the sources of the sluggish Manitch, whence it sinks gradually to the shores of the Caspian.

Shortly after leaving Rostof, we passed numbers of carts loaded with anthracite from the mines of Bakmout. It was said that when these mines were first opened by private enterprise, so large a sum was charged by government for a license to work them, that the ardour of the speculators was completely damped. However, it soon became evident that government was no less a sufferer than the public; and greater facilities are now afforded to the development of these mineral treasures.

We had crossed the boundary which separates the wild country of the Don Cossacks from the small district of Taganrog; and the road, becoming gradually worse as we approached civilisation, was almost unbearable, now that it connected two of the most important towns in this part of Russia. Precipitous ravines and interminable steppes were the only objects of contemplation; and I felt disposed entirely to agree with a witty Frenchman, who says that, to enjoy posting in Russia, the traveller requires "un corps de fer, et une imagination d'enfer." At length the Sea of Azov burst upon our wearied vision, and we were tantalised by a delay of five hours at a post-station, absolutely in sight of our journey's end. When we entered Taganrog about midnight, I could scarcely believe we had reached our destination: it seemed unnatural to ask for beds instead of horses, and to receive a civil answer in the affirmative, instead of a blunt rebuff—to make preparations for getting into said beds, and positively startling to find them supplied with sheets. Only those who, like ourselves, have been deprived of any such luxury for six weeks, can appreciate their soothing influence; and in spite of my continuing to jolt throughout the night, I did not awake until the middle of the following day, considerably refreshed, having in my dreams just succeeded in throttling a yamschik.

Taganrog is a clean, well-built town, of a most respectable appearance. Many of the houses are very handsome; and there is a new fresh look about the whole place, pleasing to the eye of a traveller in a good humour. The sea, though shallow and muddy, looked blue from the bedroom windows; and the long line of steppe over which we had journeyed, and which forms the opposite coast of a large bay, seemed quite a charming background, now that we hoped to have nothing more to do with it.

The most interesting part of the town is the Gastinni Dvor, built in the form of a square. Under these colonnades sea-faring men from every country on the Mediterranean mingle with Armenians, Tartars, and Cossacks; while the most extraordinary variety of goods are exposed for sale in the crowded shops. Every other part of the town is of course lifeless and dull; and the tall white houses, baked by the broiling sun, render the streets so intolerably hot during the day, that nobody walks in them who can help it. There are shady gardens, however, where the band plays in the afternoons, and pleasant grass-grown ramparts overhanging the sea and smaller shipping, which afford an agreeable lounge; and from hence, in clear weather, the old Turkish fortress of Azov is distinctly visible. In former days these were the outposts of Russia and Turkey; hence the extensive fortifications of Taganrog, which now, no longer necessary, are fast falling into decay.

There are few historical associations of any interest connected with Taganrog. Founded by Peter the Great in 1706, apparently for military purposes, he evidently foresaw that it would rise to a position of some mercantile importance, and bestowed more than ordinary care and attention on that account on a town of his own creation, and where his sojourn is commemorated by an oak wood of his own planting. It was here that the Emperor Alexander died. There is nothing whatever to interest, apart from this consideration, in the house where that event occurred, but which, nevertheless, all travellers are expected to visit.

The environs of Taganrog are extremely fertile, and there can be no doubt that the surrounding steppe is favourable to the growth of forest trees. In winter, of course, trade is at a stand-still, communication being alike impracticable by sea or land, except in sledges. The passage across the gulf to Azov upon the ice is then quite feasible.

The population of Taganrog amounts to about twenty-two thousand inhabitants. The trade consists chiefly in caviare, leather, tallow, corn, wool, iron, and other Siberian produce which descends the Don. Great quantities of sturgeon are caught in the Sea of Azov, which has been famous for this fish since the days of the Greek colonies.

Tallow and leather are likely always to remain important items in the exports of Taganrog; but the wool seems to hold a more precarious place in the European market. About one-third of the wool which is exported from Russia comes to England; but the increasing favour with which Australian wool is regarded, has already produced an effect upon the pastoral provinces of Russia. The quantity of wool exported from Russia to this country has steadily decreased since the year 1845, when this trade had reached its most flourishing point; and notwithstanding the exertions of the sheep-proprietors to compete with Australia, that colony has gradually mono-

147

polised the lion's share of the trade with England, while the disposition lately manifested in that quarter to extend its transactions to the Continent is causing some uneasiness to Russia. Indeed, it seems impossible that any other result can be anticipated, from the late experiences of sheep-farming in these provinces, than the decline of the wool trade.

Some years ago large quantities of merinos were introduced upon the steppes, and at first it was hoped that they would thrive, despite the inclemency of the climate. Perhaps had they been properly cared for, they would have succeeded; but Russian energy and perseverance have proved insufficient in obviating the effects of the severe snow-storms of winter and the droughts of summer, and the merinos are fast vanishing off the face of the earth. In 1849 a vast mortality prevailed; and through utter want of management on the part of the proprietors, and careless indolence on the part of the shepherds, thousands of these valuable animals were sacrificed. Unless merinos be properly housed and fed during winter, it is absurd to think of rearing them on the steppes of Russia; indeed, the fact seems pretty well established, that to have fine wool you must have a fine climate. Those hardy flocks which can endure a Russian winter, yield a wool that is barely worth exporting.

In Taurida, and the country of the Don Cossacks, the flocks are more numerous than in any other part of the empire, and they are proportionably ill cared for, the whole object being to increase the quantity of sheep, not the quality of the wool; and thus it goes on deteriorating in proportion as the flock multiplies. To add to which, the wool, being badly cleaned, and worse packed, does not realise much more than half the price of German wool in the London market, while it is being altogether superseded by that from Australia.

A steamer leaves Taganrog twice a month for Odessa, performing the voyage in ten days. A glance at the map will show that in any other country the passage would not occupy three.

148

Owing to the numerous detentions we had experienced at post-huts during the latter part of our journey, we missed the boat by two days. As we proposed exploring the Crimea, we found, to attain this object, three courses open to us;—either a long journey by land to Simpheropol, a prospect which was particularly unpleasant, after all we had just undergone,—a residence in Taganrog until the next steamer, involving a delay of twelve days, and an extremely hot, uninteresting time,—or a passage in a merchantman to Kertch, if we should be fortunate enough to find a ship ready to sail. We chose the latter alternative, and forthwith made our wants known to the sea-faring community. Through the kindness and hospitality of the English consul, we had less difficulty than might have been anticipated in passing our time agreeably in a town destitute in itself of more than a limited supply of novelty and amusement.

CHAPTER XIII

Taganrog as a port—The wheat trade—Want of labour—The prohibitive system—Its effects—Fluctuation in the price of corn—The cause of it—Supplies from India

Notwithstanding the present increasing trade and population of Taganrog, I do not think that its prosperity is at all of a permanent character. The harbour is one of the most inconvenient in Europe, and has by degrees become so shallow that ships are obliged to anchor at a distance of twelve or fifteen miles from the shore. There seems no doubt that it is rapidly filling up. So recently as the year 1793, Professor Pallas records the launch of a large frigate upon waters that lighters can now with difficulty navigate.

As if nature were not doing enough to ruin Taganrog as a port, almost every ship that arrives contributes something to the same end. The Russian government has strictly prohibited the throwing overboard of ballast, with which the majority of the vessels that annually visit it are laden; and the custom-house officials are enjoined to see that this order is complied with, by measuring the draught of water of every ship at Kertch, and comparing it with that which she requires upon her arrival at Taganrog. Of course, by this regulation government has only supplied a new source of profit to the customs' officers, without in the least attaining the object desired. A bribe at Kertch, in proportion to the amount of ballast to be discharged, has the instantaneous effect of lightening the ship; so that after she has thrown overboard a cargo of stones at the entrance of the Taganrog harbour, her draught is found to correspond with singular exactness to the measurement taken at Kertch; and thus the expense which would have been incurred by landing the ballast, is reduced to the more moderate sum to which the bribe may have amounted. The consequence of this system is, that the destruction of the harbour will proceed in exact proportion to the increase of the trade and mercantile importance of the town, until it becomes so eminently prosperous that no ship will be able to approach it at all.

But there are other reasons why Taganrog seems to me to have reached the culminating point of its prosperity. The new port of Berdianski threatens to prove a most formidable rival, as it affords facilities for discharging and loading cargo unequalled by any other harbour in the Sea of Azov. It is situated at the mouth of the Berda, and ships of considerable tonnage can lie close in-shore. Marianopol, too, is a large Greek colony, and though not possessing any great advantage as a port, it contains an indefatigable population. Indeed, to the mercantile skill and enterprise of the Greeks is to be attributed that increasing importance which the corn trade of the southern provinces of Russia has recently assumed. A new port was established four years ago at Gheïsk, upon the eastern coast of the Sea of Azov; not that its existence need cause any apprehension to Taganrog, for government seems to have chosen, as an eligible site for this town, the only bay which is filling up more rapidly even than that of Taganrog.

The most striking feature in the trade of these ports is the prominent position which the description of wheat known by the name of Ghirka is now beginning to occupy in the London market, to the exclusion of the Polish Odessa—a preference which will incalculably benefit the countries bordering upon the Sea of Azov, where alone it is produced. Mr. Mongredien says, "A few years ago red polish Odessa wheat formed by far the largest bulk of our imports from that quarter; it now barely constitutes a third. Ghirka wheats from Marianopol, Berdianski, Taganrog, and other places, have last year been imported very largely—viz., about 350,000 quarters, against 100,000 quarters in 1851. This class of wheat is daily becoming better known amongst millers; and whereas its use was once chiefly confined to Cork, Limerick, and the adjacent districts, it is now getting into general repute." It may be remarked, however, that the general decrease of this year over last, more than counterbalances this increase in Ghirka wheat.

All these ports suffer alike from the absence of any means of inland communication. So long as the transport of produce from the interior to the seacoast is attended with such difficulties as now surround it, the prosperity of these places must be retarded, and the price of grain increased. The wheat exported from Taganrog to Berdianski and Marianopol, arrives, for the most part, in carts drawn by oxen, the rate of travelling not exceeding fifteen miles a day—the roads being quite impassable, except during a few summer months. Thus it is apparent that the foreign market does not depend for the supply of grain so much upon the state of the crops in the interior of Russia, as upon the state of the roads to the seacoast.

Altogether, though the ports on this coast manifest the most determined disposition to prosper in spite of everything, I doubt whether the combination of natural and political disadvantages with which they are beset will not ultimately prove insurmountable; for, besides the want of water and the want of roads, they have just experienced a new deficiency in the want of labour. This seems rather an odd complaint for a country containing fifty millions of inhabitants, a considerable portion of whom are in great poverty; but it is absolutely the case that those of the scanty population inhabiting the steppes near these ports, who will give themselves the trouble to work, have occasionally earned as much as one silver ruble a day each.

The thousands half starving in many parts of the country, who are not altogether bound down as serfs to a particular locality, are unable to migrate to this land of plenty, on account of the system which obliges them to invest their all in a passport to bring them here, and when they have made a little money, to spend their savings in bribes to government officials, for more passports to take them back again to their own district, from which they may not be absent above a limited time; while the journey there and back would most probably occupy a considerable period, if it were not altogether impracticable for persons in their condition. But in addition to these political hindrances, the besotted and apathetic disposition of the Russian peasant, at any rate, permits him to rest content with what is barely sufficient to keep body and soul together; while in the numerous fast-days which his religion imposes, he finds abundant excuse for gratifying his indolent nature. Thus do the government and church of Russia combine to retard the advancement of the country; and instead of fostering those vast resources with which nature has blessed the land, they seem intent only upon adding to the obstacles which she has opposed to its prosperity. What reasonable motive can we assign for those enormous guild-dues to which merchants are subjected, and which seem imposed expressly to discourage the existence of such useful members of society?—or those immoderate duties upon all foreign goods, which are tantamount to a prohibition of civilisation, while they raise the price of freight to other ports, since stones are the most profitable cargo which a ship can bring to a Russian coast?—or those quarantine regulations and police dues, which must be designed to prevent vessels from coming at all, even loaded thus?

It is clear that the frosts which blockade for many months the outlets of trade—and the shallowness of the water, which makes them at all times inaccessible—and the snows, which utterly destroy the summer roads—and the indolent habits of the peasantry, which render an amelioration of their condition almost impossible—must all be regarded by government as the accessories which nature has provided to the system it is now pursuing.

It is amidst such obstacles as these that trade is expected to flourish in the south-eastern provinces; and it may be asked how it is that, in spite of them, it continues to prosper? To this it may be replied, that the corn-trade owes its vast development, within the last few years, entirely to fortuitous circumstances. It was not until Sir Robert Peel admitted foreign corn into Great Britain, freed from all fiscal regulations, that the Greek merchants, who had already monopolised in some measure the trade of the eastern shores of the Mediterranean, perceived the rich harvest that might be reaped from those fertile districts, in which their own countrymen were already located as colonists. With characteristic energy and perseverance, they opened up a trade with the shores of the Black Sea; and the produce of these provinces poured into a market in which the demand has ever been increasing, whilst other countries are only now beginning to discover their own internal resources, and their ability successfully to compete with Russia.

The Danubian provinces are already feeling their way into this lucrative trade, with telling effect. At the same time, we must not overlook the enormous extent of virgin soil in the south of Russia, capable of bearing, under a proper system of cultivation, almost enough grain to support the whole population of Europe; while in the interior, labour is cheap, or altogether forced—and thus the price of grain should *apparently* be kept low.

A closer consideration of this question proves, however, that the disadvantages attending servitude counterbalance those advantages which at first sight it seems to confer upon the proprietor. It differs materially from slavery in its effect upon agricultural operations, since the serf is possessed of a portion of land upon which he is entitled to bestow a certain amount of labour; and this is one of the causes which combine to produce the following practical result of serfdom—viz., the enormous fluctuation in the price of grain in the interior, which proves a most serious obstacle to the successful and extensive cultivation of the steppes of southern Russia and the Volga provinces.

In all other countries the *intrinsic* value of an article, as distinguished from its marketable value, is calculated by the cost of its production; and if the demand be not sufficiently extensive, and the prices of food not remunerating, the producer will cease to employ his capital and labour upon an unprofitable subject. But if, on the other hand, the demand is steady, a plentiful harvest is certain to reward him abundantly; while, if the crops be poor, the prices rise to cover the greater proportionate expense thus incurred.

In Russia, an entirely different state of things obtains. A propitious season and abundant crops do not guarantee a profitable year to the Russian farmer. The prices may suddenly have fallen so low that no physical combination of circumstances can benefit him; he is utterly unable to calculate the cost of production, and consequently unable to conjecture what would be a remunerating price. Where one part of the land is cultivated by the peasant on his own account, and another portion is cultivated by him for his proprietor, the capital employed, the rent of the land, and the work which is never paid for, become so confused that it is impossible for the farmer to have more than a general vague notion, at the end of the year, whether it has been a profitable one or not. He is thus the victim of circumstances. Totally unable to affect the price of grain himself, it depends upon the demand from foreign countries, the facilities of communication, and his position with regard to them-with many other causes incidental to an immense but thinly-peopled country, affected in its extremities by the most different temperatures, liable during the same year to famine and plenty occurring in distant quarters, between which it is matter of pure hazard whether there exist any means of communication.

To provide against such contingencies, the government has established granaries, in which the grain of prosperous years is stored in true patriarchal style. In provinces dependent upon more highly-favoured districts for supplies, private speculators lay in stores, which often accumulate to such an extent that grain becomes even more plentiful than in the producing districts, where the price falls to an absurdly low figure. This is sometimes the case with the Volga provinces, where commercial arrangements are carried on in an original manner, and the inexperienced farmer is easily disconcerted. Thus, though the wheat may be produced at a comparatively small cost, it is quite possible for the farmer of serf-grown corn to be ruined; and he probably will be, if he does not keep pace with the times, and obtain some idea of the relations subsisting between the price his grain fetches in the market, and the cost of its production. At any rate, he will discover the disadvantage under which he labours, in comparison with those who can regulate the cost and extent of cultivation according to the demand.

But it will not, surely, always be the fate of England to depend on foreign granaries alone. Is it so very extravagant to anticipate the day when she will cease to obtain corn from the shores of the Black Sea and the fertile provinces of America?— and when her own territories in the East—more abundantly prolific than either—will be intersected by railways, and yield an inexhaustible supply?—when a ship canal through the Isthmus of Suez will enable these precious cargoes to reach England in a state of preservation which is impossible under existing circumstances, since, during a passage of some months, in which the equator is twice crossed, the ravages of the weevil prove utterly destructive to grain?

When we compare the climate, soil, population, and resources of India with those of Russia, and contrast the commercial policy of the latter—so culpably Protectionist—with that of Britain, we cannot doubt the result of an enterprise so important as the formation of this canal, and are scarcely entitled to sneer at a government which does not connect the Volga and the Don, while we are deterred from carrying out a similar undertaking by difficulties which a future day will show to be not insurmountable.

CHAPTER XIV

The "Bertha"—The Sea of Azov—Our accommodation—A mercantile retrospect—Arrive at Yeni Kalè—A custom-house official—Eastern aspect of the town—Kertch: its historical associations

We had ravenously devoured whole files of *Galignani*, supplied by the kindness of the English consul—explored every shop in the Gastinni Dvor—baked ourselves in the streets, and cooled ourselves on the ramparts—paid a visit to the governor, Prince Lieven, in his summer retreat—exhausted all the luxuries of the ill-managed hotel, which seemed to grow more and more comfortless as our recollection of civilisation revived—and before two days were over, were heartily sick of Taganrog. Under these circumstances, it was welcome news to learn that the captain of a Prussian brig had been found, who offered to take us to Kertch, if we were prepared for an immediate start. We gladly closed with him upon his own terms, notwithstanding the impossibility of winding up our affairs satisfactorily upon such short notice, since it involved a forcible entry into the premises of the washerwoman, the seizure and packing of wet linen, and the abandonment of our carriage. We had tried in vain to find a purchaser for that faithful vehicle, but everybody seemed to have carriages for sale at Taganrog, and of course nobody wanted to buy ours; so we included the original price in the posting expenses, and found, after all, that the cost of the journey had not been ruinous. Indeed, we were quite satisfied with having bought a carriage which had ever arrived at the journey's end at all, and had no reason to complain of being obliged to leave it where we no longer wanted it, instead of on the dreary steppe.

We were soon ready to accompany a deaf little German to the port, and, after a three-hours' sail, reached the brig of which he styled himself captain, and which, wind and weather permitting, was to convey us to Kertch some time within the week. We accordingly proceeded to make ourselves comfortable in a hole there was under a ladder, and which was pervaded by a most unpleasant odour, containing an extremely greasy old couch, a very rickety table, an almanac, an orange, and a tumblerful of oil, to light up by night the only cabin in this filthy craft, which the skipper informed us, as he cast his eye over the accommodation with evident pride and satisfaction, was called the "Bertha," built at Königsberg, of two hundred and fifty tons burden, and laden with wool for Cork. So long as competition in the foreign carrying trade is confined to such arrant tubs as the Bertha, commanded by such careful old souls as our worthy friend and commander Kreplein, English shipowners need suffer none of those qualms which have been already caused in anticipation by the alteration in the Navigation Laws, nor fear the lower rates of freight which in some instances are charged—though, as far as I could learn, in the case of the Bertha no reduction had been made. For no possible reason that I could divine, a few hours after leaving the roads we cast anchor, on a lovely night, with a full moon to show us the way, which was anything but difficult, and a fair wind to take us along it. However, we were too much accustomed to delays to be in the least affected by one so unimportant, and I soon forgot where I was, on the dirty floor of the cabin, which might possibly be my resting-place for so many nights to come.

For four days we went edging on through the thick pea-soupy substance, of which the water seems composed, literally ploughing our way through scum, and passing over every conceivable shade of green and yellow—for the Sea of Azov can never be accused of being blue. Still and turgid, in no part attaining a depth of more than forty-two feet, the ancients appreciated its true character more correctly than we do, when they called it a marsh. We were occasionally left almost sticking in this delectable pond by the light variable airs, which seemed to delight in baffling us; and we had nothing but cloudless days and moonlight nights to compensate for so monotonous an existence.

There was no room to walk the deck, which was occupied by some pigs and the crew. The crew lived in a temporary round-house, erected for their accommodation on deck, as the wool was stowed away in their legitimate cribs below; the pigs roamed at large wherever their fancy led them, and used to dispute the ladder down to our cabin with an uncompromising tom-cat, who considered that enviable retreat as his peculiar abode. He seemed to have come to a private arrangement with Wilhelm, the cabin-boy, to be allowed a few moments upon the table alone with the dinner before we were told that it was ready—for we generally found him anticipating us in the matter of the gravy. Except for this unfair preference on Wilhelm's part, and the careless way in which he upset the oil-lamp over my bed one night, we had no reason to complain of the conduct of that simple soul, who spoke an unintelligible German patois, and who, when he was not waiting upon us, was in constant attendance upon the pigs.

For the first day we amused ourselves drying our wet clothes on the rigging, losing two pocket-handkerchiefs and a sock, which were unwarily hung too low, and devoured by pigs. The next day we tried in vain to tempt some of the fish, with which the brackish slimy water abounds, to leave their tempting element; but they were not to be deluded by our clumsy attempts, for there was no proper tackle on board. After having thus exhausted all our resources, we had nothing left but to recline on the wool sacks, watch the smoke of our cigars, and calculate the chances of a spark consuming Kreplein, Wilhelm, pigs, and all.

We were generally surrounded by country craft, in company with which we glided lazily on, while occasionally the white sails flapped idly against the tapering masts of some English merchantman, probably the only vessel of the party who really grudged the delay. Time is no object to a Russian, and the steamer takes four days to perform the voyage to Kertch, a distance of one hundred and eighty miles, touching at Marianopol, Berdianski, and Gheïsk, and remaining a day at each place—for no particular reason, as far as I could learn from those who had been unlucky enough to make the passage.

How many phases has commerce passed through upon these waters, since the first Milesian fishing-stations were established upon their shores, and exported sturgeon to Greek gourmands, when Tanais was looked upon as an *Ultima Thule*, so little known that its very existence is now almost doubtful! Many centuries after its destruction, Venetian, Genoese, and Pisan galliots sailed side by side through the Cimmerian Bosphorus, freighted with the rich merchandise of the East, while colonists of the rival republics competed upon the banks of the Don for the monopoly of trade with the celebrated Golden Horde, who were in direct communication with Samarcand. These flourishing colonies in their turn disappeared, and now for three hundred years an occasional Turkish zebeck was the only craft that crossed the sea to Azov, a fortress built on the ruins of Tana, and perhaps of Tanais.

At last a new power succeeded all these, and trade revived under circumstances altogether changed, owing its importance, not to the wealth of the East, but to the resources of the country surrounding this sea; so that vessels which traverse it now are no longer freighted with silk from China, but with corn from Taurida; and it is worthy of remark that, while the English have succeeded Greeks and Italians in monopolising, by a different route, their old Eastern trade, their ships also navigate in greater numbers than those of any other nation the once famous Palus Mæotis.

I was not sorry, on going on deck, after passing my fourth night in the close cabin, to find that we were anchored in the straits amid a host of shipping; and I was still more delighted to hear that the boat was ready to take us ashore. We quitted the bluff-built Bertha without regret, carrying away with us only a grateful recollection of the hard ship-biscuit and excellent caviare which had formed the staple of our fare. Bread was a luxury unknown on board that primitive craft. The sun was rising behind the low land which forms the Asiatic shore of the Cimmerian Bosphorus, and brought out the lights and shadows of the old Turkish fortress of Yeni Kalè, the crumbling walls of which surmounted the steep cliffs that overhang the still more crumbling village at their base.

Here, in the very teeth of a most unsatisfactory-looking custom-house official in the garb of a Russian soldier, we landed, and prepared for the ordeal which, though we were only going from one Russian town to another, seemed inevitable. We were immediately commanded to deposit ourselves and our luggage under an old wall, and there to remain until the head of the custom-house should awake, for he was not to be disturbed on any account. As it was only 6 A.M., and Russian officials are not very conscientious in their punctuality to business, we took the liberty of disobeying the soldier, in spite of his fierce injunctions to the contrary, and walked to the house of the grand personage whose slumbers were so religiously protected. A knock brought a tall man to the door, who, with an agonised expression of countenance, and walking on the tips of his toes, made violent gesticulations expressive of silence. It was evident that his master was a most ferocious personage; for when we whispered into his ear an order to awake him immediately, he started back in horror and amazement at the temerity which could suggest such a rash proceeding. Finding that our entreaties were useless, and that the man was becoming insolent, I suddenly beat a double rap with my cane, which would have done honour to a London footman, upon which his face assumed a persuasive expression, and he said something, by which I understood him to mean that he would wake his master for a ruble. This was, however, unnecessary, for in a few moments an exceedingly mild-looking person appeared in a dressing-gown, who very benignantly glanced first at our passports, then at our luggage and intimated that the ceremony was over, without manifesting the slightest displeasure, or anxiety to receive a bribe. Of course, the insolent soldier who insisted on our

161

waiting under the wall, and the servant who refused to awake his master without being paid for it, were very urgent in their request for vodka after such services.

Yeni Kalè looks like some dilapidated town on the shores of the Red Sea. The walls of the fort, and the steep cliffs, and the falling houses, and the smooth sea, were all very much the same dead colour. The varied costumes, however, which we observed as we strolled up the narrow Eastern-looking street, in some measure relieved the general sombre appearance of the place, while they seemed to transport us still more effectually into Asia. The loose trousers fastened at the ankle, the open boddices and flowing head-dresses of the women, all formed a pleasing change from the high-waisted petticoats of the Russian females; while the Turkish slippers and embroidered jackets of the men were in keeping with their swarthy hue, and indicated at once an Asiatic origin.

The population is composed entirely of Greeks and Tartars. There are a good many antiquities and remains of the old Greek colonies strewn over the country in the neighbourhood, while not far distant are some celebrated mud-springs, which we did not visit.

A sort of omnibus, devoid of seats, and half filled with straw, now appeared, to which were harnessed a pair of mules, that could easily have been put inside. However, we trusted to their capacity, though they seemed most disproportionate to the work, and commenced jolting up the steep ascent by which we left the town. From the summit the view of Kertch, and the large bay in which it is situated, was very beautiful; the broken outline of the opposite hills projected far across the straits; while the houses of the town rose one above another up the steep side of the hill of Mithridates;—the whole reminding me of Naples, to which it certainly bears a humble resemblance.

It is about seven miles from Yeni Kalè to Kertch. The country is still of the steppe nature, undulating and grassy; while the numerous tumuli scattered over it promised to be interesting subjects of future explorations.

The hotel in which we took up our quarters formed one of a handsome row of houses which faced the quay, and gives the town a somewhat more imposing aspect from the sea than it deserves.

Kertch is almost the only town in Russia built entirely of stone, and the houses look handsome and substantial. We seemed to have quitted the country of wooden cottages and green roofs, as well as of red-bearded men, with sheepskin coats, and were not sorry to be in a land where dwellings and people harmonised with the more genial temperature we now experienced. Kertch is one of the most interesting towns in the south of Russia to the antiquarian;—the Panticapeum of Strabo, it was founded about the middle of the seventh century, B.C., by the first Milesian colonists in the Taurida, and two hundred years afterwards it became the capital of the kingdom of Bosphorus, and the residence of its kings.

For three hundred years the trade of Theodosia and Panticapea flourished, for the Cimmerian Peninsula had become the granary of Greece. The conquest of that nation by the Romans, however, produced an important effect upon this kingdom, since it was dependent for its prosperity upon a market, which would soon cease to exist; and it fell an easy prey to Mithridates, at the same time that he subdued the rest of the Taurida.

To Panticapea the celebrated king of Pontus fled after his last defeat by Pompey, and here, unable to contend at once against the victorious arms of Rome and the treachery of his own son, he terminated his glorious career. And here it was that Pharnaces afterwards raised the standard of revolt, and Cæsar came, saw, and conquered him.

The successors of the son of Mithridates reigned only in accordance with the caprice of the Roman Emperors; and their territory, after being frequently devastated by the Huns and the Goths, was finally conquered in 375 A.D., by those barbaric hordes which ultimately subverted the whole civilised world, and various tribes of whom for a thousand years occupied the

163

Tauric Peninsula. Amongst these, the Khazars were the most celebrated, who seem, at one time, to have considered Kertch a place of some importance, while a great part of the peninsula took the name of Khazaria from them. In the early part of the thirteenth century a great number of Circassians established themselves in the Crimea, and the town of Kertch became subject to a prince of that nation. It was about this time that the Genoese possessed themselves of the southern shore of the Crimea, and established a colony at Caffa, with the permission of the Khan of Khazaria, whose authority they were soon in a position to set at defiance, and with whom they waged an uncertain war, until Bathi, the grandson of Zingis Khan, leader of the Golden Horde, on his way from the deserts of Tartary to the conquest of Russia, invaded the Crimea, exterminated the Comanes who then possessed it, and the Tartar capital was fixed at Eski Krim.

Crim Tartars

In 1365 the Greek colony of Soudagh, which had at one time attained an important mercantile position, enfeebled by intestine disorders, fell a prey to that all-absorbing maritime power under which Caffa had become so celebrated. A hundred years afterwards these restless adventurers became embroiled with the nation who now occupied the peninsula, and to whom they owed their deliverance. Their colonies were besieged by the Tartars by land, and blockaded by a fleet which the Porte had sent to the assistance of the Khans, who had become tributary to the Ottoman Empire. The destruction of the Genoese colonies was tantamount to an annihilation of commerce in these seas.

For three hundred years the Cimmerian Bosphorus remained closed, and the ruins of once flourishing cities lay strewn upon its shores.

CHAPTER XV

Kertch: its disadvantages as a port—Tumuli—Steppe cultivation—A Tartar conveyance—No somovar—An amusing interpreter—A railway to Theodosia: its prospects—A steppe apparition—A midnight scene—Karassu Bazaar—Approach to Simpheropol

Kertch had dwindled into a Turkish town of little importance when it was ceded to Russia by the Porte in the year 1774; but the ancient capital of the Bosphorus was destined soon to regain some of its former greatness, though at the sacrifice of those Italian colonies which had more recently engrossed the whole trade of the peninsula, and which remain to this day monuments of that adventurous spirit of commercial enterprise which called them into existence.

For some Russian reason, incomprehensible to common sense, the tribune of commerce was transferred from Theodosia, a town advantageously situated at the head of a deep capacious harbour, which is never frozen, to the shores of these straits, which are closed for four months of the year, where the anchorage is dangerous and the water shallow. Here every ship must remain and perform a four days' quarantine. The larger ones wait until their cargoes arrive from Taganrog or Rostof, in lighters; while those drawing less water cross the bar, and proceed to load at Taganrog. On their return, it becomes necessary to transfer half their cargoes into lighters at Yeni Kalè, and drop down the shallow straits to Kertch, to re-load—a proceeding which affords a rich harvest to a rapacious crew of Greek lightermen resident at the former place.

All this may be very profitable to Kertch, but it is extremely expensive to the public. For instance, supposing the produce to be Siberian iron which has descended the Don to Rostof, it is there put into lighters, and conveyed, sixty miles, to Taganrog, where it is duly landed; and when the right vessel arrives, and anchors fifteen miles from the shore, it must be put

165

on board by means of lighters again. In two days after she has been loaded in this expensive way at Taganrog, the ship probably reaches Yeni Kalè, where the process I have already described takes place, and thus the cargo has been subject to five transhipments before it can be fairly said to have left the Russian shores.

Rather than continue this absurd system, it would be better to construct a railway from Rostof to Kertch, down the eastern coast of the Sea of Azov, through the level country of the Cossacks of the Black Sea, and thus effectually terminate the existence of Taganrog, which only lives a sort of excrescence upon Rostof.

It is most unfortunate that a government which so seldom does a bit of patriotism should have misplaced its affections upon two such worthless objects as Taganrog and Kertch—that it should have fostered and protected so carefully towns which had far better never have existed. Had Rostof and Theodosia been treated in a similar manner, the price of articles exported from these shores would be incalculably diminished; for Theodosia would become an emporium for the produce not only of the Don, but of all the minor ports upon the Sea of Azov; and a vast number of small Russian craft would have been employed in concentrating freight, during the fine season, at the most highly-favoured port which Russia possesses, since it is the only one available for commercial purposes throughout the year.

That the trade of this part of the world is rapidly on the increase, is apparent from the fact that no less than one thousand vessels entered the straits of Kertch in the year 1851. It is but fair to say that the port dues, and expenses attendant on passing through the straits, are very trifling, and consist chiefly in bribes to petty officials. Unfortunately, nature has done more towards blocking up the entrance of the Sea of Azov than the government could ever have hoped to effect, even though it once established a thirty days' quarantine at Kertch, in its ardent desires to benefit that town.

During our short stay in Kertch we were much indebted to the kindness and hospitality of the English consul, Mr. Catley, with whom we drove over to inspect one of the most remarkable of the tumuli which has hitherto been opened.

The stone gallery, which is thirty-six yards long and about twenty feet high, leads to a square mausoleum, surmounted by a cupola. The whole structure, which was extremely massive, reminded me forcibly of the Cyclopean remains at Tiryns and Mycenæ. In some of these tumuli sarcophagi have been found, and their interesting contents sent either to the museum at St. Petersburg, or they are preserved in the little Temple of Theseus, which, situated on the Hill of Mithridates, is appropriated to the same purpose here.

As we crossed the steppe on our way back, it was melancholy to see thousands of acres of magnificent soil, capable of bearing the finest crops in the world, destined to remain uncultivated until the agricultural population of Russia are free to transplant themselves to those parts of the empire which offer the highest inducements, and where a new stock is wanted to replace the aboriginal Tartars, who are rapidly vanishing off the face of the earth.

It is difficult to account for this decay of a race, in a rich country absolutely lying waste for want of labour. Undoubtedly the colonisation of a territory by a civilised and industrious people has invariably led to the decrease and ultimate extermination of the original owners of the soil, where there has not been room for the two races to exist contemporaneously; but this can hardly be said to be the case in the Crimea. The barbarous Sclaves could scarcely boast a greater degree of refinement than the Tartar tribe whose country they became possessed of; while there remains still ample room for double their united population to live in plenty. The want of water is an evil only consequent upon the want of enterprise and labour sufficient to irrigate a soil which has proved itself second to none in Europe, since the buckwheat of Kertch carried off the prize at the Great

Exhibition in London; nor can justice ever be done to the Crimea while the obstacles are even greater to foreigners holding land than to Russians immigrating for the purpose of tilling it. By a recent ukase, no foreigner is allowed to hold one rood of land without becoming naturalised a Russian subject—a penalty for which, in the present state of things, nothing could compensate but a most certain and magnificent remuneration.

Kertch contains a population of ten thousand inhabitants, exporting only a little salt to some of the Russian ports. It is destitute, at present, of all intrinsic resources, and owes its prosperity to a policy which has ruined Theodosia, and immeasurably retarded commerce upon the Sea of Azov.

Our former experience of posting had been sufficiently disagreeable to determine us to avoid it for the future if possible, and so we engaged an exceedingly apathetic-looking Tartar to convey us to Simpheropol, a distance of one hundred and thirty miles, in two days, with his own vehicle and horses. Accordingly, towards evening, a long green conveyance, very much resembling a carrier's cart, appeared at the door, drawn by three diminutive rats of ponies. It was so perfectly full of

Our Tartar Waggon

straw as to appear not intended for the reception of anything else. However, we found that, after our luggage was stowed away, a remarkably comfortable bed remained for ourselves; and I was soon snugly buried in the straw, insensible alike to fleas and jolting, which my fellow-traveller told me in the morning had both been very trying. We soon found that, however eccentric might have been the appearance of our nags, they were none the less high-mettled. Our way lay over nothing but steppe, in no respect differing from the country of the Don Cossacks, except in being less undulating.

Here, at the different post-stations, the bluff Cossack was either exchanged for the indolent Tartar, or we were left without postmaster, and consequently without somovar at all. We found, to our consternation, that this was the case in a village that externally promised great things, having just accomplished seventy-five miles in a little more than twenty hours, and beginning to feel that a substantial meal had become necessary. The house which should have been devoted to the entertainment of man and beast, consisted of but two rooms, and was converted into a store for Indian corn, to insure the safety of which doors and windows had been carefully barred. The Tartar wisely carried his own and his horse's food with him. He had breakfasted off a huge watermelon and a hunch of black bread, and he was now dining off precisely similar fare. After our experience of this fruit, it was frightful to contemplate him thus engaged.

Fortunately we observed a respectable-looking mansion, and, boldly invading it, met with a cordial reception from the owner, who was evidently the squire of the place, but who was totally at a loss to divine who we were or what we wanted, until a little wizened old Frenchman suddenly appeared, and bowed himself into the office of interpreter. His success in that capacity was soon manifest, for our host vanished, and shortly afterwards a steaming somovar made its appearance, together with a bottle of excellent Crim wine and some delicious fruit, upon which, with the addition of our own stores, we made a satisfactory repast, while the little Frenchman enlivened us with his account of a visit he had made to England with Talleyrand (probably as his valet), and plied us with incessant questions as to the prospects of Louis Napoleon, and the present state of Paris, which he had not seen for thirty years. Poor old man, he was in utter ignorance of what was going on in the rest of the world, except in as far as the little Odessa newspaper supplied him with information. His present position was that of tutor to the sons of our host. That worthy individual soon after came back to us, accompanied by two unruly boys—we had observed his wife looking through a chink in the door at the unusual visitors—and commenced a conversation by an abrupt inquiry if shares in an English railway were purchased from a private company or from the crown. Upon this a discussion ensued as to our mode of managing such matters, which was somewhat confused, from the fact of our interpreter often mixing up admonitions to his pupils with the description he was giving us of a proposed line of railway from Moscow to Theodosia, which he delivered in some such fragmentary way as this: "Monsieur says, in answer to your question—why do you keep opening and shutting the door in that way, Ivan?—that the principal article is salt, for the conveyance of which from the Crimea into the interior of Russia this line would be employed—you are not the *concierge*,—but Prince Woronzoff has given it his decided opposition. He maintains that such a line would ruin Kertch, which is a far more important consideration than the welfare of the country at large—don't titter and grin, Alexis, I have said nothing for anyone to laugh at,—therefore there is no chance of a proposal for this railroad being favourably regarded by government."

Our host was evidently deeply interested in this scheme. He owned large salt-pans in the neighbourhood, and the line would necessarily pass through a great portion of his property. I was much struck with the reasons he urged in support of the superiority of this line over the one from Moscow to Odessa, which I see has since been determined on. The most palpable advantage which Theodosia possesses over all other Russian harbours, with the single exception of Sevastopol—which is devoted entirely to naval purposes—is one to which I have before alluded, viz., that it remains unfrozen all the year round. Situated in the midst of the garden of Russia, it possesses attractions denied to any other port in the kingdom; and its former opulence, as the centre of the commerce on the Black Sea, goes far to show that at the present day it would be a fitting terminus to so important a railway. The wines and the fruits of the southern coast would be thus conveyed into the interior, in addition to all those European importations necessary to render life tolerable in so barbarous and inclement a country.

But so long as government neglects such evident advantages, from an absurd dread of injuring two or three pet towns, it is checking the national prosperity, and must therefore in the long-run be found indirectly to have retarded the very towns it is thus improperly seeking to protect. However, as I remarked to our interested friend, it is useless to discuss the propriety of particular lines of railway in a country where the public is not allowed a voice in the matter. Perhaps, poor man, when he got his railway, he would not be allowed to send his salt by it; and it is yet to be proved whether a railway will pay, passing through a country which is not intersected in any one direction by a macadamized road, so that there are no lateral means of communication by which consumers and producers can conveniently convey their goods to and from the line. At least it will answer the great end and object of a rapid conveyance of soldiers and despatches: and the merchants at Odessa, as loyal subjects, will no doubt be quite contented with a goods-train to Moscow, about once a week, upon payment of the proper bribes to the managers.

We were journeying over tracts of wild thyme, grumbling at the tameness of the scenery, the solitude of the way, and the intensely hot weather, when we saw indistinctly shadowed, amid clouds of dust, a colossal apparition moving slowly and majestically towards us. Utterly at a loss to conceive what monsters of the steppe we were approaching, we were delighted to trace the uncouth forms of two camels, drawing an enormous wicker-work covered cart, which contained a group of Tartars. We had hardly time to observe the strange

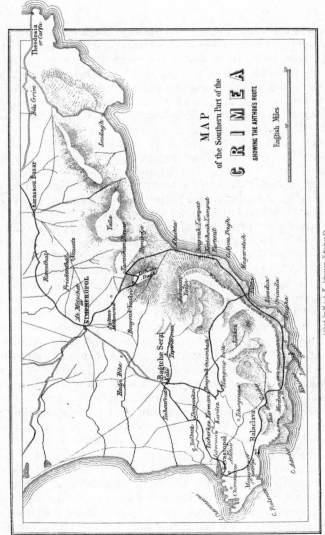

MAP

of the Southern Part of the

CRIMEA

SHOWING THE AUTHOR'S ROUTE

English Miles

Lithog. by W. & A. K. Johnston. Edinburgh.

172

appearance which this novel mode of travelling presented, when we were passed, and shrouded in our respective columns of dust, lost to each other's gaze as suddenly as we had emerged upon it. It was a rencontre—the more striking from being totally unexpected—so thoroughly in keeping with the scene, that the feeling of loneliness which I had experienced before, seemed to have been increased tenfold by this silent meeting with these wanderers of the desert.

We drove through great flocks of bustards, who manifested the utmost unconcern at our approach, merely moving aside like tame pigeons, and stalking amid the thin dry grass, as if they considered it extreme impudence in us to disturb them in the quiet possession of their own territory. I afterwards found that roast bustard was a common dish at the hotels in the Crimea, and it proved excellent fare.

Hitherto, almost the only inequalities which I had observed upon the level surface of the steppe had been composed of piles of water-melons. Those alone who have endured steppe travelling for a lengthened period, can conceive our sensations on seeing at last the beautiful irregular outline of the distant mountains, clear against the red evening sky; for we hailed them as affording a prospect, not only of a change from our present mode of travelling, but of really fine scenery only waiting to be explored.

About half-past two in the morning, I was awakened by a violent jolt, and found we were trying, with our long unwieldy equipage, to turn two corners at once, in the narrow winding streets of a Tartar town, and had naturally enough failed in the attempt. Still I was thankful to the curb-stone that had roused me, from not the most tranquil of slumbers, to a due appreciation of one of those scenes which occasionally break upon the monotony of a journey, and fully compensate to the weary traveller for the discomfort and fatigues of many days. The tortuous streets among which we were entangled, lit up here and there by the faint light of a waning moon, were pitchy dark, where the quaint old houses approached so near as almost to touch one another. The broad verandahs, casting deep shadows in every direction, seemed as silent as if the empty stalls under their eaves had never been occupied by living soul; not a solitary bark gave warning to the sleeping inhabitants of our presence; and I was wondering whether these were not the deserted habitations of a race gone by, when suddenly, from one of the dark mysterious avenues, in uniform and silent procession, marched, two and two, a body of bearded men, whose long robes and measured tread added an imposing solemnity to their occupation, which might well have been that of bewailing a people of whom they were the only survivors. Each man was distinctly visible for a moment, as he passed through a gleam of the moonlight; and so, without the sound of a footfall, the whole procession slowly vanished, and we were left to pursue our lonely way over the desolate steppe. Many hours after, I awoke to the realities of a miserable post-hut, and could scarcely believe that the spectral view I had obtained of an Armenian funeral in the old Tartar town of Karassu Bazaar was not a dream.

Karassu Bazaar is one of the largest and most characteristic of Crimean towns, containing a population of nearly fifteen thousand inhabitants. It is advantageously situated for commercial purposes; and the industrious Jews and Armenians, who, together with Tartars, compose the population, carry on extensive manufactures in morocco leather, soap, candles, &c.

The Kara Su, or black-water river, runs past the town, and through a fertile valley which grows great quantities of grain and tobacco; while the extensive pasture-lands of the surrounding steppes enable the inhabitants to maintain large herds of cattle. Near this spot the gallant Potemkin erected a palace, expressly for the reception of the Empress Catharine, who was thus surprised to find herself surrounded by all the luxuries of civilised life in this remote corner of her empire.

On the left of the post road from Karassu Bazaar to Simpheropol, and not many miles distant, are situated numerous German colonies, which have been placed upon the slopes of the mountains in the upper part of the rich valleys with which the country now begins to be continually intersected. The northern course of each rivulet was distinctly marked by a narrow belt of wood.

We had accomplished a hundred and twenty-five miles in thirty-seven hours with the same horses. The Tartar was in continual danger of dropping off his box, fatigued with hunting along his team through two consecutive nights; and the whole party were equally tired of the journey, when, after climbing up a steep ravine, the new Russian capital of the Crimea lay spread at our feet, as beautiful as it was a welcome sight. The fertile

The Tchatir Dagh

valley of the Salghir, winding from the base of the Tchatir Dagh, here expanded into a richly cultivated plain, where the white houses and handsome churches of Simpheropol seemed half buried amid luxuriant vegetation. To the left the Tchatir Dagh raised its imposing crest, to a height of five thousand feet, standing boldly out, as if unwilling to acknowledge any connection with the adjoining range. In shape it reminded me of Table Mountain at the Cape of Good Hope.

175

The cheering effects of this delightful prospect were soon manifest, alike upon ourselves, the Tartar, and the horses. The latter, sniffing their journey's end, took advantage of a gentle slope, and started off at a gallop—the Tartar vented approving shouts of their conduct—while we shook ourselves out of the dust and straw as we dashed into the valley, along avenues of tapering poplars, and terminated, with inexpressible satisfaction, our last experience of steppe travelling.

CHAPTER XVI

*Tartar quarter—Street scenes—Bactrian camels—The fair—
Costumes—Variety of races—Valley of the Salghir—Tartar
quarters—A restless night—Ascend the Tchatir Dagh—A
magnificent view—The cave of Foul Kouba—Perilous descent—
Taouchan Bazaar—The pass of Alushta*

When the Crimea was ceded to Russia in 1781, the picturesque old capital of Bagtchi Serai was considered unworthy of being the chief town of the new province, and a gay modern city was laid out upon the plains of the Salghir, dignified with an imposing ancient Greek name, and built in true Russian taste, with very broad streets, very white tall houses, decorated with very green paint. If the population consisted entirely of Russians, the interior of the town would be as far from realising the expectations which its outward appearance is calculated to produce, as Kazan or Saratov; but fortunately for Simpheropol, it was once Akmetchet, or "The White Mosque," and the inhabitants of Akmetchet still linger near the city of their ancestors, and invest the cold monotony of the new capital with an interest of which it would be otherwise quite unworthy.

Formerly the second town in the Crimea, and the residence of the Kalga Sultan, or vice-Khan, Akmetchet was a city of great importance, adorned with palaces, mosques, and public baths. It has now exchanged the Eastern magnificence of former days for the tawdry glitter of Muscovite barbarism.

About five thousand Tartars inhabit exclusively one quarter of the town, and thither we bent our steps, under the guidance of an intelligent German watchmaker, who officiated as cicerone during our stay at Simpheropol with great kindness, neglecting the duties of his shop for the pleasure of lionising the "distinguished" strangers.

The streets inhabited by Tartars are composed entirely of blank walls, and would, therefore, be the dullest places

177

imaginable were it not for the people who traverse them. The houses are only one storey high, and each is enclosed in a separate courtyard. The parchment windows which look out into it are placed so low as to be quite hidden from the street; and so the unfortunate females have not the ordinary amusement of Eastern ladies, and no black eyes glance out of latticed windows upon the passenger as he passes beneath them. The Tartar women of Akmetchet, however, do not lose much by their seclusion. The streets have none of the life and bustle of a town like Cairo. The shops are few and far between, very small and poor, and kept by ugly unveiled women. The beauties walk about covered up to the eyes with the white "fereedjè," which reaches as low as the knee. Were it not for the bright-coloured skirt which flutters beneath it, and the loose drawers that fall over tiny yellow boots, they would look precisely like animated bundles of white linen. The men occasionally wear the turban and flowing robe of the true Oriental; but their costumes, always picturesque, vary so much as to be almost indescribable.

We soon got tired of wandering through this maze of narrow lanes, always confined between high blank walls, and changed the scene by suddenly coming upon the fashionable promenade, where the band was playing in cool delicious gardens to the gay world, who delight to assemble here and stroll upon the banks of the Salghir, away from the heat and dust of the town. The present governor, Pestal, a brother to "Yes, it comes at last," is, I understand, in high favour with the Emperor. His house is a substantial handsome-looking mansion. There are extensive barracks situated a little outside the town, but the hospital alone is always in use; the rest of the building is only occupied occasionally by troops passing to and from the Caucasus. There are no less than two hotels in Simpheropol, and in the one we were at they actually gave us a sheet each, but, of course, no means of washing. Our windows looked out upon the principal street, and were always interesting posts of observation. Sometimes a lumbering nobleman's carriage, piled with luggage, and stored with provisions for a month, rattled into the town—the family being about to return to St. Petersburg for the winter, after spending the summer at their country seat in the Crimea; or an unpretending vehicle, exactly similar to ours, jogged quietly past, crammed with Armenian merchants, some of whose legs, protruding from between the curtains, were presumed to belong to Armenians, from the perfume of Turkish tobacco which was diffused over the street during their transit; or a file

Camel-Cart

of camel-carts, filled with straw, moved sedately along, stopping every now and then for a few moments while the drivers spoke to friends, when all the camels lay down; no amount of experience seemed to show them that it was hardly worth while to do this, considering how soon they would have to get up again, and the great exertion it involved. Accustomed only to the camels and dromedaries of still more Eastern countries, the appearance of this Bactrian camel was quite new to me. The two humps are generally so long, that, unable to sustain themselves, they fall over, and often hang down on each side of the animal's back. The neck and legs are covered with long thick hair, from which the Tartar women weave cloth of a soft woolly texture.

In strong contrast to these singular carts, pert droskies were continually dashing about. Though so small and light, all the public droskies here have two horses, generally very good ones, while the heat of the sun has rendered it necessary that they should, for the most part, be supplied with hoods; so that the atrocious little vehicle of St. Petersburg is converted at Simpheropol into quite a respectable conveyance. Next door to our hotel was rather a handsome Jewish synagogue, in which school seemed perpetually going on. Simpheropol contains about fourteen thousand inhabitants, of which comparatively a large proportion are members of this persuasion.

Fortunately the annual fair, which takes place in the first week of October, was being held during the period of our stay, and then it is that the greatest variety of costume, and all the characteristic features of the Crimea, are most opportunely collected for the traveller's benefit. To be properly appreciated, the fair of Nijni Novgorod should be seen before that of Simpheropol, which we found infinitely more striking, perhaps because we were completely taken by surprise when, quite unaware of its existence, we chanced to enter the market-place one afternoon. It is seldom that two races so widely differing in manners and customs, springing from origins so distinct, are brought into everyday contact in such a palpable manner as in Crim Tartary; and this mixture is the more interesting from the improbability of its existing very long in its present unnatural condition. An enormous square, many acres in extent, contained an indiscriminate mass of booths, camels, carts, droskies, oxen, and picturesque groups. Here may be seen the red-bearded Russian mujik, in jack-boots and sheepskin, in close confabulation with a gaily-dressed Tartar, who has just galloped across the steppe, and who sits his horse as if he were part and parcel of him. He wears a large white fur cap, a red striped embroidered jacket, fitting close to his body, with wide open sleeves, while his loose dark blue trousers are girded with a bright-coloured sash, amid the folds of which the massive handle of his dagger appears, and his slippered feet are thrust into clumsy stirrups at the ends of very long leathers. His horse is a wiry little animal, possessing an infinitely greater amount of intelligence than beauty. Farther on among the crowd, and distinguished by his green turban, floats the robe of some pious Hadjè; nor does he seem in the least scandalised by two young ladies in a drosky, not only devoid of fereedjè, but even of bonnets, and wearing only the jaunty little caps of the Parisian grisette. We might very fairly suggest, however, the propriety of their profiting, in some degree, from the example of the muffled females over the way, who seem afraid to expose to the profane gaze of men the dyed tips of their finger nails. In the narrow lanes formed by carts and tents, Greeks, in a no less gay though somewhat different costume from that usually worn in their own country, are haggling with Russian Jews in long black beards, and long black cloaks reaching down to their ankles. It is an even bet who will have the best of such a bargain. Savage-looking Nogays, and Cossack soldiers, are making purchases from Armenian or German shopkeepers. There are large booths, like gypsies' huts magnified, which have no connection with the ragged representatives of that wandering race who swarm at the fair, but which contain quantities of most tempting fruit, huge piles of apricots, grapes, peaches, apples, and plums, of any of which one farthing will buy more than the purchaser can conveniently carry away with him. Besides these booths, there are heavy carts, with wicker-work sides and ungreased angular wheels, which make that incessant and discordant creaking familiar to those who have ever heard a Bengal bullock-hackery. Presiding over the whole scene, not in the least disconcerted by the uncongenial forms which surround them, are hundreds of camels, in all sorts of positions, chewing the cud with Eastern philosophy, and perfectly submissive to very small ragged Tartar boys, who seem to have entire charge of them, and who do not reach higher than their knees. Rows of shops enclosed this miscellaneous assemblage, containing saddles, knives, whips, slippers, tobacco-pouches, and morocco-leather boots, all of Tartar manufacture, besides every description of European article. It was some satisfaction to feel, as we moved through the busy throng, in plaid shooting-coats

181

with mother-of-pearl buttons, that we too were adding another variety to the motley costumes of the fair at Simpheropol.

But the charm of Simpheropol does not consist in the variety of races which inhabit it. Though it seems to lie in a plain, as approached from Kertch, a great part of the town is situated upon the precipitous edge of the steppe, from whence a magnificent view is obtained immediately below; and at the foot of abrupt rocks, two hundred feet high, runs the tiny Salghir, dignified with the name of a river, and, if not entitled to it from its size, worthy the appellation by reason of the lovely valley which it has formed in its northern course. Orchards and gardens, containing every sort of fruit-trees, and abounding in rows of tall poplars, line its banks, until the hills, becoming higher and more thickly wooded, form a ridge, which is connected with the Tchatir Dagh, a noble background, and one which does full justice to this lovely picture. Nor did a closer acquaintance with the details of this view detract from our original impressions on beholding it.

We determined to take advantage of the glorious weather with which we were favoured, to make the ascent of the Tchatir Dagh, the Mountain of the Tent of the Tartars, Trapezus of the Greeks, and Palata Gora of the Russians. As mountains are rarities in Russia, a great many preparations were considered necessary before starting upon the expedition. Sending our luggage in a cart to a post-station on the road to Alushta, we hired a Tartar and three horses, and, accompanied by an excellent German, who acted as interpreter, we bid adieu to Simpheropol on a lovely afternoon, and rode up the valley shaded by the avenues we had admired from above, frequently crossing the stream, and every here and there coming upon some charming little nook, of which a picturesque cottage had taken advantage, and which, perhaps, we appreciated the more highly after our long journeys across the steppe, so totally devoid of cottages, gardens, streams, or trees. We passed through orchards, and between fields of tobacco, Indian corn, flax, and millet; and after following the main road to Alushta for nine miles, turned off at Sultan

Mahmout, and proceeding some miles across country, reached, a little after dark, the Tartar village of Bouyouk Yankoi, in which we had determined to spend the night before commencing the ascent of the mountain.

Dismounting before a very low verandah, we entered a sort of hut by a hole about three feet square, and passing through a small room and another hole, found ourselves in a somewhat more spacious apartment, carpeted with thick white felt. Raised about six inches above the floor, a sort of divan extended all round the room, above which were suspended quantities of richly embroidered cloths used as handkerchiefs or towels. I bought a very handsome one of these, with an Arabic inscription upon it, for a ruble. Upon a shelf at the further end were piled gold and silver brocades, while, hardly corresponding with such handsome garniture, earthenware vessels were ranged upon the massive beams which supported the roof, and which were placed so low that the members of the household could reach them easily, and unwary strangers knock their heads against them continually. A great many bunches of wild thyme were hanging from the rafters, but they by no means answered the purpose of overcoming the strong smell of garlic which floated round everybody and pervaded everything. We were delighted with the comfortable air of the whole establishment-nothing could have looked cleaner than the white walls, or softer than the white felt; but we had not as yet experienced one property peculiar to the latter. A very small window, with wooden bars, and touching the ground, was opposite a large old-fashioned sort of fireplace, in which an ox might have been roasted whole, and which completed the unique appearance of our quarters. Instead of the somovar, small filigree cups of thick coffee were furnished by our host, whose wife was too old and ugly to make it necessary for her to cover her face. She piled mattresses and pillows for us upon the divan in abundance, and we were soon stretched luxuriously round the room on the soft cushions, heedless of their garlicky perfume. Would that *it* had been our only annoyance—the fleas had evidently been waiting until we were well in their power, and now transferred themselves in thousands from the felt to our bodies. How little did I imagine, when I watched the old Tartar dame preparing the tempting beds, that I should toss restlessly upon them the livelong night.

Fortunately we had purposed an early start on the morrow, and were delighted to quit our downy couches at three o'clock. After another cup of coffee and a gratuity to our host, who declined to take anything until his better half interposed, we again mounted our ponies, and by the light of a very small moon, picked our way up the stony path under the guidance of two Tartars from the village. For about two hours we wound through beech-woods—in which there is said to be very good red-deer shooting—and along narrow ridges overlooking extensive valleys. Upon arriving at the last steep pitch, we left our horses with one of the guides, and clambered up amongst strewn rocks and stunted juniper-bushes for another hour, when we reached the giddy edge of the limestone cliff which forms the highest peak, a few moments after sunrise, having attained an elevation of 5135 feet above the sea.

We were well repaid for the fatigue of the ascent by the magnificent view we obtained from this point. Immediately at our feet, and so directly beneath us that a stone might be dropped perpendicularly upon the trees 2000 feet below, lay charmingly diversified woods and meadows—curling wreaths of blue smoke ascended from clumps of trees scattered over the park-like scenery, while large herds of cattle seemed from their diminutiveness to have been peppered out upon the rich pasture-land. Snug-looking Tartar villages were dotted over the well-cultivated valleys, and mountain streams meandered through them to the sea, which was scarcely discernible beneath a dense bank of clouds that altogether concealed from our view the southern horizon. Facing us, towards the west, the rival mountain of Babugan Yaila reared its stupendous crags; while far as eye could reach, in a northerly direction, stretched the undulating steppe, narrowing as it reached the Isthmus of Perecop. We could trace the wooded valley of the Salghir, discern the white houses of Simpheropol on its left bank; and nearer still we saw the beech-woods through which we had ridden in the morning, and the vast table-land of limestone rock over which we had been stumbling. We found a large stone, on which a Russian had inscribed his name; and thinking the spot undeserving of such desecration, we hurled it over a less abrupt part of the precipice, and strained our necks to see it reach the bottom; but we could only hear it crash and echo as it bounded from crag to crag. A magnificent eagle, surprised at so unusual a sound, soared majestically away from an eyrie a few feet down the cliff, and left us in undisputed possession of the summit of the Tchatir Dagh.

We soon accomplished the steep descent of the first thousand feet, and, mounting our ponies, attempted to pick our way over the rocks, to some caves, reported to be worth seeing. Our path—or rather where our path would have been, had one existed—lay over a large extent of stratified limestone, of a grey colour. The rugged surface, strewn with huge fragments of the stone, was frequently indented by hemi-spherical hollows, in which grew clumps of trees, and which, had they not occurred so frequently, might have been mistaken for the craters of extinct volcanoes.

Whatever may have been their origin, they were the cause of incessant annoyance to us as we wound round them—the rocks becoming so sharp and jagged that we were obliged to lead our horses a great part of the way. At last we descended into one, and the guides pointed to a small opening under a rock, into which we were expected to crawl, telling us it was the entrance to the Cave of Foul Kouba. Armed with a tallow candle, I forthwith crept into the hole, scrambling on hands and knees amidst a quantity of human skulls and bones, which rattled dismally as, one after another, we crawled amongst them. For twenty or thirty yards we thus proceeded, occasionally obliged to lie down perfectly flat upon the wet mud and bones, and burrow our way along—a mode of entry which reminded me of an unpleasant experience I once endured in descending into an Egyptian mummy-pit. At last we were enabled to stand upright and look around. A spacious chamber, about forty feet high, seemed supported by some huge stalactites. The largest of these was at least fifty feet in circumference; and if the cave had been lighted up with such torches as those used at Adelsburg, instead of with three tallow dips, I have no doubt their varied colours would have produced a striking effect. I followed a clear stream through a small opening into what appeared another chamber, but could get no one to accompany me on an exploring expedition, as my companion felt too unwell to enter the cave at all. Montandon, however, says that Monsieur Oudinet, a Frenchman, penetrated half a day's journey into this cave without reaching the end. The innumerable skulls and bones lying strewn about in all directions told a melancholy history;— a party of Genoese had been smoked to death here, during their wars with the Tartars in the thirteenth century.

We were glad to get into the fresh air again, and, very hot and dirty, started for Kisil Kouba, another cave not far distant. The entrance to this was magnificent; and after descending gradually for about a hundred yards, the cave increased to a breadth of thirty or forty yards, while its height could not have been less than sixty feet. Here, however, the stalactites were comparatively poor, though occasionally well-coloured. It has never been fully explored; a stream, which we did not reach, becoming too deep to allow of its extent being ascertained.

We alternately rode or led our steeds over miles more of the same elevated limestone plateau, until our guide proposed taking us a short cut to the main road, which we could discern winding through the wood about fifteen hundred feet below us. We were amazed soon after at his sudden disappearance with two of the horses, and not at all surprised at seeing one of them on the broad of his back, when we looked over the edge of a precipice and saw the rocks down which he was expected to scramble. The Tartar seemed somewhat astonished at his rapid descent, and turned round with the intention of getting back; but seeing that this was impossible, we shouted to him to try and go on: this, however, he declined, and ultimately decided upon standing stock-still.

It certainly seemed madness to attempt the descent before us; but as the horses were not very valuable, we got down to the Tartar, and each took possession of his own, leaving him to manage his pony as he liked. It was impossible for the horses to keep their footing amid the loose slabs of rock and rough stones which were strewn along the face of the mountain, and which, slipping from under them, gave them some severe falls. The chief difficulty was to avoid being tumbled upon as we pulled them after us, having found it out of the question to induce them to lead the way: thus, when both horse and man slid together for many yards without being able to gain a footing, the velocity of the former always became the greatest; and I sometimes found it necessary to let go the reins, scramble as quickly as possible to one side, and leave my horse to slide past, hoping that something would stop him soon. Becoming gradually more deeply imbedded in a mass of stony debris, he was at last altogether stopped, and so, poor beast, would remain, with every fibre quivering from fear, until I could get slowly down, and, by dint of pulling and beating, start him again on his downward course.

At last, and with no greater damage done than a few cuts and bruises, we reached the filbert woods at the bottom, and I was able again to bestride my uncomfortable Tartar saddle, which in shape was exactly like a feather pillow tied tightly round the middle, the hollow thus formed being a seat in no degree calculated to rest my aching limbs; so we limped along, weary and jaded, to the hamlet of Taouchan Bazaar, and determined to pass the night in a romantic cottage, buried in the woods and overhung by the beetling crags of the Tchatir Dagh. Here the worthy Tartar occupants gave us some excellent "yourgourt," or sour milk, which, with the addition of sufficient sugar, is very refreshing food. Half-a-dozen boiled eggs and some Tartar cake completed our simple bill of fare.

We found our German friend Richter an invaluable ally, and persuaded him to accompany us on our proposed excursions through the country. When he was not smoking, he was interpreting or making himself generally useful; and as his personal baggage only consisted of a large cloak, he was unobjectionable on that score; so he started on a trip, which was to last for an indefinite period, with perfect complacency, on my lending him a shirt to begin with.

We had taken a padaroshna at Simpheropol for Yalta, and determined to travel *in post telègas*. Accordingly, at daylight on

Post Telega

the following morning we were *en route* in one of these primitive conveyances. Precisely similar to the common cart used by the peasants, it was destitute alike of springs, seats, hood, or any sort of protection from the weather; but it was very strongly built, and admirably adapted for fine scenery, when the roughness of the road does not distract the attention. We began to toil up a steep zigzag ascent immediately upon leaving the post-house. The road winds through beech and oak woods, which thickly clothe the mountain sides, and clamber up the crevices in the rocks. Now and then we came upon an opening, from which we obtained an extensive view to the northward, and looked down upon the romantic valley of the Hangar, which we were fast leaving below us—thanks to the vigorous exertions of three sturdy horses, and the energetic shouts of our driver. The summit of the pass is two thousand eight hundred feet above the level of the Black Sea, which here bursts suddenly upon our view. The waves seem to break upon the ruined walls of Alushta, while the vale in which that village is situated stretched away from our feet in luxuriant loveliness.

An obelisk which has been erected near this spot indicates the resting-place of the Emperor Alexander at the period of his last visit to the Crimea in 1824. We commenced our descent with the utmost rapidity, our trot soon increasing into a gallop; and the cart hopping rather than rolling round the sharp, steep corners, it became quite a work of difficulty to keep our seats. The fantastic Dimirdji, with its huge crags grotesquely piled one above another, towered above us on the left—a worthy *vis-à-vis* to the Tchatir Dagh.

In an hour we had reached the bottom, and, like the mountain torrents which had dashed by our side, we glided more tranquilly on, after our stormy passage, between cypress hedges and through long avenues of poplars, casting immeasurable shadows in the morning sun, and past orchards and vineyards laden with luscious fruit. We had hardly regained our breath, when we pulled up at the door of the post-house in Alushta.

CHAPTER XVII

Tartar village of Alushta—More posting experiences—A Russo-American idiosyncrasy—A caravanserai—Coast scenery—The vineyards of Magaratsch—Yalta—An adventure in prospect—Alupka—Vine cultivation

The only remaining vestiges of the ancient dignity of Alushta are three picturesque towers, and a stone wall twelve feet high and seven feet thick, which formed part of a citadel erected by the Emperor Justinian about 465 A.D., to protect the country against the Goths and Huns. These towers seem to rise out of the flat roofs of the Tartar cottages, and produce a most singular effect.

The Alustan Phrurion of the middle ages, this town at one time contained a considerable population, and was the seat of a bishop. Under the Turkish régime it sank into the condition of a mere Tartar village. This it remains to the present day; and the massive walls of the old fortress enclose a collection of flimsy cottages, the quaint but barbarous construction of which strikingly contrasts with the solid erections of a civilised nation

Tartar Village

many centuries ago. The Tartars, unlike other people, generally prefer the steep side of a hill for the site of their villages, rather than those level situations vulgarly known as "eligible building lots." By excavating a space out of the hill, in proportion to the accommodation required, the architect is saved the trouble of building a back wall, while he simply fills up with mud the angles at the sides. The roof which thus, as it were, projects out of the hill, is perfectly flat, and covered with mould. It extends beyond the front walls, and, supported by posts, forms a sort of verandah. Thus, when the traveller passes below one of these cottages, the roof is not visible at all, while, if he be above them, they would have the effect of diminutive drying-grounds for grain or coffee, were it not for the smoke that issues from the conical mud-chimneys. These serve not only as apertures for the smoke, but also as means of verbal communication with the interior of the houses. On a dark night an equestrian might easily mistake his way, and, riding straight over one of these roofs, make his appearance at the front door in a manner too abrupt to be altogether consistent with good breeding.

The cultivation of the vine has progressed more rapidly in the valley of Alushta than in almost any other part of the

Interior of a Tartar House

191

Crimea. The soil is rich, and watered by two mountain streams, which divide the valley, and give additional effect to the charms of its luxuriant cultivation. Besides the extensive vineyards, a great deal of tobacco is also grown in the neighbourhood. A number of neat Russian houses are springing up on the various properties, and a gay new church, conspicuously placed, has just been completed. We found several travellers at the post-house waiting helplessly for horses. Two gentlemen, direct from Moscow, with padaroshnas of the most urgent description, who had been eating grapes, smoking, and sleeping for twenty-four hours, told us we were not likely to obtain horses until the following day at the earliest. They had bribed the postmaster more highly than any of the other unfortunates collected under this miserable roof, and were evidently prepared to outbribe us; so, instead of entering into a useless competition, we discussed the admirable system from which we were mutually suffering, and which, I readily conceded, was unequalled in its operation by that of any other country.

It is singular that the most striking characteristic of two people so widely dissimilar as the Americans and Russians, should be identical; that while diametrically opposed to one another in their habits and feelings, the same sentiment should predominate in the breasts of both, and find vent in a manner that soon becomes tiresome to the traveller; and yet, perhaps, although the expressions of an indiscriminating patriotism with which he is overwhelmed in both countries may scarcely differ, it would not be fair to say that the sentiment which gives rise to them is in the two cases exactly the same. It is the *personal* vanity of the American which is touched; he feels that he has individually shared in the glorious work for which he claims your admiration, and, justly proud of the position of his country and the achievements of his countrymen, he is unable to repress his satisfaction, though at the expense of good breeding: it is the genuine outburst of a mind which lacks not honesty, but refinement. The highly-polished Russian, on the

192

other hand, is disturbed by a restless consciousness of his own innate barbarism, and hopes that, by continually impressing upon you the high state of civilisation of his country and its inhabitants, you may gradually come to doubt the evidence of your own senses, and believe him instead. He is, moreover, insensibly influenced by the mode of government under which he lives; and, in a blind submission to it, deliberately deceives you with regard to the internal condition of the empire; for he feels bound to become another of the "solemn shams" which it maintains.

While experimentally testing the truth of this reflection, the postmaster came in with the news that a German colonist, on his way to Yalta with a cart-load of potatoes, had offered to exchange his load for the two Englishman. We accordingly proceeded to treat with this individual, and found him phlegmatically smoking in a sort of caravanserai, in company with a number of Armenians and Tartars. It was a large, rambling, Eastern-looking place. At one end, in a partially covered pen-fold, chibouks and coffee were supplied for the multitude. Horses, oxen, and buffaloes were tethered about the yard to the quaintly-constructed carts to which they belonged; and farmers and merchants of many different nations were congregated here, probably on their way home from the fair.

We at last persuaded the German to take us to Yalta, thirty miles distant, for a pound, and were preparing for a start, when the postmaster requested to be paid for the horses we should otherwise have had. This was looked upon as a most reasonable charge by one of our Russian friends, but indignantly demurred to by us. Finding that we were inexorable, this true specimen of a government official threw himself upon our generosity, and hoped, if we would not accede to his lawful demand, we would at any rate bestow upon him a gratuity for having found the German; so that, in fact, we were expected to pay him *one sum* as the price of horses he had refused to give us, and to make him a present of *another sum* because we were able to do without them. If he got a percentage out of the German into the bargain, he very nearly made a good thing of it. It was a trait so eminently national that I could not help wishing our Russian friends a safe deliverance from the tender mercies of their countryman, as we drove triumphantly out of the yard in our potato-cart, and left them seated in their carriage, with about as much chance of getting away as a man who goes to the House of Commons with a member's order, on the night of an interesting debate, has of ever getting into the stranger's gallery.

Our driver was a prosperous farmer of Rosenthal—a large colony, containing, from his account, about five hundred inhabitants, and cultivating a great extent of country. He was a remarkably uninteresting specimen of the race, and could give us very little information about the village in which he had been born and bred. The road begins to ascend at once from Alushta, and soon attains a considerable altitude. From the summit of the pass, before descending into Bouyouk Lambat, a magnificent view is obtained; and a few chateaux, situated on romantic spots, or in the midst of extensive vineyards, add a softness to the scenery, here very grand. The road is often overshadowed by spreading walnut-trees, and passes through Tartar villages placed on the steep sides of the hill. Near these there is generally a stone fountain, from which gushes cold sparkling water. In some of the carts which we passed, we found the camel substituted by the buffalo—a less picturesque, but more business-like animal. The road the whole way to Yalta maintains an elevation of about a thousand feet above the sea. The range to the right, two or three miles distant, is from three to four thousand feet high, and very precipitous. The Ayough Dagh, or Mountain of the Bear, is the most conspicuous peak. Rocky promontories stretch far into the sea, and form sheltered bays in which numerous little seaports were formerly situated, deriving their importance from the extensive commerce carried on upon this coast. Parthenik and Oursouf were the most considerable of these, but they now only give names to the chateaux of the noblemen in whose properties they are included.

The vineyards of Magaratsch cover a great extent of the hillside near Prince Woronzoff's chateau of Marsanda. That enlightened nobleman, wishing to offer every encouragement to the cultivation of the vine, ordered a portion of government land to be divided into a number of allotments, and permitted any person desirous of opening an estate to be put in possession of any of these which he might choose. This he was allowed to occupy for four years, upon giving the requisite security, on the condition that he should bring a certain proportion of his land under grape cultivation. If, at the expiration of this period, he had satisfied all the terms of the conditions upon which he held the lands, they became the property of himself and his heirs for ever.

Shortly after we pass the charmingly situated chateau of Marsanda, the bay of Yalta glistens at our feet, with the white town on its margin, and the thick woods clinging to the steep mountainside, until they can hold on no longer. Villas become more frequent. We meet a civilised carriage, and two or three princes and counts taking their afternoon ride. We descend the hill at a gallop, and attempt to dash into the town, but only succeed in rumbling into it, and find ourselves none the less welcome at the Hotel d'Odessa because we arrive in a potato-cart.

It is one of the unfortunate peculiarities of the Anglo-Saxon temperament, that the only species of excitement which really seems to suit it, must be attended with some degree of danger or discomfort; so that it ever affords an Englishman unspeakable gratification to be engaged in some adventure which is likely to result in what he terms "a scrape." Nowhere, indeed, is this propensity more strikingly exhibited than in the conduct of English travellers upon the continent of Europe, since nowhere can this much-desired end be more easily attained.

Perhaps it was the absence of any such excitement, for some

weeks past, in a country offering abundant facility for its enjoyment, that induced us to visit Sevastopol in the way we did. We had determined to explore the most celebrated naval station in Russia, from the moment that we heard that foreigners were not permitted to enter those mysterious precincts except upon rare occasions; and when we further learned that this permission was granted by the governor alone, and that it would be necessary to renew it every twenty-four hours during our stay, it naturally occurred to us, as Englishmen, that, to act consistently, we ought to pay a visit to so interesting a spot without any such permission at all.

In accordance with this view, we hired at Yalta a common peasant's cart, and a pair of good stout horses—an equipage altogether very similar to the one in which we had performed the journey from Alushta. We hoped that, in so unpretending a vehicle, we should be able to jog into the naval *sanctum* unnoticed. Our German friend engaged to procure *quiet* accommodation for us in the city of dockyards.

Upon leaving Yalta we ascended the hills again, and, passing through the well-laid-out grounds of Livadia, the seat of Count de Witt, had soon attained an elevation of six hundred feet above the sea, and found ourselves looking down upon Orianda, the delightful residence of the Empress, frowned upon by gigantic rocks, but redeemed from too savage a character by the taste and skill which have brought every available rood of land into a high state of cultivation. The whole way to Alupka, hedges of cypress and olive, pomegranate and laurel, line the road; handsome chateaux terminate the vistas formed by long grassy avenues; and the carefully-kept fences which enclose the pleasure-grounds are evident marks of the frequent residence here of the lords of the soil. Villages are abundantly sprinkled over the rich valleys we traverse, where the hay is quaintly stacked in the pollard trees; while tempting fruit is piled upon the roadside, and groups of picturesque Tartar maidens are clustered round some sparkling fountain, overshadowed by the spreading arms of a patriarchal walnut. But the enchantment even of such fairy land as this would be incomplete, were it not for the magnificent views which continually burst upon the delighted gaze, when the wildness and grandeur of the distance seem to add an additional charm to the surrounding loveliness.

We descended abruptly to the Castle of Alupka, the residence of Prince Woronzoff, passing through extensive vineyards which belong to this property. The numerous domes and pinnacles which peep out over the trees as we approach, indicate a palace, Oriental in its style and magnitude; while the glittering cupola and tapering minarets of the elegant mosque, which almost adjoins it, lead us to imagine that the noble owner of all this magnificence is Hadjy-Selim-Ghiri Khan at least. A few moments more, however, and we find, to our perplexity, that we are driving under the lofty walls and frowning battlements of a feudal chieftain's fortress; and as we pass through the solid gateways into the spacious courtyard, and look up at the massive square tower and belfry to correspond, we find it difficult to decide whether the building before us bears most resemblance to the stronghold of the Black Douglas, or the palace of the Great Mogul.

Notwithstanding the mixture of such incongruous styles of architecture, the general effect of this splendid chateau is charming. The Prince has spent an almost fabulous amount of silver rubles upon the house and grounds, and has succeeded in rearing an edifice worthy of the scenery amid which it stands. The taste displayed is unexceptionable. Placed almost upon the borders of Europe and Asia, the Eastern character so strongly developed throughout the structure is most appropriate; while the dash of feudalism, as suggestive of the former uncivilised condition of the West, is a graceful allusion to the present state of that country in which it is situated. The façade overlooking the sea is magnificent; terraces and gardens, ornamented with rare plants, extend down the steep slope to the water's edge, while paths are seen winding among broken rocks and between accumulated volcanic masses; and, impending over all, the stupendous crag of the Ai Petri seems to threaten annihilation to the noble edifice which nestles at its base.

It is not long since the Crimea became a fashionable resort among Russian nobility. Prince Woronzoff was the first to set the example, which has been followed by the Emperor, and the wealthier members of the aristocracy. The estates of the latter, lying for the most part between Alushta and Alupka, along the narrow strip of coast which we had followed, are charmingly diversified by the valleys which traverse them; while they are sheltered from the north winds by the high range of calcareous cliffs, to the existence of which the extraordinary fertility of this part of the peninsula is mainly attributable. It is only recently that any advantage has been taken of this prolific soil. Till within a short period, the few vineyards which existed were situated on the northern slopes of the Tauric chain, and in Soudagh and the neighbouring valleys. Owing to the energetic exertions of Prince Woronzoff, and in spite of the difficulties which always accompany experimental enterprises of this nature, wonderful advances have been made in the cultivation of the vine. Within the last ten years, however, the statistical reports show very little increase in the amount of wine exported from the Crimea. This arises probably from the difficulty of finding a market for wines of an inferior quality, which the Crim wines undoubtedly are, notwithstanding the high-sounding names with which they are dignified. The absence of any roads across the steppe renders it impossible to export wine into the interior to any great extent, although I have occasionally tasted Crim wine in St. Petersburg; while so long as the wines of the Grecian Archipelago are allowed almost free entry into the ports on the Black Sea, competition in that quarter must be quite hopeless. The present value of wine sold annually amounts to 500,000 rubles, or about twice the revenue derived from the vineyards in the country of the Don Cossacks.

CHAPTER XVIII

Stupendous cliffs—The Pass of Baidar—The Vale of Baidar—A Russian's notions of scenery—Night quarters—Tartars of the coast—Balaclava—Enter Sevastopol—Arrival at Sevastopol

We made rapid progress along the excellent new road which now connects Yalta and Sevastopol, to the great convenience of the proprietors through whose estates it passes, and whose handsome equipages we occasionally saw hurrying towards Sevastopol, where the Emperor was hourly expected. Prince Woronzoff had just arrived at Alupka from Tiflis, the present seat of his government, on his way to attend his Imperial Majesty in an inspection of the garrison and fleet. The road gradually attained an elevation of nearly two thousand feet above the sea, and became every moment more interesting. After leaving the picturesque Tartar villages of Simeis and Kikineis, it winds along the base of cliffs about fifteen hundred feet in height, and as precipitous as those down which we had looked from the summit of the Tchatir Dagh. Each turn discovered crags more stupendous than the last, until we reached the rocks of Yamen, where the road has the appearance of a narrow shelf scarped out of sheer limestone. Here we had left behind all traces of that teeming vegetation amid which we had hitherto luxuriated. Wide-spreading pines could no longer attempt to clothe the mountainsides—above were towering peaks; below, huge fragments of rock, which had fallen from the lofty range, lay strewn over the face of the rugged banks of detritus which descend abruptly to the water's edge, and project in rocky promontories far amid the breakers. Where there are occasional sheltered nooks, enterprising Tartars perch their cottages, and live in fancied security, until some tottering crag comes crashing down, and buries whole villages in its impetuous career.

Evidences of such fearful catastrophes are to be seen where the villages of Limaine and Koutchouk-Koi once stood. In the latter instance, where two mills and eight houses were destroyed, sings of an approaching convulsion of nature were perceived by the inhabitants, in the gradual sinking of the ground, which warned them to abandon their dwellings before the disaster occurred. It is little to be wondered at that the ancients found the northern shore of the Euxine most inhospitable, and that Strabo should describe it as τξαχεια παι οξειυη, παι παταιγιζουσα τοις βοξεοις.

We had no reason to complain in the latter respect. The weather was lovely; the jagged edge of the cliffs was traced sharp and clear against the blue sky; numerous white sails dotted the calm surface of the sea; and as we whirled along the wild mountainside in our independent conveyance, no care clouded our mental horizon, or breaker ruffled the placid enjoyment with which we revelled in coast scenery, unsurpassed alike by the grandeur of the Cornicè, or the softer beauties of Amalfi.

About eighteen miles from Alupka we passed through a gallery in the rock forty or fifty yards in length; then turning sharply off from the sea-coast, entered the woods, and commenced the zigzag ascent of the Pass of Baidar, at the summit of which a solid granite gateway has been erected, from whence an extensive view of the whole line of shore is obtained. The Pass of Baidar is quite a recent work. The old road, which could only be traversed on horseback, followed the coast for some distance farther, and crossed the range by the Merdven, or Devil's Staircase, the steps of which were hewn out of the living stone, or supported by trunks of trees. This pathway is compressed between huge masses of impending rock for a distance of eight hundred yards, and consists of forty zigzags almost parallel, and each only a few steps long. It is the most romantic but laborious way of reaching the Vale of Baidar, which now spread itself before us as we galloped through the forest amid showers of falling leaves. It was quite a relief, after so much that was sublime, to descend again to the picturesque, and see our night quarters

The Pass of Baidar

snugly situated in a peaceful vale, round which the wooded hills swelled back in gentle slopes, forming a strong contrast to all we had just left.

The greatest difference of opinion exists among travellers as to the merits of the valley of Baidar. Though fully prepared to do justice to its beauty, I was rather disappointed in this far-famed Crimean Tempé. It is natural that the tourist who enters the Crimea at Sevastopol, and whose first experience of Tauric scenery is Baidar, should be enchanted with a luxuriance which a journey across the steppes of Southern Russia has prepared him to appreciate more highly than it deserves. And when, for the first time, he wanders among a Tartar population, sleeps on Tartar divans, drinks Tartar coffee, sees real shepherds and shepherdesses tending their flocks, and then recalls the miseries of some Bessarabian post-hut, it is not to be wondered at if, in a state of unnatural rapture, he should designate this a Tauric Arcadia; an opinion which would be strongly supported by any Russian to whom he might express it. Apart from those patriotic considerations to which I have already alluded, this is easily accounted for. Indeed, I may say here that I once found, to my amazement, a Russian depreciate his own country. Wishing to gratify his national vanity, I expressed, in no stronger terms than I really felt, my high appreciation of the grandeur and magnificence of the rocks of Yamen. He could see nothing to admire in them!—they were too bare and rugged; but he was amazed to find I had not visited any chateau on the coast except Alupka. These very ordinary country-houses possessed charms for him which no scenery could command. Did I know that some of them were actually supplied with English stoves? "No!" I had barbarously journeyed on, admiring barren rocks. Desirous of propitiating so artificial a taste, I remarked that great judgment had been displayed in the position and arrangement of the new watering-place of Yalta. "Ah!" said my friend, "but what did you think of the Hotel d'Odessa?" I did not tell him what I thought of the Hotel d'Odessa, and have reserved an account of my experiences in that "model lodging-house" of Russians for another time.

So, when our tourist asks his Russian friend his opinion of Baidar, he answers that it is the most beautiful valley in the Crimea—it grows so many thousand tchetverts of wheat; and, doubtless, looking upon it in that light, it is quite possible the valley of Baidar, in extent and fertility, may be unrivalled in Russia. Upwards of thirty miles in circumference, watered by two limpid streams, prettily wooded, thickly populated, and richly productive, it is yet entirely deficient in that wildness so purely characteristic of the Crimea. Give me rather the narrow gorge, in which noble trees and well-cultivated gardens, pent up between overhanging rocks, singularly contrast with the harsh grey crags around. Surely the peculiar charm of the Taurida is to be found in these gems with which its mountains are studded. Let our Russian pay a visit to any second-rate Indian valley, and he will find that it is many more miles in circumference, contains more rivers, grows more tchetverts of wheat, and has double the population of his much-vaunted valley of Baidar.

We put up with a Tartar, and luxuriated in a soft-carpeted, cushioned room, which resembled nothing so much as an enormous bed, with a fireplace at the foot of it. We were furnished with a small round table, about six inches high—a mark of civilisation which quite coincided with the moderate demand of ten shillings made by our host on the following morning. He seemed, however, quite satisfied at receiving three; and perhaps his exorbitant charge proceeded more from ignorance, and a desire to err on the right side, than the innate extortion which we were at first inclined to think it evinced. The Tartars of the southern coast present a totally different appearance from those amongst whom we had journeyed upon the steppes to the north of the mountains. Here the Mongolian cast of countenance has vanished altogether. There are no high cheek-bones, wide eyes, and flat noses to bear witness of an emigration from the deserts of Tartary and Thibet; but, on the contrary, the regular features and fair complexion that tell of intercourse with the West; while such words as Tas (cup), Camera (chamber), Mangia (eat), betray with what European people these Asiatics have become so incorporated as to have lost many of the distinguishing marks of their own race.

The Tartars of the northern plains are a pastoral people, leading an active life, whose occupations are somewhat in accordance with the wandering habits of their ancestors. They are simple and hospitable, though of rough exterior. The Tartars of the coast, on the other hand, are extremely indolent, and have no inducement to exertion, finding it unnecessary to do more than gather of the abundance which their fertile soil and genial clime produces. With the Genoese blood that flows in their veins, they are imbued with the cunning of the Italian, while at the same time they are possessed of a certain polish and courtesy of manner which may be looked for in vain in the Russian boor or the savage Nogay. Thus, at Bouyouk Yankoi, where all our wants had been supplied with rough good-nature, our host at first positively refused to accept of any gratuity. At Baidar, on the other hand, we were overwhelmed with attention and civility, and charged for it in a manner that would have done credit to an English hotel-keeper.

Our road, after passing through the woods, and leaving the valley of Baidar, lay through rocky country covered with scrub, not unlike many glens in the Highlands. The scenery, though it afforded an agreeable variety, did not present any object of striking interest, until we suddenly came upon a large brig riding at anchor in what seemed, at first sight, a picturesque lake. I could hardly believe that this tranquil inlet, surrounded on all sides by steep hills, was part of the same sea that lay spread before us yesterday, which we had quitted so abruptly, and no portion of which was now visible except the pool before us.

The port of Balaclava—a name which, if it is not, ought to be, derived from "bella chiave"—is completely land-locked, and was at one time so great a resort for pirates that it was found necessary to stretch a chain across the mouth of the harbour. Any vessel, however large, having once made its way through the dangerous entrance, may ride out the severest storm in safety upon its unruffled waters, and is effectually concealed from the seaward by the projecting promontory, upon which stands the old Genoese fort, placed so as to command both the port and the entrance.

Where the ancient Greek colony of Klimatum is supposed once to have stood, the modern Greek colony of Balaclava now stands, a charming little place upon the water's edge, protected by the fortress above. It is composed of neat white houses, shaded by poplars, containing a population of Arnaouts—a name given to these Greeks by the Tartars, when, as soldiers of the Russian empire, they took part in the war which resulted in the conquest of the Crimea. In consideration of services then performed, the Empress Catharine the Second allowed them to settle in the old Genoese port of Cimbalo or Balaclava, where they reside to this day, maintaining their old religion, habits, and language, and employed on the revenue service—an occupation for which their former piratical habits have rendered them peculiarly adapted. They enjoy many privileges, and are not liable to be called out for active service, except during four months in the year. Many of them are merchants and shopkeepers in other towns of the Crimea. Balaclava itself is totally devoid of any mercantile importance; and this is probably owing in a great measure to the destructive ravages of the worm with which its waters are infested, and by which the hulls of ships remaining there for any length of time become perforated.

As we approached Sevastopol, the great curiosity which I had long felt to visit a place of which Russians speak with a kind of mysterious awe, was not unmixed with anxiety; and when, at a sudden turn of the road, we obtained an extensive view of the western shores of the Crimea, it was startling to find that the most prominent feature in the landscape was Sevastopol itself, with its lofty white houses, and frowning batteries, and green-domed churches. Far inland, and long after the houses had ceased, the tapering masts of the ships were visible above the low hills; their sails, which had been hung out to dry, were hanging idly upon them; and as we approached still nearer, we could discern the large hulls of the line-of-battle ships floating, as it were, in the very streets of the town. My expectations of Sevastopol were evidently not doomed to disappointment, whatever might be my hopes of entry. There did not seem much to fear on that score. Our clothes had been reduced, by a succession of long steppe journeys, to a worse condition than those of Richter and the driver. A thick coating of grey dust rendered all minor differences of costume imperceptible; and as we leant back, half hidden amongst bundles of hay, with our hats slouched over our eyes, as if to keep the sun off, we flattered ourselves that we looked extremely like phlegmatic German peasants from some neighbouring colony. Our accomplice smoked imperturbably and incessantly; his friend occupied himself with his horses; and so, utterly regardless of the vigilant sentinels, we passed carelessly into the town, and half an hour afterwards were eating beefsteaks at the house of a worthy German, who was delighted to receive us, having borne with the utmost firmness the scrutinising eyes of whole regiments of conscientious soldiers.

CHAPTER XIX

*The harbour of Sevastopol—The Russian fleet—Navy
contracts—The Emperor's visit—The naval review—
Fortifications of Sevastopol—Peculation in the commissariat—
The Russian army—Summary punishment—Corruption in
high places—Inkerman—The town of caverns—The vale of
Balbeck—Camel herds—Arrival at Bagtchè Serai—
Supperless to bed*

The reserved manner which, as unlawful visitors, it became us
to assume at Sevastopol, was only in keeping with the air of
mystery and distrust which pervades everything there. The
suspicious eye of each officer I passed chilled the blood in my
veins, long accustomed to a free circulation on the boundless
steppes or wild mountainside. I had not taken ten paces down
the main street, when my guilty conscience was startled, and
the last particle of romance frightened out of me, by a sentry at
my side suddenly presenting arms to the governor, who was
accidentally passing. Here no harmless ruined old tower,
perched upon the dizzy cliff, carried me back in imagination to
the days of Italian greatness. No veiled women and sedate
camels transported my roving fancy to the voluptuous East.
The only variation in the view was from the mouth of a thirty-
six-pound gun into that of a sixty-four. I was ever oppressed
with the painful consciousness of looking like an Englishman,
and suspected the groups of soldiers standing at the corners of
the streets of plotting our apprehension. We were walking in a
magazine which might explode at any moment, both literally
and figuratively.

The population of Sevastopol, including military and
marine, amounts forty thousand. The town is in fact an
immense garrison, and looks imposing because so many of the
buildings are barracks or government offices. Still I was much
struck with the substantial appearance of many of the private
houses; and, indeed, the main street was handsomer than any

I had seen since leaving Moscow, while it owed its extreme cleanliness to large gangs of military prisoners, who were employed in perpetually sweeping. New houses were springing up in every direction, government works were still going forward vigorously, and Sevastopol bids fair to rank high among Russian cities. The magnificent arm of the sea upon which it is situate, is an object worthy the millions which have been lavished in rendering it a fitting receptacle for the Russian navy.

As I stood upon the handsome stairs that lead down to the water's edge, I counted thirteen sail of the line anchored in the principal harbour. The newest of these, a noble three-decker, was lying within pistol-shot of the quay. The average breadth of this inlet is one thousand yards; two creeks branch off from it, intersecting the town in a southerly direction, and containing steamers and smaller craft, besides a long row of hulks which have been converted into magazines or prison-ships.

The hard service which has reduced so many of the handsomest ships of the Russian navy to this condition, consists in lying for eight or ten years upon the sleeping bosom of the harbour. After the expiration of that period, their timbers, composed of fir or pinewood never properly seasoned, become perfectly rotten. This result is chiefly owing to inherent decay, and in some degree to the ravages of a worm that abounds in the muddy waters of the Tchernoi Retcka, a stream which, traversing the valley of Inkerman, falls into the upper part of the main harbour. It is said that this pernicious insect—which is equally destructive in salt water as in fresh—costs the Russian government many thousands, and is one of the most serious obstacles to the formation of an efficient navy on the Black Sea.

It is difficult to see, however, why this should be the case, if the ships are copper-bottomed; and a more intimate acquaintance with the real state of matters would lead one to suspect that the attacks of the naval *employés* are more formidable to the coffers of the government than the attacks of this worm, which is used as a convenient scape-goat, when the present rotten state of the Black Sea fleet cannot otherwise be accounted for. In contradiction to this, we may be referred to the infinitely more efficient condition of the Baltic fleet; but that may arise rather from their proximity to headquarters than from the absence of the worm in the northern seas.

The wages of the seamen are so low—about sixteen rubles a year—that it is not unnatural they should desire to increase so miserable a pittance by any means in their power. The consequence is, that from the members of the naval board to the boys that blow the smiths' bellows in the dockyard, everybody shares the spoils obtained by an elaborately devised system of plunder carried on somewhat in this way:— A certain quantity of well-seasoned oak being required, government invites tenders for the supply of the requisite amount. A number of contractors submit their tenders to a board appointed for the purpose of receiving them, who are regulated in their choice of a contractor, not by the amount of his tender, but of his bribe. The fortunate individual selected immediately sub-contracts upon a somewhat similar principle. Arranging to be supplied with the timber for half the amount of his tender, the sub-contractor carries on the game, and perhaps the eighth link in this contracting chain is the man who, for an absurdly low figure, undertakes to produce the seasoned wood.

His agents in the central provinces, accordingly, float a quantity of green pines and firs down the Dnieper and Bog to Nicholaeff, which are duly handed up to the head contractor, each man pocketing the difference between his contract and that of his neighbour. When the wood is produced before the board appointed to inspect it, another bribe seasons it, and the government, after paying the price of well-seasoned oak, is surprised that the 120 gunship, of which it has been built, is unfit for service in five years.

The rich harvest that is reaped by those employed in building and fitting her up is as easily obtained; and to such an extent did the dockyard workmen trade in government stores, &c., that merchant vessels were for a long time prohibited from entering the harbour. I was not surprised, after obtaining this interesting description of Russian ingenuity, to learn that, out of the imposing array before us, there were only two ships in a condition to undertake a voyage round the Cape.

If, therefore, in estimating the strength of the Russian navy, we deduct the ships which, for all practical purposes, are unseaworthy, it will appear that the Black Sea fleet, that standing bugbear of the unfortunate Porte, will dwindle into a force more in proportion to its limited sphere of action, and to the enemy which, in the absence of any other European power, it would encounter. There is no reason to suppose that the navy forms an exception to the rule, that all the great national institutions of Russia are artificial. The Emperor and the army are not to be regarded in that light, though the latter will doubtless be glad of an early opportunity of redeeming its character, which has been somewhat shaken by the unsatisfactory displays of prowess daily exhibited in the Caucasus, and the absurd misadventures of one of the divisions, which ultimately failed in taking part in the last Hungarian campaign, for lack of a properly organised commissariat.

The greatest excitement prevailed during our stay at Sevastopol; crowds of people had been attracted from all parts of the south of Russia to receive the Emperor; the garrison had been whitewashing their barracks, and drilling themselves with praiseworthy perseverance; while the whole dockyard force had been engaged for months past in getting the ships into the presentable condition they now exhibited.

It seems that a very small complement of men is kept on board each ship while in harbour, the majority of the crews being employed on shore,—a system which is not very well calculated to keep the men in training.

As a cruise under the Emperor's personal inspection was anticipated, a great deal of exercising was necessary, to rub off the dockyard dust, for which his Imperial Majesty possesses a particularly keen eye. It is hardly natural, however, to expect that men whose maritime experience has perhaps never extended beyond the Bosphorus, should be as good sailors as those who have gone round the Horn once for every year of their lives. The seamen reared in such a nursery as our mercantile marine affords, must ever be a very different stamp of men from those reared in the dockyard of Sevastopol. It is maliciously said, that upon the few occasions that the Russian fleet in the Black Sea have encountered a gale of wind, the greater part of the officers and men were always sea-sick.

It is certain that they have sometimes been unable to tell whereabouts they were on their extensive cruising-ground; and once between Sevastopol and Odessa, it is currently and libellously reported that the admiral was so utterly at a loss, that the flag-lieutenant, observing a village on shore, proposed to land and ask the way.

I regretted not being able to stay in Sevastopol to witness the naval review, which the presence of the Emperor himself would have rendered additionally interesting. As, however, our chance of detection would have been considerably increased by the prominent exposure which this exhibition must have entailed, we thought it prudent to beat a timely retreat, and, to Richter's great disappointment, escaped from Sevastopol the day before the great event was to take place, thus obliging him to picture in imagination the manifestations of loyalty with which his Imperial Majesty would be welcomed. The Emperor, as we afterwards heard, did not accompany the fleet on their short cruise outside the port, but expressed himself very much dissatisfied with their performances.

Nothing can be more formidable than the appearance of Sevastopol from the seaward. Upon a future occasion we visited it in a steamer, and found that at one point we were commanded by twelve hundred pieces of artillery: fortunately for a hostile fleet, we afterwards heard that these could not be discharged without bringing down the rotten batteries upon which they are placed, and which are so badly constructed that they look as if they had been done by contract. Four of the forts consist of three tiers of batteries. We were, of course, unable to do more than take a very general survey of these celebrated fortifications, and therefore cannot vouch for the truth of the assertion, that the rooms in which the guns are worked are so narrow and ill-ventilated, that the artillerymen would be inevitably stifled in the attempt to discharge their guns and their duty; but of one fact there was no doubt, that however well fortified may be the approaches to Sevastopol by sea, there is nothing whatever to prevent any number of troops landing a few miles to the south of the town, in one of the six convenient bays with which the coast, as far as Cape Kherson, is indented, and marching down the main street (provided they were strong enough to defeat any military force that might be opposed to them in the open field), sack the town, and burn the fleet.

Notwithstanding the large numerical force which occupies the south of Russia, the greatest difficulty must attend the concentration of the army upon any one point, until railroads intersect the empire, and its water communication is improved. At present, except during four months in the year, the climate alone offers obstacles almost insurmountable to the movements of large bodies of men; the roads are impassable for pedestrians in spring and autumn, and in winter the severity of the weather precludes the possibility of troops crossing the dreary steppes. But in addition to the natural impediments presented by the configuration of the country, the absence of roads, and the rigour of the climate, all military operations are crippled by that same system of wholesale corruption so successfully carried on in the naval department.

Indeed, it would be most unfair if one service monopolised all the profits arising from this source. The accounts I received of the war in the Caucasus, from those who had been present, exceeded anything of the sort I could have conceived possible.

The frightful mortality among the troops employed there amounts to nearly twenty thousand annually. Of these, far the greater part fall victims to disease and starvation, attributable to the rapacity of their commanding officers, who trade in the commissariat so extensively that they speedily acquire large fortunes. As they are subject to no control in their dealings with contractors for supplying their requirements, there is nothing to check the ardour of speculation; and the profits enjoyed by the colonel of a regiment are calculated at £3000 or £4000 a year, besides his pay. It is scarcely possible to apprehend at a glance the full effect of a process so paralysing to the thews and sinews of war; or at once to realise the fact, that the Russian army, numerically so far superior to that of any European power, and supplied from sources which appear inexhaustible, is really in a most inefficient condition, and scarcely worthy of that exaggerated estimate which the British public seem to have formed of its capabilities. It is not upon the plains of Krasna Selo or Vosnesensck, amid the dazzling glitter of a grand field-day in the Emperor's presence, that any correct notion can be formed of the Russian army. The imperial plaything assumes a very different appearance in the remote Cossack guard-house, where I have scarcely been able to recognise the soldier in the tattered and miserably equipped being before me, or on a harassing march, or in the presence of an indomitable enemy.

We have only to remember that the present position of Russia in the Caucasus has remained unaltered for the last twenty-two years, notwithstanding the vast resources which have been brought to bear upon this interminable war, to perceive that the brilliant appearance of the Russian soldier on parade affords no criterion of his efficiency in the field of battle; while no more convincing proof could be desired of the gross corruption and mismanagement which characterises the proceedings of this campaign, than the fact of an over-whelming force of two hundred thousand men being held in check for so long a period by the small but gallant band who are fighting for their snow-clad mountains and their liberty.

A striking view is obtained from the ridge of the hill upon which the governor's house is situated. Upon one side the streets run parallel down to the water's edge; upon the other they descend into the old town, once known by the name of Achtiar. There is nothing to interest in this collection of dirty lanes inhabited by the filthy and disreputable population for which a large military or naval station always serves as a nucleus.

When we returned to Sevastopol not long afterwards, we heard that the Emperor had left the military portion of the community a reminiscence that was calculated to produce a deep impression. He had scarcely terminated his flying visit, and the smoke of the steamer by which he returned to Odessa still hung upon the horizon, when, in a smothered whisper, one soldier confided to another that their ranks had received an addition; and when we returned to Sevastopol it was said that the late governor, in a significant white costume, was employed with the rest of the gang upon the streets he had a fortnight before rolled proudly through, with all the pomp and circumstance befitting his high position. No dilatory trial had reduced him to the condition in which he now appeared before the inhabitants of his late government. The fiat had gone forth, and the general commanding became the convict sweeping. I was very anxious to discover what crime had been deemed worthy of so severe a punishment, but upon no two occasions was the same reason assigned, so it was very clear that nobody knew; and probably no one found it more difficult than the sufferer himself to single out the particular misdemeanour for which he was disgraced. The general opinion seemed to be that the unfortunate man had been lulled into security in his remote province, and, fancying himself unnoticed in this distant corner of the empire, had neglected to practise that customary caution, in the appropriation of his bribes and other perquisites, which is the first qualification of a man in an elevated position in Russia, and without which he can never look for promotion in the army, or make a successful governor. At the same time, the expenses attendant upon this latter position are generally so very heavy that it does not answer to be too timid or fastidious.

I think it is De Custine who says that no half-measures in plundering will do here. If a man has not, during the time of his holding an appointment, sufficiently enriched himself to be able to bribe the judges who try him for his dishonest practices, he will certainly end his days in Siberia; so that, if the fraud has not been extensive, the margin left will barely remunerate him for his trouble and anxiety. The probability is, that General —— had calculated upon the usual court of inquiry, and was consequently quite unprepared for the decided measures of his imperial master.

Reseating ourselves on our bundles of hay, we jolted away from Sevastopol, passing the celebrated docks, which have been constructed at an enormous expense under the able superintendence of Colonel Upton, and soon after descended into the lovely valley of Inkerman, from which they are supplied by a canal twelve miles long. The tunnel at Inkerman, through which it is carried, is about three hundred yards in

Inkerman

length. The hills that enclose this valley supply the freestone of which the town and docks of Sevastopol have been built, the quarries being so situated as to command water-carriage for the entire distance. But the curiosities of Inkerman—the "Town of Caverns"—are to be found rather in the remains which still exist there, to tell of races long since departed, than in those constructions which display the perseverance and ingenuity of modern times.

The precipitous cliffs, between which flows the Tchernoi Retcka, are positively honeycombed with cells and chapels. The origin of these singular caves is uncertain; but they are supposed to have been excavated by monks during the reigns of the Emperors in the middle or later ages. When the Arians who inhabited the Chersonesus were persecuted by the Greek Church, then predominant, the members of that sect took refuge in these singular dwellings, whose lofty and inaccessible position rendered them to a certain degree secure.

The largest chapel, which presents all the characteristics of Byzantine architecture, is about twenty-four feet long by twelve broad. Sarcophagi, usually quite empty, have been found in many of the cells; these latter are often connected with each other, and are approached by stairs cut in the living rock.

Perched upon the same cliff, and of much earlier date than the caverns which undermine them, are the ruined walls of an old fort. Whether they are the remains of the Ctenus of the ancients, built by Diophantes, Mithridates' general, to strengthen the Heraclean Wall, or of the Theodori of the Greeks, or of some Genoese stronghold, is still a very open question.

There can be no doubt that the seat of government of the principality of Theodori stood formerly on this spot, though I think that Mrs Guthrie is mistaken in imagining that it was composed of Circassians. The site of the Circassian colony was Tcherkess Kermen, the town of the Circassians, the remains of which are situated to the eastward of Inkerman, so that they are not, as she thinks, identical; and if, as she supposes, the fortresses of Theodori (Inkerman) and Gothie (Mangoup) maintained their independence until the sixteenth century, the Genoese could never have possessed them, as they had been expelled by the Ottoman power from the Crimea before that period; but there are undoubted evidences of their occupation of Mangoup; and it is more probable that the population of these two fortresses consisted of Greeks, who were to some extent dependent upon the famous Greek colony of Soudagh, or Soldaya; and when the Genoese, in the fourteenth century, possessed themselves of this mercantile emporium, it is not likely that two petty principalities should be able to resist the Italian adventurers, then in the zenith of their power.

The view from the high-road to Bagtchè Serai of the valley of Inkerman, with its perforated cliffs and ruined fortress, in as remarkable as it is beautiful. A romantic old bridge in the foreground spans the sluggish stream, which winds amidst the most luxuriant vegetation.

The plains of Baidar did not seem to me comparable either to this valley or to the vale of Balbeck, into which we shortly after descended, and the richness of which exceeded anything we had yet seen. The road follows the course of the Balbeck for some miles, overshadowed by wide-spreading trees, and passing through gardens, the production of which it would be equally tiresome and hopeless to attempt to enumerate.

We met great numbers of waggons, all filled with loyal subjects, hurrying to Sevastopol; many of them were friends of Richter's. They seemed so amazed at the company he was in, and the direction he was going, that they forgot to return his salutation. We had scarcely passed his friends before we met some of our own. A long string of horse telègas, driven by Russian mujiks in beards and sheepskins, appeared slowly traversing the valley; and when we found that they were laden with merchandise from the fair of Nijni, we regarded those familiar figures as old acquaintances, whom, under the circumstances, it was advisable not to acknowledge. They return laden chiefly with dried fruit and Crim wine.

At the large and picturesque village of Davonkoi we left the valley, and shortly afterwards passed the mansion of a Tartar nobleman, celebrated for his great wealth. His riches seemed patriarchal in their character, for an enormous herd of camels, scattered over the face of the country, were being collected into groups by the herdsmen, who were driving them home for the night. It was an interesting sight, in the still evening, to watch these ungainly creatures stalking over the extensive grass prairies, mingled with flocks of sheep, distinguished from those of any other country by their short curly wool, of a bluishgrey colour. The breed which produces this wool is very highly prized in the Crimea, in certain portions of which alone it is reared. Great quantities of the lamb skins, called "shumski," are exported annually into Poland and the neighbouring countries. They are valued on the spot at from ten to fifteen shillings a-piece.

It was so dark when we entered the narrow valley in which the old Tartar capital of Bagtchè Serai is situated, that we had great difficulty in finding the dilapidated archway, through which it was necessary to pass into the main street; then we rumbled over its uneven pavement, between low deserted-looking tenements, for an interminable time. At length Richter and the driver, who had been looking in vain for a gleam of light, which is the only evidence in a Tartar town of a house of public entertainment, descended to explore, and left us stationary in the narrow silent street. Here we waited, until my imagination, wearied with the excitement of the day, peopled the sleeping city with the veiled ghosts of Tartar women, whom I thought I could perceive haunting the black alleys, which opened up to the right and left of our position, in company with sundry monks whose bones lay whitening in the caverns of Inkerman.

A sudden jolt aroused me to a sense of the impropriety of which my fancy had been guilty, and I found that our spies had returned, sheered by a ray of hope so feeble that no doubt it corresponded with the ray of light which had given rise to it.

However, upon entering the courtyard we found ourselves in an indisputable khan. It was filled with every conceivable description of vehicle, while a number of small doors opened upon a low wooden balcony which extended all round it, and beneath which a quantity of horses were stalled. The rooms were in proportion to the size of the doors, and we obtained the most sumptuously furnished apartment, in which there was barely space for three greasy stretchers.

As we had not tasted anything since leaving Sevastopol, and found that the khan did not supply food, we made an expedition into the town, in a vague but desperate hope of finding something to eat somewhere. All our efforts, however, to knock up bakers and butchers were unsuccessful; we only received abusive answers from behind unopened shutters, and so were obliged to return to our khan, and make a supper of thick coffee, and bread more black and sour than usual. After some consolatory chibouks we stretched ourselves upon the wooden frames, and were lulled to sleep by the low monotonous tones of an old moullah, in the adjoining coffee-room, who, to judge by the imperturbable countenances of his smoking auditory, was relating a history calculated before long to produce a similar effect upon them.

CHAPTER XX

The change from Sevastopol, the city of barracks and
dockyards, to Bagtchè Serai, "the Seraglio of Gardens," was as
agreeable as it was sudden. Here, in a sequestered dell, shut out
from the world by the fantastic crags which surround it, the
ancient capital of Crim Tartary lies embowered amid the most
luxuriant vegetation; overtopping which, a forest of tapering
minarets and waving poplars extends far up the narrow valley,
forming the only signs which lead us to suspect the existence
of dwellings concealed beneath.

The population is precisely the same as it ever was; there is
no visible evidence of the great change which has passed over
the condition of the Tartar—nothing significant of the power to
which he now owes his allegiance. The Crescent and the Cross
do not here compete with one another; venerable mosques are
not jostled by green domes bespattered with stars; nor is the
cry of the muezzin drowned in the clang of unmusical bells; no
reckless drosky threatens the foot-passenger with instant
destruction; no reeling mujik overwhelms him with besotted
caresses; no importunate shopkeeper bawls loudly after him.
Were it not for the Cossack who stands sentinel in the archway
of the Palace of the Khans, those deserted halls might yet be
filled with the turbaned retinue of former years, and the empty
harem still occupied by dark-eyed houris.

It was pleasant to emerge from the savage rudeness of
Northern barbarism into even a low state of Eastern civilisation;
but how difficult to realise the fact, that the dignified Tartar who
saluted us with "Sabani khair," was a fellow-subject of the pigmy
Laplander; and that not thirty miles distant their common ruler,

surrounded by his Muscovite subjects, seemed to be ignoring the existence of this town, the former capital of a kingdom whose princes had once made his ancestors tremble. A word to the forces he was now inspecting might change the destinies of Europe; but the inhabitants of Bagtchè Serai were as proudly indifferent to their Emperor as he was to them, and cared nothing whatever for the destinies of Europe.

The main street, so silent upon the previous evening, was now full of life and activity. It is nearly a mile long, and so narrow that two carts can scarcely pass. Fortunately this is a contingency which does not often arise; and the busy throng that traverses the street, which consists almost entirely of Tartars, Karaïte Jews, and Gypsies, is extremely inconvenienced by the appearance of a wheeled vehicle at all.

As we mixed with this nondescript populace, our attention was divided between the variety of feature and costume which it exhibited, and the wonderful display of goods exposed for sale in the open shops. These are devoid of any front wall, and are closed at night by the wooden shutters which in the daytime form a sort of counter. Upon this the owner sits cross-legged, earnestly engaged in the manufacture of the article he sells, and only allowing himself to be distracted from his occupation by the arrival of a customer.

From the manner in which these shops were arranged, I concluded that the members of each craft were collected into divisions specially appropriated to them. Thus, immediately on leaving our khan, and turning up the principal street towards the Palace, we passed a bazaar in which sheepskin caps were fabricated. Here the purchaser, if he find none ready made to suit his taste, has simply to choose his skin and strike his bargain, and is furnished with the genuine article before an hour has elapsed. The most characteristic are those made of the shumski or lambskin, with the short curling wool, of a bluish-grey colour, which I have already mentioned. Beyond these come the workers in leather, encompassed by piles of saddles, richly embroidered belts, tobacco-pouches, and absurd-looking whips,

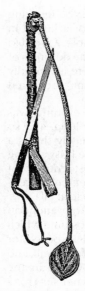

with a large flat piece of leather at the end of the lash, and a knife concealed in the handle. Opposite are slipper-makers and tailors; while the cutlers occupy a great extent of territory, and are famed for the excellent Tartar knives which they manufacture.

It adds immensely to the interest of shopping to witness the process of manufacturing the article one wishes to buy, and I have no doubt it proves a most profitable plan thus to expose the interior economy of a craft. It was impossible to watch a man make a cap, and not buy it after it was done.

We were so long moving about from one set of these affable shopkeepers to another, that it was late in the day before I began to wonder whether we were never coming to a food quarter. Hitherto, since leaving Sevastopol, we had feasted our eyes only, while Richter had subsisted entirely on pipes. Upon his now suggesting that we should go to a cook-shop, we willingly proceeded in search of one, and were attracted, by sundry whiffs redolent of mutton, to a large corner-house, whence arose a cloud of fragrant steam. Here a number of people were standing in the open street, diving into huge projecting cauldrons of soup, from whence they extracted square pieces of fat, which they devoured with great relish while strolling about among the crowd. Not entirely approving of this *al fresco* mode of dining, and fearing that we might stand a chance of being run over while discussing an interesting morsel, we were glad to discover that it was not necessary to present a ticket of admission to a Bagtchè Serai soup-kitchen; so we entered, and seated ourselves on a narrow bench, behind a very filthy plank intended to serve as a festive board. Being fully exposed to the street, we were in a most convenient position for the loungers in it to satisfy their curiosity regarding us, and accordingly we were mutually edified by staring at one another.

Our attention, however, was soon diverted to the head cook, who brought us a boiled sheep's head in one hand, while with the other he attempted to catch the gravy that trickled through his fingers upon a loaf of black bread. These he set down before us on the cleanest part of the plank we could pick out, and evidently considered that our every want was supplied. We forthwith proceeded with our penknives to discuss the sheep's head, which seemed to have been previously stripped of everything but the eyes; and with the addition of some kibaubs (square pieces of fat strung upon a reed), succeeded in accomplishing a meal, which sustained us for the rest of the day;—not that it would be possible to starve in Bagtchè Serai; the heaps of delicious fruit with which the street is lined for some hundreds of yards, would always furnish an abundant, if somewhat unwholesome meal. Grapes, figs, pomegranates, peaches, nectarines, and apricots, tempt the passenger to refresh himself at every step; while, as if in gentle remonstrance with his imprudence, innumerable fountains of the purest water gush out of the hillside, murmuring invitations to the thirsty soul which it is difficult to resist.

From one of these, which has ten spouts, the sparkling streams fall upon slabs of marble. A continual babbling goes on in every direction as the clear little rivulets seem hurrying away from the filth of the town, determined to lose themselves as speedily as possible in the waters of the Djurouk Su, upon the banks of which stream Bagtchè Serai is situate.

Our conduct was shameful in seeking something more potent, after our unsatisfactory meal, than the refreshment these tiny cascades could afford; and we deserved to be half-poisoned by the extraordinary concoction with which we were supplied at the "Booza" cellar, whither we resorted. Here hogsheads of this liquor, which is extracted from fermented millet-seed, and highly esteemed among the Tartars, were ranged around a low room, and served to us in earthenware jugs. Its excessive astringency rendered it anything but an agreeable beverage.

We had now traversed the entire length of the main street, and reached a small square, the right side of which was occupied by the far-famed Palace of the Khans. My attention was, however, more immediately directed to a number of women who were collected here, and who displayed at once the varieties of race most commonly observed in Bagtchè Serai. It must be a great comfort to Tartar ladies that their religion obliges them to remain veiled in public, for I have little doubt that they would be fairly eclipsed by the lovely Jewesses, whose graceful costume in the group before us contrasted favourably with that of their waddling companions. There is nothing Israelitish about these Karaïte maidens—the Grecian nose and fiery nostril, the short proud upper lip, and exquisitely turned mouth, seem almost to belie their Hebrew origin; while those large eyes, so deeply set, require no white fereedjè to give additional effect to their lustre.

They are congregated under an old archway, and laughingly criticising the strangers, an occupation which would not meet with the approval of their lord and master, who, in common with the rest of his sect, shares the prejudices of true believers in jealously guarding the female part of his establishment. Near them some gypsies in wild array, with dishevelled hair, prowl restlessly about, having left their caves in the rocks to follow their universally recognised occupation of begging and stealing.

It seemed to me that the only Russians in Bagtchè Serai were the soldiers in charge of the Palace. I afterwards heard that, by an imperial ukase, Russians were forbidden to settle in the valley; a most unusual instance of generosity and consideration on the part of the government.

We half regretted, after seeing the officer in command, that we had not taken up our abode in the rooms furnished for the accommodation of strangers in the Palace; but we scarcely thought it worth while now to desert our present characteristic abode, even for the apartments of royalty, and so contented ourselves with inspecting the former habitation of the Khans, under the guidance of a garrulous old soldier.

Crossing the moat, we passed through a massive painted gateway with projecting eaves, and I was no less astonished than delighted with the singular collection of buildings that met my eye on every side. To the right of a large grass-grown court stands the rambling disjointed palace, with gaudy walls and highly decorated trellis-work festooned with vines, and small lattice windows looking out upon fragrant gardens; while above all is an octagonal wooden tower, with a Chinese-looking roof. On the left are a number of two-storeyed buildings, with verandahs supported by ornamented posts, and near them a mausoleum and mosque, with two tall minarets—the mark of royalty. A handsome fountain, shaded by willows, stands

Palace of the Khans

opposite the private entrance; behind it, the court is enclosed by the walls of an orchard, situated on a rising ground, which is intersected by terraces. Looking beyond the objects immediately surrounding us, the view was no less striking. We seemed to be in the arena of an amphitheatre, of which the flat roofs of the Tartar houses—stuck, as it were, in rows against the sides of the mountains—represented the seats. All over these mountains caves occurred frequently, resembling pigeon-holes.

Nothing can be more unique than the aspect of the town from the courtyard of the palace, while gigantic rocks, of grotesque shape, are poised in mid air, threatening destruction to all that remains of the capital of this once mighty empire.

The iron gate at the entry of the palace bears this inscription:—

"The Master of this gate, who has acquired this province, is the most exalted personage, Hadji Ghiri Khan, son of Mingli Ghiri Khan. May the Lord God deign to accord supreme happiness to Mingli Ghiri Khan, as well as to his father and mother."

Entering the principal vestibule, we observed the celebrated Fountain of Tears, immortalised among Russians by the poem of Nicholas Pushkin. This hall opens, by means of arches, to the gardens of the Seraglio; and from it, dark staircases ascend and terminate in narrow passages, which again lead to spacious galleries, brilliantly decorated.

Wandering through the latter, we lose ourselves at last in a labyrinth of small apartments, scarcely differing from one another, connected by doorways, in which swing heavy satin brocades. We glide noiselessly through them over the soft Turkish carpets, as if treading the chamber of death. There was something appropriate in the mysterious silence which characterised all our movements, surrounded as we were by a luxury so fresh-looking and real, that it seemed as though its possessors had but just vanished for ever from the fairy scenes they had conjured around them. Here were broad crimson divans, richly embroidered curtains carefully suspended over the latticed windows, and tapestry of costly satin elaborately worked, concealing the walls, or hanging quaintly from semicircular projections over the fireplaces—a flimsy splendour, which was not allowed to fade and vanish with its original possessors, but was retained in all its gaudy colouring, as if to mock the memory of those to whose effeminate tastes it once had ministered.

But Muscovite sovereigns have condescended to lodge in the former abode of the Khans; and the guide, of course, imagines that the most interesting object in the palace is the bed in which the Empress Catharine slept. We hurried him on to the room of Maria Potoski, fraught with more romantic associations. Here for ten years the infatuated countess resided, hoping to effect a compromise between her conscience and her passion for the Khan, by a life devoted to religious exercises, while content to reign, at the same time, supreme in the palace of the infidel. The apartments appropriated to her are luxuriously arranged; and a lofty hall, with fountains plashing upon slabs of marble, bears her name. Adjoining it is a Roman Catholic chapel, which was built expressly for her use by the amorous Khan.

They must have been somewhat lax Mahomedans altogether these Khans. Many of the rooms are ornamented with representations of birds and beasts and creeping things, in every variation of grotesque form; while, as if to compensate for this direct violation of the Koran, fragments of that sacred record are inscribed upon the walls. One of the most singular chambers in this most singular palace is a large glass summer-house, surrounded by a divan, and decorated in a most unorthodox manner, in which a fountain plays into a porphyry basin. It opens upon a flower-garden, at the farther end of which, shaded by a magnificent old vine, is a marble bath, prepared for the Empress Catharine by the considerate gallantry of Potemkin, and supplied by cascades from the fountain of Selsabil. The favourite lived enclosed among delicious gardens, in the now deserted harem, during the residence of his royal mistress in the palace, from which it is approached by a succession of pavilions and verandahs. Attached to it is the octagonal tower; and authorities differ as to whether the Khans reserved it for the use of their women or their falcons. As it is exactly like a large wooden cage, no light is thrown upon the subject from its construction. From between the bars a singular panoramic view is obtained of the town and palace.

We entered the royal mosque by the royal staircase, and descended—to speak in Christian language—to the royal pew, from behind the lattice of which the dancing dervishes and religious ceremonies of the church may be witnessed unseen. It is a spacious edifice, and over the principal door, facing the street, is this characteristic inscription:

"Who is Hadji Selim? He who is the most illustrious of all the Khans, the favoured of God. May the Lord God accord him every benefit as a reward for the erection of this mosque. Selim Ghiri Khan is in his existence comparable to the rose-tree. His son is a rose. Each in his turn has been crowned with the honours of the seraglio. The rose-tree has flourished anew; its only fresh rose has become the lion of the Padishah of the Crimea—Sehlamet Ghiri Khan. God has fulfilled my wish in this inscription. It is to the Lord God alone that this mosque has been erected by Sehlamet Ghiri Khan."

Having seen the former abode of the Khans, we thought we would now visit their present resting-place. So, leaving the fountains to play and babble in silent halls, and the divans to grace untenanted rooms, and the trees to blossom and perfume the deserted gardens, we entered the vaulted chambers in which the most illustrious Khans repose. Here a venerable old Hadjè held tremulously aloft the dim flickering light, to enable us to look over the turbaned tombstones. Passing out, we walked through the cemetery, where vines cluster over the crumbling ruins that tell of departed greatness; and all seemed travelling the same road which the occupants of these sculptured sepultures have already taken.

Mausoleum of the Khans

228

CHAPTER XXI

*Annexation of the Crimea—Intriguing policy of Russia—
Murder of Devlit Ghiri Khan—Novel mode of catering—Scenes
in the Khan—A Tartar bath—Valley of Jehoshaphat—Tchoufut
Kalè—The Synagogue—Karaïte Jews: their peculiar tenets—The
Jewish fortress—The monastery of Uspenskoï—The Seraglio of
Gardens*

The Seraglio of Gardens possesses other charms than those
with which it is invested by virtue of its romantic position, its
Tartar population, and Oriental palace.

The historical associations connected with the former
capital of Little Tartary are not devoid of interest. From the
period of the total annihilation of the Bosphorian empire in
the fourth century, until the occupation of the Crimea by the
advanced guard of the Golden Horde in the thirteenth, the
history of this country presents little else than a series of
invasions by those barbarians, who, on their way to occupy the
fertile plains of eastern Europe, had made the Tauric peninsula
their first resting-place, and established in it a supremacy
which only existed until some new host swept along this great
highway with irresistible violence, overturned the institutions,
and succeeded to the territories of their savage precursors.
Thus the kingdom of Bosphorus had no sooner fallen a prey to
the incessant ravages of the Alans, the Goths, and the Huns,
than they were succeeded by the Khazars, the Pétchenègues,
and the Comanes, who each in turn occupied the Crimea, until
the grandson of Zingis Khan succeeded in establishing a more
durable empire, amid the remains of which we were now
wandering; and it was melancholy to think that the strange
destiny of this devoted province had not yet been
accomplished, and that, while other European countries are
rejoicing in the sunlight of civilisation, it should have fallen a
prey scarcely seventy years since to a new power from the
north, more overwhelming and rapacious than any of those

Asiatic hordes to whose incursions it had hitherto been exposed.

Nor is the condition of the Crimea improved under the sway of a government professing a higher state of moral and intellectual advancement than had characterised its Mongolian predecessors. Indeed, this questionable superiority only evidenced itself in the means Russia employed to acquire this much-coveted territory, since to the destructive inroads of barbarians she added those political intrigues which are more in accordance with the notions of modern times, and of a people eminently qualified to practise them.

The Khans of Crim Tartary had moved the seat of government from the rocky fortress of Tchoufut Kalè to the lovely valley of the Djurouk Su, and, as tributaries to the Porte, had reigned in their palace of Bagtchè Serai for nearly three centuries, when the bloody war which had been relentlessly carried on between Russia and Turkey, and of which the Crimea had been in some degree the theatre, terminated in the treaty of Kainarjè. Devlit Ghiri, who had been invested with the dignity of Khan by the Sultan, was now deposed, and his brother Jehan, who for some time past had been retained a hostage at St. Petersburg (though he nominally held the office of a captain in the imperial guard), was placed upon the throne by the Empress Catharine—an act which was in direct violation of the principal article in this treaty, in which the independence of the Crimea, as well as the free choice of its sovereigns, had been expressly stipulated.

But it was not enough that a prince should be thus forced upon a country, in opposition to the will of the people; a mere puppet in the hands of Russia, he was compelled to show a marked preference for the power to which he owed his crown, and to introduce so many Russians into his service, that he soon increased the hatred and disgust of his subjects, whose feelings of disaffection were secretly fomented by Russian emissaries, until they broke out into an open revolt of so serious a character as to oblige the Khan to fly to Taman, where he remained until assistance arrived in the shape of a Russian army, which invaded the Crimea, and restored him to the throne from which he had been forced.

During this period of the occupation of the province by the Russians, the most atrocious cruelties were perpetrated upon those who had been instigated to share in the revolt. So anxious did Russia profess herself to prevent the recurrence of such an event, that a proposal was made to the Khan to retire from the throne upon a pension of 100,000 rubles a year, resigning his crown into the safe keeping of the imperial government—an offer which was entitled to some consideration in the presence of an overwhelming army ready to enforce its acceptance. The luckless prince, whose residence at the Russian court had taught him to estimate truly the value of promises emanating from such a quarter, persisted for some time in his refusal, but he found himself ultimately obliged to submit to the terms proposed, and, as he had but too justly anticipated, was confined as a prisoner at Kaluga, in which character he was, of course, considered undeserving of his pension.

After in vain petitioning to be sent to St. Petersburg, he was consigned, at his own request, to the tender mercies of the Turks. By them he was banished to Rhodes, where he soon after fell a victim to the bow-string;—so terminated the inglorious career of the last of the Khans. An imperial ukase, issued by the Empress Catharine, annexed this magnificent province to her fast-extending empire. No wonder she thought it necessary to congratulate the Prince Potemkin, in the words of the Russian chronicler, "upon the address and good fortune with which he had managed this important operation."

As my friend was attacked with a return of the fever and ague from which he had suffered on the Volga, we remained at Bagtchè Serai some days. I could not but rejoice at the delay, however much I regretted its cause, and the discomforts of our lodging for an invalid. Although it was now getting late in the year, the heat was excessive; and the swarms of flies, which seem to delight in Mahomedans more than in the professors of any other faith, rendered rest by day almost out of the question.

Our manner of living, however, was wonderfully improved. After our first experience of Tartar kitchens, we determined to attempt a new mode of proceeding. Accordingly, we first paid a visit to the butcher, selecting, at his recommendation, the most eligible joint. Next we proceeded to the baker, where, after tasting every description of Tartar fancy-bread, we at last discovered one species that we could tolerate. Thence we resorted to the vegetable market, which was well supplied. I observed great quantities of bringals and other tropical produce. Contenting ourselves with some potatoes, we returned heavily laden to the soup-kitchen, and deposited our purchases with the cook, who seemed utterly at a loss to divine our intentions. He promised, however, implicitly to follow our directions in trying to roast the mutton; and in the evening, upon our return from the day's sight-seeing, we picked up our dinner, which was presented to us in a large tin dish, and, bearing aloft our steaming mutton and potatoes, triumphantly paraded the main street of the town for a quarter of a mile, and found, upon reaching our khan, that we had every reason to congratulate ourselves on our success.

As our little crib adjoined the public coffee-room, we had only to open the door to be spectators of the novel scenes it usually afforded. Here were collected a number of picturesque old Tartars, seated cross-legged in little wooden pens, incessantly smoking chibouks or nargillehs, and drinking their thick coffee out of cups resembling large brass thimbles. They seldom spoke to one another, but puffed away most imperturbably on their carpeted divans, where I used often to join them.

There is a pleasant dreaminess in all Oriental habits which insensibly asserts its influence over the stranger. I was disappointed, however, to find that the deliciously-enervating Turkish bath was modified by the Tartar into a series of ablutions far less luxurious. At the same time, I much preferred it to the extravagant treatment of the Russians: for the birch twigs which they energetically apply to produce a healthy glow (a result very soon attained) are here substituted woollen gloves; and a bunch of cotton dipped in soap-suds performs the cleansing process, instead of that violent hydropathic treatment—those alternate buckets of boiling and iced water, which render a Russian bath a terrifying ordeal to a novice. So far the mode of proceeding in a Tartar bath is *à la Turque*; but in the middle of the Tauric sudatorium there is no deep pool of water ever increasing in temperature, in which the bather revels for an indefinite time, in a parboiled condition. Here he stretches himself, in a state of nudity, upon an unbearably hot slab of marble, upon which he is rolled about, and scrubbed, and splashed. In fact, the difference between a Turkish and a Tartar bath is simply this, that in the one you are boiled, in the other fried. I infinitely prefer the boiling process, particularly when it is succeeded by shampooing and coffee, which are not the invariable accompaniments among the Tartars.

One day we strolled up the valley in which Bagtchè Serai lies almost concealed; and passing through the narrow gorge in which it terminates, and which contains caverns occupied only by gypsies, we suddenly emerged from the deep shadow of precipitous cliffs upon a dark mysterious glen, heavily wooded with majestic oaks and beech trees. A winding path dived into its sombre recesses, and we were soon wandering through a maze of tombstones, formed in the shape of sarcophagi, and covered with Hebrew inscriptions. This was the valley of Jehoshaphat—for centuries the cemetery of the Karaïte Jews, who still love to lay their bones beside those of their ancestors; so that the sleeping inhabitants of the valley of Jehoshaphat far outnumber the population of Karaïtes in any one town in the Crimea.

For nearly a mile did we follow the little path, always surrounded by these touching mementoes of a race who, in whatever part of the world they may be scattered, still retain the profoundest veneration for a spot hallowed by such sacred associations. The grove terminates suddenly near a frightful precipice, from the dizzy edge of which a magnificent view is obtained.

A few miles distant, the conical rock of Tepekerman rises abruptly from the broken country, its beetling crags perforated with innumerable mysterious caverns and chambers. Beyond, the Tchatir Dagh, with the elevated sea-range of which it is part, forms the background to the rich and varied landscape.

Following the line of the calcareous cliffs upon which we stood, we reached a point where the prospect in the opposite direction was still more striking. To the right, the dilapidated

The Jewish Fortress of Tchoufut Kale

old fortress of Tchoufut Kalè crowned the nearest height, while the monastery of Uspenskoï, built into the face of the overhanging rock, looked as if it had been excavated by the inhabitants of stony Petra, rather than by monks of the Greek Church. Here, too, compressed within narrow limits, lay the old Tartar capital, almost hidden by the gardens which clothe the valley in a mantle of richest green. Lower down, the precipices soften into gentle slopes, and the cultivation spreads over a great extent of country, through which the Djurouk Su meanders until it falls into the Black Sea, that bounds the western horizon.

When the Tartar Khans deserted Tchoufut Kalè for the lovely vale below, this singular stronghold became again exclusively the residence of the Karaïte Jews, who had lived there from time immemorial, and who are naturally bound to it by the strongest feelings of reverence and affection, since it has been alike the cradle of their sect, and the rock upon which they have ever found a secure refuge in times of persecution.

As the population was said to be entirely Jewish, we expected to find Tchoufut Kalè filled with picturesque groups of handsomely dressed men and lovely maidens; but we passed through the archway, and along the streets, to which the living rock answered the purpose of pavement, and still, to our astonishment, not a soul was to be seen. A few dogs flew at us, and obliged us to perambulate the rest of the town armed with stones. It seemed quite empty, for not only were the public thoroughfares deserted, but we could get no answer at any of the doors at which we knocked; so that I was beginning to suspect that the last inhabitant must have recently got some-one to bury him in the valley of Jehoshaphat, when a husky voice murmured something through a crack in a shutter, and presently a decrepid stoneblind old man, who might have been the individual in question, hobbled out with a stick, and offered to conduct us to the synagogue. On our way we came upon quite a crowd, consisting of two more old men and a boy, who attached themselves to us. With them we entered a mausoleum containing the tomb of a Tartar princess, who had been seduced by a nobleman, and carried off to a Genoese fortress: her melancholy history formed the subject of the long inscription which covered the tombstone.

The venerable rabbi, who now appeared to conduct us to the synagogue, was the highest ecclesiastical authority of the Karaïte church; and it was strange to find perched upon this inaccessible cliff the headquarters of a sect whose members are scattered over Russia, Poland, and Egypt.

The synagogue was a plain building, differing in no respect, to my uninitiated eye, from an ordinary Jewish place of worship. We looked at some magnificently bound copies of the Old Testament in manuscript. The books of Moses only are printed and taught in the schools. The Karaïtes profess to have the Old Testament in its most genuine state.

The derivation of their name I took upon Richter's authority to be *kara* and *ite*; words signifying, in Arabic, black dog—a not unlikely epithet to be applied by Mahomedans to this despised race. A more generally received and probably correct derivation, however, seems to be from the word *kara*, Scripture—because they hold simply to the letter of Scripture, not admitting the authority of the Talmud, or the interpretations of the rabbis. The Talmudists accuse the Karaïtes of retaining the errors of the Sadducees. This is not entitled to much weight, coming from so hostile a quarter. There is, however, no doubt that the two sects differ in many material points from one another; as, for instance, in the different degrees of relationship forbidden in marriage, in their rules controlling the succession of inheritance, and more especially in the entire recognition of polygamy. According to Rabbinists, their schism is of comparatively recent date; the Karaïtes themselves, however, contend that their separation from the main stem took place prior to the return from the Babylonish captivity. Like all Jews, they display extraordinary care in the education of their children, who are publicly instructed in the synagogues.

About five thousand Karaïtes are resident in Poland, who acknowledge the old rabbi of Tchoufut Kalè as their spiritual chief. They are said originally to have emigrated from the Crimea.

But it is not by the difference which exists upon points of doctrine or civil discipline that the stranger can at once distinguish the Karaïte from the Talmudist, but by the strange contrast which is invariably presented in the lives and characters of the members of these opposing sects. The Karaïte merchant enjoys everywhere so high a reputation for probity, that throughout the Crimea his word is considered equal to his bond. How singular that branches of the same tree should bear fruit so dissimilar, as to be distinguished by those extremes of honesty and dishonesty which have become a proverbial characteristic in each case. To what can we ascribe this honourable distinction which the Karaïtes have thus acquired, but to their principles of strict adherence to the letter of the Old Testament alone, to the exclusion of those traditions and rabbinical interpretations which their brethren have allowed to supersede the authority of the inspired record?— and this is a conclusion which, however palpable, it is not superfluous to draw, since there are those who, in our own day, in an enlightened country, and in a Christian church, may be supposed to have a fellow-feeling for the Talmudist, as they themselves are engaged in a somewhat similar process.

As almost all the Karaïtes are engaged in trade or manufacture, and as they observe the most scrupulous honesty in their dealings, it has naturally followed that they are a prosperous and thriving community; while, as if an exception had been made in favour of this portion of that interesting people whose unhappy destiny has been so wonderfully accomplished, probably the only settlement exclusively Jewish which still exists is the fortress of Tchoufut Kalè—a refuge which God seems to have provided for those only who worship Him purely and in the manner of their forefathers. The population of Tchoufut Kalè has, however, dwindled down to a very small remnant, since trade has increased, and additional facilities have been afforded for settling in more convenient positions than upon the summit of one of the highest crags in the Crimea. The population of the seaport of Eupatoria is composed mainly of Karaïtes, nearly two thousand of whom are now resident there—and some of these are wealthy merchants.

I no longer wondered that the streets were silent, or that the valley of Jehoshaphat was so fully garnished with tombstones, when I learnt that all devout Karaïtes scattered through the Crimea, when increasing infirmities warn them of approaching dissolution, are brought hither to die. There was something touching in this last tribute to the spot endeared by so many associations; and I could not accuse of a mawkish sentimentality those members of this singular sect who desired to lay their bones beside those of their forefathers in this lovely vale of Jehoshaphat.

There are only two entrances to the fort; and the massive gates are locked every night. We descended a long flight of steps cut out of the living rock to the well of delicious water which supplies the inhabitants, the situation of which, at the bottom of a valley, and far below the walls, would render the impregnable position of the fort utterly valueless in time of war. At this well is usually stationed a man who fills the water-skins borne by donkeys to their master above, both the consigner and the consignee being probably too old to accompany these sagacious animals on the numerous trips which are, nevertheless, so essential to the comfort of the inhabitants.

Following the left bank of the ravine, we reached the monastery of the Uspenskoï, or the Assumption of the Virgin Mary, where galleries are suspended upon the face of a lofty precipice, beneath the stupendous rocks out of which the chambers are hewn, and out of which also are cut the flight of steps by which they are approached. There are only ten rooms and a small church at present excavated; but the work is progressing, and the limited number of monks which now compose the fraternity will probably be augmented with the accommodation.

The monastery is said to have originated at the time of the persecution of the Greek Church by the Mahomedans, when its members were not allowed to worship in buildings. In some places the windows are mere holes in the face of the rock, while in others the front is composed of solid masonry. A wooden verandah before the church is supported over the massive bells.

About twenty thousand pilgrims resort hither annually in the month of August. Altogether it is a curious place, and harmonises well with the strange scenery in which it is situated; so that the monks deserve some credit for adding to the charms of a spot already possessing so many attractions; and this is probably the only benefit their presence is likely to confer upon the community.

We mounted the steep crags above the town to take one last look at the Seraglio of Gardens before we bade it adieu; and as the rays of the setting sun tinged the whole sky, and shed a warm glow over the palace of the Khans, we were reminded of their glory, so short-lived, and so bright while it lasted, of which all that remained was the lovely scene before us: but the glory of the Khans was set for ever!

Tartar Guide

CHAPTER XXII

Ascent to a deserted fortress—Mangoup Kalè: its history—The Cape of the Winds—Picturesque ruins—An agreeable road—Tartar travelling—Shoeing a bullock—Prospects of Crim Tartary—The Oesembash pass—View from the summit—Descent to Yalta

It was no easy matter to get away from Bagtchè Serai. We had been in treaty with sundry Tartars for horses to take us over the mountains to Yalta; but, like true Easterns, they were most unflinching in driving a bargain; and it was not until a wholesome competition was established that we came to terms with a man who showed us some wiry-looking nags, and promised to come to the khan sufficiently early to enable us to accomplish the long day's work in prospect.

As we were going back to Yalta, we thought we could dispense with the services of Richter for the future, and he accordingly took his departure for Simpheropol, when we rode out of the town on our way to Mangoup. We had been most fortunate in stumbling upon so useful an ally: he was thoroughly good-natured and honest, though a Russian subject. As he came from the German provinces on the Baltic, he was distinguished by none of the national characteristics, except that of never changing his clothes while travelling; a circumstance which, while it reconciled me to the separation, was, it is fair to say, almost unavoidable in his case.

It was a beautiful morning as we jogged, for the last time, down the main street, seated on uncomfortable saddles, behind which our bags were strapped. Our road lay to the eastward of that by which we had come from Sevastopol, and in a few hours we re-entered the lonely vale of Balbeck, just where it emerged from the mountains; and following the bed of the stream, wound through rich gardens, between lofty precipices, until we reached the base of the noble hill that terminates the glen, and looking up at the ruined walls that crown it, perceived that this

Mangoup Kalè

was indeed the celebrated fortress of Mangoup Kalè. There is a deliciously cold spring at the romantic little village of Karolez, at which we refreshed ourselves before commencing the sharp ascent. We found it was impossible to ride up the short cuts which we preferred taking, and were soon all scrambling along the steep face of the hill, despising the winding paths, and caring only for the glorious old ruins above. When we reached the walls, we were for some time at a loss to find a gap by which to enter the fortress. At last we stormed a breach, where the huge stones which had composed the massive walls were heaped together, and found ourselves surrounded on all sides by ruin and desolation.

The uncertainty which hangs over the history of these fragments of former greatness, tends to invest them with a mysterious interest peculiar to themselves. They are strewn so extensively over the surface of the rock, as to leave no doubt of the magnitude and importance which once distinguished the city that crowned this mountain top. They bear the traces of almost every race which has inhabited the Crimea, are pervaded by the very essence of antiquity, and regarded by the Tartars with the profoundest veneration. And they are worthy of it, for they are their own historians; and an account of their former owners, and the vicissitudes these stones have undergone since they were first hewn from the solid rock, may at a future time be extracted from them by some antiquarian who has made it the study of his lifetime to worm himself into the confidence of such impenetrable records. Meantime, authorities differ very widely upon this matter. The name is frequently pronounced Mangoute. The latter syllable, signifying Goths, may perhaps lead us to suppose that it was derived from the possessors of that principality, of which this was at one time the capital. The Goths were expelled from the low lands by the Huns in the fourth century, and still continued to live in an independent condition, defending themselves in their fastnesses from the attacks of those barbarians who successively possessed themselves of the remainder of the Tauric peninsula. According to some authorities, Mangoup remained the capital of the Gothic principality until it was taken by the Turks in the sixteenth century; while others suppose that, after the conquest of the Crimea by the Khazars, it became a Greek fortress, and so remained until it fell into the hands of the Genoese, at the same time with the Greek colonies on the coast. This is probably the correct view, as the greater part of the remains are Grecian. Professor Pallas calls Mangoup "an ancient Genoese city, which appears to have been the last resort of the Ligurians after they were driven from the coast." Still the chapel, which is here excavated from the rock, and the images of saints, which he describes as painted on the walls, but which I did not observe, may be traces of the Christian Goths no less than of the Genoese; but it is extremely improbable that such is the case.

In 1745 Mangoup was occupied by a Turkish garrison for twenty years, after which it was taken possession of by the Khan of the Crimea. It had been for many years inhabited almost exclusively by Karaïte Jews. These gradually dwindled away, until they totally disappeared about sixty years ago, and have left nothing behind them but the ruins of their synagogue and a large cemetery, containing tombs similar to those amid which we had wandered in the valley of Jehoshaphat.

There is very little left of the massive buildings which once adorned this famous town, except the foundations. It was quite a work of difficulty to pick our way through the maze of ruins which were scattered around us. The lofty calcareous promontory upon which the fortress is perched, is about a mile long, and a quarter of a mile broad. Upon three sides it is surrounded by frightful precipices, while that by which alone it is accessible is defended by castellated towers, placed at intervals in the massive wall through which we had entered. At right angles with it, and intersecting the narrow promontory, are the remains of another wall; and the most perfect building now existing is a square fort built into it, two storeys high, and pierced with loopholes for musketry. Passing through another opening, we reached the most eastern point, and discovered for the first time that the whole length of the upper edge of the plateau was perforated by small chambers cut out of the solid rock, and approached by stairs from the upper surface. Descending into one of these chambers, at the most projecting

Cape of the Winds, with Sevastopol in the distance

point of the promontory, called the Cape of the Winds, I tremblingly approached the aperture, which had once served for a window, but was now broken away to a level with the floor, and from the dizzy height gazed over wild ravines, and peaceful valleys, and undulating plains. At last I perceived the harbour of Sevastopol, with little black specks upon its surface, significant of the change which has come over the destinies of this singular country, where an impregnable fort has been superseded by an *invincible* armada, and the castellated walls of the Genoese stronghold have given place to the three-tiered batteries of a Russian arsenal.

Many of the chambers I was now inspecting are from fifteen to twenty feet square, and connected by stairs; but the work of exploring required nerves rather stronger than people who inhabit houses instead of eagles' nests usually possess, and the steps hewn out of the face of the giddy cliff were more picturesque to look at than agreeable to traverse. Who the dwellers in these singular cells can have been, it is difficult to conjecture; but they were probably inhabited before the town was built upon the rock above.

If the ruins of Mangoup Kalè possessed no other merit, they serve at least as an attraction to mount the cliffs upon which they are situated, and the labour of the ascent would be amply repaid by the view alone. But when to the beauties of the distant landscape we could ever add a romantic foreground— when we could hide in the mysterious caverns, and look through the jagged clefts in the rock as from some prison window—or, sheltering ourselves under an old tower, bring the ruins of the synagogue into the corner of the picture—we felt that they themselves formed the greatest charm of the view to which they had allured us, and could only regret being obliged so soon to leave a spot thus richly endowed with all that could compensate to the traveller for the annoyances to be met with in the country which it serves to adorn.

We descended another road, and passed through an old arched gateway, once the principal entrance to the citadel. I was able to gain a more correct idea of the configuration of this part of the Crimea from the fortress of Mangoup Kalè than I had yet obtained. A precipitous limestone range extends nearly east and west, parallel to the sea range; and upon the edge of the stupendous cliffs are perched the forts of Tchoufut Kalè and Mangoup Kalè. The whole of the country intervening between these ranges, through which our road now lay, is intersected by lovely valleys, and watered by clear mountain-streams; their banks are highly cultivated, and frequent tufted groves betray the existence of the villages which they conceal. This tract is inhabited solely by Tartars, who seem to cling to their highland glens with the tenacity characteristic of mountaineers. They are a hardy hospitable race, totally different from their lowland brethren.

Although the sun was still very powerful, our narrow road was in general completely protected from its rays by the spreading boughs of noble trees that met overhead and formed a covered avenue. Occasionally we wound round a hillside, and entered upon a new valley more enchanting than the last. Our path being often incommoded by so much luxuriant foliage and vegetation, we adopted the rocky bed of the stream, and so paddled ankle-deep through the clear sparkling water, the mountains from which it flowed becoming more and more distinct as we approached their base. These brooks, so convenient and harmless now, become furious torrents in the winter.

We did not often enter the villages, but picked up an equestrian or two, who joined us out of curiosity, and rode on ahead with our guide, discussing such unusual visitors, no doubt. No Tartar ever dreams of walking from one village to another; but when he wants to pay a visit to his neighbour, like a true country gentleman he rides over to him; and if he has not so good a horse as the squire, he has scenery at least which the other might covet, and can beguile the way with a contemplation of its beauties, if competent so to enjoy himself. To the traveller furnished with a government order, the Tartars are bound to provide horses at any village where it may be produced. These are often poor-looking animals, but active and sure-footed, and admirably adapted for the rocky passes which they are obliged to traverse; indeed, they deserve great credit for the way in which they seem to cling to a mountain side, for they are shod with a flat plate of iron, with a hole at the frog, which may be useful in stony deserts for protecting the hoof, but must cause many a slip over the smooth rock.

Not content with shoeing their horses thus, the Tartars treat their oxen in like manner. I saw the process at Bagtchè Serai, and was at a loss to conceive at first what was going on. The animal was upon the broad of his back, and there secured—a man sitting upon the head. The four legs, tied together, were sticking straight up in the air, and the smith was hammering away, enabled by his convenient position to operate all the more skilfully. There was something excessively ludicrous in the whole scene, though, to judge from the low moaning

Shoeing a Bullock

which issued from beneath the assistant seated on the animal's head, the poor brute found it no laughing matter.

It was melancholy to think that the inhabitants of these lovely valleys were gradually disappearing under the blighting influence which Russia appears to exercise over her Moslem subjects. Of late years the Tartars have been rapidly diminishing, and now number about a hundred thousand, or scarcely half the entire population of the Crimea. Their energy, too, seems declining with their numbers. Whole tracts of country susceptible of a high state of cultivation, and once producing abundantly, are now lying waste; their manufactures deteriorating, their territorial wealth destroyed, their noble families becoming extinct, their poor ground down by Russian tax-gatherers, and swindled out of their substance by dishonest sub-officials.

Ere long the flat-roofed cottages, now buried amid the luxuriant vegetation of clustering fruit-trees, will crumble into dust, and with them the last remains of that nation who once occupied an important position among European powers. Is the only Mahomedan state still existing in the West to share the same fate as the kingdom of Crim Tartary?

It was late in the afternoon when we arrived at the romantic village of Oesembash, situate at the foot of the mountains, and our guide insisted that it was impossible to cross over the pass to Yalta after the day's work we had already performed. However, though the village looked very clean and respectable, we had promised ourselves a nearer approach to civilisation in our night-quarters than it could afford. Dreading, besides, an encounter with Tartar fleas, more than the dangers of the Oesembash pass upon a dark night, we held our guide to his engagement, and pushed on up the steep ravine, in spite of the remonstrances of the villagers, who were disappointed at losing such profitable-looking guests. We followed the water-course until it became too rugged and precipitous, and then took a more winding path; even this was, however, frequently so steep as to render it advisable to dismount. Our guide was comforted by an old Tartar who took advantage of our escort at so late an hour to continue his journey.

The pass from the valley of Oesembash to Yalta is undoubtedly the most beautiful in the Crimea. The views over the country towards Bagtchè Serai are only surpassed by the sublime panorama which meets the eye on reaching the summit. Here, in whatever direction we turn, we are surrounded by magnificent peaks and crags, below which dark pine-woods thickly clothe the mountain side, until, the temperature becoming more genial, they are succeeded upon the south by the vine cultivation of the coast, amid which is placed the little town of Yalta, its white houses reflected in the smooth sea, which here forms a charming bay. To the north, the fertile valleys along which we had been journeying seemed shut out from the rest of the world by lofty walls of limestone, upon which were perched inaccessible forts, to guard the entrance into this enchanted land. Beyond this singular range the distant steppe, like a sea of another colour, stretched away until it became confused and lost in the dim haze which obscured the horizon. It was a picture in which many different elements seemed combined. The magnificent timber that clothed some of these mountains, to a height of three thousand feet, transported me in imagination back again to tropical scenery; but the bright autumn tints soon dispelled the delusion of an evergreen jungle. The dark pine-forest which stretched around us might have sheltered the hillsides of some Norwegian valley, and the cold grey crags above head harmonised with those harsh scenes; but this was no Norwegian sunset—it was Italian! and so were those gentle slopes terraced with vines to the shores of the sea that was blue as the sky above it.

The gloom of the fir woods through which our downward path led us was soon merged in the shades of evening; and at last it became so dark that we were obliged to lead our horses warily down the precipitous gullies, directed by the occasional shouts of our guide, whom we could no longer see. We quite sympathised with our poor beasts as we crawled together into the inn-yard at Yalta. They had carried us for thirteen hours without halt or bait of any sort; and I have no doubt they experienced better treatment after their hard day's work in the Tartar's stable than we did at the Hotel d'Odessa.

CHAPTER XXIII

*Yalta—The grand hotel: its accommodation—Voyage from
Yalta—The ancient city of Chersonesus—Our fellow-
passengers—The war in the Caucasus, and its results—The
object of the war: its effects on our Indian possessions—
Reflections on Russian aggression in the East—Eupatoria—A
startling occurrence, and unpleasant results—Novel mode of
supporting a theatre—Arrival at Odessa—First impressions—
The use of a medical board*

Yalta is a presuming sort of little place; but though so
beautifully situated, to judge from the style of architecture
which prevails, the inhabitants do not seem inclined to build in
harmony with the lovely scenery by which they are
surrounded. It possesses, moreover, all the attributes of
Cockneyism, and this is at first a little interesting to the
stranger, as he has an opportunity of comparing the
Cockneyism of Russia with that of his own country; besides
which, there is a sort of civilisation in its very extravagance that
savours of home.

There is one attempt at a bathing-machine, which does not
look as if it had ever been used; at any rate, we thought it an
invasion of the rights of the retired bay, the beauties of which
we could occasionally contemplate while swimming about it.
There are quantities of ponies, whose persevering owners
follow you all over the place with tempting descriptions of
Alupka and Orianda. There are a few officers lounging upon
the quay in the evening; and if the steamer should chance to be
in the bay, the passengers ride about in detachments, staring at
everything, like overland travellers at Cairo. There are great
quantities of fruit-stalls, the contents of which are most
temptingly arranged; but the prices are enormously high, if the
stranger should be unwary enough to attempt to buy any of
them himself. One street of glaring white houses, in which the
principal building is the hotel—a few shops and government

offices, erected along the sea-shore, with a most fantastic church, picturesquely situated on a hill above them—at present complete the town of Yalta. It seems, however, destined soon to become a fashionable watering-place for the inhabitants of Sevastopol and Odessa. Scaffoldings are erected in every direction, and the work of building more glaring white houses goes on apace.

The pretensions of the hotel are quite characteristic of the growing importance of the place. It is not a bad type of Russian hotel generally. Upon arriving, the traveller walks through an archway and up a stair, in hopes of seeing somebody. In this he is for some time disappointed; nor does he gain anything when he at last discovers a slovenly-looking servant, and points indignantly to his baggage below. The answer is extremely polite, expressive of the deepest sympathy on the part of the speaker, who at the same time gently insinuates that he is Prince Galitzen! (There are about three hundred Prince Galitzens in Russia.) Escaping under cover of a profusion of apologies, our traveller opens a number more doors, goes up and down more stairs, and sees another man with a cigar in his mouth. Determined to avoid a similar mistake, he respectfully addresses him in French or German, or, if he can muster enough Russian, in that tongue, and intimates a wish to find the master of the hotel, or some servant. Upon this the gentleman walks off, evidently offended. However, he is soon after heard shouting down the long passages, and turns out to be none other than the landlord himself. Now begins a search for rooms, ending in the occupancy of a small uncarpeted chamber, with a very dirty floor, containing a hard couch, a harder stretcher (dignified with the name of "bed"), a table, and a chair! This accommodation is cheap at 3s. 4d. a night. After some wrangling, a basin and jug are thrown into the bargain, and, by way of a piece of extra luxury, one sheet is spread upon the hard mattress on the stretcher, but this has evidently been a good deal used already. Milk and butter were luxuries quite unknown at the Grand Hotel at Yalta; and eggs were only procurable at an enormous price, while vegetables were unheard—of accompaniments to dinner. There are no means of calling the servant, except by wandering through the passages shouting "Chelaviek." Of course the "chelaviek" is always in a distant part of the establishment when he is wanted; indeed, considering that there is only one, this is not extraordinary.

If he is wise, our traveller will cultivate the acquaintance of Prince Galitzen, who is not the least annoyed at having been mistaken for a servant, but only anxious to maintain the credit of Russian hotels, and the character of his country for civilisation generally. He says that foreigners find the accommodation bad, because they do not travel as he does. With a view of giving his unenlightened English friend the benefit of his experience, he ushers him into the small room occupied by "Madame la Princesse" and five children. The lady, however, is hardly visible amid the piles of bedding with which she is surrounded, and which a number of servants are engaged in unpacking. The cook is rummaging among the sacks of provisions that block up the passage; the children are clustered round their own somovar; and hence it is quite clear that our friend the Prince is independent of everything except a roof; and as the hotel does not leak, he, of course, is perfectly contented with the accommodation it affords.

Those who travel in Russia, and more particularly in the Crimea, must be prepared not only to rough it, but to pay the prices of first-rate hotels. It is almost to be regretted that the very limited amount of civilisation with which the traveller in the Crimea is tormented, should ever have penetrated to this remote corner of Europe. I infinitely preferred to it the quiet hospitality of a Tartar cottage, where we were entertained by an unsophisticated people, and led an Eastern sort of life. The Crimea is in a most unsatisfactory state, just awakening to a sense of its beauty, and consequently of its capacity to prey upon the few strangers who annually visit it. The day will probably come when the Oesembash will be crossed in a summer as often as the Grimsel, and the Tartar village at its foot converted into a second Lauterbrun. Even now steamers run to Odessa two or three times a month, from Taganrog or Redout Kalè in the Caucasus, touching at the various ports of Kertch, Theodosia, and Yalta. It was late one evening that we exchanged our comfortless bedroom for a crowded saloon in one of these; and here, having secured a few square feet of floor as soon as we came on board, we stretched ourselves amid a host of snorers.

Morning found us rounding Cape Chersonesus, the most western point of the Heracleotic Peninsula. Upon these shores, for nearly twelve centuries, the celebrated colony of Cherson flourished, rivalling the Bosphorites who possessed the eastern extremity of Taurida. A strongly fortified wall, extending from Inkerman to Balaclava, the remains of which still exist, protected the inhabitants of this populous promontory from the inroads of the Tauric and other barbarians. The stupendous cape called by the Tartars Ai Bûrûm, or "The Holy Promontory," has been fixed upon by Pallas as the Parthenium of Strabo; and here, therefore, the priestess Iphigenia celebrated her bloody rites at the fane of the demon goddess; while the shipwreck upon these rocks of Orestes, and her escape with him, led to the colonisation of this part of Taurida by the Heracleans.

The monastery of St. George, with its green-domed church, its terraces and gardens, are suspended many hundred feet above the sea, and occupy nearly the same position with the ancient Temple of Diana; while, still farther to the westward, and upon the Peninsula of Phanary, are strewn the ruins of the ancient city of Chersonesus. The whole of this coast has been explored by Pallas, who was guided in his researches by the minute descriptions of Strabo, and who gives a most interesting account of the extensive remains of the new city of Chersonesus, which flourished in the time of the historian. These existed until quite recently in a high state of preservation. Muscovite Vandalism has now, however, demolished the noble gates, together with two forts, and a great portion of the handsome wall by which the city was surrounded; and the blocks of freestone of which they were composed have been degraded into turning arches in the fortress of Sevastopol—conduct which these venerable stones would not have expected at the hands of the Tauri, whose attacks they had once defied.

After the conquest of Taurida by Rome, Cherson continued to flourish pre-eminently under the rule of princes substantially independent. These ultimately, however, sought the protection of the Byzantine emperors, and in 840 Cherson was made the capital of Khazaria, under the Emperor Theophilus, and remained a place of some importance until the conquest of Taurida by the Tartars, when it became incorporated into the empire of Little Tartary.

We touched at Sevastopol, and picked up a cargo of general officers and ministers of state returning from the grand review. Altogether, we had a most miscellaneous assemblage of passengers on board: hypochondriac old gentlemen from the far-famed baths of Pettiagorsk in the Caucasus, with delicate ladies returning from the same waters, and improving their effect by smoking incessantly; officers in Cossack regiments, big with the doings of their corps; German travellers from Circassia, dressed in true Lesghi costume, whose experience there had taught them to be as sceptical as was consistent with politeness of those tales of Russian valour, while they were loud in praises of their foes, and of the country they inhabit, and tell wonderful stories of Schamyl Bey, the indomitable chief, whose residence is the impregnable fortress of Dargo.

It seemed quite the opinion of these impartial spectators of the war in the Caucasus, that the position of Russia in that quarter is every year surrounded with increasing difficulty. The triumphs of the army, which are incessantly sounded in the government papers, generally originate in some disaster, which it is necessary to convert into a victory. According to these veracious records, the Russians have won upon an average about twelve battles a year for the last twenty-two years, in which the number of Circassians slain must far exceed what the total population of the country was at the commencement of the war. It will be necessary soon to discover some miraculous source from which to draw the inexhaustible supply of mountaineers ever ready to repel their attacks, and to ascribe to some mysterious agency their power of resisting the might of Russia. To us, however, who do not believe these reports, and who have been somewhat enlightened by our experience of a Caffre war, this problem requires no such unnatural solution. It is evident that a nation in which all the males have been following war as an occupation for twenty-two years, must be in first-rate fighting condition; while the fact of their having during that period always contended with the same enemy, enables them to form a pretty correct estimate of his prowess as compared with their own,—a comparison which cannot but be favourable to themselves, when we look at the results of the war. Each year of successful resistance inspires these tribes with fresh energy and courage, while it dispirits their invaders. Meantime they are learning the art of war at an enormous expense to Russia, whose efforts to prevent them from obtaining ammunition have driven them to manufacture it themselves.

Hitherto they have been divided by intestine discord, but it was rumoured that Schamyl had at last come to an understanding with some of the other tribes: this was, however, mere report. There can be no doubt that, if a reconciliation could be effected, the organisation of a combined force under the command of the European officers who have long directed the operations of the Circassian army would prove most formidable to Russia. Many of these officers are Poles; while a fellow-passenger who had visited the mines in Siberia assured me that he had himself spoken to two Englishmen who had been taken prisoners while fighting with the mountaineers, and who are now condemned to perpetual labour in chains. Death at the hands of a Cossack would be infinitely preferable to such a fate as this.

If we ask a Russian how it is that the enormous army now serving in the Caucasus does not speedily reduce this tiny province to subjection, we are told that the war might be thus terminated at any moment, but that it is required as a nursery for imperial troops—that it is an institution of the state, so to speak, where raw levies learn their duty, and disaffected soldiers are reduced at once to skeletons and subjection—a sort of military penal settlement absolutely necessary to the well-being of the army. Without staying to consider whether it be true or not that Russia requires a permanent foreign war—a sort of external chronic irritation—to insure the healthy condition of her naval and military forces (which, to say the least of it, will always render her an extremely unpleasant neighbour), I think there can be no doubt that, if it were possible, she would gladly terminate *this* struggle at any rate, since it is said to have absorbed almost the entire revenue of Poland for many years; and, indeed, that such is the case is proved by the frequent overtures for peace which have been made to the Circassian chiefs, who desire nothing better than to be left alone upon their own terms. At the same time, it is evident that the only termination to this war which could be satisfactory to Russia must be the entire subjection of the province, and this she has hitherto been absolutely unable to accomplish.

It is not for the value of this mountainous scrap of territory that Russia desires its annexation; its total revenue would not furnish one-half the amount that is annually expended upon its conquest. Nor is it because she has any right or title to these mountains. It is said, that it is because the Emperor is piqued by a resistance so obstinate and determined, that he sacrifices thousands of his fellow-creatures here annually. We will do him the justice to suppose that he is actuated by no such unworthy motive, while more substantial reasons exist. It is evidently the independent existence here of restless tribes, in the midst of provinces so recently subjected to Russian rule, who possess so many sympathies in common with the conquered people which causes the Russian government uneasiness.

So long as these mountaineers have it in their power to bar the only passages by which Russia obtains access to one portion of her vast dominions, so long must the value of the trans-Caucasian provinces be diminished, and the Emperor frustrated in his cherished project of extending the frontier to the southward; for in case of the dismemberment of the Turkish Empire, until Russia conquers Circassia she is clearly not in a position to annex with equal advantage those provinces which, when that dismemberment takes place, she will doubtless expect to fall to her share. At present, therefore, Circassian independence seems to be a formidable barrier to Russian aggression. But when Russian troops can march with impunity across those mighty passes, and acquire new provinces to the south and eastward—when her frontier is conterminous with that of Persia in a great part of that country which is now Turkish, and when her influence over that state will increase with her frontier—when Persia is no longer able to resist her demands, and Cabul only anxious to aid her designs, the tenure by which Great Britain holds her dominion in India will be materially affected, and it may be thus affected sooner than we anticipate; for surely, during the present crisis of Eastern affairs, these results are not to be deemed altogether speculative. Let it be remembered that Russian aggression is not confined to Turkey in Europe alone—that the Asiatic frontier of the Empire reaches a parallel of latitude two hundred miles to the south of that in which Constantinople is situated—that it is a longer march from the Pruth to Orsova than from the Araxes to the Tigris—that the Muscovite soldiers now stationed on the banks of the former river are more than half-way from Moscow to Peshawur—that the extent of territory which intervenes between Russia and the British provinces in India is not so great as that already acquired from Turkey alone, while the greater portion of it belongs to a power whose fate is indissolubly linked with the tottering fabric of Ottoman independence, now crumbling to pieces under the repeated and vigorous assaults of a most relentless foe. When facts such as these are taken into consideration, the contingency of Russian influence becoming dominant in Persia does not seem very remote, or the extension of the southern frontier of the empire to Herat altogether a chimera; and even then it is not the probability of an invasion that is to be dreaded, but rather the effect upon the northern provinces of India of the proximity of this new and powerful neighbour, whose secret agents would overrun our provinces, foment disaffection, disturb the whole system of government, and worthily accomplish the insidious designs of rulers as unscrupulous as themselves.

A further result of Russian aggression in Eastern Turkey, and one more immediate than those to which I have already alluded, would be the severe blow which our commerce in the Black Sea would inevitably sustain by the annexation of the provinces of Kars and Erzeroum. The enormous trade now carried on by us through Trebisond is all the more jealously regarded by Russia, because the prohibitive system of the empire, and the inferior quality of her own productions, render her incapable of competing with us in securing and maintaining the commerce of the East. Should these provinces be obtained, however, she will again attempt to monopolise that trade which was thrown into our hands by the blind policy that has already closed the route through the trans-Caucasian provinces. These were topics, however, upon which it was almost impossible to touch, in conversing with our fellow-passengers, who were never to be betrayed into giving an opinion upon a political subject by any plot, however insidiously designed to entrap them.

We touched at Eupatoria, an uninteresting town situated upon the low steppe, but considered the most thriving port in the Crimea. It owes its prosperity to the great number of Karaïte Jews resident here. These successful traders compose the greater part of the population, and the handsomest synagogue of which the sect can boast adorns the town.

It is a run of eighteen hours from Eupatoria to Odessa, and

the wind, which freshened to a sharp breeze before evening, produced effects which rendered the crowded saloon anything but a pleasant resting-place. Too well accustomed to such scenes, however, to be affected, my sound slumber was only disturbed once during the night by a confused murmur of earnest voices and some heavy treading near me. The whole seemed so mixed up with a disagreeable dream, that upon awaking in the morning I easily accounted for a vague feeling of discomfort which seemed to oppress me, and was rather surprised upon looking into the faces of those who were awake, and probably had never been asleep, to discover an uneasy expression, denoting feelings somewhat akin to my own; and someone said that, restlessly tossing upon the hard floor of the saloon, he had suddenly stretched out his hand, a few hours before, and started as it came in contact with the cold clammy face of his next neighbour. The low moaning which we could hear through the half-opened door of the ladies' cabin, proceeded from the wife of the unhappy man who had thus suddenly expired without having given a moment's warning to the roomful of people by whom he was surrounded. He was a quiet, retiring person, and few people had spoken to him, though he had been on board three or four days; those who had were evidently proud of the distinction, and gave the result of their observations to knots of nervous inquirers. It is not often that Russians moralise; but one conceited old privy-councillor, who generally confined his conversation to a discussion of his own merits, favoured the company with a few remarks which he considered appropriate, and incidentally mentioned the death of the Duke of Wellington.

Had I ever doubted that the effect produced by a piece of thrilling intelligence depends in a great measure on the circumstances under which it is received, I should cease to do so since that hour on which I first heard that two people were dead, neither of whom I had ever spoken to in my life. In the one case, personal contiguity with the deceased invested the

258

circumstance of his death with a strange and peculiar interest; in the other, how many old associations were revived and recollections called up by the mention of a name so familiar and so deeply venerated—while the tidings seemed all the more startling, since they were uttered by those who could sympathise with none of these feelings.

The news that we were close to Odessa soon changed the current of ideas on board. It was a glorious morning, and people easily succeeded in shaking off their gloom as we entered the noble harbour and anchored beneath the walls of the chief mercantile city in the empire. The young ladies from the baths were gathered in groups upon deck, as they said they found the ladies' cabin and the company of the widow *triste*, and talked gaily in anticipation of the approaching season. The quay, only a few yards distant, was crowded with happy faces, as friends long parted discovered one another. Soon it became apparent that their embraces were to be postponed, and one by one the crowd vanished. The young ladies experienced a violent revulsion of feeling, and really began to wish from their hearts that the poor man had not died, as the cause of our detention dawned upon them. The privy-councillor looked unutterable things, and was evidently determined not to be kept on board by anything so purely unimportant. An aide-de-camp of Prince Woronzoff's said that he and his despatches should land though nobody else did, except the privy-councillor, whose rank, he admitted, rendered it out of the question that he should carry the infection. The other passengers for the most part said that they had expected this all along, but had never thought it worth while to say so. A boat-load of medical officers now raised the excitement to its utmost pitch. They were to report upon the infectious nature of the disease of which our fellow-passenger had died.

I was not in a position at that time, from my ignorance of the true circumstances upon which our destinies depended, to sympathise fully with the alternations of hope and despair which agitated the breasts of my fellow-passengers. Those trembled for our fate who knew that the person who supplied the quarantine with provisions was also the lessee of the Odessa theatre. As this Odessa theatre pays very badly, it is a government regulation that the same man who obtains the lucrative contract for supplying the quarantine shall also rent the theatre. The consequence is, that no opportunity is lost of discovering the infectious nature of the diseases which may exist on board any of the ships in the harbour, while the number of persons thus imprisoned, the long duration of their quarantine, and the exorbitant prices charged, produce more than is sufficient to set off against the losses incurred by a bad season; and so it is evident that in proportion to the increase of sickness in the year is the company at the Odessa theatre improved, and the enjoyment of the Odessa public heightened. Indeed, it was rumoured that in the event of another unusually severe plague at Constantinople, the manager had expressed his intention of engaging Rachel.

Presently a more cheerful report went abroad, and people were delighted to discover that the deceased was brother-in-law to the governor of Odessa. Of course it was out of the question to suppose that the unhappy widow could now be put in quarantine. Such, indeed, turned out to be the case. The victualling officer of that establishment was utterly unable to compete with the overwhelming interest thus brought to bear. The medical board found that the disease was not infectious, according to instructions probably received before leaving the shore; and those who pleased were thus enabled to honour the theatre that very night with their presence, and share directly in that entertainment, to the support of which we had all been so nearly obliged to contribute.

CHAPTER XXIV

Arrival at Odessa—First impressions—European aspect of the town—The internal commerce of the Empire: its influence on foreign markets—The Moscow and Odessa railway— Aristocratic beetroot-growers—The Odessa police-office—How to bribe judiciously—The Isle of Serpents—The Soulina mouth of the Danube—The fair at Ismael—The condition of Bessarabia, as compared with the Danubian principalities

It was with mingled feelings of gratitude and triumph that I found myself climbing the steep hill which leads from the quay into the town of Odessa. I felt thankful that we had escaped three weeks' quarantine; that we had passed through the custom-house without having our luggage examined; that there was a prospect at last of a return to some of the luxuries of civilised life after a somewhat arduous journey. And I felt triumphant, because I could now for the future fearlessly condemn Russian hotels, discuss the merits of Russian shops, and depreciate Muscovite civilisation in general, without being told that I was not in a position to judge of any of these subjects from never having been at Odessa.

Hitherto my life had been rendered miserable by repeated allusions to the "Russian Florence." Some infatuated Odessans on board the steamer impressed upon me for two days and nights that nothing I had seen at Moscow or St. Petersburg could give me even a faint conception of the glories of Odessa, which, according to them, combined in itself the charms of all the capitals in Europe. The statues and the opera were Italian; the boulevards and shops, French; the clubs conducted upon English principles; and the hotels unequalled in Europe—the whole forming attractions which may surpass my most sanguine anticipations.

It struck me as somewhat singular, notwithstanding, to be told, upon asking what means existed of leaving this enchanting spot, that we should find it necessary to buy a carriage and post, as no diligence had as yet been established. Odessa, probably, is the only town in Europe containing upwards of a hundred thousand inhabitants, which cannot boast some public means of conveyance other than a post telèga, which is infinitely more barbarous than a Cape bullock-waggon, and only meant for the conveyance of feld-jägers and despatches.

It was evident that these benighted inhabitants of Odessa praised their city in utter ignorance of the merits of others. It could not seem strange to them that a pair of sheets should be charged a ruble extra in the best hotels, since they seldom or ever made use of them at home; while it was not to be wondered at that jugs and basins should seem superfluities to those who followed the mode of washing adopted on board the Russian steamer, which consisted in each man's trickling a little water into his friend's hands—so little, indeed, that but a very few drops of the precious liquid were spilt. Our exertions to obtain a basin on board evidently caused us to be looked upon as bad travellers, who did not conform to the manners of the country they were in.

The change from the climate, inhabitants, and customs of the East, to those of the bleak North, was very marked on our arrival at Odessa. We were again surrounded by sheepskins, and pierced with a sharp east wind that howled over the desolate steppe. Here were no lofty peaks to shelter us, nor summer sun to warm us; winter seemed fairly to have set in the day we arrived, with the view of chasing us out of Russia. However, we could not go until we had been advertised a certain number of days in the papers, for the benefit of imaginary creditors. Fortunately we had given notice of our intended departure before we arrived, whereby the length of our stay was considerably diminished. Meantime we found plenty to amuse us in the greatest mercantile emporium in Russia.

It must be admitted that Odessa is very cosmopolitan in its character. Almost every country in Europe has its representative here, and the principal streets are filled with an immense variety of costume. Indeed, Odessa has an air of business and activity about it quite foreign to Russian towns generally; and this is doubtless owing to its rapid growth and mixed population. There is a great deal more liberty enjoyed by the inhabitants than by those of any other town in the empire; and I was struck by the unwonted freedom of smoking and conversation which prevailed among those with whom I mixed. The evident effort made to be as little Russian as possible, is a significant comment upon the inconsistency of the inhabitants, who, while they maintain the superior excellence of everything national, seem chiefly desirous of sinking their nationality, and, with that facility of imitation peculiar to the Russian character, seek to assimilate themselves as much as possible to other European nations. It follows therefore, that, apart from the novelty with which this city is invested by its commercial character, in a country affording no encouragement to trade, there is little to interest in its broad glaring streets, where clouds of white dust overwhelm the passengers, and rows of stumpy trees are reduced almost to the same colour as the tall houses behind them.

Odessa has existed to serve a definite purpose, and in that respect its case is altogether an exceptional one: it has been forced on in spite of government, by virtue of being a free port, and of possessing the most saleable commodity in Europe as its principal article of commerce. As its exports exceed the imports by two-thirds, its prosperity cannot be said to have a very firm foundation; indeed, a war with Russia would be fraught with more serious consequences to these provinces than to the country which derives its supply of corn from them. In the one case the ruin would be permanent and irretrievable; in the other, the temporary inconvenience would doubtless be very great, but a new source of supply would surely be found, and one in all probability not liable to such sudden and violent interruptions. However, a consideration of the commercial interests of the Russian empire would never turn the scale with government one way or the other in a question of peace or war.

The mere fact that the great proportion of the trade of Russia is in the hands of foreign merchants, while it tends to render the government indifferent to consequences affecting their prosperity, proves how little worthy the natives themselves are of any other treatment than that which they now experience. But Russia alone is not injured by those influences of despotic government and an apathetic population, which, reacting upon each other, are fatal to the commerce of the empire. Unfortunately for the rest of Europe, they conspire to raise the price of Russian productions to an inconceivable degree; nor is it difficult to trace the origin of such a result.

The only merchants who are able to engage directly in foreign commerce are those belonging to the first or second guilds—the latter only to a limited extent. The duty for a license which confers this advantage is so high, and the capital required by government, before it can be obtained, is so great, that comparatively few are enabled to embark in the extensive transactions involved by foreign trade. So effectually is this system calculated to prevent any addition to the Russian mercantile community, that notwithstanding the Black Sea trade, so extensive and so recently called into existence, there are only four more merchants in the first guild now than there were fifteen years ago; while, on the other hand, the number of peasants holding certificates enabling them to trade *within* the empire, is increased by one-third during the same time,—thus showing that the commercial relations of the interior have improved by virtue of that foreign trade, which has not benefited the merchants of a higher order. At the same time, it is evident that it is highly prejudicial to the true interests of commerce that it should be so largely exercised by an ignorant and half-civilised peasantry, who are only allowed certificates by the year, and are still in the condition of serfs. The palpable effect of such a state of things must be a total absence of that credit which is a primary condition to the mercantile prosperity of a country; and the merchants on the coast are to a great extent at the mercy of these petty traders, who scruple at no species of dishonest practice which may insure them quick returns. It is this class who frequent the numerous large fairs throughout the country, and by means of them exercise an indirect influence upon the foreign markets; and when, therefore, we find that the supplemental value with which articles are burdened, before they reach the port of export, is sixty per cent upon the productions of the soil, and twenty-five per cent on those of industry, no other result can be expected in a country where the want of capital, the want of enterprise, the want of liberty, the want of roads, and the want of honesty, combine to produce it.

Although there is no macadamized road leading in any one direction out of Odessa, yet even the magnificent rivers which afford such evident means of communication with the interior are not taken advantage of. The Pruth, the Dnieper, the Dniester, and the Bug, are all either navigable or might easily be made so. At present little else but wood-rafts float down their broad waters. No private company has enterprise, or rather hardihood enough, to attempt an undertaking which government might at any moment ruin; and even now, almost all speculations in Russia are carried on by rash foreigners, who have not lived long enough in the country to know better. I think, therefore, it will be some time before a railway is completed to Moscow, though government now offers a guarantee of four per cent. It will be a singular anomaly if a railway should connect Moscow and Odessa in the absence of any macadamized road between the two; and one none the less striking, because only to be found elsewhere in America.

Private speculations, however, if undertaken by men of rank, are occasionally protected at the expense of the whole community. Thus, lately, in the neighbourhood of Odessa, the cultivation of beetroot, and extraction of sugar from it, was carried on to a considerable extent by the large landed proprietors of the adjoining provinces. Notwithstanding most praiseworthy exertions, these aristocratic beetroot-growers were totally unable to make their speculation remunerative, and many of them must have been ruined had not the legislature stepped in and prohibited the sale of any other sugar. The consequence is, that the inhabitants are obliged to buy sugar at a hundred per cent higher than the price at which our colonial sugar could be imported into the country. It is some satisfaction to know that, notwithstanding this iniquitous regulation, combined with the system of forced labour, the beetroot-growers are unable to cultivate with profit.

And yet these very nobles are none the less objects of commiseration. If, instead of attempting to protect their speculation, government would take off some of the heavy taxes under which they groan, far more lasting benefit would be conferred on them. The tax levied on the nobility, for instance, by means of passports, would be looked upon as unendurable in any other country. In the first place, it is with the greatest difficulty that a permission to travel, or leave of absence for two years, is obtained by a Russian, however high his rank; and then it is only granted upon payment of a sum amounting to eighty pounds a-head for each member of the family.

Fortunately for strangers, the government does not make a similar demand upon them. Still it costs travellers no little trouble and annoyance to go through the formalities necessary to enable them to quit the empire. The ordeal is more severe here than in any other country in Europe; while the corruption and insolence of the *employés* do not facilitate the working of a system sufficiently intricate in itself. These clerks are, by virtue of their office, nobles of the fourteenth class, and, as such, think themselves entitled to treat all foreigners as serfs.

A police-office experience at Odessa affords the traveller a pretty correct notion of what he will have to encounter at all the large towns throughout the empire. At the top of a dingy flight of stairs is an antechamber, containing a crowd of bareheaded men and women waiting in the most suppliant manner at a sort of barrier, where two soldiers are placed to prevent indiscriminate intrusion. If the traveller be an Englishman, his resolute appearance daunts these two cerberi, and he passes into an extremely dirty room, where a number of worn-out, ragged-looking men are scribbling in a dejected manner, regardless alike of him or his passport. At last he follows the direction of the point of a pen, and finds himself in a similar room, where the coats of the writers look a little less threadbare; and here a man seizes the document, and looks through a pile of portfolios, among which he chooses one, and begins leisurely reading. Our traveller stands patiently waiting the result, which is probably the passing on of the passport to the next writer, who reads it through in rather an interested manner, and hands it back. Meantime the original man has found something in the portfolio, which seems to have some reference to the passport, for he inscribes something thereon, and, giving it to its owner, directs him to another man, who, upon receiving it, makes the government charge, puts it on one side, as if he never meant to look at it again, and goes on attending to numerous other applicants, regardless of the entreaties of his victim, who at last bethinks him of trying the effect of a bribe. This the nobleman complacently pockets, and tells him to come back in three hours. If time is valuable, however, on doubling his bribe the traveller is rejoiced with the sound of "sichass," which, if he has just come to Russia, he will have learnt means literally *immediately*; but if he has remained there any time, he will have discovered that it has practically the opposite signification.

Some time having elapsed, and the same routine having been gone through with three or four more rusty-looking members of the aristocracy, who confer continually with one another, as if his were a most exceptional case, the traveller, in despair, finally refuses to bestow another bribe, and, relinquishing his passport, determines to complain to the governor. This functionary, notwithstanding the fact of his having amassed considerable wealth by these very means, displays much righteous indignation, and orders an immediate restitution of the passport to the peppery Englishman, who has thus succeeded in scraping through one office in an incredibly short time, and has probably three more in prospect. It thus happened that we were fully occupied during our three days' stay in Odessa with trying to get away from it; while no doubt the kind exertions in our behalf of the British consul, Mr. Yeames, much facilitated our departure.

We had still a voyage in a Russian steamer before us, the next most terrible prospect to a residence in a Russian hotel, as it is always impossible to predicate the length of the voyage. The run to Galatz is usually performed in twenty-four hours; in that case we expected to find ourselves in the Danube by daylight. At seven o'clock, however, on emerging from an extremely unpleasant cabin, I found that we had cast anchor off the Isle of Serpents, exposed to the violence of an unmerciful sea, on which we tossed and rolled in a way which laid up nearly all the passengers and some of the cabin servants. We were thirty miles from the mouth of the river, and were destined to look at the barren rock before us until the sea should calm or the wind change. Nobody seemed to have heard of the possibility of such an occurrence, which, indeed, could only have happened under the grossest mismanagement. It seems that, during the prevalence of a west wind, there are only nine feet of water on the bar of the Soulina branch of the Danube. We drew nine and a half, and so were doomed to lie at anchor thirty miles off, until there should be water enough to float us over.

For twenty-four hours, our only consolation consisted in expressing our opinions upon the arrangements which could incur such a misadventure, when the establishment of a smaller steamer on the line would have obviated it at once. The delay of one day which had thus been caused, was sufficient to run out the supply of provisions; and had the same wind lasted as much longer, we should have returned to Odessa, to satisfy our hunger, absolutely unable to perform our voyaye of twenty-four hours.

There is nothing interesting in the first view of the Danube, on the marshy shores of which is situated the unhappy-looking town of Soulina—a veritable American Eden. But the shipping is abundant, and the costume of the crews varied. Though the river is so deep as to render it impossible for us to find a sandbank, we manage cleverly to put one paddle-wheel high and dry on the right shore, which gives us time to look over a vast expanse of bulrushes, and to admire the original manner in which unfortunate crews are obliged to tow up their barks in default of tug-boats, and we sympathise with the rows of Englishmen we see now attached to the tow-rope, after having been always accustomed to have such work done for them.

There was a grand fair going on at the large Bessarabian town of Ismael when we arrived, the third we had witnessed in Russia, and frequented by a population almost equally varied and characteristic with that attending the others. Here quaint covered passages, extemporaneously got up, were crowded with Moldavians, Cossacks, Germans, Bulgarians, Gypsies, Greeks, and Armenians. An infinite quantity of nondescript merchandise loaded the counters, and uncouth garments fluttered overhead. Grapes were piled in heaps at the corners of the streets; for Bessarabia is a great vine-growing province, and Swiss vine-dressers have emigrated here in numbers. The town of Ismael is mean and straggling, and contains about forty thousand inhabitants; but it boasts a respectable fortress, numerously garrisoned,—while some gun-boats are anchored under its walls.

The principal port of a very fertile province, Ismael carries on a considerable trade; but the resources of Bessarabia are but feebly developed, and it is in a far more depressed condition than the neighbouring districts. The Russian political economist contends that this is owing entirely to the abrupt emancipation of all the serfs, and regards the result as a triumphant vindication of the system of serfdom. But a very slight consideration of the circumstances under which this wholesale liberation took place is sufficient to show the unsound nature of the argument, and to prove that a measure, though indisputably beneficial in itself, must ever be greatly influenced in its practical effects by the motives which prompt it, and may be so carried out as to produce widely differing results. And where a measure such as this has originated, not in a desire on the part of the government to give freedom to the agricultural population, but to ruin their owners, the Moldavian Boyars, or old landed aristocracy, its wholesome tendency must be to some extent neutralised; while the mal-administration of the local government, the intrigues and chicanery of the Russian *employés*, and the introduction of the prohibitive system of the empire into a country previously enjoying a liberal commercial policy, form a combination of evil influences more than sufficient to account for the unhappy state of this poverty-stricken province.

It is interesting to observe the present condition of Bessarabia, as affording us some idea of the probable result of the annexation of the Danubian principalities by Russia, should that event ever take place. We have only now to look at the prosperous state of those provinces, as compared with Bessarabia, to perceive how disastrous must be the effects of such an occurrence.

It is not to be wondered at that the inhabitants of Moldavia and Wallachia dread the day when the blighting influence of Russian administration will be extended along the shores of the Danube as far as the Austrian frontier; for in the past history of Bessarabia they foresee their own unhappy future. Should the Emperor grant them a constitution, they can compare it with that which Alexander granted to the Boyars of Bessarabia, and need be under no uncertainty as to the extent of its duration. Should he accord them *special privileges*, they will at once be able to estimate them at their true value, to anticipate their fatal effects, and to calculate exactly how long it will be before protection in trade shall reduce them to a state of Bessarabian depression.

CHAPTER XXV

Trade of Moldavia—Jealousy of Russia: her policy with
reference to the mouths of the Danube: its effects upon
England—Proposed canal from Rassova to Kustendji—
Galatz—The "Boreas"—Voyage up the Danube—Execrable
accommodation—Herr Sippel distinguishes himself—
We arrive at Orsova, and are put under arrest—
Triumphant release—The "Livre Noir"

From Ismael we retraced our steps up the Kilia branch of the
Danube, and re-entered the main stream at the picturesque
Turkish town of Tultcha. Solitary Cossack guard-houses occur
every three versts, almost hidden among the reeds by which
they are surrounded. Their sickly-looking occupants crawl out
to gaze at the steamer as she passes; and the dejected sentry is
evidently glad of the opportunity thus afforded of presenting
arms.

Early in the morning the shallow pools upon the river banks
are coated with ice. A week ago we were roasting at Yalta, with
the thermometer at 80° in the shade. At last we reached Galatz.
I was glad to exchange the ragged Cossack for the slouching
Moldavian soldier, who was here perambulating the quay, and
to find that we had passed from the imperial dominions into
those of a quasi-independent prince, where I might light a
cigar in public with impunity—where there was no examination either of luggage or passports—where, in fact,
everything seemed conducted upon most liberal principles.

But though, while in Moldavia, the traveller is released from
those annoyances which he anticipates as inevitable, when he
remembers that he is surrounded by Russia, Austria, and
Turkey, the government does not act with the same liberality
towards its own subjects. At present, sufficient facility is not
afforded for the exercise of that trade to which Moldavia owes
its prosperity, and which should render it one of the richest, as
it is one of the most fertile, countries in Europe.

Intersected by noble rivers, it only requires the properly directed skill of the engineer to render them navigable; blessed with a most magnificent soil, it only awaits the operations of some enterprising capitalist to yield its abundance, and, in addition to the finest wheat and Indian corn, produce flax and other crops, which have not as yet been even tried.

Again, it appears self-evident that every advantage should be taken of the limited frontage which this country possesses upon the mighty stream by means of which its trade finds vent; and while the only port of which it can boast is made the emporium of all the produce of the interior, it should act in a like capacity for the grain of the neighbouring provinces. With an almost incredible blindness, the importation of all foreign corn, even for the purpose of transhipment, is prohibited at Galatz; and, in consequence of this, Ibraila, a town sixteen miles farther up the river, is increasing with fourfold rapidity, representing a country which extends for more than three hundred miles along the margin of the river; and the prosperity of Galatz, instead of arising in a great degree from the contiguity of its rich neighbour, is dependent entirely upon the small country at its rear, which, owing to the difficulty of inland transport, and the scarcity of capital and labour, is not in a condition to profit by the richness of the soil.

Just now the most increasing export of the Danubian principalities is Indian corn. An almost entirely new trade has recently sprung up in this article, Ireland having hitherto been the principal consumer. It is evident that these provinces are annually becoming more formidable as rivals to the south of Russia. Wheat exported from the Danube ranks higher, and obtains better prices, in the London market than Polish Odessa; while there can be no doubt that, if the encouragement hitherto afforded by foreign markets to these provinces be continued, Moldavia, Wallachia, and Roumelia will soon equally divide with Russia the corn trade of the Black Sea.

A full conviction of the ruinous consequences of such a result to the southern shores of the empire has no doubt operated powerfully in conducing towards the present unjustifiable occupation of the principalities; and even should the designs of permanent annexation now entertained be frustrated, and an evacuation of these provinces ultimately prove to be inevitable, Russia will be compensated for the inconvenience of the movement by the soothing consciousness that she has retarded for many years the commercial prosperity of her most dreaded rivals.

At present, not the slightest effort is made to improve the navigation of the Danube. Prior to the treaty of Adrianople the depth of water upon the bar at the mouth of the river was about sixteen feet. There is little more than nine feet of water there now. The bar is formed principally of alluvial deposit, and not of sand washed up by the sea, consequently nothing could be effected more easily than its removal. As, however, it was not stipulated in the treaty of Adrianople upon whom this duty was to devolve, in the year 1840 Austria entered into a convention with Russia, whereby it was agreed that a tax should be levied by this latter power upon all ships entering the river at Soulina; and, in consideration of this privilege, Russia became bound to keep the mouth of the river free from all such impediments as now exist. Since that period, the tax, which has fallen very heavily upon British ships, has been duly levied; while not only has the obligation arising out of it been totally neglected, but it has ever been the end and aim of Russia to allow this channel-which she is not allowed to fortify-to fill up, with a view of forcing the river and the trade through the northern or Kilia branch. This branch was formerly the deepest, and therefore that preferred by ships. In the hands of the Russians it silted up, and the waters thus turned into the Soulina branch, which became the more available. If the Soulina should silt up, it is probable that the Kilia branch would again be opened, and the fortress of Ismael would command the trade of the Danube.

So long as the Soulina mouth was in the possession of Turkey, every vessel leaving the river was compelled to drag a large rake behind her. This was sufficient to stir up the mud, which was thus carried away by the mere force of the current. Since then, vessels have offered to continue this practice, but have been positively prohibited from so doing. Indeed, it is absurd to suppose that Russia will take any steps tending to increase the trade of rival countries, by improving the navigation of the river on which their prosperity depends, simply because she is bound by treaty to do so. The consequence is, that the difficulty of entering the Danube is far greater than it used formerly to be, and numbers of English ships are lost upon the bar every year. But Russia is not satisfied with allowing nature to monopolise the work of destroying the Danubian trade; she has raised an artificial barrier, which is even more ruinous to commerce than that at the mouth of the river. The stringent quarantine regulations which have been imposed by her, render it impossible for the produce of the Turkish provinces to find an outlet in this direction, which is consequently forced, at a needless expense, to Varna and other ports on the Black Sea.

Galatz and Ibraila do not suffer only from the neglect and jealousy of Russia: Austria possesses an entire control over the steam navigation of the river; and so long as the Danube Steam Navigation Company continues to hold the monopoly it at present exercises, so long will an insurmountable obstacle exist to the increasing prosperity of these provinces, which are thus victimised by their unfortunate position between powers so opposed to a liberal and enlightened commercial system.

But a consideration of the dismal prospect in store for these corn-growing districts, renders it also evident that those countries which are in any degree dependent upon them for grain, are no less affected by the injurious influences at present exercised upon Danubian navigation. If England is ever to be independent of Russia for her annual supply of corn, it is chiefly from the western shores of the Black Sea that she must look to obtaining sufficient to satisfy the ever-increasing demand. There can be no doubt that, if the resources of these provinces were allowed a free development, they would be found adequate to meet that demand; but if the mouths of the Danube are to be neglected or blocked up by one power, and the steam navigation monopolised by another, the corn-consuming and corn-producing countries are equally at the mercy of those who, from whatever motive, may be desirous of impeding the important trade at present existing.

It may yet prove necessary, for the interests of Europe, that a canal should be cut from Rassova on the Danube to Kustendji on the Black Sea—a work of great comparative facility, and one which, if properly carried out, would serve a double purpose in removing the line of traffic to a distance from any portion of the Russian frontier; while a circuit of more than two hundred miles, and a great deal of intricate navigation, would be saved by so simple a proceeding. The proposed outlet, which does not exceed forty miles in length, passes chiefly through a highly fertile country.

The day does not seem far distant when new treaties must be entered into with reference to this portion of Europe; and it is to be hoped that then the defects in the treaty of Adrianople will be remedied, and the free and unimpeded navigation of one of the finest rivers in Europe secured to the world.

Galatz is picturesquely situated upon the side of a steep hill rising abruptly from the river's edge. It contains a mixed population, amounting to about thirty thousand inhabitants. There is one establishment here on which the English traveller looks with some interest, when he discovers that it is the preserved-meat manufactory which obtained for Mr. Goldner so unenviable a notoriety, and which is again being carried on under the superintendence of two Englishmen. There is probably no place in Europe where provisions are cheaper, or the prices paid for labour higher. A silver ruble a day may frequently be earned by a common porter; while, after selling the hides and tallow, the meat which was preserved for the benefit of the Admiralty did not cost Mr. Goldner more than a halfpenny a pound.

I should not have been so anxious for the arrival of the steamer by which we were destined to ascend the Danube, had I foreseen the discomforts in store for me. In happy ignorance of this, after remaining two days at Galatz, I hailed with delight the intelligence that the steamer had arrived from Vienna, and was already preparing for a return voyage. Meantime, passengers had been accumulating from various directions, and we formed a goodly company on board the "Boreas." The representatives of eleven different nations jostled one another in her crowded saloon, and a Babel of languages resounded throughout the ship from morning till night: the pre-ponderating tongues I discovered to be Greek, Moldavian, Italian, German, French, Russian, and Arabic.

Life on board the Boreas was as different from life on board the Samson as the rivers traversed were dissimilar. On the Volga we reigned supreme, with an affable captain to dine with, and a good-natured old woman to take care of us. On the Danube we were lost amid a crowd of others, all treated alike contemptuously by the Austrian officer in command, and the Austrian stewards who did us the honour to wait at table.

There is not much to interest on the Danube below the "Iron Gate." As usual, one side monopolises all the beauty; and the picturesque Turkish towns, with their mosques perched upon the steep hillsides, or peeping out from amid woods and vineyards, cause those passengers, who are susceptible of them, passing emotions.

Few, however, find time or inclination to trouble themselves with the beauties of the river. The system upon which the Danubian Steam Navigation Company's boats are managed, affords ample occupation of another description to those who are unfortunate enough to travel by them. Throughout the voyage there is one continued selfish scramble, and each succeeding day and night is enlivened by the varied and exciting scenes which occur amongst ourselves.

At the Wallachian towns at which we touch, we receive numerous additions to our party, and soon the small triangular cabin, miscalled a saloon, is inconveniently crowded. There are only two or three private cabins to be procured, which are pounced upon at an enormous price, and the weather if far too cold to admit of sleeping on deck. The consequence is, that, as night draws on, preparations for turning in are apparent. Those who wish to secure a few feet of *infested* sofa, wisely take possession about six o'clock. Those who prefer a cigar in the calm moonlight on deck may esteem themselves fortunate if, upon going below, they can find an unoccupied space on the floor.

For about two hours the greatest confusion prevails. Everybody is either fighting for his bed, or making it, or snoring in it, such as it is. Some people do not think it necessary to undress at all; others go to an opposite extreme, and expose themselves to a needless risk of catching cold.

When, having enjoyed the fresh evening air as long as possible, I quit the deck about midnight, I seem to be entering a badly-managed hospital rather than the saloon of a steam-ship. I know my bed is secured to me, because three of us have entered into partnership to watch over one another's interest, and we mount guard alternately. It is not so, however, with my Prussian friend Sippel, a good-natured farmer, whose acquaintance I had first made at Odessa, where he was being victimised in the same police-office with myself,—he now makes a point of always offering me his bed, for he is the most yielding and amiable of men. Tonight, however, he finds the corner, to which he supposed he had obtained a prescriptive right, occupied by a burly Austrian, with whom all entreaties and remonstrances seem unavailing. Suddenly we observe our friend stoop down, as if to whisper something into the ear of the usurper; a moment more, and he has seized him with a gripe that renders resistance hopeless, and has flung him violently across the cabin. We were wondering at the want of spirit manifested by the large mustached man who had thus been summarily ejected, and were applauding Sippel's energetic behaviour somewhat loudly, when, as if by magic, appear two gendarmes with fixed bayonets by the side of the couch he had so nobly won. A most impressive silence is caused by this apparition, broken only by the snores of those who wish it to be supposed that they have never been awake. Everybody is awe-struck but Sippel, who, stretched upon his back, is evidently determined to remain there in spite of the whole Austrian army. However, upon giving up his passport, he is allowed quiet possession, and the gendarmes vanish as suddenly as they had appeared. Though we had been some days on board, we never suspected the existence of these gentry, whose presence amongst an unsuspecting set of travellers was somewhat significant, and people began to speak in suppressed whispers and look mysterious. I was advised to cut Sippel forthwith, but did not follow this well-meant counsel, though many of the other passengers did.

If it was difficult to sleep on board the Boreas, it was still more difficult to wash. The only basin supplied by the company was required at nine o'clock A.M. by the stewards, so that the crockery might be washed in it immediately after the passengers. It was therefore necessary for some of the party to begin their ablutions before daylight—as we had scarcely done fighting for the basin when we began to fight for places at the breakfast-table; and then the food was so atrocious, that at last, in despair, we determined to commit the audacious proceeding of entering a complaint in the book. Such a piece of hardihood had never been perpetrated before on board the Boreas; but as everybody signed the important document except one man, people flattered themselves that there was safety in a multitude. This one exception was a gay young gentleman on his way to Pesth, where he was to be imprisoned for five years, according to his own account, for having talked politics in a café at Bucharest. He was very proud of his notoriety, and gambled incessantly. He was suspected of being a spy; but if he acted in that capacity, his object probably was merely to curry favour with those whom he wished to propitiate.

We had just passed through a severe examination at the Orsova custom-house, which lasted for about three hours, when, a little after midnight, I passed along the quay to return to the steamer in company with a Hungarian noble who had joined us first in the Crimea. He was revisiting his native land after an absence of five years. During this period a terrible change had come over the condition of his unfortunate countrymen; but this was a topic he carefully avoided discussing; and whatever may have been his feelings upon a subject in which he was so deeply interested, he had seen too much of the world to give vent to them. A few moment ago I fancied, as he indignantly twisted up his long-pointed mustache, that his Magyar blood was rising while he watched the custom-house officials overhaul his wardrobe. And now that the ordeal was over, and we were strolling silently along in the calm still moonlight, I strove to analyse his feelings by imagining what my own would be under similar circumstances, and had just arrived at the conclusion that it was impossible for me to realise sentiments so foreign to the nature of an Englishman, when a remark he made induced me to suppose that his thoughts were running in the same direction. Perhaps it was fancy: but the words had scarcely escaped his lips when we were surrounded by gendarmes; and so sudden and appropriate was their appearance that, as far as my thoughts were concerned, it might have been the effect of clairvoyance. My friend was no less startled than myself at this unexpected reception to his fatherland, and was at first disposed to enter into indignant remonstrance. This was evidently useless, as those by whom he was arrested professed ignorance of his crime, further than that he was the friend of two Englishmen whom they also had orders to arrest. Upon this he was instantly marched off, and I was ordered to return to the steamer and remain there "until called for." As the police were in possession of our passports, there was nowhere else to go to, and I accordingly carried the agreeable intelligence to my travelling companion and the other passengers, and was in some degree consoled by the panic it created among some of the latter.

People did not seem inclined to sleep much that night as we lay alongside the quay, but envied sundry new arrivals, who came on board and took possession of sofas without opposition, their sound slumbers.

A little before daybreak the Count returned in great triumph. The governor, at whose order he had been arrested, proved to be an old friend and companion-in-arms, who had arrested him upon information, as we inferred, received from the captain and purser. These worthies had taken advantage of our detention at the custom-house to report to the governor, in their capacity of spies, certain political conversations alleged to have been overheard as passing between the Count and ourselves. These conversations the Count assured his Excellency were purely imaginary; and our friend went on to supply a reason for this piece of malignity, so very probable, that the governor was constrained to believe him. The three names which headed the celebrated manifesto of our grievances on board were, singularly enough, identical with those of the so-called politicians. Our complaints had been so well founded, and our language so decided to those in authority on board, that they attempted thus to revenge themselves, and would no doubt have succeeded in causing us to be arrested had not this lucky friendship subsisted.

A slight revulsion of feeling, however, was created when it was whispered, upon undoubted authority, that the whole ship-load of passengers were inscribed in the "Livre noir" as suspected persons; that, in fact, we were looked upon as a most factious and rebellious crew, maintaining opinions calculated to subvert the empire, because we objected to remaining on board a government steamer for more than a week without washing.

CHAPTER XXVI

Orsova: its political associations—Effects of Russian aggression in the West upon Great Britain, as compared with other European countries—The traditionary policy of the Empire successful, and Russia mistress of the Dardanelles—Results of a dominant influence over Turkey upon the rest of Europe

The scenery at Orsova is very fine. Here the Danube seems to have gathered up its mighty forces, and burst a passage through the rocky barrier which composes the Iron Gate. Sweeping past the walls of the little town, the river expands into a noble reach; and from the eddying waters rise the quaint turreted battlements of an island fortress, where tapering minarets tell of a mosque embowered amid the poplars and cypresses which adorn it. On either side lofty cliffs frown upon the picturesque old castle. An inconsiderable brook flows into the Danube a little below the island; and beneath the range in which it takes its rise, nestle the white houses of Orsova. But though forming part of the finest river-scenery in Europe, the intrinsic merits of the landscape do not now claim our attention, but rather the associations connected with it, and which are absorbing to the whole civilised world.

The island fortress once contained a Turkish garrison. The cliffs on the south are the highlands of Servia; the little stream opposite is the Bagna, which separates Wallachia from Austria; and the mountain range from which it issues is *the present limit of Russian aggression*.

The island may soon prove a stepping-stone for her troops to invade a province which they have never yet occupied; and the prospect which Muscovite soldiers now obtain from those mountain-tops may serve as a stimulus, such as they already experienced when, surmounting the steep passes of the Caucasus, they first gazed on the sunny countries lying stretched at their feet.

Only sixty years ago the most westerly point of the Russian

empire was still two hundred miles from the Austrian frontier; at present the Russian and Austrian frontiers are conterminous for a distance of five hundred miles; and if Russia be allowed to complete her long-cherished designs upon the Danubian principalities, that extent will be doubled, and for a distance of one thousand miles, or more than one-third of its entire circumference, will Russia clasp in one giant embrace an empire of magnitude scarcely equal to that enormous territory of Poland which the last half-century has seen absorbed within her vast dominions. Hitherto Russia has possessed only the swampy delta of the Danube, and her frontier is conterminous with that of Turkey in Europe for about eighty miles; but, if the contemplated annexation takes place, it will extend along the shores of that river for nearly five hundred miles to this little town of Orsova; and her acquisitions from Turkey since the treaty of Kainardji, in 1774, will comprise a greater extent of territory than all that remains in Europe of the ill-fated empire from which they have been successively wrested.

These are facts which a mere glance at the map will confirm. They are the apparent and undoubted results of the fulfilment of those designs which are now openly avowed by Russia—which have been entertained in the deliberate prosecution of a policy which, through a long course of years, has never been changed, for it has been invariably successful—but which, though scarce heeded in its earlier stages, has now assumed a character calculated to fill all Europe with dismay.

In the violence of that universal agitation which the present aspect of the Eastern question has excited, the entire Continent seems to be united in impressing upon Great Britain the fact, that the interests which she has at stake are more vitally concerned than those of any other nation; and the English public, as if glorying in the unenviable distinction, at once appropriate the position thus anxiously conceded. Having agreed, however, to monopolise the lion's share of the evil consequences which must result from Russian aggression, their unanimity ceases; and while the Peace party, on the one hand, indignantly assert that the "domestic" interests involving the commercial prosperity of Great Britain are paramount to all others, the War party, on the other hand, insist no less earnestly that a peace, enjoyed at the expense of Turkish independence, will be attended with consequences infinitely more disastrous to ourselves than to our Continental neighbours. The importance of this question to England is not to be disputed; but to contend that, because she is the only nation in Europe possessing an Indian Empire and an extensive Black Sea trade, therefore she is the only power interested in maintaining the integrity of the Ottoman power, is almost as absurd as to say that, because she possesses the largest mercantile marine in the world, therefore she need not stir in the matter at all, but may calmly contemplate a struggle by which her commercial operations will be seriously retarded.

It must ever be most injurious to our own country to exaggerate her stake in the eyes of Europe, and, by giving an undue prominence to those interests of hers which will be the most deeply affected by the solution of the Eastern problem, to cause the task of solving it to devolve chiefly upon her. A very cursory examination of the facts will, I think, tend to show how materially other nations are affected by a question so essentially European.

The history of Europe for the last century testifies, that upon six previous occasions has Turkey been despoiled by Russia of as many separate portions of her dominions; and we have only to examine a little more narrowly the system which Russia has pursued in her encroachments, not only upon Turkey, but upon Persia, to discover that her present designs are dictated by the same policy which has ever guided her cabinet; to perceive, in fact, that it is not by actual conquest only that Russia may subvert the independence of nations, and convert their resources to her own use, but that she seeks rather to govern them through their natural rulers, till the time shall have arrived for annexing them to her dominions; and by pressing her influence upon their weakness until it becomes paramount, succeed in establishing an *imperium in imperio*.

It is not now a question of the conquest of Turkey physically;—*that* is not yet contemplated. It is not necessary for Russian troops to garrison Constantinople, in order to secure the passage of the Dardanelles to a Russian fleet; and the right of way through the Bosphorus will be held by a tenure perfectly in accordance with the designs of the Czar, so soon as the Sultan officiates as his janitor. The artfully-contrived plan by which he hoped to effect this darling project has just been developed, and Europe is now called upon to check, before it be too late, the last of a series of encroachments which have been surely, but fatally, sapping the foundations of Ottoman independence: for the long-cherished schemes of Russia are almost realised; her traditionary policy may again be crowned with success, and a dominant influence obtained over Turkey by means of a succession of petty robberies, none of which has been of sufficient importance to rouse Europe to a sense of its insecurity, or to call forth the indignation of a Continent upon this power, so inexhaustible in its intrigues, so insatiable in its demands, so unscrupulous in its designs, and so indefatigable in their execution.

Let Russia once become mistress of the Dardanelles, and the advantages of her position are incalculable. The means of internal communication throughout the empire would be improved, and its vast and military naval resources concentrated upon Constantinople with a rapidity which cannot now be conceived, when the same inducement does not exist for facilitating the conveyance of the material of the army to any given point. The noble rivers flowing into the Black Sea, by which the empire is intersected, would now become available, and Russia, secure behind a barricade where the application of engineering skill has improved natural advantages such as do not exist elsewhere in the world, would maintain within this impregnable position such a force as would insure to her the command of the Mediterranean, and invest her with the supreme control of the destinies of Europe.

Who, then, will pretend that England alone is vitally affected by Russian aggression?

I have already alluded to the position of Austria in the event of the annexation of the Danubian principalities. It is easy to see how she would be affected by the next step of Muscovite progress in the West. If the resources of Turkey in Europe were available to Russia, the Austrian empire, in a military point of view, would become indefensible; and, composed of so many heterogeneous and even hostile nationalities, could exist only as a dependency of Russia. And if, therefore, the spirit of freedom were to kindle afresh in Austria or Italy, Russia could turn the scale in favour of despotism, as she has already done, and quench for ever any spark of liberty still smouldering in those unhappy countries. It were easy for Spain to call in to the support of oppression a similar force.

The next revolution in France would see Italy occupied by Russian troops, reinforcing those of dependent Austria—would see Sardinia crushed, and the Russians again driving the French eagle over the Alps. In every civil commotion that might occur, the shores of the Mediterranean would be as open to invasion as the banks of the Rhine, and Algeria would be lost. The mere knowledge that the whole military and naval power of Russia, Turkey, and Austria could be brought to bear in one united mass upon any point to which the will of one man might direct it, would change the whole relations of parties in France and in every other country, and would give an inevitable preponderance to that party whose cause he should espouse. Prussia and the minor states of Germany could then offer no effectual resistance, either to the arms or the influence of the Colossus; and if the revolutions of the wheel of fortune—the lottery of political changes—should place a creature of Russia on the throne of France, England alone, of all the nations of Europe, could hope to maintain her independence. We have already seen one man exercise a dominant influence over the whole continent of Europe, whose birth and original status in society gave no warrant for anticipating so marvellous a destiny. Should a similar power again be vested in one man, it will be under circumstances less extraordinary, but scarcely less appalling; for the thrones of continental Europe would be occupied by tyrants dependent on the omnipotent will of one who would have at his disposal an immense army, and a perfect facility for conveying it to any country where freedom still struggled for existence. And when this principle is at stake, it is not for England to remain a passive spectator while justice is trampled on, and liberty is crushed so that it may never rise again, because she cannot afford to see consols at 90. May it be in defence of a noble cause that she now takes up arms, if a peaceful solution of the difficulty should prove impossible! And then if she magnify the interest at stake, and appropriate it to herself, it will be because this country alone has the love of freedom at heart, since she alone has experienced its blessed influences.

CHAPTER XXVII

Travellers' privileges—Last impressions—Policy of Russia in the present question—Motives which influence the Czar—The religious character of the war—Disaffection in Bessarabia: in the country of the Don Cossacks: in the Crimea: in the Caucasus—Consequences of a blockade of the shores of the Black Sea—Importance of these considerations

In the course of a disagreeable and somewhat tedious voyage up the Danube, if there is but slender opportunity afforded of observing the social habits or political feelings of the inhabitants who dwell upon its banks, there is at least abundant leisure for reflection; and if the traveller has been exploring some of the bypaths of the East, he will feel, as he journeys along the greatest of European highways, that his physical labours are at an end. He will then be able to indulge, for the first time, in all the delights of retrospection, and reap that reward to which the hardships and discomforts he has undergone have entitled him—the pleasure of recurring in imagination to those scenes, still fresh in his memory, which occupy the most prominent position there, because they afforded the keenest enjoyment when witnessed. He will conjure up a picture which time cannot efface. It must ever grow brighter as it grows older, since the dark shade which many unpleasant recollections cast over it will gradually be dissipated. That faculty of forgetting the miseries, and remembering only the joys of his wandering life, is the traveller's happy privilege, and invests his favourite pursuit with a peculiar fascination.

If, in the foregoing relation of my Russian experiences, I have enlarged too fully upon the want of comfort and civilisation which so eminently characterised them, it is more with a view of giving what I conceived to be a faithful impression of the country than in a spirit of complaint; and though I must confess that my journal contains more allusions to our hardships than I have thought it necessary to record, there is no longer the same reality in those reminiscences as in others of a more pleasant nature.

I have sometimes been puzzled to decide which sensation is most enjoyable—the glorious excitement of setting foot for the first time in an interesting country hitherto unvisited, or that delightful repose consequent upon a return to old haunts, when the inquisitive faculties are thankful to be rested, and the agreeable task presents itself of filling in rough sketches taken under difficulties—of arranging and combining loose impressions—of collecting and condensing scraps of information hastily jotted down in miserable night-quarters—and coming to some general conclusion, whether right or wrong, upon the condition, manners, and customs of the newly-explored land and its inhabitants.

After all the passengers on board the Boreas had overhauled my sketch-book, I was allowed to amuse myself with it unmolested; and not until everybody had sapiently remarked, "Ah, monsieur fait ses impressions de voyage," and I had shown to a few "mes impressions du Boreas," was I permitted to resume an occupation which seemed to promise much interest—that of comparing information gained from Russian sources with what I had obtained from people likely to be honest and impartial, and of judging how far both agreed with those general impressions which my own observation had led me to form. However cursory the traveller's survey of the more distant provinces of Russia may have been, he will not long have escaped the seductive influences of St. Petersburg and Moscow before he begins to make discoveries affecting the social polity of the empire, which he never could have arrived at had he viewed it only through the distorted medium prepared for him at the chateaux of the nobility, or at the Imperial Court. As he penetrates farther into the country, he will penetrate also, in some degree, farther into the true origin of those moral and physical evils which beset his path, and obtain some insight into the workings of that political system which distinguishes the government of the Autocrat by what he sees of its practical results. He must estimate the value of the information he receives upon all that still lies hidden from his own observation by the source from whence it springs. The accounts which all foreigners give from their own experimental knowledge of the internal economy of the Empire is generally consistent, while no two Russians ever agree in their statements; and in order to arrive at the truth, it is necessary, so far as possible, to conceal the real design and bearing of the question.

My own inquiries and observation were rather directed to the commercial than to the military capabilities of the country, partly because I could more easily acquire information about them, and partly because I had then no reason for supposing that the latter were in a few months to be so severely tried. It was soon evident that I had chosen the inferior and subservient interest as a subject of inquiry. The military resources of Russia are developed *at the expense* of civilisation and commerce. The discoveries of science are only tolerated, and the spirit of mercantile enterprise only encouraged, because they supply agencies powerful, not for the enlightenment of the people, but for the support of that system which, concentrating in itself all light and intelligence, employs the powers thus gained to maintain an unhappy country in a state of the grossest darkness.

Thus, while the export trade is protected, because it replenishes the Exchequer, the import trade is virtually prohibited, and the advantages sacrificed which the people (and therefore indirectly the government) would reap from it, in order that its civilising tendencies may not be experienced by those whose obedience is insured by their barbarism and ignorance. Therefore, if it be true that Russia watches with anxiety over her mercantile interests just so far as she considers them a most powerful auxiliary to her military designs, it is not inconsistent with her policy that she should regard with the utmost jealousy those countries on the shores of the Black Sea or the Danube, whose rapidly-increasing commercial prosperity seems likely to interfere with her own. How far this consideration may have prompted the Czar's recent proceedings, or how far those proceedings were the result of a scheme long since concerted, in accordance with a policy in which he has been educated, it is difficult to determine. The present war has *ostensibly* originated upon purely religious grounds; and the crusade in which Russian soldiers believe themselves to be embarked, is prosecuted in the name of that faith to which a large proportion of the imperial subjects are said to be devoted.

There are certain *facts*, powerfully affecting this religious aspect of the question, which have been confirmed by my own observation in Russia, and their importance seems scarcely to have been recognised. Now they carry with them a significance which they did not possess in my eyes twelve months ago. Although I feel quite incompetent to offer any opinion upon the real designs or probable results of that war which is engaging the attention of Europe, yet I venture to suggest these considerations, because they must enter into the calculations of the Czar in deciding upon a future line of conduct, should the alternative ever be presented to him of terminating the war by the acceptance of those terms which the allied powers of England and France may think fit to dictate; and whatever tends to throw light upon the motives which influence him, upon whom so much depends, acquires a value peculiar to itself.

Hostilities having once commenced, there can be little doubt that, whatever their result may be, the warlike sentiments of a large portion of the Russian aristocracy would, in the first instance, be readily responded to by those of the Czar; and should the views which they mutually entertain be adopted, reverse will only serve as a stimulant to greater exertion, and victory be regarded as an earnest of a complete success. At the same time, the experience of former occasions has proved that the policy of Russia is characterised by a caution which is rarely at fault—which seems to rest in abeyance so long as, by a haughty blustering, she may impose upon Europe, and secure thereby her own ends, but which, so soon as the horizon assumes a threatening aspect, springs into active exercise, to avert the disastrous consequences which her too extravagant pretensions may entail.

European statesmen may weigh the motives which will influence the policy of Russia by those considerations which press upon her from without; they may speculate on the effect upon her cabinet of an alliance so unexpected, and so impracticable to Muscovite diplomacy, as that now subsisting between England and France; they may appreciate correctly the embarrassment of Austria and Prussia, and predict how long those countries are likely to maintain their present attitude, and they may attach the importance which is due to the unlooked-for displays of energy and prowess recently exhibited by the Ottoman army. But the Russian Autocrat is also keenly alive to the critical position of matters at home. Before he decides upon prolonging indefinitely a hazardous contest, he will consider the present aspect of the internal condition of the Empire as attentively as its external relations. He cannot forget that an extent of territory, comprising one-half of what is now called Russia in Europe, has been annexed within the last sixty years—that, consequently, more than half of the European inhabitants of the Empire, having been recently subjugated, are more or less disaffected; *that of these, sixteen millions, or about one-fourth of the entire population of Russia, do not profess the Greek faith;* that his Mahomedan subjects alone amount to two millions and a half; and that the protection of the Greek religion has been proclaimed as the ground upon which the present anti-Mahomedan crusade was commenced.

With respect to the various populations of the conquered provinces, there are many reflections connected with this question which must suggest themselves as readily to the English traveller as to the Russian Emperor. The Lutheran and

Roman Catholic inhabitants of the Baltic provinces may regard the war with the utmost indifference, so long as its operations are confined to the banks of the Danube; but should it become necessary to blockade and harass the shores of the Baltic, the unorthodox agriculturists must inevitably be ruined in the cause of a religion they despise, and to gratify the ambition of the despot who oppresses them. Under such circumstances, it is probable that they would sympathise with the neighbouring Poles, whose conduct at such a crisis it is not very difficult to predict. Approaching still nearer to the present seat of war, we reach that vast tract of corn-growing country, which, stretching along the shores of the Black Sea for two thousand miles, is entirely composed of provinces that have been successively wrested from the Turkish empire; while, though in the richly productive district of Bessarabia the inhabitants profess the Greek faith, the imperial sway is as obnoxious to them as to the Mahomedans of the Crimea; and the frequent but unavailing remonstrances of the ancient aristocracy, together with the demonstrations of discontent manifested by the peasantry, prove how galling is the Muscovite yoke, and how cheerfully the oppressed population would return to their old allegiance to the Hospodars of Jassy, and enjoy again the old delusion of believing in the security of the Ottoman protectorate.

At the easterly extremity of the corn-growing provinces on the Black Sea lies the formerly republican country of the Don Cossacks, containing a disaffected population of eight hundred thousand inhabitants, bound to an onerous military service, which, while it adds to their discontent, furnishes the Russian Government with a powerful engine for enforcing their submission; to retain which, the levies that are drawn from its boundless steppes are hostages in the Russian army! And over all that country, from the more western province of Taurida, and the fertile shores of the Sea of Azov to the salt deserts of the Caspian, restlessly wander half a million of Calmucks and Nogays, who, hovering upon the northern frontier of the Caucasus, are a continual source of suspicion and uneasiness to the Government, which has plundered them of all their ancient rights, and reduced to a state of degradation the miserable remnant of a tribe that has escaped from the yoke of the Czar, to find a refuge under the milder sway of His Celestial Majesty.

In the centre, a settled Tartar population inhabit Taurida and the Crimea, and bear witness to the former existence there of an independent and powerful state, whose influence spread from the Volga to the Vistula; for the Czar and the Sultan alike respected the Khans of Crim Tartary. Then these luxuriant valleys, guarded by impregnable fortresses, were thickly inhabited by a hardy and courageous race, whom Muscovite persecution has not altogether succeeded in exterminating, but who still cling with affection to the mountains and glens of their romantic country, and who, remembering the days of their former chivalry, may perhaps now cherish the hope that they may be called upon to take up arms in defence of the faith that is dear to them. Nor does this seem to be a very extravagant expectation. Ottoman troops have before now landed upon the rocky coast of Taurida, and should they do so again, they may hope to be welcomed by a nation stimulated to exertion by a prospect of at length regaining their independence—faithful followers of the Prophet, who, inspired by a religious enthusiasm, gain confidence as the cause of the true believer triumphs, and who, well versed in the local features of their mountainous peninsula, will prove valuable allies and formidable foes. If the Russian troops in the Crimea were beaten,[1] and all communication by sea with the mainland intercepted, the only means of approach for a Russian army would be across the inhospitable steppes of Taurida; and if the narrow isthmus of Perecop (which is protected by a fort) was properly defended, the Crimea might be permanently occupied by the Turks.

1 When I visited Simpheropol, the barracks were quite empty, with the exception of a few invalids in hospital; and the only garrison in the Crimea, at which troops were permanently stationed, was Sevastopol.

The position of Russia in the Trans-Caucasian provinces has lately been brought too prominently before the public to need much comment. It seems evident that if the Turkish expedition upon Tiflis is successful, and Prince Woronzoff's division of 30,000 men gives way under a combined attack of Circassians and Ottomans, the difficulty of retaking the country will prove almost insurmountable. When the eastern shore of the Black Sea is blockaded, an invading army could enter Georgia only by forcing the passes of Mozdok or Derbent. The imperial troops now stationed in the Caucasus and Daghestan would be incompetent to attempt this; a force which the indomitable Schamyl has for so long held at bay, could scarcely hope to surmount the rocky passes of Circassia, when a powerful ally was aiding in their defence. It would, therefore, be necessary to send large reinforcements to the assistance of the invading army, and these would be compelled to march a distance of 500 miles from the nearest government where troops are recruited, over the dreary steppe of the Cossack, and the arid desert of the Calmuck,—the nature of the country being such as to render any cantonment of reserves impossible.

Under these circumstances, it is not unlikely that troops would be conveyed down the Volga to Astrakhan, and thence by sea to Derbent. In that case another division would attempt to land at Bakou. But, apart from the length of time which these movements would entail, on account of the extremely intricate navigation of these distant waters, there might be some difficulty in procuring reinforcements large enough to co-operate effectually with the army of the Caucasus, while warlike operations upon a grander scale were being carried on upon the whole length of the European frontier of the empire.

If the Russians failed in reconquering their possessions in this direction, the prestige of that name, which for half a century has caused every Eastern potentate to tremble for his throne, *would be lost*.

Such is the present condition of those provinces which compose the European frontier of this vast empire. From the

Baltic to the Black Sea—from the shores of the Danube to the banks of the Phasis—extends an indissoluble bond of common sympathy—a deep-rooted hatred of Russia, which nothing less than the dread of incurring the vengeance of a despotism almost omnipotent could have restrained so long; and when at last the auspicious time arrives for giving vent to this feeling, the flame will kindle wildly in the recently acquired kingdom of Poland, for there the revolutionary spark has never been extinguished. It is true that in the southern provinces of the empire all hope of freedom has long disappeared, and terror and oppression have reigned so long, that the inhabitants of the thinly-populated steppe have lost much of the energy of their Mongolian ancestors; but while they may hesitate to start at once into open rebellion, they will not fail to use measures of passive resistance as a means of opposing the designs of Russia. Opportunities will not be wanting to insure some degree of success. When the presence of the allied fleets in the Black Sea denies to the Czar transport for his troops from the ports upon its margin in any one direction, divisions of the Russian army will often be compelled to march across the inhospitable steppes of the south; and here, dependent for food and transport upon whatever a barren and thinly-populated country can supply, it is probable that they will find their wants altogether disregarded. The Tartars have only to remove their families and their cattle out of the line of march, to render the onward progress of the army a· matter of the utmost difficulty, if not altogether impossible; and thus they will be able to gratify at the same time their natural hatred to the Russians, and their no less natural desire of retaining possession of their own flocks and herds. Even this dejected race might be stimulated to more active measures, by the presence upon their coasts of an overwhelming fleet hostile to Russia. It is impossible to foretell what the result may be of so novel a contingency. It rests with his Imperial Majesty to decide whether it will ever arise; but whatever weight he may attach to these considerations, and whatever may be the conclusion at which he may ultimately arrive, the facts, in so far as they illustrate the present internal condition of the empire, are important; for if, on the one hand, they combine to form any of the grounds upon which Russia may ever be induced to acquiesce in conditions proposed by the allied powers of Europe, a due appreciation of the difficulties by which he is surrounded, and which have compelled her to pursue a course so repugnant to Muscovite pride, must materially influence those upon whom the important task devolves of framing terms, the nature of which will depend in some measure upon the relative physical and moral condition of the hostile countries. But if, on the other hand, the attitude of Europe remains such that the Czar does not shrink from hazarding a war which must test the inmost resources of his Empire, then it is well for the Powers who are engaged in the struggle to know what those resources are, lest, measuring them only by a standard provided by Russia, and judging of their value by reports which emanate from a source totally unworthy of credit, they forget that, when the different elements of which the nation is composed are incohesive as sand, the extent of a country which comprises scattered populations of various kindreds, differing in faith, habits, and interests, is really its weakness.

A JOURNEY TO KATMANDU

PREFACE

The interest which was manifested in the Nepaulese Embassy during the short residence of Jung Bahadoor in England leads me to hope that a description of the romantic country and independent Court which he came to represent, as well as some account of his own previous eventful career, may not be unacceptable to the English public—more especially as no work upon Nepaul has been published in this country, that I am aware of, since Dr. Hamilton's, which appeared about the year 1819.

Through the kindness and friendship of the Nepaulese Ambassador, I was enabled to visit Katmandu under most favourable circumstances; and during the journey thither in his company I had abundant opportunity of obtaining much interesting information, and of gaining an insight into the character of the people, and their mode of everyday life, for which a residence in camp was peculiarly favourable.

In the Terai I was fortunate enough to witness the Nepaulese mode of elephant-catching, so totally unlike that of any other country, while the grand scale on which our hunting party was organised was equally novel.

I therefore venture to submit this volume to the public, in the hope that the novelty of a portion of the matter contained in it will in some degree compensate for its manifold defects.

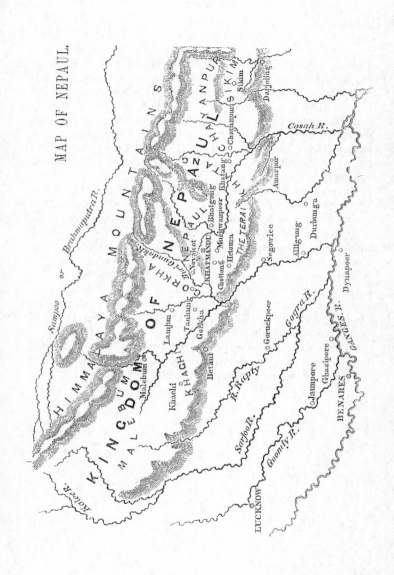

MAP OF NEPAUL.

CHAPTER I

Arrival of Jung Bahadoor in Ceylon—Voyage to Calcutta—Rifle practice on board the Atalanta—Rifle-shooting—Colonel Dhere Shum Shere—A journey along the Grand Trunk Road of Bengal—The experimental railway—The explosion at Benares

Towards the close of the year 1850 a considerable sensation was created in the usually quiet town of Colombo by the arrival in Ceylon of His Excellency General Jung Bahadoor, the Nepaulese Ambassador, on his return to Nepaul, bearing the letter of the Queen of England to the Rajah of that country.

The accounts which had preceded him of the magnificence of the jewels with which his person was generally adorned, had raised expectations amongst the natives which were doomed to disappointment: intelligence had been received by Jung of the death of the Queen of Nepaul, and the whole Embassy was in deep mourning, so that their appearance on landing created no little astonishment, clad, as they all were, in spotless white, excepting their shoes, which were of black cloth—leather not being allowed to form part of the Nepaulese mourning costume.

His Excellency had a careworn expression of countenance, which might have been caused either by the dissipation attendant upon the gaieties of his visit to London, by grief for his deceased Queen, or by sea-sickness during his recent stormy passage across the Gulf of Manaar. He had been visiting sundry Hindoo shrines, and it was for the purpose of worshipping at the temple of Ramiseram, which is situate on the island of that name, in the Gulf of Manaar, forming part of Adam's Bridge, that he touched at Colombo. Here I was fortunate enough to make his acquaintance, and, attracted by his glowing description of sport in Nepaul, accepted an invitation to accompany him to that country, in order to judge of it for myself.

So good an opportunity is indeed rarely afforded to a European of visiting Nepaul, and of inspecting the internal economy of its semi-barbarous Court. I soon found that Jung Bahadoor excelled no less as a travelling companion than he had done as Premier and Ambassador.

As doubts had arisen and some misapprehension had prevailed in England as to his position in his own country, I was anxious to ascertain what was his real rank and how he would be received there. It was reported that he had risked his temporal welfare by quitting his country, while, in order that his eternal welfare should in no way be compromised by this bold and novel proceeding, he had obtained an express reservation to be made in his favour at Benares, overcoming, by means of considerable presents, the scruples of a rapacious and not very conscientious priesthood.

The ostensible object of the mission had reference, as far as I could learn, to a portion of the Terai (a district lying upon the northern frontier of British India) which formerly belonged to Nepaul, and which was annexed by the Indian Government after the war of 1815-16; but it is probable that other motives than any so purely patriotic actuated the Prime Minister. His observant and inquiring mind had long regarded the British power in India with wonder and admiration—sentiments almost unknown amongst the apathetic Orientals, who, for the most part, have become too much accustomed to the English to look upon them with the same feelings as are entertained towards them by the hardy and almost savage race inhabiting the wild valleys of the Himalayas.

But besides the wish to gratify his curiosity, there existed yet another incentive which induced him to undertake this expedition. The precarious nature of his high position in Nepaul urged on him the good policy, if not the necessity, of a visit to England, for he doubtless felt, and with good reason, that the Native Durbar would be inclined to respect a man who had been honoured with an interview with the Queen of so mighty a nation, and had had opportunities of securing the support of her government, should he ever be driven to seek its aid.

The Atalanta, one of the oldest steam frigates in the Indian navy, had been placed at the disposal of His Excellency, and, upon the evening of the 9th of December 1850, was lying in the Colombo Roads, getting up her steam as speedily as possible, while I was uneasily perambulating the wooden jetty, which is all the little harbour can boast in the shape of a pier, endeavouring to induce some apathetic boatmen to row me over the bar, a pull of three miles, against a stiff breeze. It was bright moonlight, and the fire from the funnel of the old ship seemed rushing out more fast and furious in proportion as the boatmen became more drowsy and immovable; finally they protested that it was an unheard-of proceeding for anybody to wish to go on board ship on such a night at such an hour, and insinuated that all verbal or pecuniary persuasions would be alike unavailing. It is very evident that Colombo boatmen are a thriving community; still they seem a timid race, for upon my having recourse to threats containing fearful allusions, which there was not the remotest possibility of my being able to carry into execution, a wonderful revolution was effected in the feelings of the sleepers around me; they forthwith began to unwind themselves from the linen wrappers in which natives always swathe themselves at night like so many hydropathic patients, and, converting their recent sheets into turbans and waistcloths, they got with many grumblings into a tub-like boat, just as the smoke from the steamer was becoming ominously black. Their eyes once open, the men went to work in good earnest, and an hour afterwards I had the satisfaction of walking the deck of the Atalanta, which was going at her utmost speed, some seven knots an hour.

In the morning we were off Point de Galle, and put in there for General Jung Bahadoor, who, with some of his suite, had made the journey thither by land.

All the world make voyages nowadays; and nobody thinks of describing a voyage to India any more than he would an excursion on the Thames, unless he is shipwrecked, or the vessel he is in is burnt and he escapes in an open boat, or has some such exciting incident to relate. We were *unfortunate* in these respects, but in our passengers we found much to interest and amuse us; and as everything regarding the Nepaulese Ambassador is received with interest in England, a description of the proceedings of one day, as a sample of the ten we spent on board the "Atalanta," may not be altogether uninteresting.

Time never seemed to hang heavy on the hands of the Minister Sahib, for that was his more ordinary appellation; rifle practice was a daily occupation with him, and usually lasted two hours. Surrounded by those of his suite in whose peculiar department was the charge of the magnificent battery he had on board, he used to take up his station on the poop, and the crack of the rifle was almost invariably followed by an exclamation of delight from some of his attendants, as the bottle, bobbing far astern, was sunk for ever, or the three strung, one below the other, from the end of the fore-yard-arm, were shattered by three successive bullets in almost the same number of seconds. Pistol practice succeeded that of the rifle, and the ace of hearts at 15 paces was a mark he rarely missed.

Then the dogs were to be trained, and in a very peculiar manner; a kid was dragged along the deck before the noses of two handsome stag hounds, who, little suspecting that a huge hunting-whip was concealed in the folds of their master's dress, were unable to resist so tempting a victim and invariably made a rush upon it, a proceeding which brought down upon them the heavy thong of the Minister Sahib's whip in the most remorseless manner. That task accomplished to his satisfaction, and not being able to think of anything else wherewith to amuse himself, it would occur to him that his horse, having thrown out a splint from standing so long, ought to be physicked. He was accordingly made to swallow a quantity of raw brandy! It was useless to suggest any other mode of treatment, either of horse or dogs. The General laughed at my ignorance, and challenged me to a game of backgammon. Occasionally gymnastics or jumping were the order of the day, and he was so lithe and active that few could compete with him at either.

While smoking his evening pipe he used to talk with delight of his visit to Europe, looking back with regret on the gaieties of the English and French capitals, and recounting with admiration the wonders of civilization he had seen in those cities. He was loudest in his praise of England. This may have arisen from a wish to gratify his auditory, and it certainly had that effect. He had not thought it necessary, however, to perfect himself in the language of either country beyond a few of what he considered the more important phrases. His stock consisted chiefly of—How do you do?—Very well, thank you—Will you sit down?—You are very pretty—which pithy sentences he used to rattle out with great volubility, fortunately not making an indiscriminate use of them.

But my particular friend was the youngest of his two fat brothers, whose merits, alas! were unknown in England, the more elevated position of the Minister Sahib monopolizing all the attention of the lion-loving public. Colonel Dhere Shum Shere, such was his name, was the most jovial, light-hearted, and thoroughly unselfish being imaginable, brave as a lion, as recent events in Nepaul have proved, always anxious to please, and full of amusing conversation, which, however, from my limited knowledge of Hindostanee, I was unable fully to appreciate.

It is considered a breach of hospitality to make invidious remarks affecting the character of the mansion in which you are a guest; but although my recollections of the Atalanta are most agreeable in reference to the kindness of the officers, I must say she was a most indisputable tub; and if there is an individual who deserves to be turned slowly before the fires in her engine-room, so as to be kept in a state of perpetual blister, it is the Parsee contractor who furnished the provisions, for so meagre was the supply that we could barely satisfy the cravings of hunger.

On the morning of the tenth day after leaving Ceylon we came in sight of the city of palaces, and, sweeping up its magnificent river, soon after anchored amidst a host of other shipping.

Of Calcutta I need say nothing; Chouringhee Road is almost as well known in these days of quick communication as Piccadilly; this is not quite the case with towns in the interior: if it is easy to get to Calcutta, it is not so easy to get beyond, and the means of locomotion by which the traveller makes the journey to Benares are of the most original nature.

The morning of New Year's Day found me comfortably ensconced in a roomy carriage, built almost upon the model of an English stage-coach, in which, with my fellow-traveller, I had passed the night, and which was being dragged along at the rate of about four miles an hour by ten coolies, harnessed to it in what the well-meaning philanthropist of Exeter Hall would call a most barbarous way.

The road along which we were travelling in this extraordinary manner was not, as might be expected, impassable for horses; on the contrary, it was an excellent macadamized and perfectly level road, denominated the Great Trunk Road of Bengal.

The country through which this road led us was flat, stale, but not unprofitable, since on either side were paddy-fields extending *ad infinitum*, studded here and there with clumps of palms.

The climate was delightful, and the morning air tempted us to uncoil ourselves from our night-wrappers, and take a brisk walk in the dust; after which we mounted the coach-box, and devised sundry practical methods for accelerating our team, who however were equally ingenious in contriving to save themselves fatigue.

The midday sun at last ridded them of their tormentors, and we once more betook ourselves to our comfortable beds in the interior of the conveyance, there to moralize over the barbarism of a man, calling himself an enlightened Englishman, in employing men instead of horses to drag along two of his fellow-countrymen, who showed themselves even more dead to every feeling of humanity by the way in which they urged on their unfortunate fellow-creatures. These coolies were certainly very well paid, and need not have been so employed had they not chosen—for they had all applied for their several appointments—but then the ignominy of the thing!

And so we rolled lazily along, hoping to reach Benares some time within the next fortnight. Before dark we passed through Burdwan, where a few Bengal civilians vegetate on large salaries, to do the work of the rajah, who is still more highly paid not to interfere. He lives magnificently in his palace, and they live magnificently in theirs. We arrived at a small rest-house at night, where we had the satisfaction of eating a fowl in cutlets an hour after it had been enjoying the sweets of life.

There is a considerable amount of enjoyment in suddenly coming to hills after you have for a long time seen nothing but flat country—in first toiling up one and then bowling down the other side, at the imminent peril of the coolies' necks—in seeing streams when you have seen nothing but wells—in coming amidst wood and water and diversified scenery, when every mile that you have travelled for a week past has been the same as the last. Such were our feelings as we woke at daylight one morning in the midst of the Rajmahal hills.

There were a good many carts passing with coal from the Burdwan coal-mines; moreover, we saw sticks, and from the top of each fluttered a little white flag, suggestive of a railway, whereby our present mode of conveyance would be knocked on the head, and all the poor coolies who were pushing us along would be put out of employ. Notwithstanding the disastrous results which must accrue, a railway is really contemplated; but I have heard doubts thrown out as to the present line being the best that could be obtained. It is urged that it has to contend against water carriage—that, with the exception of the Burdwan mines, the coal of which is of an inferior quality, there is no mineral produce—that immense tracts of country through which it passes are totally uncultivated, and from a want of water will in all probability remain so—and it has been calculated that, even if the whole traffic at present passing along the great trunk road of Bengal was to become quadrupled, and if all the Bengal civilians were to travel up and down every day, and various rajahs to take express trains once a week, it would not pay: all these things being considered, were it not that its merits and demerits have been maturely considered by wiser, or at least better-informed men than the passing travellers, one might have been inclined to think that those who expressed doubts regarding its success had some good foundation for them.

However, it is better to have a railway on a doubtful line than none at all; the shareholders are guaranteed 5 per cent., and the Government is rich and can afford to pay them. So let us wish success to the experimental railway, and hope that the means of transport may soon be more expeditious than they are at present.

It will doubtless open out the resources of the country, though I cannot but think, for many reasons, that it would have been more judicious to have made the line from Allahabad to Delhi the commencement of the railway system in this part of India, instead of leaving it for a continuation of the line that is now being made.

The bridges we passed over are all on the suspension principle, and do credit to the government; the rivers are difficult to bridge in any other way, as the rains flood them to such an extent that arches will not remain standing for any length of time. It took us two hours to cross the Soan, which we forded or ferried according as the streams between the sand-banks were deep or shallow. This large river is at times flooded to so great an extent that it is one of the most serious obstructions to the railway.

It was not until the morning of the seventh day after leaving Calcutta that we found ourselves on the banks of the Ganges. The Holy City loomed large in the grey dawn of morning, with its tapering minarets barely discernible above it, looking like elongated ghosts.

We were ferried across in a boat of antique construction, better suited for any other purpose than the one to which it was applied, and landed in the midst of the ruins caused by the dreadful explosion of gunpowder that had taken place the previous year: it had occasioned a fearful destruction of property and loss of life, and many hair-breadth escapes were recounted to us. We were told, indeed, that two children, after being buried for five days, were dug out alive; two officers were blown out of the window of an hotel, one of whom was uninjured, the other was only wounded by a splinter, whilst the Kitmutgar, who was drawing a cork close to them at the time, was killed on the spot.

In the course of an hour after leaving this scene of desolation we reached the hospitable mansion which was destined to be our home during our short stay in Benares.

CHAPTER II

*Benares—Cashmere Mull's House—The Chouk—The
Bisheshwan Temple, and Maido Rai Minar—Jung Bahadoor
in Benares—A Rajah's visit—The marriage of Jung Bahadoor—
Review of the Nepaul Rifle Regiment—Benares College*

Whatever may be said of the large salaries of the Bengal
civilians, they certainly deserve great credit for the
praiseworthy employment of their wealth; and making
amends as it were for the backwardness of India as regards
hotels, they supply their places to the friendless traveller, in a
way which our frigid friends at home might imitate with
advantage. I look back upon my stay in Benares with the
greatest pleasure, and shall long remember the kindness I
there experienced.

There is much to be seen in the Holy City, and the means of
locomotion which I should recommend the sight-seer to adopt
are Tom Johns, or chairs swung upon poles, with or without
hoods, as the case may be. Upon arriving at the Chouk or
Marketplace, we hired two of these conveyances and started to
see the residence of Cashmere Mull. But first I must make an
attempt, however unsuccessful, to describe the Chouk: it is a
large square, studded with raised oblong platforms without
walls, the roofs being supported by fluted Ionic columns. The
Police Court, in which a Native magistrate presides, forms one
side of the square. On the platforms sit the vendors of shawls,
skull-caps, toys, shells, sugar-cane, and various other
commodities; but to enumerate the extraordinary diversity of
goods exposed for sale, or to describe the Babel of tongues
which confound the visitor as he wanders through the motley
crowd, would be impossible.

We turned out of the Chouk down a narrow street about
three feet broad, gloomy from the height of the houses, and
unpleasant from the great crowd and close atmosphere; every
now and then we got jammed into a corner by some

Brahminee bull, who would insist upon standing across the street to eat the fine cauliflower he had just plundered from the stall of an unresisting greengrocer, and who, exercising the proud rights of citizenship, could only be politely coaxed to move his unwieldy carcase out of the way.

We wended our way through pipe bazaars and vegetable bazaars, where each shopkeeper has a sort of stall, with about three feet frontage to the street, but of unknown depth, and a narrow balcony supported by carved wood-work over his head, out of the latticed windows of which bright eyes look down upon the passengers. Whenever there is a piece of wall not otherwise occupied in this compact and busy city, you see depicted, in gaudy colours, elephants rushing along with dislocated joints in hot pursuit of sedate parrots, or brilliant peacocks looking with calm composure upon camels going express, who must inevitably crush them in their headlong career, but the vain birds, apparently taken up with admiration of their own tails, are blind to the impending danger, thereby reading a good lesson both to the passers-by and to the shopkeepers opposite. Now a sudden jerk prevents you from further moralizing, as you find that you are going round a corner so sharp that you must get bumped either before or behind. There are ugly women carrying brass water-vessels, rich merchants on ponies, sirwahs on horses, here and there in the wider streets a camel or an elephant, but very seldom, as few streets would accommodate either of them; finally there are chuprassies who disperse the crowd with their swords in a most peremptory manner, smiting everything indiscriminately, except the Brahminee bulls, which, although they are much the most serious impediments, are left "alone in their glory."

By the exertions of these city police we reached Cashmere Mull's house, noted as a specimen of antique Oriental architecture.

The courtyard into which we were first ushered reminded me of an old English "hostelrie;" it was small and uncovered, and round each story ran a curiously worked balcony, on to which opened doors and windows, carved with strange devices, and all the nooks and crannies formed by so much intricate carving were filled with dust and cobwebs. Passing up a narrow, dark, and steep stone stair, we reached a second courtyard, upon the balcony of which we emerged, and which was so very like the last, that I imagined it to be the same, until I remarked that it was smaller, and, if possible, more dirty. We thence ascended to the flat roof of the house, and on our way looked through half-open doors into dark dungeons of rooms, which one would not for the world have ventured into at night.

There was a raised stage with steps up to it, which we ascended and found ourselves on a level with a great many similar stages on the tops of a great many similar houses. A stone parapet about 8 feet high, with beautiful open carving, enclosed this stage, so that we could inspect our neighbours through our stone screen with impunity. On the next roof to where we were was a boy training pigeons, and the numerous crates or frames on the surrounding house-tops showed this to be a favourite amusement. The young gentleman in question certainly made his flock obey him in a wonderful manner, his chief object being to take prisoner a pigeon from his neighbour's flock. He directed their gyrations by loud shrill cries, and, as there were numbers of other members of "Young Benares" employed in like manner, it seemed wonderful how he could recognize his pigeons, or they their master.

Leaving this antique specimen of a nobleman's town house, we passed through a maze of narrow streets; and bobbing under low archways at the imminent peril of fracturing our skulls, we arrived at the Bisheshwan Temple, which was crowded with Hindoos worshipping the Lingum, represent-ations of which met the eye in every direction.

A well in the yard behind the temple was surrounded by worshippers of the god, who is supposed to have plunged down it and never to have come up again. If so, he must find the smell of decayed vegetation very oppressive, as garlands of flowers and handfuls of rice are continually being offered up, or rather down, to him. From this well we had a good view of the temple, which was covered with gold by Runjeet Singh, and presents a gorgeous and dazzling appearance.

In close vicinity to this temple is a mosque built by Arungzebe to annoy the Hindoos. I ascended the Maido Rai Minar or minaret, and from its giddy height had a magnificent panorama of the city and its environs, with the Ganges flowing majestically beneath, its left bank teeming with life, while the opposite bank seemed desolate.

The observatory, or man mundil, is on the river's bank, and affords a pretty view from its terraces, which are covered with disks and semicircles and magical figures cut in stone.

Gopenate Dore Peshad is the great dealer in Benares embroidery, as well as its manufacturer. We paid him a visit and were delighted with the rich variety of embroidered goods which were displayed; we saw pieces valued at from 10,000 rupees downwards: magnificent smoking carpets, housings and trappings for horses, shawls, caps, kenkabs, and other articles of eastern attire, were spread out before us in gorgeous profusion. After eating a cardamum, and touching with our pocket-handkerchief some cotton on which had been dropped otto of roses, we ascended to the house-top, and found it built upon much the same plan as Cashmere Mull's, without its antique carving and quaint appearance.

We were not a little glad when the bustle and heat attendant on so much sight-seeing was over, and we forced our way back through the crowded streets.

The population of Benares is estimated by Mr. Prinsep at nearly 200,000; its trade consists chiefly in sugar, saltpetre, indigo, opium, and embroidered cloths; besides which, the city has advantages in its position on the great river, making it, jointly with Mirzapore, the depôt for the commerce of the Dukkum and interior of Hindostan.

General Jung Bahadoor had reached Benares a few days before I arrived there, and I found him installed in a handsome house, the envy of all rajahs, the wonder of the natives, and the admiration of his own countrymen, some thousands of whom had come thus far to meet him. If he had been a *lion* in London, he was not less an object of interest at Benares—his house was always crowded with visitors of high degree, Indian and European; one old native rajah in particular was frequently to be seen in close conference with him; and the result was, that the Prime Minister of Nepaul became the husband of the second daughter of his Highness the ex-Rajah of Coorg. Upon the day following his nuptials my friend and I called upon him, and to our surprise he offered to present us to his newly-wedded bride. We, of course, expressed our sense of the honour he was doing us; and had just reached the balcony, the stairs leading up to which were on the outside of the house, when our friend the bridegroom perceived his father-in-law, the Coorg rajah, coming in a most dignified manner down the approach. Like a schoolboy caught in the master's orchard, he at once retreated and unceremoniously hurried us back—and just in time, for no doubt, if the old Coorg had detected him thus exhibiting his daughter the day after he had married her, he would have mightily disapproved of so improper a proceeding. This incident shows how utterly Jung despised those prejudices which enthralled his bigoted father-in-law. He was, in fact, the most European Oriental, if I may so speak, that I ever met with, and more thoroughly unaffected and unreserved in his communication with us than is the habit with eastern great men, who always seem afraid of compromising themselves by too much condescension. An instance of this occurred during another visit. While we were chatting on indifferent subjects a native rajah was announced, as being desirous of paying a visit of ceremony. Jung immediately stepped forward to receive him with much politeness. The rajah commenced apologising for not having called sooner, excusing himself on the plea of the present being the only auspicious hour which had been available since his Excellency's arrival; a compliment which the latter returned by remarking that it was unfortunate that his immediate departure would preclude the possibility of his returning his visit, which he the more regretted, as he was at present most particularly engaged in matters of a pressing nature with the English gentlemen, and he therefore hoped he would be excused thus abruptly, but unavoidably, terminating an interview which it would otherwise have given him the greatest pleasure to have prolonged. Thus saying, he politely rose and led the rajah in the most graceful manner to the front door, which was no sooner closed behind him than he returned, rubbing his hands with great glee, as he knowingly remarked, "That is the way to get over an interview with one of these natives."

A detachment of a regiment had come to Benares to escort the General on his journey to Katmandu, and he accordingly determined to favour the inhabitants generally, and the English in particular, with a review.

The men were tall and well-made, and were dressed in a light-green uniform with yellow facings. They went through various evolutions with tolerable regularity; but the performance which excited the most interest was the platoon exercise, no word of command being given, but everything done with the utmost precision at different notes of the music, the men beating time the whole while and giving a swaying motion to their bodies, which produced a most curious effect. The origin of this novel proceeding, his Excellency told us, was a request by the Ranee that some other means should be invented of putting the men through their exercises than by hoarse shouts, which grated upon her ear. The minister immediately substituted this more euphonious but less business-like method.

At this review Jung Bahadoor and his brothers were dressed in the costume they wore when in England: the handsome diamonds in their turbans glittering in the sunshine.

I accompanied him one day on a visit to the Benares college, a handsome building in process of erection by the Indian Government. The Gothic and Oriental styles of architecture are most happily combined, and there is an airiness about the building; but this did not in any way detract from its solidity. The cost of the college and professor's house is not to exceed £13,000; the length of the large school-room is 260 feet, its breadth 35; and there are six large class-rooms on each side.

CHAPTER III

*Jaunpore—A shooting-party—Scenes in camp and on the
march—A Nepaulese dinner—Ghazipore—The Company's
stud—Indian roads—Passage of the Gograh—Jung Bahadoor's
mode of despatching an alligator*

Being anxious to visit Jaunpore, I left Benares one evening
after dinner, and accomplished the distance, 36 miles, with one
set of bearers, in seven hours and a half.

The first object that attracts the eye of the traveller as he
enters Jaunpore is the many-arched bridge thrown by the
Mahometans over the Goomte, and considered the finest built
by them in India; on each side are stalls, in which sit the vendors
of various wares, after the fashion of old London Bridge. On an
island in the middle of the river was discovered a huge figure of
a winged lion guarding an elephant, which would suggest some
connexion with the sculptures found at Nineveh, and must date
much further back than the erection of the bridge.

Passing through a serai, which was filled with travellers, we
reached the fort, built, it is supposed, by Khan Kan, or one of
the kings of the Shirkee dynasty, about the year 1260. From one
of its turrets we had a magnificent view of the town and the
surrounding country, while immediately below is seen the
river, spanned by the picturesque old bridge, unmoved by the
fierce floods which so constantly destroy those arched bridges
that have been erected in India by Europeans.

The appearance of the town is diminished in size, but
increased in beauty, by the many stately trees which are
planted throughout it, while here and there a huge screen of
some musjid rears its Egyptian-looking crest, and gives to the
town an appearance peculiar to itself; Jaunpore is, in fact, the
only city in India in which this style of architecture prevails.

On our way out of the fort we passed a monolithe, on which
was an inscription in the same character as that on
Ferozeshah's Lath at Delhi, which has been recently translated

by Mr. Prinsep. In the main gateway were some porcelain slabs which had at one time formed part of a Jain temple.

The Itala musjid, to which we next bent our steps, has been built on the site of one of these temples; its cloisters remain untouched, and the figures on almost every slab bear undoubted testimony to the previous existence of a Jain temple on this spot. The large square rooms, which were filled during our visit with true believers, were curiously roofed; a dome was ingeniously thrown over the square. An octagon, placed on solid buttresses, supported a 16-sided figure, which in its turn supported the dome. The Jumma musjid, which we also visited, was remarkable for its magnificent screen, 120 feet in height by 70 in breadth, and covered with curious inscriptions and fantastic devices; the top is slightly narrower than the base, tapering in depth as well as in breadth.

The population of Jaunpore is about 35,000; there is a small European station near the town. In the course of the evening's drive I saw a specimen of the Addansonia or baobab-tree: the trunk, measuring 23 feet in circumference, was perfectly smooth and the branches were destitute of leaves. There are but five other specimens in India, and not many in Java, where the tree was discovered by Mr. Addanson; it is said to have attained, in some instances, the enormous age of 2000 years.

Leaving Jaunpore about midnight, I reached the camp of Jung Bahadoor on the following day. The scene as we approached was in the highest degree picturesque; 5000 Nepaulese were here collected, followers, in various capacities, of the Prime Minister, whose tents were pitched at a little distance from the grove of mango-trees which sheltered his army and retainers. On our arrival he was out shooting, so, mounting an elephant, we proceeded to join him. We heard such frequent reports of fire-arms that we fully expected to find excellent sport; great was my disappointment, therefore, when I saw him surrounded by some 20 or 30 followers, who held umbrellas, loaded his guns, rushed to pick up the *game*, or looked on applaudingly while he stealthily crept up to take a deliberate pot shot at some unlucky parrot or small bird that might catch his eye as it perched on a branch, or fluttered unconsciously amongst the leaves. But the most interesting object in the group was the lately-wedded bride, who was seated in a howdah. Jung introduced her to me as "his beautiful Missis"—a description she fully deserved. She was very handsome, and reflected much credit on the taste of the happy bridegroom, who seemed pleased when we expressed our approval of his choice.

Before quitting the subject of Jung's shooting-party, I must remark, in justice to him as a sportsman, that he considers nothing less than a deer to be game at all. Tiger or rhinoceros shooting is his favourite sport, and he looks upon shooting a parrot, a snipe, a hawk, or a partridge as being equally unworthy of the name of sport, nor does he understand why some of those birds should be dignified with the name of "game," and the others not.

At dawn on the following morning the stir and bustle in camp announced an early start, and our elephant appeared at the tent door just as the gallant rifle corps marched past, the band playing the "British Grenadiers." Mounting the elephant, we picked our way through the débris of the camp, now almost deserted; some few of the coolies were still engaged packing the conical baskets which they carry on their backs, one strap passing over the forehead, and two others over the shoulders. The appearance of a hill coolie as he thus staggers along under his tremendous burden is singular enough, and so totally unlike that of the coolies of the plains, that it was a sort of promise of there being in store for us more curiosities, both of Nepaulese men and manners, in their native country, and we looked with no little interest upon the first specimens we had seen of the Newar race—the aborigines of Nepaul. Short and compact, the full development of their muscle bore evidence to their almost Herculean strength. Their flat noses, high cheek-bones, small eyes, and copper-coloured complexion are unequivocal signs of a Mongolian origin, whilst the calves of their legs, which I never saw equalled in size, indicate the mountainous character of their country.

Threading our way on our wary elephant through nearly 5000 of these singular-looking beings, all heavily loaded with the appurtenances of the camp, we soon overtook the cortège of the Minister and his brothers, which consisted of three or four carriages dragged along by coolies, over a road which, in many places, must have severely tried the carriage springs, as well as nearly dislocated the joints of Jung's "beautiful little Missis," whom I saw peeping out of one of the windows. The rest of this motley crowd, with which we were destined to march for the next three weeks, was made up of Nepaul gentlemen in various capacities, who cantered past on spirited little horses, or squatted cross-legged in the clumsy, oddly constructed "Ecce," a sort of native gig; besides these, there were merchants and pedlers, who followed the camp as a matter of speculation. Amidst an indiscriminate horde, our elephant jogged lazily along, generally surrounded by eight or ten others, with whom we marched for company's sake. We usually arrived at the mango tope destined to be our camping-ground about ten o'clock in the morning, and lounged away the heat of the day in tents; towards the afternoon Jung generally went out with his gun or rifle, shooting with the former at parrots at ten yards distance, and with the latter at bottles at a hundred. There was not much attraction for the sportsman throughout the whole line of march, and I only bagged a few couple of snipe, partridges, wild-duck, and quail.

Our dinner was always supplied from Jung's own carpet, for he does not use a table, and it was with no little curiosity that at the end of the first day's march I looked forward to the productions of a Nepaul cuisine. We had not forgotten to provide ourselves with a sufficient *stand-by* in case it should not prove altogether palatable. Towards evening an enormous dish, containing rice enough to have satisfied the whole of the gallant rifle corps, was brought into our tent, closely followed by about 20 little cups formed of leaves, one inside the other, each containing about a thimbleful of some exquisite condiment; also three or four saucers containing some cold gravy, of unpleasant colour, in which floated about six minute particles of meat.

Filling my plate with rice, which had been well and carefully greased to improve its flavour, and scientifically mixing the various other ingredients therewith, I unhesitatingly launched a spoonful into my mouth, when I was severely punished for my temerity, and almost overcome by the detestable compound of tastes and smells that at once assailed both nose and palate: it was a pungent, sour, bitter, and particularly greasy mouthful; but what chiefly astonished me, so much as to prevent my swallowing it for some time, was the perfume of Colonel Dhere Shum Shere, the fat brother, which I was immediately sensible of, as overpowering everything else. Not that I would for a moment wish to insinuate that it was a nasty smell; on the contrary, it would have been delicious on a pocket-handkerchief; but to imagine it going down one's throat, in company with an immense amount of grease and gravy, was nearly enough to prevent its doing so at all.

Our march to Ghazipore was through country richly cultivated and pleasing, if not absolutely pretty. The numerous poppy-plantations were evidence of our proximity to the headquarters of one of the largest opium agencies in India. Ghazipore is approached by an avenue of handsome trees, more ornamental than useful, seeing how utterly destructive it is to the permanent welfare of a road.

The mausoleum, containing a monument to Lord Cornwallis, is solid but not ungraceful: upon one side of the monument are sculptured the figures of a Hindoo and a Mussulman, and on the other a British and a native grenadier, all of whom are weeping. The building is prettily situated near the bank of the Ganges, on a large plain or maidan, across which pleasant avenues lead in all directions; the one which we followed brought us to the stables of the Company's stud, containing 700 horses. On our way we remarked a number of handsome houses now unoccupied and falling rapidly into decay, the military force at the station having of late been much reduced. The horses were being exercised, notwithstanding which they carried a good deal of superfluous fat, and vented their spirits by occasionally breaking loose, and dashing pellmell through rings of their companions, who, grudging them the sweets of liberty, made vigorous efforts to partake of them, and in some instances succeeded. I saw not less than eight at once dashing about in the large training enclosure. My friend having already bought three, we thought it best to withdraw ourselves from further temptation, and set out to join the camp at Cossimabad, 16 miles distant, still passing through richly cultivated country, which was as pretty as a dead level ever can be.

The crops most generally reared are, sugar-cane, poppies, rare (a species of pulse), wheat, often with a delicate border of blue-flowered flax, tobacco, mustard, peas, and sometimes vetches. The large rose-gardens for which Ghazipore is celebrated lay to the right. I regretted that our way did not lead us through them, but we had evidence of their existence in some delicious otto of roses, which is easily procured here.

The road by which we were now travelling was what is called in India a cutcher-road, which means unmetalled. It is a pity that Government should spend so much in macadamizing roads, when cutcher-roads answer just as well for all the wants of native traffic. The rocks here are of limestone formation, and consequently, as there is not much traffic on any road in India, if the trees were cut down, roads on a limestone formation would always keep themselves in repair, provided the side drains were properly kept open. The bridges are all good, and, if the line of road was well bridged throughout, the country conveyances could always make their way along it with perfect ease. If the money now spent in macadamizing were spent in making the necessary bridges, the resources of the country would be much more fully opened out than they are at present; a garre-waller, or cart-man, can always appreciate a bridge, never a macadamized road. At present the bridges on this road are all wooden, and liable to be carried away by the first heavy flood.

The whole way to the frontier of Nepaul we travelled along a cutcher-road, accompanied by a train of at least a hundred hackerys, without the slightest inconvenience; and until the style of cart at present used by the natives becomes wonderfully improved, this road may well be used, except of course during the rains.

A few days' march brought us to the banks of the Gograh, a large river rising in the western Terai, and measuring, at the point where we crossed, at least half a mile in breadth. As we came upon the cliff overlooking the river, the scene was novel and amusing. As 5000 persons had to reach the opposite bank, and no preparations had been made for their transit, the confusion may be easily imagined. The good-humour of the hillmen, however, was imperturbable, and, though there was plenty of loud talking, the remarks made were usually of a facetious nature.

The stream was rapid, and carried the boats down some distance. Ten elephants, with nothing visible but the tips of their trunks and the crowns of their heads, on which latter squatted the mahouts, made the passage gallantly. On the opposite side we passed through a village, the little square of which was absolutely filled with monkeys. They resort thither by hundreds from the neighbouring jungles to be fed by the villagers, and are most independent in their behaviour, unscrupulously attacking the man who brings their daily allowance, and, as they are accounted sacred, they are of course unmolested. We saw some serious fights amongst them, young and old mixing indiscriminately in the mêlée; a mother was frequently seen making a rapid but orderly retreat with her young one on her back.

We occasionally passed picturesque villages, the inhabitants of which were of course all attracted by so novel a spectacle. The system pursued by the villagers here is the same as may be observed in many parts of the Continent of Europe: they invariably congregate in a collection of mud-built closely packed huts, showing a gregarious disposition, and great aversion to living alone. I do not remember to have passed one solitary house. As the whole of the country is richly cultivated, the distance of their dwellings from the scene of their daily labour must in some instances be considerable.

The Gandaki, over which we were ferried, is a large stream rising in Nepaul, and as broad as the Gograh. We went some distance up its banks, in the hopes of finding wild-pig, but were unsuccessful.

The minister, however, being determined not to go home empty handed, doomed to destruction a huge alligator, unconsciously basking on a sand-bank. Accordingly, arming eight of us with double-barrelled rifles, he marched us in an orderly manner to the bank, when, at a given signal, 16 balls whistled through the air, arousing in a most unpleasant manner the monster from his midday slumbers, who plunged into the stream and disappeared almost instantaneously, and the Minister Sahib, coolly pulling out the wallet which contained his tiffin, remarked that we might profitably employ ourselves in that way until he came up to breathe, when he should receive another dose. Retiring therefore a few yards from me—for a Hindoo may not eat in the presence of a Christian—he and his brothers were soon deep in the mysteries of curious viands. Perceiving, however, that I was not prepared for an alfresco luncheon, he shared with me some grapes, pomegranates, &c., as well as a piece of green-looking meat, which I found very delightfully scented. As we were in the middle of our repast, our wounded friend showed his nose above the water, when he was immediately struck by a splendid shot from the minister, who was in no way disconcerted by having his mouth full at the time. Lashing the water furiously with his tail, the alligator once more disappeared: he came up shortly after, and the same scene was enacted three times before his huge form floated lifeless down the stream.

CHAPTER IV

A picnic on the Nepaul frontier—A boar-hunt—The Terai and its resources—Our shooting quarters—Incidents of sport—A tiger-hunt—The great elephant exhibition of 1851—Camp Bechiacor

Pitched under the shade of some wide-spreading mangoes are a variety of tents of all sizes, from the handsome and spacious marquee to the snug sleeping tent; near them are picqueted a number of fine-looking Arab horses in prime condition, while the large barouche, which is standing close by, might have just emerged from a coach-house in a London mews; a few servants are loitering about, and give life to this otherwise tranquil scene.

Nobody can for an instant suppose that this is the camp of Jung Bahadoor; his tents are green and red and generally surrounded by soldiers; his horses do not look so sleek and fresh as these; he has not got a barouche belonging to him, far less a piano, and I think I hear the music of one proceeding from yonder large tent.—No—this is an Indian picnic—none of your scrambling, hurried pleasure parties to last for a wet day, when everybody brings his own food, and eats it uncomfortably with his fingers, with some leaves for a plate and an umbrella for a roof, and then persuades himself and others that he has been enjoying himself. Let such an one come and make trial of a deliberate, well-organized picnic of a fortnight's duration, such as the one now before us, with plenty of sport in the neighbourhood, while the presence of the fair sex in camp renders the pleasures of the drawing-room doubly delightful after those of the chase.

Boar-hunting, or, as it is commonly called, pigsticking, is essentially an Indian sport, and I could not have partaken of it under more favourable auspices than I did at Hirsede, when, having obtained intelligence of a wild boar, and having been supplied with steeds, some five or six of us proceeded in pursuit of the denizen of the jungles. We soon roused and pressed him closely through the fields of castor-oil and rare-cates. The thick stalks of the former often balked our aim. He received repeated thrusts notwithstanding, and charged three or four times viciously, slightly wounding my horse, and more severely that of one of my companions. After being mortally wounded, the brute unfortunately dodged into a thick jungle, where, hiding himself in the bushes, he baffled all our efforts to dislodge him. In their attempts to do so, however, the beaters turned out a fine young boar, who gave us a splendid run of upwards of a mile at top speed—for a pig is a much faster animal than his appearance indicates, and one would little imagine, as he scuttles along, that he could keep a horse at full gallop. However, he soon became blown, and, no friendly patch of jungle being near for him to take refuge in, was quickly despatched.

Our revels having been kept up to a late hour, I left Hirsede in the small hours of the morning, and came up to Jung Bahadoor's camp on the Nepaul frontier.

A small stream divides the Company's from the Nepaulese dominions, and on crossing it the change of government was at once obvious. The villages looked more wretched, the people more dirty, the country was almost totally uncultivated, and nearly all traces of roads disappeared as we traversed the green sward of the Terai of Nepaul, scattered over which were large herds of cattle, grazing on the short grass, which extended in all directions over the vast expanse of flat country.

This province is governed by Krishna Bahadoor, a younger brother of the prime minister, an active and energetic officer. Any complaint of the peasantry is in the first instance brought to his notice, and referred by him to his brother, if his decision does not give satisfaction. His subordinates are a sirdar, or judge, and several subahs, or collectors.

The Terai is a long narrow strip of territory, extending for three hundred miles along the northern frontier of British India, and is about twenty miles in breadth. The whole tract is a dead level. For the first ten miles after crossing the frontier the country is used chiefly for grazing by the inhabitants of the adjoining British provinces, who drive thousands of cattle across the border, paying a considerable revenue to the Nepaul government for the privilege of so doing.

Ten miles from the frontier commences the great saul forest, which is also ten miles in breadth. It is composed almost entirely of the valuable saul-tree, and a great quantity of timber is annually exported to Calcutta down the Gandaki, which is navigable to the foot of the Cheriagotty hills. The licence to fell the saul timber is confined exclusively to Nepaul merchants, and the payment demanded by Government for such permission is so enormous that the trade is not very profitable.

The principal sources of revenue derived from this district are the land-tax and the receipts from the sale of licences for felling timber and for grazing cattle. The large amount thus received, together with the number of elephants which are annually caught in the great forest, renders the Terai a most valuable appendage to the Nepaul dominions.

It is, however, entirely owing to the excellent management of Jung that the revenue of the Terai is now so considerable. In 1816 this province did not yield more than one-tenth its present revenue, which is now computed to amount to fifty lacs (£500,000). Still the Terai might be made yet more profitable. At present no use whatever is made of the hides and horns of the hundreds of head of cattle that die daily in this district, which are left to rot on the carcases of the beasts. It would remain to be proved however whether, even if permission were granted by the Nepaul Government, any would be found possessing the capital or enterprise to engage in a speculation which would, unquestionably, ensure a handsome return.

It is not, however, in a pecuniary point of view alone that the Terai is considered by the Nepaulese as contributing to the prosperity of their dominions; it is looked upon as one of their chief safeguards against invasion. For nine or ten months a disease, denominated by the natives the "Ayul," renders the Terai impassable to man, so deadly are its effects even to the natives of the country. It would appear that might be obviated—if we are to believe the native theory somewhat gravely recorded by Mr. Hamilton (who made a journey through this province with a mission sent by Government in 1803)—by going in search of and killing certain serpents, which are said to poison the atmosphere with their breath. I should be inclined to recommend the cutting down of the jungle in preference to the cutting up of the serpents; and I have little doubt that, were parts of the great forest cleared, and wide roads cut through it, it would cease to be so pestilential a locality as it is at present. In case of a war, there would be no difficulty, even now, in our troops possessing themselves of the whole territory to the foot of the Cheriagotty hills in the cold season; but as we should have to maintain some position throughout the year, the top of those hills themselves would be the only one available, and here, in the heart of an enemy's country, and cut off from all communication with India, the position of the garrison would be anything but enviable.

I observed several of the natives of this district afflicted with goître, and I was informed that cretinism was also prevalent,— a fact which proves clearly the fallacy of the old doctrine that these complaints are attributable to snow-water, for all the water drunk by the inhabitants of the Terai rises in the Cheriagotty hills, on which snow rarely if ever falls. This would be strongly corroborative of the correctness of the idea that malaria is the origin of goître and cretinism, even if the experiment which has been tried at Interlacken, of building a hospital on the hills, above the influence of the infectious atmosphere in the valley, had not proved completely successful.

The camp which was destined to be our headquarters during a few days' shooting was pitched in the plain near the village of Bisoleah, distant about two miles from the borders of the grand jungle. Its appearance was totally different from those already described; two more regiments were here in attendance upon the Minister; the men were all comfortably lodged in grass huts got up for the occasion, and the innumerable host of camp followers, who on the march had been contented with wrapping themselves up in their thick cloths, and sleeping in groups round the various fires, were now engaged in erecting like temporary habitations, forming by these means a grass village of considerable extent.

Horses, oxen, camels, elephants, were tethered in every direction, or wandering in search of sweeter tufts of grass. The village itself was close and dirty; the largest house, which stood near a temple, was occupied by some half-dozen wives of the Minister, who had come to the borders of their country to welcome home their lord and master.

Our tents were pitched between the camp and a small clump of trees, near which upwards of 300 elephants were tethered; a stream divided us from them, the banks of which presented a continual scene of confusion, as men and animals, at all hours, passed along in crowds, while the motley groups, collecting as the Minister moved about to inspect various parts of his establishment, indicated the whereabouts of that great personage. The scene struck us as particularly novel and attractive when we arrived from Hirsede about midday; as we approached from one direction, the Minister Sahib arrived from another, mounted in a handsome howdah, the trophy of the morning being a tiger which he had just killed, and which was lashed on to the elephant following him, while a hundred more hustled one another up the steep bank and through the crowded street, greatly to the inconvenience of his dutiful subjects, who were salaaming vociferously.

We immediately started in quest of like game, and commenced beating the heavy jungle, by which the plain was bounded as by a wall, but fortune did not smile upon our efforts, and we only succeeded in killing a deer and a pig. I found my first experience in shooting from a howdah to be anything but agreeable: the deer bounds through the long grass as a rabbit would through turnips; and, at the moment one catches a glimpse of his head, the elephant is sure to be going down a steep place, or stopping or going on suddenly, or trumpeting, or doing something which completely balks a sportsman accustomed to be on his own legs, and sends the ball flying in any direction but the right one. Our line of elephants consisted of upwards of one hundred, and they beat regularly and silently enough, except when the behaviour of one of them irritated some passionate mahout, who would vent his wrath upon the head of the animal by a blow from a short iron rod, or would catch him sharply under the ear with a huge hook, which he dexterously applied to a sore kept open for that purpose; then a loud roar of pain would sound through the jungle for a moment, much to our disgust, as it startled the deer we were silently and gradually approaching.

The pig, which formed part of the game-bag of the afternoon, was, in the first instance, only severely wounded, and an elephant was commanded to finish the poor brute; as he lay, grimly surveying us, his glistening tusks looked rather formidable,—so at least the elephant seemed to think, as for some time he strongly objected to approach him. At last he went timidly up and gave the boar a severe kick with his fore-foot, drawing it back quickly with a significant grunt, which plainly intimated his opinion that he had done as much as could reasonably be expected of him. His mahout, however, thought otherwise, and, by dint of severe irritation on the sore behind his ear, seemed to drive him to desperation, as the elephant suddenly backed upon the pig, and, getting him between his hind legs, ground them together, and absolutely broke him up. After this we went crashing home, regardless of the thick jungle through which we passed, as the impending boughs were snapped, at the word of the mahouts, by the obedient and sagacious animals they bestrode.

Daybreak of the 30th of January found us not foot in stirrup, but foot on ladder, for we were mounting our elephants to proceed in search of the monarch of the Indian jungles, intelligence of the lair of a male and female having been brought into camp overnight. A hundred elephants followed in a line, forming a picturesque procession, towards the long grass jungle in which our noble game was reported to be ensconced. On reaching the scene of action we formed into a line and beat regularly the whole length of the patch. We were not destined to wait long, and the crack of my friend's rifle soon sounded in my ears. He had wounded the tiger severely, and the animal had again disappeared in the long grass. We were now on the alert, as it was impossible he could escape us; and in a few moments I had the satisfaction of seeing him bounding through the grass at about thirty yards' distance. The report of my rifle was quickly followed by three more shots as he passed down the line, and he fell dead at the feet of the minister, with five balls in his body.

In the evening, after our return from a good day's sport, we paid Jung Bahadoor a visit in his tent, and went with him to see the elephants which had been caught for the service of the Government during his year's absence from the country. In a square enclosure were upwards of two hundred elephants of all sorts and sizes. Here might be seen an elephant fastened between two others, and kept quiet only by being dragged continually in two different directions at once, no mahout having yet ventured to mount him; while, in evident terror at her proximity to such a monster, stood an anxious mother performing maternal duties to a young one not much larger than a calf, who was in no way puzzled by the position of the udder between her fore legs, but by a dexterous use of his trunk helped himself in a manner wonderfully precocious for so young a baby; indeed, he seemed very much pleased with having a trunk to play with, and certainly had a great advantage over most babies in possessing so permanent a plaything. Behind this interesting party stood a large elephant, with huge tusks, which had been chiefly instrumental in the capture of the victims he was now grimly surveying at a considerable distance, it not being safe to let him approach too near, as he seemed to be under the delusion that every elephant he saw still required to be caught. Each mahout now brought forward the prizes he had captured since the commencement of the year, and they were severally inspected: those which had no tufts of hair at the tips of their tails, or were in any way deformed, were put aside to be sold to unwary purchasers in India; while those approved by his Excellency were reserved for the use of government, or, to speak in plainer language, for his shooting parties.

As I do not know the points of an elephant as well as those of a horse, the want of the tuft was the only mark I could distinguish. However, the science of elephant-flesh seemed to be as deep and full of mysteries as that of horse-flesh.

Having finished our inspection, and the pay of an unsuccessful mahout or two having been stopped, Jung entered into a long disquisition upon the subject of the wild sports of the Terai. He told us, amongst other things, that he had forbidden all deer-shooting here, although the revenue to Government upon the skins amounted to £400 or £500 a year, in order that he might enjoy better shooting. Of course, we praised the love of sport which could prompt such an order, and said nothing of the love of country which might perhaps have prevented it. I was often struck by the despotic tone which the prime minister assumed, and it only confirmed my previous opinion as to his substantially possessing the sovereign power.

We killed five or six more deer and pigs before quitting Bisoleah on the following day, our road to Bechiacor leading us through the great forest, at this season perfectly healthy. We found our camp pitched in the broad dry bed of a mountain torrent, which I observed to be filled with fragments of granite and micacious schist.

As the shades of evening closed in upon the valley, the scene became extremely interesting: high upon the hillsides,—for we had reached the base of the Cheriagotty hills,—groups of natives, crouching round their fires, were sheltered only by grass huts, the labour of an hour. While lights twinkled in the minister's camp, soldiers were gathered round their watch-fires, and the villagers were assembled near a huge crackling blaze to witness so unusual, and to them so exciting a scene, as 5000 souls encamped in their solitary valley.

CHAPTER V

March to Hetowra—Cross the Cheriagotty Hills—Scenes of the
war of 1815-16—Preparations for a wild-elephant hunt—The
herd in full cry—A breakneck country—Furious charges of wild
elephants—The lost child—Return to camp

Early on the following morning we were on the march, and for
five miles did our clumsy elephant trip it heavily over the large
stones forming the bed of the stream in which we had been
encamped the previous night. I fear the beauty of the scenery
did not so well compensate him for the badness of the road as
his more fortunate riders. To see a hill at a distance after having
travelled so long over a dead level was refreshing; but when we
began to wind round the base of precipitous cliffs, or clamber
up some romantic mountain pass, the effect was most
animating.

The cliffs which now frowned over us were about 500 feet in
height; a few larches crowning the summit indicated the
elevation of the country, and almost reminded us of home,
until some monkeys swinging about amongst the branches at
once dispelled the illusion.

The hills themselves consist entirely of clay mixed with
sandstone, mica, and gravel; and the effect of the mountain
torrents during the rainy season upon such soft material had
been to form precipitous gullies, along which we were now
passing, while the grotesque pinnacles which constantly met
the eye reminded us of the dolomite formation of the Tyrol. In
many places were strata, sometimes horizontal, but more
frequently inclined at an angle of about forty-five degrees,
consisting of limestone, hornstone, and conglomerate.

This range is called by Hodgson the sandstone range; it does
not rise more than 600 feet from its immediate base, its
elevation above the sea being about 3000 feet. The pass itself,
by which we crossed the Cheriagotty hills, was a mere
watercourse, sometimes so narrow that the banks on each side

might be touched from the back of the elephant, and so steep and rocky that, both in ascending and descending into the dry bed of a torrent, the animal found no little difficulty in keeping his footing.

It was in this place that some of the severest fighting took place in 1816 during the Nepaulese war. Commanded by the surrounding heights and crowned by the temporary stockades of the Ghorkas, it was a dangerous and formidable obstacle to the progress of our army; but the able tactics of Sir David Ochterlony successfully overcame it. In the very watercourse we were now traversing the carcase of a dead elephant had, on one occasion during that campaign, fallen in such a manner as effectually to block up the way; and so narrow is the path, and so steep the banks on each side, that the army was absolutely delayed some time until this cumbrous impediment was removed.

After descending into the bed of the Chyria Nuddee our road lay through the saul forest, the magnificent trees of which served as a grateful shade for some miles, while, the road being comparatively level and free from impediments, our journey was most agreeable. A short distance from our destination we crossed the Kurroo Nuddee, by a picturesque wooden bridge peculiar to the Himalayas.

Hetowra is a place of considerable importance in a mercantile point of view, but it is not gay except during the season; it is, in fact, fashionable only while it is healthy. Form this place two roads lead to Katmandu. The whole of our week's stay in the Terai was rendered interesting to us from the recollection that in this province originated a war as disastrous to our troops as it was unprovoked by us. Never in our eastern experience have we commenced hostilities with a native power upon more justifiable grounds, and seldom have we paid more dearly for the satisfaction of at last dictating terms, from which indeed we have since reaped no great advantage. At Persa, but a short distance from Bisoleah, Captain Sibley and his detachment fell into the hands of the enemy, losing two guns and three-fourths of his men. Major-General Gillespie fell at the storming of Kalunga, while gallantly cheering on his men; our casualties here amounting to 225, twenty of whom were officers. Beaten back on this occasion, we were no less unsuccessful in a second attempt, losing in killed and wounded 483 men, including eleven officers. It was only when General Ochterlony assumed the command that affairs began to wear a brighter aspect. The energy and ability of this officer were displayed in a series of operations which daunted the enemy in proportion as they inspired confidence amongst our own ranks, and the result of the campaign was the expulsion of the Ghorkas from a large tract of country, which was subsequently annexed to British India. Attempts at negotiation were then made, which ultimately proved futile, and after the usual amount of delay, specious professions, and deceit common to native Courts generally had been practised by the Nepaul Durbar with a view to gain time, open hostilities broke out with redoubled vigour on both sides. General Ochterlony assumed the command of an army of 36,000 men, and commenced the campaign by moving the main body at once across the Cheriagotty hills, an operation involving incredible toil and difficulty, but which was, nevertheless, performed with the greatest rapidity. From Hetowra he advanced upon Muckwanpore, which, after two engagements, fell into his hands, our loss amounting to nearly 300. This fort commands the valley of Katmandu, and the Durbar therefore thought it advisable to treat as speedily as possible. The terms which were finally agreed upon differed little from those proposed on the former occasion, leaving in our hands a portion of the Terai, and, what was more important, giving the Ghorkas a more correct notion of the enemy they had to deal with than they had gained from their experience in the first campaign.

We found our camp prettily situated at the village of Hetowra, on the Rapti, surrounded by hills clothed to their summits with evergreen jungle, not unlike those I had lately left in Ceylon.

The Minister Sahib, having received information that a herd of wild elephants were in the neighbourhood, paid us a visit immediately on our arrival at camp, in a great state of excitement, and enjoined on us the necessity of an early start if we wished to partake of a sport which he promised would exceed anything we had ever witnessed, and prove such as no European had ever before had an opportunity of joining in.

I was aroused about 3 on the following morning, by the tune of the 'British Grenadiers,' played by the bands of the two regiments, which marched past my tent on their way to beat the jungle, and I wondered whether its composer ever imagined that its inspiriting effects would be exercised upon men bound on so singular a duty as those whose tramp we now heard becoming fainter and fainter as they wound up the valley. This was a signal for us to abandon our mattresses, which were always spread on the ground, in default of a four-poster, but were none the less comfortable or fascinating to their drowsy occupants on that account. It was necessary to make such a morning's meal as should be sufficient to last for 24 hours. This was rather a difficult matter at that early hour, as we had eaten a large dinner over-night; however, we accomplished it to the best of our power, and, jumping into our howdah, soon overtook Jung, whom we accompanied to what was to be the scene of action, a thick saul jungle on the banks of the Curroo Nuddee, here a considerable stream.

Down a hill before us, and by a particular pass, the wild elephants were to be driven by the united efforts of the gallant rifle corps, a regiment of infantry, and a hundred elephants; while our party, which comprised an equal number of these animals, was prepared to receive their brethren of the woods.

Our patience as sportsmen was destined to be severely tried, and midday came without any elephants having made their appearance: we therefore lit a huge fire, and, dismounting, partook with Jung of some very nice sweet biscuits and various specimens of native confectionery, declining the green-looking mutton which was kindly pressed upon us. Had the elephants chosen that moment to come down upon us, a curious scene must have ensued: Jung's grapes would have gone one way and his curry-powder the other—he was eating and curry-powder at the time; and his brother, who was toasting a large piece of mutton on a reed, must have either burnt his mouth or lost the precious morsel: however, the elephants did not come, so Jung finished his grapes and curry-powder, and his brother waited till the mutton was cool, ate it in peace, and went through the necessary ablutions. He then gave me a lesson in cutting down trees with a kukri, a sort of bill-hook, in the use of which the Nepaulese are peculiarly expert. The Minister Sahib at one stroke cut through a saul-tree which was 13 inches in circumference, while sundry unsuccessful attempts which I made on very small branches created great amusement among the bystanders skilled in the use of the weapon.

At last a dropping shot or two were heard in the distance: this was the signal of the approach of the herd, and I was put by the minister through the exercises necessary to be acquired before commencing the novel chase.

Taking off my shoes and tying a towel round my head, I was told to suppose an immense branch to be in front of me, and was taught to escape its sweeping effects by sliding down the crupper of the elephant, and keeping the whole of my body below the level of his back, thus allowing the branch to pass within an inch above it without touching me. In the same manner, upon a branch threatening me from the right or left, it was necessary to throw myself on the opposite side, hanging only by my hands, and swinging myself into my original position by a most violent exertion, which required at the same time considerable knack. Having perfected myself in these accomplishments to the utmost of my power, I awaited in patience the arrival of the elephants.

Looking round, I saw Jung himself, seated in the place of the mahout, guiding the elephant which he bestrode very cleverly. When silence was required he made a peculiar clucking noise with his tongue; whereupon these docile creatures immediately became still and motionless: one would drop the tuft of grass which he was tearing up, another would stop instantly from shaking the dust out of the roots which he was preparing to eat, others left off chewing their food. When a few seconds of the most perfect calm had elapsed, the rooting up and dusting out went on more briskly than ever, and the mouthful was doubly sweet to those who were now allowed to finish the noisy process of mastication.

At last our patience was rewarded, and Jung gave the signal for us to advance.

On each elephant there were now two riders, the mahout and a man behind, who, armed with a piece of hard wood into which two or three spikes were inserted, hammered the animal about the root of the tail as with a mallet. He was furnished with a looped rope to hold on by, and a sack stuffed with straw to sit upon, and was expected to belabour the elephant with one hand while he kept himself on its back with the other.

This was the position I filled on this trying occasion; but my elephant fared well as regarded the instrument of torture, for I was much too fully occupied in taking care of myself to think of using it. Away we went at full speed, jostling one another up banks and through streams, and I frequently was all but jolted off the diminutive sack which ought to have formed my seat, but did not, for I found it impossible to sit. Being quite unable to maintain any position for two moments together, I looked upon it as a miracle that every bone in my body was not broken. Sometimes I was suddenly jerked into a sitting posture, and, not being able to get my heels from under me in time, they received a violent blow. A moment after I was thrown forward on my face, only righting myself in time to see a huge impending branch, which I had to escape by slipping rapidly down the crupper, taking all the skin off my toes in so doing, and, what would have been more serious, the branch nearly taking my head off if I did not stoop low enough. When I could look about me, the scene was most extraordinary and indescribable: a hundred elephants were tearing through the jungle as rapidly as their unwieldy forms would let them, crushing down the heavy jungle in their headlong career, while their riders where gesticulating violently, each man punishing his elephant, or making a bolster of himself as he flung his body on one side or the other to avoid branches; while some, Ducrow-like, and confident in their activity, were standing on the bare backs of their elephants, holding only by the looped rope,—a feat I found easy enough in the open country, but fearfully dangerous in the jungle. A few yards in front of us was a wild elephant with her young one, both going away in fine style, the pace being 8 or 9 miles an hour. I was just beginning to appreciate the sport, and was contemplating hammering my elephant so as to be up amongst the foremost, when we, in company with about half a dozen others, suddenly disappeared from the scene. A nullah, or deep drain, hidden in the long grass, had engulfed elephants and riders. The suddenness of the shock unseated me, but fortunately I did not lose my hold of the rope, and more fortunately still my elephant did not roll over, but, balancing himself on his knees, with the assistance of his trunk, made a violent effort, and succeeded in getting out of his uncomfortable position.

The main body of the chase had escaped this nullah by going round the top of it; but we were not so much thrown out as I expected, for we arrived in time to see the wild elephant charging and struggling in the midst of her pursuers, who, after several attempts, finally succeeded in noosing her, and dragging her away in triumph between two tame elephants, each attached to the wild one by a rope, and pulling different ways whenever she was inclined to be unmanageable. I was watching the struggles which the huge beast made, and wondering how the young one, who was generally almost under the mother, had escaped being crushed in the mêlée, when a perfect roll of small arms turned our attention to another quarter, and I saw an elephant with an imposing pair of tusks charging down upon us through a square of soldiers, which had just been broken by it, and who were now taking to the trees in all directions. I ought to remark, lest the gallant riflemen should be under the imputation of want of valour in this proceeding, that they were only allowed to fire blank cartridge. The elephant next to me stood the brunt of the charge, which was pretty severe, while mine created a diversion by butting him violently in the side, and, being armed with a formidable pair of tusks, made a considerable impression; the wild one was soon completely overpowered by numbers, after throwing up his trunk and charging wildly in all directions. Of the violence of one of these charges I have retained visible proof, for a splintered tusk, which had been broken short off in the combat, was afterwards picked up and given to me as a trophy. Having succeeded in noosing this elephant also, we were dragging him away in the usual manner between two others, when he snapped one of the ropes and started off, pulling after him the elephant that still remained attached to him, and dashed through the jungle at full speed, notwithstanding the struggles of the involuntary companion of his flight. For a moment I feared that the courage of the mahout would give way in that pell-mell career, and that he would slip the rope which bound the two animals together. But he held on manfully, and after another exciting chase we succeeded in surrounding the maddened monster; my elephant jostled him so closely that I could touch him as we went neck and neck. It is a curious fact that the elephants never seem to think of uncurling their trunks, and sweeping their persecutors from the backs of their tame brethren: this they have never been known to do, though it has not unfrequently occurred that a wild herd have proved more than a match for the tame one, and then there is nothing for it but to turn and make off in an ignominious retreat as fast as the blows of the mahouts can urge them. It is only under these circumstances that there is any danger to the riders, and such an occurrence can take place only when the tame herd is small, and encounters an unusually large number of the wild elephants.

Upon this occasion we mustered so strong that defeat was out of the question.

We now heard a terrific bellowing at a short distance, which, in my ignorance, I thought proceeded from a huge tusker making a gallant resistance somewhere; I was rather disappointed, therefore, to find that the object of interest to a large group of men and elephants was only a young one struggling on his back in a deep hole into which he had fallen, and from which he was totally unable to extricate himself. Lying on his back, and kicking his legs wildly about in the air, he looked the most ridiculous object imaginable, and certainly made more noise in proportion to his size than any baby I ever heard. So incessant was his roaring that we could scarcely hear each other speak; at last, by means of ropes attached to various parts of his body, and by dint of a great deal of pulling and hauling, we extricated the unfortunate infant from his awkward position.

The poor little animal had not had a long life before experiencing its ups and downs, and it now looked excessively bewildered at not finding its mother, who had escaped with the rest of the herd. He was soon consoled, however, by being allotted to a tame matron, who did not seem particularly pleased at being thus installed in the office of foster mother whether she liked it or not.

We now all jogged home in great spirits, and, though Jung professed himself dissatisfied with only having captured four out of a herd of twelve, we were perfectly contented with a day's work which my elephant-shooting experience in Ceylon had never seen equalled, and which so fully realised the promise made by the minister at starting, that we should be the first to partake of a sport to be met with only in the noble forests of his native country.

CHAPTER VI

March to Bhimphede—National defences—The Cheesapany pass—Lovely scenery—Night adventure—The watch-fire— Reception at camp—Arrival at Katmandu

We had looked forward with no little anxiety to the morning following our elephant-hunt, as we were to go in search of rhinoceros: it was therefore a severe disappointment to us when Jung entered our tent at daylight, and informed us that it was necessary we should at once proceed on our way to Katmandu. The reason he gave us was, that we should have to go too far out of our route before we could find our game: however that might be, there was no help for it, and we commenced our march up the valley of the Rapti, along the narrow rocky path leading to Bhimphede, our next halting-place. It was a five hours' march, and we crossed the river thirty-two times before we came in sight of the picturesque Durumsolah, or native rest-house, which is situated at the head of the valley. Hills clothed to their summits with variegated jungle rose above us to an immense but not uniform height, and the scenery looked bolder as we became more enclosed among the mountains.

Bhimphede is a Newar village, the inhabitants being the aborigines of the country. It is said to derive its name from a Hindoo divinity named Bheem having on some occasion happened to step there. It is distant from Hetowra about 18 miles, and the road might be much improved by a little engineering.

The present policy of the Nepaul government is to keep the roads by which their country is approached in as impassable a state as possible, vainly imagining that, in case of a war, the badness of the roads would offer an insuperable obstacle to our progress, and compel us to relinquish any attempt to penetrate to Katmandu. This delusion ought to have been dispelled by the occupation of Muckwanpore by Sir David

347

Ochterlony; not that it is a contingency they need take much trouble to provide against, since it would never be worth our while to do more than take possession of the Terai.

The present state of the roads renders it impossible for goods to be conveyed into Nepaul, except upon men's backs; and as the traffic would be considerable in various articles of commerce, the prosperity and wealth of the country would be incalculably increased by an improvement in the means of transit.

Jung Bahadoor is quite alive to the real state of the case, and sees at once the absurdity of the policy pursued by the Nepaul government, but he feels that any innovation of the sort would be too unpopular for him to attempt in his present position. His recently imbibed liberal notions coincide but little with the cramped ideas of a semi-barbarous durbar. He is well aware that neither bad roads, troops, nor any other obstacle that he could oppose to our advance, would avail in case of our invading Nepaul. His feeling as regards a war with the British was not inaptly expressed in a remark he once made to me,— "If a cat is pushed into a corner it will fly at an elephant, but it will always try to keep out of the corner as long as possible."

At Bhimphede, where we arrived about midday, I dismounted from the elephant on which I had journeyed comfortably for 200 miles, and for which I had begun to feel quite an affection, and was soon high up the precipitous ascent of the Cheesapany pass. It crosses a mountain which rises nearly 2000 feet above the village at its base; the path is so steep that a horse can barely scramble up it; and the ascent of the Rigi, in Switzerland, seemed a mere nothing in comparison: this pass in its turn is not nearly so steep as the Chandernagiri, which is the last pass before you descend into the valley of Katmandu.

Having so much mountain work before me, I determined on walking the rest of the journey, that being the most satisfactory and enjoyable way of travelling across a highland country and viewing its scenery; my companion betook himself to a cot or dandy swung on a pole, preferring that method of getting carried over the hills to the one in general use amongst the natives, which I imagine is peculiar to Nepaul. An open-mouthed conical basket, like that of the Parisian chiffonnier, but with contents in some respects different, since this contains the traveller and not the shreds of his exploded journal, is fastened upon the back of a bearer by a strap across his forehead and two others over his shoulders; the occupant sits with his legs over the rim of the basket, and his back almost resting against the head of his bearer, who, bending forward under the weight of his load, and grasping a long stick, looks like some decrepit old man—a delusion which vanishes the instant you commence the ascent of a mountain by his side, when his endurance and vigour astonish you, if they do not knock you up.

Before we had toiled half way up the precipitous ascent, the view, that great alleviator of fatigue to the mountain traveller, was suddenly hidden from us by a thick mist in which we became enveloped, and which, rolling slowly over the hills, hid from our gaze a magnificent panorama of the lovely valley along which our morning's march had led us, and which lay stretched at our feet. With its broad stream winding down its centre, it reminded me of many similar valleys in Switzerland and the Tyrol, more particularly the Engadine, as seen from the hill above Nauders; while the hills, richly clad with masses of dark foliage, and rising to a height of two or three thousand feet, more nearly resembled those of the Cinnamon Isle. There is a fort near the summit of the pass with a few hundred soldiers, and a sort of custom-house, at which two sentries are placed for the purpose of levying a tax amounting to about sixpence upon every bundle passing either in or out of the Nepaul dominions; whether it be a bundle of grass or a bale of the valuable fabric manufactured from the shawl-goat of Thibet, the same charge is made, rendering it a grievously heavy tax upon the poor man with his load of wood, while it is a matter of no importance to the rich merchant whose coolies are freighted with rare and valuable merchandize.

Having accomplished nearly half the descent of the opposite side, we emerged from the mist, and a view of a wilder valley opened up, in which the streams were more rapid and furious, and the mountains which enclosed it more rugged and precipitous. A few trees, principally firs, were here and there scattered over the bare face of the mountain wherever they could find a sufficiently-sheltered nook. Enterprising settlers had perched themselves upon the naked shoulders of the hills, or were more snugly ensconced below by the side of the brawling stream, which was crossed here and there by primitive bridges, consisting of a log or two thrown from one heap of stones to another, which a few turfs laid upon them.

I observed in the Nepaul valleys—what must be the case in every country in which the hills are composed of a soft material—deltas formed by the soil which is washed down by the mountain torrents. The mass of débris in the valley often extends quite across it, and forces the stream through a gorge, frequently of considerable grandeur in those places where the power of the torrent during the rains is very great.

This circumstance adds greatly to the beauty of the scenery in the Tyrol, where the limestone formation of the hills thus worked upon spreads a soil in swelling knolls over the valley, on which the most luxuriant vineyards are picturesquely terraced. The effect, however, is very different in Nepaul, where the hills are composed chiefly of gravel and conglomerate; the deltas, consequently, produce crops of stones more frequently than of anything else. Notwithstanding the want of cultivation in the valley on which we were now looking down, it was full of a sublime beauty, the mountains at either end towering to a height of three or four thousand feet, while the path we were to follow was to be seen on the opposite side, winding over a formidable range, and always appearing to mount the steepest hills and to go down unnecessarily into innumerable valleys. It was with no little regret then that we made the almost interminable descent, apparently for the mere purpose of starting fair from the bottom of the valley, before we commenced the arduous climb in store for us over a range still higher than the one we had just traversed.

We crossed the stream at the bottom by a single-arched bridge of curious mechanism and peculiar to the Himalayas, the chief advantage being the large span, which admits of an immense body of water rushing through; a necessary precaution in the case of a mountain torrent. We then toiled up the hillside by a fearfully narrow path. At times my companion seemed absolutely hanging over the precipice; and our path was not in some places above twelve inches broad; had we slipped we must inevitably have become food for the fishes in the Pomonia, which was gliding rapidly along some hundreds of feet below, and which we were informed was a good trouting stream.

At last we reached the summit of the range, from which we had a lovely view of the surrounding country; the hills were just tipped by the setting sun; but this fact, while it added to the beauty of the scene, materially detracted from our enjoyment of it. In a few moments more we should be benighted, and we had still two hours' walk to the village for which we were bound. Accordingly, we had scarcely commenced the descent when it became so dark that it was no longer possible to distinguish the path; and having a vivid recollection of the precipices I had already passed, I felt no inclination to risk a fall of a few hundred feet. After making some little progress by feeling our way with sticks, we found it hopeless, and fairly gave in, having no alternative but to make the narrow path we were on our resting-place for the remainder of the night. This was a most disagreeable prospect, and we regretted that we had allowed Jung and his suite to ride on. The minister had recommended us to follow in cots, as he thought the road was too bad for men accustomed to level country to ride along. It was vain to tell him that we could ride where he could, or that we had seen hills before we came to Nepaul; he insisted that he was responsible for our safety, and would not hear of our riding. As we had little anticipated so arduous a march at starting, we had not thought it worth while further to contest the point with one who knew the country so well; and now, when it was too late, we sincerely wished ourselves comfortably lodged in his camp.

I had already walked for six consecutive hours over roads exceeding in danger and difficulty most of the mountain passes in Switzerland, and began to feel fatigued and not a little hungry, seeing that I had not touched a morsel of food since daybreak, with the exception of a crust of bread that I had found in my pocket. Thus the prospect of stretching myself out on a slippery path, with a stone for my pillow, and the contemplation of my miseries for my supper, was anything but agreeable.

As we were in this humour it was not to be wondered at that an intelligent soldier, whom we had for a guide, came in for a certain amount of our indignation when he informed us that it was still four coss (eight miles) to Pheer Phing, the place to which we were bound. Base deceiver !—he had told us at starting that it was not quite four coss, and now, after walking hard for six hours, we had got rather farther from it than we were at starting. It was impossible, at this rate, to say when our journey would come to an end. Nor could we get him to admit his error, and own that one or other of his statements must be wrong. He was a good-hearted fellow withal, and bore us no malice for our ill temper, but gave me a walking-stick and an orange as peace-offerings. However, he rigidly maintained his assertion as to the distance, at the same time suggesting that we should push on, encouraging us with the assurance that the rest of the path was a maidan or dead level. As he had made a similar statement at starting, and as the only bit of level walking we could remember was a log bridge, over which we had crossed, we knew too well what amount of confidence to put in this assertion.

At last one of the bearers who had gone on to explore the path ahead came back with the animating intelligence "that he saw a fire." We therefore determined to make for it with all diligence, and soon perceived the bright glare of a large watch-fire, with a party of soldiers crowded round it. We gladly joined them, and while one of their number was sent forward for torches we rolled ourselves in our cloaks near the crackling blaze, for the night was bitterly cold; and, heaping up fresh logs upon the fire, a bright flame lit up the wild scene.

We forgot our miseries as we watched the picturesque group of weather-beaten Ghorkas, or gathered what we could from their conversation, of their opinions upon the politics of the country, and the trip of the prime minister, on both which subjects they expressed themselves pretty freely, and took pains to impress upon us how anxious they were for our safe arrival in camp, informing us that their heads would be the price of any accident that should happen to us. At last the torches were seen flickering on the opposite hill, and soon afterwards we commenced our march in picturesque procession, passing over rugged ascents, across brawling rocky streams, and down dark romantic glens, until we began to think that the existence of Pheer Phing was a fiction.

It was about nine o'clock when I perceived we had entered a town which, by its brick pavement and high houses, I concluded to be a large one. After crossing three ranges of mountains, each nearly two thousand feet high, we did not much speculate upon anything but the distance still to be travelled; and the numerous lights twinkling in the distance were a welcome evidence of the proximity of Jung's encampment. The minister came out and received us cordially, expressing his regret at our misadventure and the anxiety he had been in as to our fate; for the route we had taken was not the ordinary one, but one of those short cuts which so often prove the unwary traveller's greatest misfortune. As our servants had not yet come up, he insisted upon our partaking of the repast he had prepared for us. I did not require a second invitation, and all scruples vanished as I looked with delight at the little leaf cups containing the scented greasy condiments formerly despised, and unhesitatingly plunged my fingers (for of course there were no spoons or forks) into a mass of rice and mixed it incontinently with everything within reach, disregarding the Jung's remonstrances, that this was salt-fish and the other sweetmeat, and that they would not be good together. After fasting for fifteen hours, and being in hard exercise the greater part of that time, one is not disposed to be particular, and to this day I have not the slightest conception what I devoured for the first ten minutes; at the end of that time my first sensation was peculiarly disagreeable—namely, that my hunger was sufficiently appeased to allow me to consider what I was eating; at this point I stopped, still rather hungry, but better off than my companion, who, having retained his presence of mind, had not touched anything.

We now got into palanquins prepared for us, and arrived at the residency at Katmandu at three in the morning, in a comatose state, arising partly from fatigue, partly from drowsiness, but chiefly, I imagine, from peculiar feeding.

CHAPTER VII

The British residency—Houses at the temple of Pusputnath—
Unprepossessing appearance of the Newar population—Their
dress and characteristic features—Ghorkas—Temple of
Pusputnath—View from the hill above it—The temple of
Bhood—Worshippers from Thibet and Chinese Tartary—Their
singular and disgusting appearance—Striking scene in the
grand square of the city of Katmandu

I did not awake until the day was far advanced, and my first
impulse was to look out of my window, with no little curiosity,
expecting to see the Snowy Range somewhere in the heavens
near the sun; in this I was disappointed, for the mist was so
dense that neither sun nor Snowy Range was visible; we
therefore determined to go in search of less exalted objects of
interest.

But ere we canter away from the door of the residency upon
the shaggy little ponies which had been provided for our use
by the Durbar, the Company's establishment in Nepaul
demands a moment's attention. In the only thoroughly
independent state extant in India the British Government is
represented by a Resident, to whose hospitality we were much
indebted during our delightful stay in Katmandu. His house, a
Gothic mansion of a rather gingerbread appearance, is
situated in a well laid-out park-like enclosure, which forms the
residency grounds, and which contains two or three neat
substantial houses, the habitations of the two officers of the
embassy. One of them kindly accompanied us in our search
after sights, and directed our steps in the first instance to the
temple of Pusputnath. We passed through the suburbs of
Katmandu by a road beautifully paved, in some places with
brick, in others with granite. It was along this road that the
body of Martiber Singh, the late prime minister, and uncle of
Jung Bahadoor, was dragged after he had been shot by his
nephew, and was burned on the bank of the Bhagmutty before

the soldiery (with whom he was an especial favourite) had any idea of his having been killed.

As I approached the temple I remarked some handsome houses, three or four stories in height, which we were informed were the residences of some of the priests. As they were good specimens of the architecture of this country, I may as well describe them here.

The whole front of the Nepaulese houses presented a mass of curiously carved wood-work, so that the beautiful flat brick of which they were built (and for the manufacture of which Nepaul is famous) was scarcely discernible amidst the intricate tracery which surrounded every window, and hung in broad wooden fringes from the balconies: these are formed under the eaves, which project five or six feet, and are supported by rafters, on which quaint figures are depicted in all sorts of impossible postures; the space between the rafters is also filled by carved wood, forming a sort of balcony or small room, generally occupied by the women of the establishment, and flat faces peer out of grotesque windows as you pass beneath.

But it must not be imagined that the same attraction exists here as in other Oriental countries to induce you to return their gaze. On the contrary, the female portion of the Nepaulese community is anything but attractive. I have seldom seen a race look more debased and squalid. Sometimes a florid tint about the nose and cheek-bones seems to hint at an affection for the bottle; while their flowing or rather tangled locks, and slovenly dress, might fairly induce the suspicion that they had but lately parted company with it. The Newar women, however, were ladylike in their appearance, when compared with some of the Bootya tribe with whom I afterwards made acquaintance.

It would, perhaps, be hardly fair to these copper-coloured ladies to judge entirely from their appearance, but, from what I could learn, it did not belie them, except, of course, as regards their friendship for the bottle, drunkenness being a vice which is not prevalent, though the strictness with respect to intoxicating liquors, so remarkable amongst the Hindoos of the plains, is by no means observable among the hill tribes.

The dress of the men consists of a short coat, not unlike a shooting-coat, reaching about half-way to the knees, and composed of a coarse cotton fabric manufactured in the country, from a tree which is a native of some of the lower valleys, but which I did not see in the valley of Katmandu.

In the colder months they wear home-spun woollen clothes. The dress of the women differs little from that of the men, except that the coat is longer, resembling a dressing-gown, and a sort of bodice is generally worn beneath it; a white shawl wrapped round the waist completes one of the most ungraceful costumes imaginable. All the men and some of the women are armed with the kukri, a heavy-bladed weapon or knife of singular shape. But lest this be too unprepossessing a picture of the Newars, or aborigines of Nepaul (for the Ghorkas are a superior and very different race), I should remark that I had no opportunity of seeing any of the females of the higher orders of either nation. The Ghorkas, being, for the most part, bigoted Hindoos, are prevented by their religion from allowing the women to appear in public. The Newars, not fettered by any such restraint, can now boast very few noble families; the ancient grandees of the Newar dynasty are extirpated, with the exception of one or two of the old aristocracy, who are in the last stage of decay. I cannot agree with Colonel Kirkpatrick (who wrote an account of his visit to Nepaul in 1803) in thinking that, "though the Newars have round and rather flat faces, small eyes, and low spreading noses, they bear no resemblance to Chinese features"; on the contrary, I was much struck with the great similarity of the mass of the lower order to the Chinese. Their imperturbable good humour and unaffected simplicity as plainly proved them a hill race, as did their picturesque dwellings and sturdy limbs. Altogether this class of the inhabitants of Nepaul are a cheerful, happy race, for whom one could feel a sort of affection after becoming reconciled to their appearance; but a woman is certainly not fascinating when what ought to be nose is nothing but cheek with two holes in it, and what ought to be neck is almost body as well. If people have protuberances in wrong places, it of course requires a little time for the eye to become accustomed to them. It may be that a goître is a beauty in the eyes of many a young Nepaulese swain. It matters little, however, to a young Newar bride whether her husband admires her or not, for she is at liberty to claim a divorce whenever she pleases, and, if her second choice be not of lower caste than herself, she may leave him at pleasure and return to her original spouse, resuming the charge of any family she may have had by him.

The Ghorkas are the conquerors of Nepaul, and now compose the army; they have grants of land called jaghires, on which they live when not actually on service. They are a handsome and independent race, priding themselves upon not being able to do anything but fight; and in their free and sometimes noble carriage often reminded me of the Tyrolese.

Besides the Ghorkas and Newars there are two or three other tribes, each consisting of but a limited number, and possessing no peculiar distinguishing marks, except the differences to be found in their religious opinions, which are generally a mixture of the Bhuddist and Hindoo creeds.

But to return to the temple of Pusputnath. This celebrated edifice is said to have been erected by Pussoopush Deoth, the fourth prince of the Soorijbunsee dynasty; and so sacred is the temple considered, that a pilgrimage to its shrines is held to be more meritorious than any other act that can be performed by a Hindoo. As the massive folding-doors opened before us, the view of the courtyard was certainly more striking than anything I had yet seen of the sort. Immediately opposite the handsome gateway, and situated in the centre of the courtyard, was the temple, roofed with lead, while the edges were ornamented with a profusion of gold leaf. Beside the large doors of massive silver were finely carved windows, covered in all directions with devices in the same precious metal.

Four sculptured lions guarded the double flight of steps, while at the bottom of the principal flight was a large figure of a kneeling bull (nanda), executed in copper, and superbly gilt. The rest of the courtyard was filled with images and shrines of various descriptions; a kneeling figure of Siva, a huge bell, more lions, and other sacred objects being studded throughout it in odd confusion. After looking at the varied and somewhat brilliant objects about us, our attention was directed to the roof of the temple, and certainly the transition from the sublime to the ridiculous was extraordinary. Pots, pans, old kukris, dusty-looking musical instruments, goods and chattels of all descriptions, such as one might imagine would form the contents of a Nepaulese pawnbroker's shop, if there is any such establishment here, were wedged together indiscriminately beneath the projecting roof of the pagoda, for of that Chinese form was this much venerated *Hindoo* temple. This mass of incongruous wares, as far as I could learn, was composed of the unclaimed goods of pious worshippers, persons dying without known heirs, and certainly, to judge from their appearance, the heirs did not lose much by not establishing their claims.

We ascended the hill, immediately under which the temple is situated, and were charmed with the lovely prospect which it commanded. On the left, and clothing with its brilliant colours a gentle slope, was the grove sacred to Siva, divided by the equally sacred Bhagmutty from the temple we had just visited, and into which we now looked down. The Bhagmutty was crossed by two narrow Chinese-looking bridges, resembling those we have such frequent opportunities of admiring on the willow-pattern plates. It is at this sacred spot that devout Hindoos wish to die with their feet in the water. Here it is that the bodies of the great are burnt; Martibar Singh was reduced to ashes at the end of the bridge, and so was the Ranee not three months before my visit, together with two favourite female slaves, whose society she did not wish to relinquish.

Beyond this interesting foreground stretched the luxuriant valley, its gentle slopes and eminences terraced to their summits, which were often crowned by some old fortified Newar town: the terraces, tinged with the brilliant green of the young crops, rose one above another to the base of the walls, while beneath the Bhagmutty wound its tortuous course to the romantic gorge in the mountains, through which it leaves this favoured valley to traverse lazily the uninteresting plains of upper India.

A peak of the gigantic Himaleh, bursting through the bank of clouds which had hitherto obscured it, reared its snow-capped summit far up towards the skies, and completed this noble prospect.

Crossing the river, we proceeded to visit the temple sacred to Bhood, the resort of the numerous tribes of Bhootiyas, or inhabitants of the highlands of Thibet and Chinese Tartary, who perform annual pilgrimages hither in the winter, but are obliged to return to their homes early in the spring, being unable to endure the heat of a Nepaulese summer.

This remarkable building was visible some time before we reached it, and is of the form peculiar to Bhuddist places of worship in other parts of the world, but more particularly in Anuradhupoora and the ancient cities of Ceylon, the ruins of which bear testimony to the existence of larger Dagobas than that before which the followers of the Bhuddist faith worship in the valley of Katmandu.

The pyramidal summit was gorgeously gilt, and terminated in a huge bell adorned in the same glittering manner, producing a brilliant effect as it brightly reflected the rays of the noonday sun. The massive stone platform on which the Dagoba stood was square; the ascent to it on each side was by a broad flight of steps, but, on the lower part of the pyramid, staring Chinese-looking eyes, painted in brilliant colours, detracted considerably from the imposing effect which a massive pile of stone and brick, not less than 120 feet high, would otherwise have produced.

We rode round it in a sort of courtyard, enclosed by small two-storied houses, which were very filthy, and out of which emerged men, women, and children, very filthy also; we were soon encompassed by a crowd of the most disreputable, dissolute-looking wretches imaginable. The women were dressed in thick woollen gowns, which had once been red, and reached a little below the knee; these were loosely fastened round the waist, remaining open or closed above as the case might be. The children, notwithstanding the inclement temperature, were in the cool and airy costume common to the rising generation in the East. The men were dressed exactly like the women; their matted hair and beard, flat noses, and wide eyes, generally bloodshot, giving them a disgusting appearance. Both sexes wore a sort of woollen gaiter, open at the calf, the protruding muscle of which looked as if nothing could have confined it; their shoes, as far as the dust would allow me to see, were of the same material. They seemed good-natured and inoffensive, but are not free from the vice of drunkenness; they consume quantities of tea prepared with rancid lard.

Had I been asked to determine the origin of this race, I should have pronounced it to be a mixture of Naples lazzaroni with the scum of an Irish regiment. The ruddy complexions of some of the women, and the swarthy look of many of the men, might fairly warrant such a conclusion. They were so importunate and offensive as they pressed round me that I hurried over my sketch of the temple, and made my escape from them, not, however, without once more looking round with interest on the crowd of beings whose distant habitations were upon the northern slope of the Himalayan chain, hitherto unvisited by any European, except Dr. Hooker, and consequently almost totally unknown.

I quite envied them the journey they were about to undertake, which would occupy them three weeks; the large droves of sheep by which they are always accompanied carried their limited worldly possessions, together with the various tokens of civilization which they had procured in the (to them) highly civilized country they were now visiting, and on which no doubt their Bhootan friends would look with no little awe and wonderment.

This wandering and singular race do not visit Nepaul solely to worship at the temple of Bhood, but have an eye to business as well as religion. I shall have occasion by and by to speak of the numerous articles which they import into Nepaul, on the backs of sheep, over the rocky passes which lead from the cold region they inhabit.

On our way from the temple of Bhood, which, by the by, had just been furbished up and whitewashed by a great man from H'Lassa, an emissary of the Grand Lama's, we passed through the town of Katmandu, which was entered by a massive gateway, the city being surrounded by a wall. Long narrow streets, very fairly paved, lead in all directions; the houses are not so high as those of Benares or Cairo, the streets are broader, and some of them would admit of the passage of a carriage. They are all well drained and comparatively clean, contrasting most favourably in that respect with any other Oriental town I have ever seen. The streets were filled with foot-passengers, in bright and variegated costumes, passing busily on, or stopping to make purchases at the shops, which were on the ground-floor, with the whole front open, and the merchant sitting in the midst of his wares. The next story is inhabited, I believe, by his family; but I did not gain an entrance into any of the common houses. The outside front generally presented a mass of wood carving, each small window surrounded by a border two or three feet broad, while under the eaves of the house projected the singular balcony I have already described.

The great square, in which is situated the Durbar, or palace of the King, presented in itself almost all the characteristic features of a Nepaul town. As it suddenly burst upon us on turning the corner of the long street leading from the city-gate, the view was in every respect most striking. This square, or court, is well paved, and contains the Chinese pagoda, composed entirely of wood, from which it is said the town derives its name. Its three or four roofs, glittering one above another, are supported by grotesque representations of unknown deities, and figures of all sizes and colours, not always of the most proper description. The whole formed a mass of green, gold leaf, and vermilion; and was guarded by a sentry, who, in order to be in keeping with his charge, wore a long flowing gown of bright colours, reaching to his ankles, and marched backwards and forwards at the top of a long flight of steps. A couple of well-carved lions, in grey sandstone, guarded the lower steps as efficiently as he did the upper ones. There were at least four pagodas, painted in like way, and guarded in like manner, in the great square of Katmandu. The guard-house contained a large stand of arms of antique construction. There was also the Durbar, the residence of the Rajah, a straggling building, almost European in its style, and gaudy enough to please even the late King of Bavaria; close to it was a huge deformed image of Siva, sitting in an uncomfortable posture on a square stone, violently gesticulating with her fourteen arms, perhaps at a party of heretical Bhootyas who were passing tranquilly by, leading along their sheep, decidedly the cleanest and most respectable-looking members of the group. Beyond, high and gloomy houses almost touched, their wooden fringes creaking responsively to one another across the narrow streets, while the owners of the cobwebby tenements, peeping out of the narrow windows in their balconies, made their remarks upon the strangers in not much more melodious tones; in an old courtyard a little way above, was visible an unwieldy rhinoceros, placidly contemplating a bundle of grass, from which it had satisfied its hunger, in happy ignorance that its life is dependent on that of the Rajah; for in Nepaul it is a rule that the death of one great animal should be immediately followed by that of another, and, when a Rajah dies, a rhinoceros is forthwith killed to keep him company. As he stood tethered almost under the palace windows, we thought him at once a fitting moral and a characteristic background to this novel and interesting picture.

CHAPTER VIII

*The temple of Sumboonath–View from the platform of the
temple–The valley of Nepaul and its resources–Tradition
respecting it–Entrance of the Prime Minister into Katmandu–
The two kings–A brilliant reception*

The temple of Sumboonath, which we next visited, is situated
on the summit of a woody eminence; it is approached by a
long flight of steps, the trouble of ascending which is amply
compensated by the lovely view which the platform of the
temple commands, as well as by an inspection of the curious
construction of the building itself.

Sumboonath is looked upon as one of the oldest temples in
Nepaul, and was erected, according to Kirkpatrick, when
Nepaul was ruled by a race of Thibetians; its possession was at
one time claimed by the Dalai Lama, or Sovereign Pontiff of
H'Lassa, but he has since been obliged to abandon the claim.

The Dagoba resembles the temple of Bhood, but is only
about half its size; the spire is covered with plates of copper,
gilt. It is surrounded by pagodas, as well as numerous more
modern shrines of a bastard Hindoo class, to which Bhootyas
and Bhamas, a tribe of Newars, resort in great numbers.
Occasionally the Ghorkas visit these shrines; the thunderbolt
of Indra, which is here exhibited, being, I suppose, the object
of attraction to them, as they pride themselves on being
orthodox Hindoos.

This collection of temples is surrounded by rickety old
houses, inhabited by Bhootyas and priests. All around small
images sit upon wet stones, holding in their hands everlasting
tapers, and look out of their niches upon the dirty worshippers
who smother them with faded flowers. Turning our backs
upon these little divinities, we obtained the first panoramic
view we had yet had of the valley and city of Katmandu.

The valley is of an oval shape; its circumference is nearly 50
miles, and the hills by which it is enclosed vary from one to two

thousand feet in height. Sheopoorie, the most lofty of these, is clothed to the summit with evergreen jungle, and rises abruptly behind the town. Behind it the fantastically shaped Jib Jibia shows its craggy summit thickly powdered with snow, while the still loftier Gosain-Thān, at a distance of about 30 miles, rears its ever white and glittering peak to a height of 25,000 feet, and seems majestically to preside over this glorious scene.

The town of Katmandu, situated at the junction of the Bhagmutty and Bishmutty, and containing a population of 50,000 inhabitants, lay spread at our feet, and we could discern the passengers on the narrow fragile-looking bridges which span the two rivers, at this time containing scarcely any water. Innumerable temples, Bhuddist and Hindoo, and mixtures of both, occupied hillocks, or were situated near the sacred fonts or groves with which the valley abounds, and which adds much to the beauty of its appearance. The number of the edifices affords strong proof of the superstition of the people, and warrants the remark of Colonel Kirkpatrick, who says that there seem to be in Nepaul as many shrines as houses, and as many idols as inhabitants.

A tradition is current in Nepaul that the valley of Katmandu was at some former period a lake, and it is difficult to say in which character it would have appeared the most beautiful. The knolls, wooded or terraced, with romantic old Newar towns crowning their summits,—the five rivers of the valley winding amongst verdant meadows,—the banks here and there precipitous, where the soft clayey soil had yielded to the action of the torrent in the rains,—the glittering city itself,—the narrow paved ways leading between high hedges of prickly pear,—the pagodas and temples studded in all directions, presented a scene as picturesque and perhaps more interesting than would have been afforded by the still lake embedded in wild mountains, and frowned upon by snow-capped peaks; while the richly cultivated knolls in the valley formed fertile islands, the luxuriant vegetation of which would have softened the scene into one of exquisite beauty.

Whether the rich and wonderfully prolific soil of the valley is the alluvial deposit of this lake, I cannot say, but there is no doubt that, whatever may be the cause, the valley of Nepaul is almost unrivalled in its fertility, supporting as it does in comfort and plenty a population of 400,000 inhabitants, being 300 persons to the square mile.

There is not, I conceive, any other mountainous country in the world that can boast of possessing so favoured a spot. Throughout its whole length and breadth, not a stone is to be found: it is well watered; its temperature is delightful, the thermometer in the hottest month seldom reaches 75°, in the coldest never falls below 30°; it is sufficiently near the tropics to rejoice in the presence of the warm bright sun even in the depth of winter, while the proximity of the ever snow-capped "Himaleh" prevents the heat being too severely felt in the middle of summer. It rarely freezes in the valley, and never snows, although the hills around, some of which do not exceed 1000 feet, are frequently powdered.

It is impossible to conceive a more enjoyable climate, and the numerous productions of which the valley can boast betoken its genial influences.

I am sorry that I cannot from my own observation testify to the rich variety of its vegetable productions, as the time of year during which I was in Nepaul was unfavourable, but many English forest-trees flourish here,—amongst them, oaks, chestnuts, and pines; rhododendrons also abound, and I observed almost every species of English fruit-tree: in the residency garden all the European vegetables are raised to perfection.

But to return from this digression on the advantages of soil and climate which the valley possesses. The lovely view before us comprised in a glance the grand and majestic scenery of the mountains, with the softer but still animating view of the luxuriant plain, bearing evidence of that large and industrious population whose habitations were so picturesquely grouped throughout it.

We had not nearly satisfied our desire to gaze upon so much that was new and interesting, when we were informed by our attendants that the astrologers had announced the auspicious moment at which the Minister Sahib, or, as we must now call him, Jung Bahadoor Comaranagee, should leave the camp outside the city walls and make an imposing entry into Katmandu.

This lucky hour was now close at hand; and as the entrance of the prime minister into the capital was a scene not to be lost, we hurried down to be in time for the ceremony of his reception.

In a few moments we were rattling in one of the only carriages in Nepaul over one of the only carriage-roads of which it can boast, and soon reached the bridge, near which was pitched a spacious tent. On our way we passed a square lined with soldiers, and the streets were crowded with a motley population, such as it would be vain to endeavour to describe, but which increased in density as we approached the centre of attraction, near which we were obliged to leave the carriage, and were conducted between rows of soldiers by various members of the royal household, each of us being led by the hand in the most affectionate manner. My conductor was a brother of Jung Bahadoor's, who distinguished himself about a week afterwards by a base attempt to assassinate the minister. I was unfortunate in my friends in other instances besides this: one old man, who had accompanied the minister to Europe, and was an especial ally of mine on board ship, was implicated in the same vile plot against the life of the man towards whom he had every reason to feel gratitude, if such a sentiment is known amongst Orientals. Poor old Kurbeer Kutrie was a venerable-looking dignified old man, bigoted to an excess, and thoroughly disgusted with his trip to the land of the beef-eaters, though he could not but admit that what he saw was wonderful! The ignominious punishment which was inflicted upon him for his share in the conspiracy, and by which he lost caste, was doubtless more severely felt by him than death would have been. Not that it signifies in the least in Nepaul whether a man is a fratricide or prefers making away with more distant relatives. If you do not associate with assassins, you must give up the pleasures of Nepaul society. Among the natives assassination is not looked upon as a crime, but as a matter of course; the minister, however, with those of his suite who accompanied him on his recent mission, have become more enlightened in this respect, and have found to their astonishment that indiscriminate murder is not the usual mode adopted in the civilized world for bringing about political changes or accomplishing private ends.

Jung Bahadoor, no doubt, now wishes that more of the Durbar had made the same trip, and profited by it in like manner, since the custom above alluded to must be highly inconvenient to him, more particularly since he has eight brothers, most of whom cast a longing eye towards the premiership; a man's chance of filling this office not depending upon his power "to form a ministry," so much as upon his accuracy in taking aim and his skill in seizing any opportunity offered by his rival of showing his dexterity in a manner more personal than pleasant. Jung Bahadoor may well exclaim, "Save me from my brothers!" Already has one of them attempted his life; but the Minister has learned mercy in England, and, to the astonishment of everyone, Budreenath Sing and his fellow conspirators are only banished for life. It is said that the minister resisted all the representations of his friends as to the propriety of executing the conspirators by the argument of "What would the 'Times' say?"—which must have appeared to the majority of the members of the Nepaul Durbar to be a very extraordinary reason for leniency.

Bum Bahadoor had acted as prime minister during the absence of his brother in England, and had just learnt to value the possession of power when the return of the minister put an end to his short-lived greatness, and he would have sunk at once into comparative insignificance, had not Jung, who knew enough of human nature to guess the sentiments of a man in such a position, judiciously gilded the pill by making him Commander-in-Chief of the Forces.

Grasping the friendly hand of my conductor, in happy ignorance of his fratricidal intentions, I followed immediately behind the Minister, whose return to Nepaul, after he had encountered the perils of land and sea, and paid a visit to the Queen of the greatest country in the world, not even excepting China, was a matter of so much importance, that the Rajah himself came from his palace to the spot where we were now assembled, to meet one who had been favoured with an interview with so mighty a monarch, and who had in his possession the letter from her majesty of England to his majesty of Nepaul. We were, therefore, prepared to see the king seated on a divan, and arrayed in gorgeous attire; but who the old gentleman was who was sitting with most perfect sang froid next him on his elevated seat, I was at a loss to conceive. Whoever he was, he seemed most perfectly at home, and I found on inquiry it was natural he should be so, for the old man was sitting on his own throne, which had been usurped by his son, he having been dethroned on the score of imbecility. Such being the case, why he was allowed to occupy the place he did was inexplicable, unless it were to prove that he really was unfit to sit upon the throne alone, since he was content to share it upon grand occasions with his son, whenever this latter precocious young gentleman, who was, as it were, the representative of "Young Nepaul," chose to give his venerable father a treat.

But it would be useless to speculate on the cause of this proceeding, since it is impossible ever to understand, and hopeless to attempt to discover, the motives or secret springs which actuate a native Durbar; and no doubt Jung himself, who is the real manager of everything, had some good reason for the present double occupancy of the throne. It struck me that it would answer one purpose at any rate: it would show the people that the young king looked as imbecile as the old one, while his countenance was far less prepossessing, as he seemed only to have just sense enough to be able to gratify the brutal and sensual passions to which he is a prey; whether the stories of wholesale executions of slaves taking place in his courtyard merely for his amusement are true or not, I cannot say, but he looked capable of any wickedness, and, though not more than twenty-two or twenty-three years old, had already rivalled the atrocities of Nero. His countenance was not unlike those depicted on the walls of Indian towns, with the same large staring eyes, thin twisted moustache, sensual lips, and thick bull neck. His dress was handsome, and his jewels were magnificent; but in dress, in carriage, and in dignity of manner, the prime minister was unquestionably the most distinguished-looking man in Durbar. He wore a magnificent robe of white silk embroidered with gold, and tight pantaloons of rich brocade, which set off his slim figure to advantage; his turban was a mass of sparkling diamonds, and his whole person seemed loaded with jewels. His sturdy body-guard, all armed with double-barrelled rifles, stood close behind his chair, and were the only soldiers in the tent; the nonchalant way in which he addressed the rajah, with folded arms and unbended knee, betokened the unbounded power he possesses in the state. Perhaps it is not very politic in him to arrogate so much to himself in a land where every man's hand is against him, in proportion as he is feared by everyone from his majesty downwards.

On each side of the tent stood a row of grandees of the realm, amongst whom the eight brothers of Jung Bahadoor held conspicuous places, while kasies and sirdars continued the line, until they were lost in the crowd of minor officers.

The blaze of jewels, and the glitter of gold and silver, were calculated to strike an European spectator with astonishment, and he might well be startled at so magnificent a display in a highland court.

I observed a few English and French uniforms, covered with a great deal more of gold and silver lace than they were entitled to; all which gaudy array was the more striking to me when I remembered that I had on a plaid shooting-coat and felt hat. I had no opportunity of explaining to his majesty that plaid shooting-coats and felt hats are the court costume in England, but no doubt he thought it all correct. It is, moreover, the prerogative of Englishmen to sit in the presence of Oriental potentates with their hats on, which prevented my secreting my shabby old wide-awake as I had intended.

As I sat next but one to the minister, I was under the immediate protection of the rifles and pistols, which latter implements protruded in a most formidable manner from the belts of the body-guard. As various Nepaulese nobles of doubtful politics sat in front of his Excellency, he felt these gentlemen-at-arms were peculiarly valuable additions to his retinue, as being ready to act either on the offensive or defensive at a moment's notice. Everything, however, went off with the most perfect harmony; a few compliments were exchanged between himself and his sovereign, and the meeting broke up after the usual ceremony of giving and receiving pawn. This consisted in the presentation by both the kings, to every stranger present, of a small pyramidal packet of leaves, which, when opened by the favoured recipient, was found to contain a few other leaves, stuck together by slimy substances, of unpleasant appearance and aromatic odour. Fortunately, you were not compelled to partake of this in the presence of the royal donor, and means were found to dispose of it slily on leaving his majesty's audience-chamber.

As we were driving back to the Residency, it struck me that the history of a man who, at so early an age, had raised himself from being an ensign in the army to the powerful position which the grand display at his reception had just proved him to hold in his own country, would be interesting, if it were possible to gain any information on the subject that could be relied upon. I therefore determined to collect the best that it was in my power to obtain; and the following particulars, gathered partly from himself, and partly from one who has had many opportunities of becoming acquainted with his history, form, I believe, a trustworthy account of a career which, from its tragic nature, is invested with a thrilling interest, while it faithfully portrays the eventful changes usually attending the life of an Oriental statesman.

CHAPTER IX

Sketch of the career of His Excellency General Jung Bahadoor, Prime Minister of Nepaul

It will be necessary before commencing an account of the career of Jung Bahadoor to describe the state in which the political affairs of Nepaul were when his ambition and daring prompted him to play so important a part in its government. Cool, courageous, and an adept in all arts of intrigue, he possessed every qualification necessary to render a man successful in the East, where native courts are incessantly torn asunder by rival factions, and scenes of violence and bloodshed are the result of plots and counterplots, as each party becomes for the time predominant, and its leading man assumes the office of premier, to be soon after deprived of his short-lived greatness by a successful conspiracy of the opposing party. These in their turn share the same fate, the King and country remaining passive spectators of the struggles between the opposing factions. They are indeed uninteresting to the King, for he is only too delighted to get anyone to take the cares of government off his shoulders, and considers his prerogative to consist in enjoying himself as much as possible. They are equally uninteresting to the country, for these violent dissensions do not arise upon questions of policy, in any way affecting its government. Ministerial explanations are never asked for nor given in the East. The power of the prime minister is absolute till he is shot, when it becomes unnecessary to question the expediency of his measures, and the people are only interested to this extent, that, generally speaking, the longer a premier can maintain his position, by so much is their prosperity increased.

The two rival factions in Nepaul were the Pandees and Thapas, and in the early part of this century the reins of government were held by one of the most enlightened men that ever attained to the position of prime minister. Bheem

Singh Thapa has left behind him numerous monuments of his greatness, calculating, like Napoleon, that his fame would last at least as long as they did. For an unusual number of years did this able minister retain the management of affairs. He was ultimately placed in confinement, on the charge of being accessory to the murder of the Rajah's children by poison. His enemies resorted to an ingenious, though cruel device, to rid themselves altogether of so dreaded a rival. Knowing his high spirit and keen sense of honour, they spread the report that the sanctity of his Zenana had been violated by the soldiery, which so exasperated him that he committed suicide, and was found in his cell with his throat cut from ear to ear; this occurred in the year 1839. His property was of course confiscated, and the greater part of his family banished. His successor, Ram Singh Pandee, did not long enjoy his ill-gotten power, for, having been discovered intriguing against the British with the ministers of other native courts, he was removed at the representations of our government. Mahtabar Singh, a nephew of the former prime minister, Bheem Singh Thapa, had meantime ingratiated himself with the Ranee (Queen), and through her influence succeeded in getting himself appointed to the vacant post of premier—when, as was to be expected, his first act was to decapitate his predecessor, and as many of the Pandee's family as possible.

The brother of Mahtabar Singh was a kazi, commanding a portion of the army stationed on the northwest frontier of Nepaul, and the second of his eight sons was Jung Bahadoor, then a subadar, or ensign. The independent spirit which the young man had manifested from a boy led him into frequent scrapes with the old kazi, and he used to escape the punishments which they entailed by absconding altogether, and remaining absent until he thought his father's wrath had subsided, or until, as was oftener the case, his own resources were expended. These, however, he usually found means to replenish by his expertness at all games of chance with cards and dice, and early in life he became an accomplished gambler.

He was moreover a great favourite amongst the soldiers, as well from his readiness to join them in any wild scheme, as from his skill in all manly exercises and accomplishments. At last the young officer, impatient of being under command, decided upon a bolder step than a mere temporary absence without leave, and thinking, no doubt, that it was a duty he owed to society to improve himself as much as possible by seeing the world, he walked across the Nepaul frontier into Upper India, and profitably employed his time by turning his powers of observation to account, thereby gaining considerable insight into the mode of government and resources of our Indian possessions.

After a time his own resources became so greatly diminished that he was obliged to return, trusting to his powers of acting the repentant prodigal to avert the torrent of his father's wrath. The breach of discipline which he had committed was as readily overlooked in Nepaul as it would have been in other more civilised countries, when the offender has good interest to back him; and promotion to the command of a company was given him as the reward of his services while ensign. About this period Jung Bahadoor received the intelligence of the advancement of his uncle, Mahtabar Singh, to the office of prime minister. So fine a chance for an adventurous spirit to push his fortune at court was not to be lost, and once more bidding adieu to the dull out-station at which he was posted, to the constraint of discipline and to the grumblings of the old martinet, his father, he followed the example of many great men before him, and betook himself to the capital, thinking it the only place in which his talents could be appreciated. Here he possessed frequent opportunities of displaying that aptitude for intrigue to which he mainly owes his present position, coupled as it was with a daring that hesitated not at the performance of any act which his keen perception and subtle understanding pointed out as necessary for the advancement of his own interests. Jung soon after accompanied a secret mission to Benares, to meet one from the north-west, with the view of organising a war against the British. The vigilance of our authorities, however, discovered the existence of this conspiracy, and Jung, together with his compatriots, was ignominiously taken back to his own frontier, and there liberated. On his return to the capital he led much the same life as before, dabbling not a little in politics; and the ambitious views which now began to actuate him rendered him obnoxious to the young prince, then a mere boy of eighteen, who, nevertheless, seemed to share with his father a portion of the executive. Indeed it was difficult to say in whom the sovereign authority rested; for the Ranee, or wife of the old King, had, with the assistance of Mahtabar Singh, the prime minister, gained a great influence over the mind of the monarch, who seems to have become nearly imbecile.

It was perhaps the near relationship of Jung to the Prime Minister that brought upon him the ill-will of the Prince, who treated him with the most unmitigated animosity, and used every means in his power surreptitiously to destroy him. On one occasion he ordered him to cross a flooded mountain torrent on horseback, and when he had reached the middle of the current, which was so furiously rapid that his horse could with difficulty keep his footing, the young Prince suddenly called him back, hoping that, in the act of turning, the force of the stream would overpower both horse and rider. This danger Jung escaped, owing to his great nerve and presence of mind. In relating this anecdote he seemed to think that his life had been in more imminent peril than on any other occasion; though the following struck me as being a much more hazardous exploit. After the affair of the torrent the Prince was no longer at any pains to conceal his designs upon the life of the young adventurer, and that life being of no particular value to anyone but Jung himself, it was a matter of perfect indifference to anybody and everybody whether the Prince amused himself by sacrificing Jung to his own dislikes or not. It is by no means an uncommon mode of execution in Nepaul to throw the unfortunate victim down a well: Jung had often thought that it was entirely the fault of the aforesaid victim if he did not come up again alive and unhurt. In order to prove the matter satisfactorily, and also be prepared for any case of future emergency, he practised the art of jumping down wells, and finally perfected himself therein. When, therefore, he heard that it was the intention of the Prince to throw him down a well, he was in no way dismayed, and only made one last request, in a very desponding tone, which was, that an exception might be made in his favour as regarded the being cast down, and that he might be permitted to throw himself down. This was so reasonable a request that it was at once granted; and, surrounded by a large concourse of people—the Prince himself being present by way of a morning's recreation—Jung repaired to the well, where, divesting himself of all superfluous articles of clothing, and looking very much as if he were bidding adieu for ever to the happy valley of Nepaul, he crossed his legs, and, jumping boldly down, was lost to the view of the prince and nobles, a dull splash alone testifying to his arrival at the bottom. Fortunately for Jung there was plenty of water—a fact of which most probably he was well aware—and there were, moreover, many chinks and crannies in the porous stone of which the well was built; so, having learnt his lesson, Jung clung dexterously to the side of the well until midnight, when his friends, who had been previously apprized of the part they were to perform, came and rescued him from his uncomfortable position, and secreted him until affairs took such a turn as rendered it safe for Jung Bahadoor to resuscitate himself. Such was the adventure of the well, which, marvellous as it may appear, was gravely related to me by his Excellency, who would have been very much scandalised if I had doubted it, which of course I did not.

While in a story-telling mood, I may as well relate an account that was given me of the manner in which Jung distinguished himself on one occasion with a musk elephant. The story is interesting, as it was by such daring feats that he won for himself the reputation of being the most undaunted sportsman in Nepaul. The elephant in question had been for some time the terror of the neighbourhood, nor was anyone found hardy enough to attempt the capture of the rabid monster. At last, so notorious became his destruction of life and property that Jung heard of it, and at once determined to encounter him. The animal was in the habit of passing along the narrow street of a village in the course of his nocturnal depredations. One night Jung posted himself on the roof of a low outhouse, and, as the huge brute walked under the roof, made a vigorous leap, which landed him on the neck of the elephant, and, in spite of all the efforts of the infuriated animal, there he maintained his position until he succeeded in blindfolding him with a cloth, and in securing him to a tree, amidst the shouts of the populace. Lest this story should seem too improbable to be credited, it may be remarked that a musk elephant is often, as was the case in this instance, a tame one, which at a particular season becomes rabid, and, breaking loose, is the terror of the neighbourhood until recaptured.

During this eventful period in Jung Bahadoor's life, his uncle, Mahtabar Singh, continued to administer the affairs of government with tolerable success; but the Ranee, to whom he was beholden for the position he occupied, turned the influence she had thus obtained over him to a bad account, and this gallant soldier and popular minister ultimately became distrusted and feared by his own friends, with whom the Ranee was no favourite. This unprincipled woman ill repaid the devotion of her minister, for, on his refusing to comply with her request that he should put to death some of her personal enemies, she became at once his implacable foe, and ruthlessly resolved upon the destruction of her hitherto devoted ally. Thus Mahtabar Singh found himself alienated from and distrusted by his own faction, while he was abandoned by his former patroness, for whose favour he had sacrificed their adherence. The Ranee did not hesitate to apply to this very party for assistance in the furtherance of her nefarious design, and the prime minister was doomed to fall a victim to his own indecision by the hands of his favourite nephew.

One night, about eleven o'clock, a messenger came from the palace to inform him that his services were required by their Majesties—for the Queen had always kept up a semblance of friendship with him. Without the slightest suspicion he repaired to the palace, but scarcely had he ascended the great staircase, and was entering the room in which their Majesties were seated, when the report of a pistol rung through the room; the fatal bullet pierced the heart of the gallant old man, who staggered forward, and fell at the feet of the wretched woman who had been the instigator of the cruel murder.

It is difficult to say what were the motives that prompted Jung Bahadoor to the perpetration of this detestable act, of which he always speaks now in terms of the deepest regret, but asserts that it was an act of necessity, from which there was no escaping. The plea which he invariably uses when referring to the catastrophe is, that either his life or his uncle's must have been sacrificed, and he naturally preferred that it should be the latter. However that may be, the immediate effect was, the formation of a new ministry, in which Jung held office in the capacity of commander-in-chief. The premier, Guggum Singh, was associated with two colleagues. A year had hardly elapsed before Guggun Singh was shot while sitting in his own room. This occurred in the year 1846; a sirdar was taken up on suspicion of having committed this murder, and Abiman Singh, one of the premier's colleagues, was ordered by the Queen to put him to death; as, however, the Rajah would not sanction the execution, Abiman Singh refused to obey the command—a proceeding on his part which seems to have raised a suspicion in the mind of Jung that he had been concerned in the assassination. This suspicion he communicated to Futteh Jung, the other colleague of the late prime minister, suggesting that Abiman Singh and the sirdar already in custody should be forthwith executed, and Futteh Jung installed as prime minister. Futteh Jung, however, refused to accede to so strong a measure; and Jung, who was not of a nature to be thwarted in his plans, determined upon temporarily depriving him of his liberty, in order to enable him to put the design into execution himself.

He had no sooner decided upon his line of conduct than he displayed the utmost resolution in carrying it out. On the same night, and while at the palace, the suspicions which Jung already entertained were confirmed by his observing that Abiman Singh ordered his men to load. It was no time for hesitation. The two colleagues, with many of their adherents, were assembled in the large hall, where the Queen, in a highly-excited state, was insisting upon an immediate disclosure of the murderer of Guggun Singh, who was supposed to have been her paramour. At this moment Jung gave the signal for the seizure of Futteh Jung. The attempt was no sooner made than his son, Karak Bikram Sah, imagining that his father's life was at stake, rushed forward to save him, and seizing a kukri, had already dealt Bum Bahadoor a severe blow, when he was cut down by Dere Shum Shere Bahadoor, then a youth of sixteen or seventeen.

Futteh Jung, vowing vengeance on the murderers of his son, sprang forward to avenge his death, and in another moment Bum Bahadoor, already seriously wounded, would have fallen at his feet, when the report of a rifle rang through the hall, and the timely bullet sped by the hand of Jung Bahadoor laid the gallant father by the side of his no less gallant son.

Thus Jung's *coup d'état* had taken rather a different turn from what he had intended; the die, however, was cast, and everything depended upon his coolness and decision in the trying circumstances in which he was placed. Though he may have felt that his life was in most imminent peril, it is difficult to conceive how any man could attain to such a pitch of cool desperation as to enact the scene which closed this frightful tragedy. There still confronted him fourteen of the nobles whose leader had been slain before their eyes, and who thirsted for vengeance; but the appearance at his side of that faithful body-guard, on whose fidelity the safety of the minister has more than once depended, precluded them from seizing the murderer of their chief. It was but too clear to those unhappy men what was to be the last act of this tragedy. Jung received the rifle from the hand of the man next him, and levelled it at the foremost of the little band. Fourteen times did that fatal report ring through the hall as one by one the rifles were handed to one who would trust no eye but his own, and at each shot another noble lay stretched on the ground. Abiman Singh alone escaped the deadly aim; he managed to reach the door, but there he was cut almost in two by the sword of Krishn Bahadoor.

Thus, in a few moments, and by his own hand, had Jung rid himself of those whom he most feared. In that one room lay the corpses of the highest nobles of the land, shrouded by the dense smoke still hanging in the confined atmosphere, as if to hide the horrors of a tragedy that would not bear the light of day. The massacre now went on in all parts of the building. One hundred and fifty sirdars perished on that eventful night, and the panic was widespread and general. Before day had dawned Jung Bahadoor had been appointed prime minister of Nepaul, and had placed guards over the arsenal, treasury, and palace.

In the morning the troops were all drawn up on parade; before them were placed, in a ghastly heap, the bodies of their late commanders, to which Jung pointed, as he assured the army that it would find in him all that it had ever found in them, and he consoled many of the officers in a great measure for the loss they had just sustained by granting them immediate promotion. It seems as easy for a daring adventurer to gain the affections of an army in India as in Europe, and Jung found no difficulty in reconciling his Ghorkas to a change of commanders, and they have ever since professed the greatest devotion to his person.

The utmost caution was now necessary on the part of the new premier, who was obliged still to be on his guard, lest the partizans of those whom he had massacred should succeed in organizing a conspiracy against his life; a sirdar was put to death simply because he had a private audience with the King. Circumstances soon showed that Jung had good reason to feel the insecurity of his position. The two elder Princes, sons of a former Queen, had been for some time in confinement, and the Ranee now attempted to induce Jung to put them to death, in order to secure the throne for one of her own sons. This he positively refused to do, and his refusal brought upon him the wrath of this vindictive woman, whose vengeance had already been so signally wreaked on his uncle by his own instrumentality.

He had not played so prominent a part on that occasion without profiting by the lesson he had learnt; and knowing well the character of the woman with whom he had to deal, he took care to obtain accurate intelligence of all that transpired at court.

Information soon reached him that a plot was formed against his life, and that the post of premier had already been promised to his intended murderer, as a reward for so dangerous a service. Once more the command, which had proved so fatal to Mahtabar Singh, issued from the palace, desiring the immediate attendance of the minister; the messenger was the very man at whose hand Jung was to meet his doom. He had scarcely delivered his treacherous message, when he was struck to the ground by one of the attendants of the prime minister. Jung then proceeded on his way to the palace, where he at once demanded of the Rajah to be dismissed from office, or to be furnished with authority to order the destruction of all the enemies of the heir-apparent. The King could not refuse to grant the authority demanded; and it was no sooner granted than Jung seized and beheaded all the adherents of the conspirator.

As the Ranee herself was the most inveterate enemy of the young Prince, the Rajah's order was at once carried into effect against her, and, to her infinite astonishment, she was informed by Jung that she was to leave Nepaul immediately, accompanied by her two sons. It was of no use to resist the successful young adventurer, whose indomitable courage and good fortune had triumphed over the plots and intrigues of his enemies, and who thus saw himself freed from every obstacle to his quiet possession of the government.

The Rajah accompanied the Queen to Benares. Meantime the heir-apparent was raised to the throne, and the whole administrative power vested in his minister.

Upon hearing of the installation of his son as Rajah, the old Monarch seemed to evince, for the first and last time in his life, some little interest in proceedings by which he himself was so seriously affected, and the result was a feeble determination not to relinquish his throne without a final struggle. Urged to this course probably by the persuasions of the ambitious and disappointed Ranee, he collected a few followers, and crossed the southern frontier of Nepaul. Jung, however, had received timely notice of his intention, and the luckless King had no sooner encamped in the Nepaul dominions, than he was surprized at night by the troops of the minister, and his small forces utterly routed, four or five hundred remaining killed or wounded upon the field. The Rajah himself was taken prisoner, and placed in confinement by the dutiful son who now occupies the throne, and who sometimes allows him, on grand occasions, to take his seat upon it next to himself.

The vacillating conduct of the imbecile old man throughout his whole reign, the apathy with which he was contented to remain a passive spectator of those bloody dramas of which his court was for so long a period the theatre, deprive him of all claim to commiseration in his present degraded position, which, in fact, is the natural result of his indifference to the game so eagerly played by the contending parties, and of which the stake was his own throne.

If, on the other hand, in a country where common humanity, and, still more, every kind of principle, is unknown, daring and intrepid conduct merits a reward, Jung has fairly earned for himself the position he now holds; and though his path to greatness has been deluged with the blood of the bravest nobles of the land, it must be admitted that the peace and prosperity which Nepaul now enjoys would never have been possessed by her while distracted and convulsed by the struggles of hostile factions; and much less would she ever have experienced the blessings of an enlightened administration, if these struggles had not resulted in the elevation of General Jung Bahadoor to the office of prime minister.

And now, for the first time in the history of Nepaul, the Durbar was to a certain extent united; internal machinations were no longer to be feared; and the country was ruled over by different members of that family, the elevation of which was due to one of their own number, who possessed sufficient daring and resolution to execute the bold, though unscrupulous schemes his undoubted genius had conceived.

Such was the rapid rise to power at the early age of thirty of General Jung Bahadoor, the Nepaulese ambassador to England, who would have been invested with a deeper interest than the mere colour of his face or brilliancy of his diamonds entitled him to, had the British public known the foregoing particulars of his eventful career. But, perhaps, it was as well for him that they did not, since our occidental notions as to the legitimate method of carrying political measures might have altogether excluded him from the favour of those who delighted to honour him during his visit to England; but, in extenuation of his conduct, it must be remembered that the mode employed by him of gaining power is the common one in his country, and that his early training had induced a disregard of life and recklessness of consequences; for he is not, I am convinced, naturally cruel. Impetuous and thoughtless, he has many generous and noble qualities; and in a companionship of two months I discovered so many estimable traits in him, that I could not help making allowances for the defects in a character entirely self-formed by one ignorant of all moral responsibilities, the half-tamed son of an almost totally uncivilised country.

And while thus unreservedly relating his history, I do so in the belief that he has no desire to conceal what, in his own mind and that of his countrymen, is not regarded as crime, since I have frequently heard him refer, with all the simplicity of conscious innocence, to many of the facts I have related, and for some of which he himself is my authority.

Having thus given a short account of the previous career of this remarkable man, a few words on his present position and future prospects may not be uninteresting, the more so as he purposes, since he has visited the courts of Europe, to become an enlightened ruler of his countrymen.

CHAPTER X

*The titles of his Excellency General Jung Bahadoor
Coomaranagee in England—Extraordinary notions of the
British public on Indian affairs—Jung Bahadoor's
conciliatory policy—Our unsuccessful attempt to penetrate
beyond the permitted boundaries—Dangerous position of the
Prime Minister—His philanthropic designs—Great opposition
on the part of Durbar—Native punishments—A Nepaulese
chief-justice—Jung's popularity with the peasantry and army*

The rumours in England during Jung Bahadoor's short
residence there—of who he was, of what position he held, of
his having taken his greatest enemies with him to keep them
from conspiring against him while absent—of his being at least
a Prince, if not the Rajah himself in disguise—were as far from
correct, and as improbable, as were the numerous stories
related of him in the newspapers, many of which had no
foundation whatever, and in no way redounded to his credit.

The subject, however, of so much speculation was generally
too much pleased with his notoriety to care for the means
which in some measure obtained it for him; and I have heard
him repeat with great glee some imaginary anecdote of
himself, or laughingly enumerate the various appellations by
which he had been known. Amongst the few words of English
which he could pronounce were those by which he was most
frequently addressed—such as, the Prince, the Ambassador,
your Highness, your Excellency, the Minister, Jung Bahadoor,
Jung, or more often "the Jung." Whilst the appearance of the
Coomaranagee Polkas showed an unusual amount of correct
information on the part of the publisher.

Such ignorance might have been expected from the utter
indifference manifested in England towards Indian affairs. The
ideas of John Bull upon the subject are often ludicrous in the
extreme, as he finds it impossible to divest himself of the
preconceived notions which he surely must have been born

with when he pertinaciously imagines that all dark-coloured people have woolly heads and thick lips, and speak the broken English of the negro; nor has he the slightest conception of the relative position of great towns in India, or which States are independent; or who the Nizam is, or if his contingent is not some part of his dress; or whether the Taj is not the husband of the Begum mentioned in Pendennis. He has a vague notion that nabobs come from India, and has heard perhaps of cabobs, but what the difference is, or whether they are not articles of Indian export usually packed in casks, he has not the most remote conception. For all the light, therefore, that John Bull could throw upon the subject of who or what Jung Bahadoor was, besides being the Nepaulese ambassador, or where the country was that he came to represent, it might remain a mystery to the present day.

But even supposing the public were better informed on Indian affairs, it would not be a matter of surprise that they should be under a misconception as to what Jung's position in his own country might be, seeing that it is not usual amongst European nations to send their prime ministers on foreign missions. But to estimate correctly the minister's power and authority, the word "send" perhaps ought not to be used in this case, since he was a self-appointed ambassador; and his next brother was left by him to perform the arduous duties attendant on the important office which he vacated for a while.

And now that he is returned to resume the reins of government, and once more become involved in the petty intrigues of his highland court, it is natural that he should look back with delight, not unmingled with regret, at the wonders he has so lately witnessed—the, to him, magical effects of the operations of steam—the still more incomprehensible electric telegraph—our institutions—our court—the magnificence of the successive entertainments, of which he could say "Magna pars fui," and at which he was not more the spectator than the spectacle: but, above all, was it a matter of astonishment to him that such hospitality should have been shown to an unknown and ignorant stranger by a nation whose enterprise is no less stirring than her resources are vast, and in the midst of a social machinery to him so incomprehensibly intricate in its details.

"Why," he would observe after his return to Katmandu, "should I attempt to tell these poor ignorant people what I have seen? It would be as ridiculous in me to suppose they would believe it as it is hopeless to attempt to make them understand it." And he feels that the information he has acquired has been too extensive to allow him to sink to the level of those by whom he is surrounded. But, while anxious to increase his popularity, with his attempts at conciliation is combined a patronizing air, which he cannot conceal, and which is calculated to render him unpopular, even could he bring himself to return to the old system of embracing instead of shaking hands; of taking off his shoes when entering the Durbar; of salaaming ere he addresses his Monarch—all which acts of devotion and homage are repugnant to the man who has had an interview with the Queen of England, and received a visit from the Duke of Wellington. "When that great warrior called upon me," he says, "I felt it to be the proudest moment of my life": and at Benares, when, upon the occasion of his visiting a native Rajah, there was a question of whether he should go in state or not, he decided the matter by saying, "I shall go just as I went to return the Duke's visit"; or, at another time, "I will receive the Rajah in a friendly way, just as I did the Duke when he called upon me." Nothing seemed to impress him so deeply as the absence of all display where genuine greatness rendered it unnecessary; and he looks with no slight contempt upon the pomp to which he in common with his court was formerly so much attached. That court, however, retaining of course its old unenlightened sentiments, looks with suspicion and distrust on the independent manners of the returned prime minister. "He has become a Feringhee."—"He wants to introduce their barbarous customs amongst us."—"He brings visitors, and is making friends with the English, in order to betray us to them." This is said by his enemies at court;

and, while they watch his every action, esteem him a traitor, who, if they did but know it, is the best friend of their country. Thus, in spite of his earnest desire to promote its welfare, he is likely to be thwarted, and his ardent and somewhat impatient temperament will not, it is to be feared, improve matters, however good his intentions may be. That he is already careful lest he offend any prejudices, I had a convincing and most annoying proof.

On the journey through India, while in high spirits, out shooting, he had promised to allow us to travel over any part of Nepaul we might wish to visit—a permission never yet granted to any European. To the fulfilment of this promise we naturally looked with no small pleasure; but, after a residence of a week in Nepaul, the anti-Anglican feeling was so strongly manifested, that the mere fact of four or five European visitors having been in Katmandu (for Lord G—— and his party were among his guests) brought upon him a certain degree of odium.

To allow strangers to visit Nepaul, and reside at Katmandu, was unusual, but bearable; the idea of a common beef-eater infringing the limits of a circle beyond which no British resident, much less traveller, had ever penetrated, was so monstrous a heresy on the part of the prime minister—so serious an infraction of a well-established rule—that even Jung felt it to be too unpopular an act by which to celebrate his return to his country. It was with much regret that we were obliged to relinquish so interesting an enterprise. I must not, however, forget his offer to adhere to his promise if we wished it, saying at the same time that his doing so would seriously compromise him. But, as *compromise* and *decapitate* may be looked upon as synonymous terms in Nepaul, we felt that it was hardly fair to our kind host to place him in such an awkward position; and as, moreover, the effect of his being so compromised in Katmandu would have probably entailed upon us a precisely similar fate, we considered it hardly fair to the guests either. But while thus hanging back from his promise on the score of compromising himself, I am fully persuaded that personal considerations had but little to do in the matter. He is looking out for means of usefulness, and it was more the fear of retarding his schemes of improvement by thus increasing the popular discontent that induced him to change his mind, than any hope of retaining his head upon his shoulders. The difficulty of doing this can be but very slightly increased; and it must be admitted that he esteems life as lightly in his own case as he formerly did when others were concerned.

It cannot but be regretted that with so pure an object he should be totally without co-operation from any quarter. The young King, capable only of aiding in nefarious schemes, such as those already recounted, can in no way comprehend the new-fangled philanthropic views of the prime minister. He cares little about the welfare of his country; his amusement seems to consist in concocting and executing bloody designs, and his mind must be so accustomed to his species of excitement that it can scarce do without it. It is unfortunate that the Rajah's hobby should lie in this peculiar direction, more unfortunate still that the contemplated victim should be Jung; for I presume that there is little doubt that the King's brother, who was engaged in the last conspiracy against the minister's life—which took place a few days after my visit—must have acted with the knowledge, and most probably at the instigation, of his Majesty.

Nor can Jung look to his brothers for support as in times of old: one of them, whom he esteemed amongst the most faithful, was, as before mentioned, deeply implicated in the same attempt on his life; and there is no one now on whom he can confidently depend in the hour of need except the two youngest of the family, who accompanied him to England, and whom I consider thoroughly devoted to his interests. Deserted by his King, who owes his throne to him, his life, conspired against by one of his own brothers, bound to him by the yet stronger ties of blood, he stands alone a mark for the dagger of anyone who would win the approval of his degraded Sovereign. But his bearing is not the less bold, or his eye less piercing, as he makes the man quail before him who is that moment planning his destruction. He anticipates the fate of his fourteen predecessors; they were all assassinated! His predecessors, however, did not surround themselves with a guard armed with rifles always loaded[1]. In all probability the man who takes the life of the prime minister will do so at the price of his own. So securely guarded is he, and so careful of his own safety, that I cannot but hope he may live to frustrate the designs of his enemies, and to carry out that enlightened policy which, while it morally elevates the people, would develop the resources of a country possessing many natural advantages, in its delightful climate, fertile soil, and industrious population. Valleys unvisited by civilization save as received through the medium of a few semi-barbarous travellers, may contain treasures which they are now unknown to possess; mines of copper, lead, and antimony, now clumsily worked, may be made to yield of their abundance; tracts of uncultivated lands be brought into rich cultivation, and efficient means of transport would carry their produce far and wide through the country. Katmandu itself would be on the high road for the costly trade of Chinese Tartary and Thibet with the provinces of Upper India.

In fact it is impossible to enumerate the various benefits which would accrue to the country were a different system of government adopted; and it is much to be feared that unless the present prime minister lives to accomplish the task he has undertaken, no one of his successors, for some time to come at least, will have either the will or the ability requisite for its successful consummation.

In some of his legislative acts Jung had shown himself to be in advance of his age before he left Nepaul. No less than twenty-two punishments for various crimes, principally consisting of different modes of torture, were abolished. A

1 The arms of his body-guard were bought in London, of Purdy, Lancaster, and other eminent rifle-makers, and cost Jung about £ 2000.

thief must have been three times convicted of the crime ere he can suffer the penalty entailed upon the offence, viz., loss of his hand; and after it is cut off, he has his choice between having it bound up or allowing himself to bleed to death. I understood the latter alternative to be the one usually chosen by the culprit. Gambling is strictly prohibited in Nepaul, except for four or five days during the celebration of the Devali.

Women are not liable to capital punishment. The mutilation of noses no longer exists, although some years ago it was the most usual punishment, and one village was entirely peopled by the unfortunate victims of such barbarous treatment.

The amount of labour which his position as prime minister entails upon Jung is almost incredible; the simplest bargain cannot be struck, nor a cooly engaged, nor can a departure or an arrival take place, without his sign manual. In fact he comprises within himself the whole of the ministry, besides doing the entire duty of the several departments, and the office of premier in Nepaul can be no more a sinecure than it is in England. One can only wonder that a position fraught with such imminent danger to its possessor, and bringing upon him such incessant trouble and responsibility, should be so eagerly sought, when it entails the almost absolute certainty of a violent death. With us moral courage is an indispensable quality for a prime minister; in Nepaul, physical courage is no less needed. If he is a good shot, and expert with his kukri and kora, so much the better for him. As regards both these accomplishments Jung was eminently qualified for the post he now holds; but his literary acquirements were of a very low order, for upon becoming prime minister he could neither read nor write. Finding great inconvenience from his incapacity in these respects, he applied himself diligently to his alphabet, and was soon able to carry on all official corres-pondence of any importance to himself. The whole of the political, fiscal, and judicial communications are submitted to him, and the departments controlled by him, very little regard being had to the Rajah's will on the subject.

The next officer in rank to Jung Bahadoor is his brother, Bum Bahadoor, who bears the mark on his hand of the horrible action in Durbar already recorded. He appeared inferior in ability to his brother, but it is difficult to judge of the talent of anyone who is in a subordinate position in Nepaul.

The Raj Guru is the highest spiritual dignitary in Nepaul, and in that capacity received the greatest deference from everyone, including Jung, whose popularity in some measure rests on his intimate relations with the chief priest, to whom he invariably paid every mark of respect. The Raj Guru met us at Benares, and granted indulgences to those who had visited England. So great is the respect shown him, that upon entering his presence the prime minister invariably touched with his forehead the foot of the holy man. To the office of spiritual adviser to the Rajah is added that of judge of the spiritual court, which is one of great emolument, arising chiefly from fines levied on the infraction of religious ceremonies or ordinances—such as the killing or maltreating of a cow and other like enormities.

Next in order follow the Kazies, or "Patres conscripti," who ought to possess some voice in the administration of affairs, but are content to remain silent during the independent rule of the Minister Sahib. They number thirty or forty, and their duty is to consult upon all weighty matters connected with the Government, while some act as governors of provinces, others as judges in important causes.

Then come the Sirdars, who also decide causes, and possess considerable authority in the more remote districts, governing some of the provinces, and superintending the collection of revenue. Their number is far larger than that of the Kazies.

We visited the supreme court one day and saw the Chief-justice, or Durma Dikar, sitting cross-legged (smoking his hookah on the verandah), the court having adjourned. The old man bore that venerable appearance which is everywhere esteemed inseparable from the judicial character, and I doubted whether his long grey beard was not a more imposing, as it certainly was a more natural and graceful, appendage than a wig.

There are six law courts in Katmandu, presided over by Sirdars and Bicharees, and the laws and modes of punishment are very effectual for the prevention of crime; for although a prisoner cannot be convicted except upon his own confession, he may be subjected to an ordeal which will most probably extort it; and, perhaps, in an eastern country justice is more effectually administered by such methods than where the judge decides on the guilt or innocence of a man by speculating on the character of the witnesses, and believing those who look most as if they were telling the truth; and where, although he knows that all the witnesses are more or less bribed, he is not allowed to take any but a voluntary admission from the prisoner, when perhaps a little gentle persuasion would save a great deal of unnecessary trouble, to say nothing of the amount of lying that might thus be dispensed with. Whatever the laws may be, they seem to give perfect satisfaction to the inhabitants, who cannot be called a litigious race.

While we were at Bisoleah, on our way to Katmandu, an interesting instance occurred of the prime minister taking the law into his own hands; and, as far as we could judge, complete justice was done to the parties. A complaint was preferred by a deputation of the peasantry of the Terai against one of the sirdars who was a member of his suite, and who had been governor of some part of the district before he had accompanied the minister on his expedition to England. It was alleged that he had, in connection with his brother, who was an especial favourite with Jung, defrauded them of 25,000 rupees. This charge was indignantly denied by the two sirdars. The case was fully entered into, and the result was, that Jung became convinced of the justice of the claim of the peasantry. He had no sooner satisfied himself on this point than he ordered both the noblemen to be placed in confinement, where they were to remain until the required sum was forthcoming. The affair delayed us twenty-four hours; and I perfectly well remember wondering at the time what could be the cause of a detention for so long a period in so unpleasant a locality; more especially as by it we lost the chance of a day's rhinoceros shooting, which was, doubtless, as great a disappointment to Jung as to myself.

By thus carefully protecting the interests of the peasantry he has endeared himself to them, since they are always sure of a ready and attentive hearing of any complaint, although it may affect the highest nobles in the land. In talking to a man who acted as guide on our return through the Terai, we discovered that the popularity of Jung, arising from this cause, had extended across the frontier, and had induced my informant to migrate into the Nepaul dominions, so that he might benefit by the paternal rule of its prime minister. He said the taxes were lighter, and he led altogether a more happy and independent life than in the Company's dominions, where the native officers employed as tax-gatherers do not always display the most scrupulous honesty.

But it is not with the peasantry alone that Jung is so deservedly a favourite. With the soldiers he is, if possible, still more popular. An admirer of Napoleon, he has profited by the perusal of his life, and turns to advantage his knowledge of the influence possessed in so wonderful a manner by one whom he seeks in every respect to imitate, so far as the difference of position admits. That he has succeeded admirably with the army there is no doubt. His personal feats of daring and known courage are considerable aids to an imitation of the more scientific means employed by his great model.

Thus, firmly seated in the affections of the most important portions of the community over which he rules with unlimited power, and a most ardent wish to improve their condition, it will be on all accounts most deplorable if the country is deprived of the services of so valuable a man by some vile plot, emanating from the petty intrigue of a jealous and disappointed Durbar.

CHAPTER XI

The temple of Balajee—The old Newar capital—The houses and temples of Patan—View from the city gates—Nepaulese festivals—The Newars skilful artisans—The arsenal—The magazine and cannon-foundry

One afternoon we strolled across some verdant meadows, and along narrow shady avenues, to visit the temple of Balajee. There is nothing in the building itself worthy of notice; but near it is a tank of beautifully clear water, filled with sacred fishes, *which* crowd near the visitor as he stands on the brink, expecting to be fed with grain, which some old women at the gate sell for their especial benefit. Balajee is one of those sheltered nooks which make the scenery of Nepaul so attractive. Immediately under a wooded knoll the trees dip into the tank, from whence the water leaps in three tiny cascades into the courtyard of the temple, quaint and singular itself, and rendered still more interesting from its connexion with the sacred fonts and groves near which it is so romantically situated.

Hitherto we had seen no Newar town. Katmandu, the capital of Nepaul, was built by the conquering Ghorkas, and is comparatively modern. The old Newar capital is Patan: situated on a green slope, and fortified by a high wall, it looks picturesque when seen from the modern city, from which it is distant about two miles.

Crossing the narrow brick bridge which spans the Bhagmutty, outside the walls of the town, we shortly after entered the massive old gates of the ancient capital. As we trotted past the high rickety houses, along the brick pavement of the narrow streets, still slippery from the morning dew, we encountered troops of girls with garlands in their hair, for this was some festive day. At the corners of the streets were beings of both sexes, as decrepit as the houses under which they crouched, presiding over baskets full of beautiful flowers. The entire population were Newars, except a few fierce mustachioed Ghorkas, who stood sentinels over the temples, or loitered about the guardhouse. The long street looked deserted; there was not a single shop in it; and the foot-passengers were few and far between. But the grand square was the chief feature of the place, and was well worthy of a visit. We looked with astonishment and delight at the incongruous mass of buildings, of the most varied and fantastic construction, yet massive and substantial; but whence the designs originated, or in what other part of the known world anything is to be seen approaching to the style of Newar architecture, it would be impossible to conjecture. Houses built of horn are said to exist at Lassa; and from Lassa, I should imagine, came the designs for the temples and houses of Patan. Time has mellowed their bright colours— if they were ever painted at all like those at Katmandu—into a sombre, quiet grey. The Durbar, a huge, massive building, is absolutely covered with black wood-carving. The care displayed in its execution is still apparent through the mass of dust and cobwebs which almost conceal it; for the old Durbar of Patan is deserted. The residence of the monarchs who ruled the happy valley is in strong contrast with the smiling appearance of their former territory. It alone seems to have gone into mourning for its former occupants, while the valley seems to thrive as well under the rule of the Ghorkas as it did under that of the Newars. The Durbar is of great extent, and occupies one side of the square, in the centre of which stand two monoliths, between 30 and 40 feet high: on one of them is the figure of an angel, represented in all respects as angels usually are, with the addition of a magnificent gilt tail; this, together with a pair of large gilt wings, gave it a most gorgeous appearance. My Ghorka guide could give me no information as to what particular divinity this figure was intended to represent. The other pillar was crowned by the figure of a Newar monarch with an unpronounceable name, who was watched over by a cobra, standing upon its tail, and looking over his head with its mouth wide open.

On the opposite side to that on which the Durbar was situated were two temples: one of them, built of grey sandstone, was an imposing structure, altogether different from any building, lay or ecclesiastical, that I had ever seen before. The lower story consisted of massive verandahs or cloisters; the pillars were all of grey sandstone, very simple in form; and the connecting arch was somewhat Saracenic in its appearance. The temple was square, and the corridor which ran round it was elevated considerably above the level of the court: the ascent to it was by two flights of steps, each guarded by a pair of sculptured winged lions. Three stories of light belfry-like temples, three upon each side of the square, surmounted each other in rows; in the centre was a mass of architecture between a dome and a spire, rising to a height of upwards of 100 feet above the level of the court: the whole formed a pyramidal structure ornamented with fantastic devices, and undoubtedly Bhuddist in its character.

The other temple was a two-storied pagoda; its bright colours were faded, and it appeared far inferior to those of more recent construction. There were also ruined pyramidal shrines of no known architecture, and difficult to describe from their complicated nature—antique specimens of the masonry of ages long gone by, and memorials of a religion doubtless impure, although Bhuddist in its character and origin.

No less singular were the residences of the old Newar nobility, a race which no longer exists, and the only remains of which now extant are their ruined habitations, evidently destined to succumb before long to the same all-destroying power which has long since obliterated every trace of their former owners.

How different was the peculiar yet handsome style which distinguished the dwellings of the Newar nobles at Patan from the tawdry glitter which characterises the mansions of the present Ghorka chiefs in the modern capital! Here the carving is more rich, the ornaments more massive, the houses themselves are more lofty and capacious. Sometimes two or three elaborately-carved balconies adorn the sombre but not less imposing exterior; from the projecting eaves wooden tassels, forming a sort of fringe, swing to and fro over the windows.

The roofs are beautifully tiled, each tile having a double curvature, while the corners of the buildings are quaintly turned up, giving a Chinese look to the building. The whole appearance of the houses and temples carries one far from the mud-huts or close cities of the plains of India, into the land of chopsticks and small feet, and the traveller feels much nearer to Pekin than to Calcutta as he wanders along the empty streets under the frowning houses and indescribable temples of the Newar town of Patan.

Everything seemed to have been blighted by time; besides all the old temples, old houses, old gates, and old streets, there were numbers of old people. Everything seemed to sympathise with everything else, and had evidently come to the conclusion that there was nothing worth living for, and the sooner they all took themselves off and quitted the bright valley of Nepaul the better. And indeed it was difficult to realize the existence of anything half so cheerful inside the town as the prospect which met our view as we emerged from its gloomy entrance, and looked upon the luxuriant plain, the glittering capital shining in its midst, whose gaudy pagodas, hung round with bells and adorned with flags, were very different from those just visited; the industrious population were going light-hearted to their work as we rode through smiling fields, and we ceased to wonder at Patan looking deserted, for it was evident that all the cheerfully disposed inhabitants had flitted away, unable to bear its depressing influence, and leaving behind them only the crabbed old people at the corners of the streets, and the tattered beggars, who must make a meagre livelihood out of the falling temples and 24,000 rotten houses of the once handsome capital of Nepaul.

It was a clear frosty morning, and, as we rode down the gentle slope on which the old city stands, the snowy range of the Himalaya burst upon us with inexpressible grandeur. The Gosain-than, a mass of glistening snow, looked contemptuously down upon the Jibjibia, itself covered with snow: though 13,000 feet lower than the Gosain-than, the Jibjibia in turn overtopped the Sheopoorie, which rises abruptly from the valley to a height of 2000 feet. On a peninsula, formed by the junction of the Bhagmutty and Bishmutty, stands the town of Katmandu, surrounded by a high wall in which are four gates: to the east the snow-capped peaks extend as far as the eye can reach; to the west the Dawalogiri, the highest mountain in the world, is in clear weather distinctly visible; in that direction the valley is shut in by lofty hills, the steepest of which is crossed by the Chandanagiri pass.

The exhilarating effect of so glorious a scene seemed not to be lost upon the inhabitants themselves, and we observed among them the same merry and contented appearance as that which is so remarkable amongst the inhabitants of Switzerland and the Tyrol; indeed mountaineers in general either have much fewer troubles than lowlanders, or take them less to heart.

The Nepaulese, in common with most highland tribes, have strong religious feelings, and are bigoted adherents to a faith which they would find it somewhat difficult to define. One use to which they put their religion, and in which they far exceed even the Roman Catholics of the Alps, is, in making it furnish them with an almost unlimited number of holidays and festivals: no opportunity of merry-making is lost by the light-hearted inhabitants of Nepaul, and in this respect they are at once distinguishable from their more gloomy and saturnine conquerors, the Ghorkas, who, glorying only in the art of war, look with contempt on what they consider the frivolity of the Newars.

There can be no doubt of the warlike character of the Ghorkas, even had not our own experience testified to the fact in a most unpleasant way. Not only are they brave and skilful soldiers, but, for a barbarous nation, they are wonderfully advanced in the art of fabricating the implements of war; they cast their own ordnance, manufacture their own muskets, shot, powder, and cartridge-boxes; in fact, every instrument or weapon used in civilized warfare is manufactured in Nepaul, often clumsily enough, but the mere fact of their being capable of being used, and used with effect, is highly creditable to the ingenuity of the Ghorkas.

The Newars are still more skilful artisans than the Ghorkas, but their talent does not lie in the same direction. The bricks of Nepaul are deservedly famed; whether the virtue lies in the clay of which they are formed, or the skill with which they are made, I do not know—most probably in both. The Newars excel also in bell-making; it is the trade of the land; they are all bell-makers from their youth, and proofs of their skill are exhibited hanging at the corners of pagodas, swinging from the roofs of houses, surmounting Dagobas—in fact, the device upon a Nepaulese banner should be a bell. In jewellery they are no less expert, and are elaborate workmen in all metals. A species of coarse paper is manufactured by them from the bark of a tree, which is first reduced to a pulp and then spread over a sheet and dried.

They are as excellent agriculturists as tradesmen, and the rich soil of the valley is not allowed by the industrious peasants to lie fallow a moment longer than is necessary.

At certain seasons every inhabitant capable of wielding the hoe is at work, and there is much incentive to such industry, for the soil is inexhaustible, and seems as if it could go on for an indefinite period yielding its four crops a year—namely, wheat, rice, Indian corn, and vegetables—supporting thereby a double population. The plough is never used. It struck me that the introduction of buffaloes from the plains would be advantageous in assisting the worthy Newar, whose religious scruples prevent his using the bullock. There is a species of small baffalo, which is a native of the Himalayas, but it is never brought down by the Bhootyas into the plains, nor even to Katmandu.

We went one day to visit the arsenal, which a veteran of the Nepaul army took an especial delight in exhibiting, and naturally looked for expressions of wonder and delight from the barbarians. But the only astonishment we felt was, that such a mass of fire-arms, so excessively old and so excessively dirty, should be thought worthy of being carefully ranged throughout the long dark rooms. In a corner of one of these rooms the light streamed brightly through a window on some old-fashioned firelocks bearing an English maker's name; they were trophies of the war with the British, and were held worthy of conspicuous places in the Nepaul arsenal. The delighted old Colonel pointed these out to us with a laudable pride; he said the arsenal contained 100,000 stand of arms, and expected us to believe it. Had they been in proper order, the collection would have been of importance numerically considered.

Their artillery was insignificant, but they possessed trophies denied to many more powerful nations in a pair of brass 2-pounders, also taken from the British in the same disastrous campaign. I looked as abashed and mortified as I could, and pleased the Colonel exceedingly thereby. In the same establishment was carried on the process of manufacturing powder of a very coarse grain, and we were shown sundry store-rooms containing grape and canister.

Leaving the arsenal, we mounted our elephants, crossed the parade-ground and the river, and, passing through the massive gateway, reached the magazine, situated in the interior of the city, where we had an opportunity of witnessing the process of hammering iron into balls. The Nepaulese can produce no heat sufficient to cast balls, and are, consequently, obliged to beat them into the required shape, an almost endless operation. By this tedious process the making of each two-pound ball occupies two men a whole day, and costs, including other incidental charges, about a rupee, so that the expenses of a siege would come rather heavy upon the Government. All round the courtyard blacksmiths were forging and hammering, while in the middle of it a number of men were employed beating leather, so as to render it sufficiently pliable to undergo the process of being trodden soft, a curious operation, and fatiguing to the muscles of any other legs than those of the Nepaulese, who keep continually doubling up the leather and treading it out again, and putting their feet to all sorts of uses, in which, if we had properly cultivated the gifts of nature, we should, doubtless, be equally skilled. At present our great object is to make our feet look smaller than they naturally are, and even in that the Chinese excel us, civilized though we be. The result of so much beating and treading was a number of leather cartridge-boxes, which could not have been harder had they been deal; so the means did not justify the end, and perhaps after all we make better use of our feet than the Nepaulese tanners do.

In another part of the establishment was a gang of men engaged in twisting gun-barrels, turning out wonderful productions, considering the rude method employed.

The stocks were more easily fabricated, and the whole musket justified the pride with which it was exhibited; but Jung is no longer satisfied with the productions of the Nepaulese gunmakers. He visited a gun-manufactory at Birmingham, and was most disagreeably surprised by finding how different was the English mode of manufacturing the implements of war from that employed in Nepaul.

In England Jung had seen brass guns cast by the score during his short visit to the foundry. Here they were being cast at the rate of one every two or three months. The metal is not allowed to run into the mould in a continuous stream, but is ladled in, thereby rendering the gun liable to flaws. There were many other improvements which it would have been obvious to a practised eye were needed in the gun-factory of Nepaul; and it was plain enough that everything was rough and clumsy; but Jung had paid especial attention to these subjects while in England, and intends speedily to introduce an improved system. How long it will be ere he will have a steam-foundry established in Katmandu time alone can show.

CHAPTER XII

Kindness of the Mahila Sahib—His motive—Drawing-room ornaments—Visit to the palace of Jung Bahadoor—A trophy of the London season—Grand Durbar at the reading of the Queen of England's letter—Dress of the officers—Review of troops—Dancing boys

The Mahila Sahib, the younger brother of his Majesty, was a very pleasant-looking young man, with a much more amiable expression of countenance than his royal brother, and professed to be one of Jung's greatest friends and allies. As a compliment to the minister, he politely requested us to pay him a visit, an invitation of which we were glad to avail ourselves, since it proved his kindly feeling towards our host, whilst it gave us an opportunity of inspecting the ménage of a Nepaulese Prince Royal.

It is worth while to make a trip to Nepaul, not only for the delight of viewing the romantic beauty of its scenery, of wondering at the stupendous height of its mountains, of roaming amidst its ancient cities, ruined palaces, and glittering pagodas, but in order to take a lesson in human nature, for we are not at liberty to suppose that the princes and nobles of this country are a more depraved class than any other body of men, the fact being that a Nepaulese follows his natural impulses, unfettered by the restraints of our standard of civilization and morality, and the results are apparent. Is not the more civilized inhabitant of western lands actuated by the same feelings, and would he not behave in the same manner as his swarthy brother in the East, had he been brought up in the same code of morality, and were he as fearless of the consequences of his following the bent of his own inclination? But if so, then the visitor to Nepaul simply sees the game of human life played openly and unconstrainedly, and in no way hampered by the rules which prevail in more civilized countries; and the unsophisticated tyro has only to come here and learn in a month what would cost him a lifetime of anxious study in a country enjoying the blessings of civilization.

The palace of the Mahila Sahib is situated in a courtyard, and is entered by a small doorway, by no means in keeping with the handsome staircase, lined with muskets, up which we followed the prince, who had come to the entrance to meet us. We were ushered into a long narrow room, similar in shape to the reception-room in all other Nepaulese palaces, and adorned in like manner with a profusion of pictures, occidental as well as oriental, while in the midst, upon a round table, and displayed as drawing-room ornaments, was an incongruous collection of articles, amongst which I remarked three leaden spoons, an old cruet-stand, a Bohemian glass scent-bottle, an old hair-brush and tooth-brush on some hot-water plates, a pair of brass candlesticks, and other wares usually found in kitchens, pantries, and bedrooms. Some English prints and pictures of a particularly pothouse appearance attracted me into a little side room, where a handsome telescope stood pointed out of the open window, from which there was a lovely and extensive view, and while my friend and the prince were chatting in the next room I took advantage of the means thus afforded me of enjoying the prospect.

On looking through the telescope the first object which met my eye was the roof of a handsome house, on which figures were moving briskly to and fro. All the windows of this mansion were commanded by the glass, and I almost imagined I could see the female figures flitting about in the more gloomy and secluded part, which seemed to be the harem. The house thus under observation struck me as being known to me, and upon looking at the neighbouring objects I perceived that it was the palace of the Minister Sahib.

The fact of the glass being thus pointed to his house was in itself a suspicious circumstance, but I little thought that the bland owner of the leaden spoons and pothouse pictures was then deliberately contemplating the vile plot he so soon afterwards nearly succeeded in executing. Within a week after this visit I heard that our polite entertainer was in confinement for an attempt to assassinate the minister, towards whom he had so recently professed the profoundest sentiments of regard.

We descended into the well laid-out garden attached to the palace and devoured the delicious mandarin oranges, with which hundreds of trees were loaded, until our attention was diverted from them by a luscious fruit, in appearance something like a medlar: this fruit is rare in Nepaul, the tree being a native of Thibet.

It cost us an effort to bid adieu to the polite prince and his attractive garden; but at length we remounted our elephants and proceeded on our way to the Minister's house. Passing through the handsome gateway, guarded by a magnificent tiger, that prowled restlessly up and down his cage, a vigilant-looking sentinel, we entered a yard filled with the soldiers and retainers of the illustrious man whom we had come to visit.

We were greeted cordially by the Minister Sahib, who was surrounded by a crowd of brothers, only three of whom I knew, viz. the two fat travellers and the future would-be assassin.

Jung's house was a large white building, which looked as if a Chinaman had mixed together a Birmingham factory and an Italian villa, every now and then throwing in a strong dash of the style of his own country by way of improvement. It is three stories high, and one wing is devoted to the six "beautiful missises" who compose the female part of his establishment.

The state-room was very similar in shape and appearance to that in the palace of the Mahila Sahib, but was, if possible, still more fantastically ornamented. A picture of her Majesty's Coronation was supported on the one side by a lady's bonnet, on the other by a carpet-bag, while a lady's riding-habit, an officer's red jacket, and various other articles of attire were hung round the walls upon pegs; here and there, perhaps partly hidden by the folds of a lady's dress, was to be seen the portrait of some sedate old Nepaulese noble.

Jung called our attention to one of these; it was the portrait of a strikingly handsome man, whose keen eye and lofty brow seemed almost to entitle him to the position he held between the Duke of Wellington and the Queen. "See," said Jung, enthusiastically, "here is the Queen of England, and she has not got a more loyal subject than I am." Then turning to the picture of the man with the keen eyes and high forehead, he remarked, "That is my poor uncle Mahtiber Singh, whom I shot; it is very like him." After which he launched into a discussion upon the comparative merits of the Duke of Wellington and Napoleon, and, skipping two cocked hats and a bonnet, went on to some Purdy's rifles, of which he spoke in glowing terms and with all the enthusiasm of a true sportsman.

My friend Colonel Dhere Shum Shere now came up, whistling the Sturm Marsch, and challenged me to a game of billiards: he was in his manner more thoroughly English than any native I ever knew, and both in appearance and disposition looked as if he was an Anglo-Saxon who had been dyed by mistake. When in Europe he used to dress like an Englishman, and in company with his brother, the Minister Sahib, in similar attire, patronized Vauxhall, Cremorne, and other places of fashionable resort usually frequented by such fast men as they showed themselves to be. Like Jung, he used to say he could not bear the abominable screeching at the Opera, and consequently never made his appearance until the commencement of the ballet, which was much more in their line.

Having profited by his visits to European houses, Jung intends to show his enlightenment by substituting pictures for the articles of vertu with which the walls of his room are at present adorned, and to exchange kitchen ware for albums, in order to prove that he has travelled to some purpose. While examining these table ornaments, I observed a civilized looking little square piece of satin, and on taking it up found I was inspecting the first invitation to Her Majesty's Opera that had ever reached Nepaul.

In one apartment £700 worth of ladies' dresses, purchased in England, were spread upon the floor, destined, I presume, to adorn some sable beauties on whom the fashionable flounces of Madame Devy would be anything but becoming.

Jung informed us that a grand ceremony was to take place on the following day. The Queen of England's letter, of which he was the bearer, was to be read in full Durbar under a salute of twenty-one guns—a greater honour than is shown even to a communication from his Imperial Majesty of the celestial empire.

We accordingly repaired at the appointed hour next morning to the palace of the King, in the great square of Katmandu, and were ushered into the narrow room appropriated to the Durbar. It was hung round with pictures that a tavern would be ashamed of, and altogether looked so dirty that, had it been a tavern, it would have had but little custom.

Seated on a throne were the two Kings gorgeously apparelled and bedizened with jewels, while the Minister Sahib wore nothing but the simple bukkoo, or fur-robe, of great value but unassuming appearance.

There was to be a review of the troops after Durbar, and, as nearly all the nobility of Nepaul hold rank in the army, the whole assemblage was in uniform, certainly one of the most dazzling that I ever saw collected together. Each man had twice as many feathers as he was entitled to wear, and, while their cocked hats were always completely hid, the bodies of the more diminutive officers almost shared the same fate. The English dragoon and the French hussar might here recognize portions of their uniform, adorned with gold and silver lace to an extent which field-marshals alone have, with us, a right to indulge in, and often mixed up with some Oriental finery—a pair of glittering slippers that consorted but ill with the tightly strapped-down gold lace trowsers, or a handsome shawl that clumsily supported the jewelled sabre.

The ceremony of presentation having been gone through, a

select party, consisting of the two Kings, the English Resident and one or two officers of the Embassy, and the Prime Minister, adjourned to an upper room. This seemed to me a curious proceeding, and one which the remaining portion of the legislators must have thought particularly unsatisfactory: however they looked as if they did not care, or could not help it; and while the coterie above were solemnly perusing Her Majesty's epistle, and the guns were booming in honour of it, we below were chatting upon indifferent matters, until the Royal party returned, when, in addition to the pawn usually given on such occasions, we were presented by their Majesties with some Nepaulese weapons, and amidst more firing of cannon left the palace in the Minister's phaëton to witness a grand review.

The parade-ground was situated immediately under the city walls, and upon it 6000 men were drawn up: the uniforms differed in some instances; the "rifles" were in a pea-green suit which hung about them loosely, while the regiments of the line wore red coats, with trowsers ample enough to please a Turk. Upon their turbans or caps were the distinguishing badges of their respective corps—a half-moon, a lion, the sun, and various other devices. The regiments were not numbered as with us, but adopted some magniloquent high-sounding title suggestive of their valour in war, fearlessness of danger, and other martial qualities.

There was no cavalry, the country not being adapted to that arm of the service, but the artillery seemed very fairly handled; there was an immense deal of firing, both of small arms and great guns, which I believer was very good; and there were a great number of evolutions performed, which, as I am not a soldier, did not seem to me more incomprehensible than such manœuvring usually is, but I was informed by those who were capable of judging, that in this instance they really were altogether without meaning. Regiment after regiment marched past, the men swinging their arms regularly as they moved, and trying to persuade themselves they were British grenadiers. At all events the band was playing that tune. Suddenly the music changed; they struck up a lively polka, and a number of little boys in a sort of penwiper costume, clasping one another like civilized ladies and gentlemen, began to caper about, after which they went through various antics that surpassed even the wildest notions of our highly civilized community: all this while the troops were manœuvring as vehemently as ever, and the boys were dancing as fantastically; and the whole thing was so eminently ridiculous and looked so very like a farce, that it was difficult to maintain that dignified and sedate appearance which was expected from the spectators of a scene so imposing.

Jung alone looked for no expressions of surprise or admiration from us, but was evidently disappointed and chagrined at the inferiority of his own soldiers to those he had seen in Europe and amongst our Indian troops. He could indeed point with pride to the stalwart bearing and soldierlike appearance of his men, but he had seen "the Guards" reviewed, he had been present at an inspection of 15,000 of the French army at Versailles, and he seemed half ashamed of the display we were witnessing, notwithstanding our efforts to comfort him by telling him that we had little thought the art of war was so far advanced in the wild valleys and rocky mountains of Nepaul.

CHAPTER XIII

Distinguishing features of the races of Nepaul—The Ghorkas—Conquest by them of Katmandu—Maintenance of the Nepaul army—Bheem Singh's monument—A feast at the minister's—We bid him adieu—Ascent of the Sheopoori—Magnificent view of the Himalayas from its summit

The grand review over, we availed ourselves of the opportunity to inspect the regiments composed of men recruited in some of the most distant provinces of Nepaul. They bore in their countenances little resemblance either to the Ghorkas or Newars. We examined their faces, and tried to imagine what sort of a looking country was likely to produce this sort of a looking man. A regiment of dark-visaged stalwart Ghorkas would march past, followed by a diminutive race from the north-western frontier, little, ill-made, and abominably ugly. The same cast of countenance was prevalent throughout the regiments that had been recruited there; all the men had the same high cheek-bones, or wide mouths, or whatever their peculiarity might be. The insignificant Newars looked majestic by the side of these men, while in their turn their own strong Chinese characteristics were thrown completely into the shade by some regiment from the north-east, almost pure Bootyan or Mongolian.

There are not, however, many Newars employed as soldiers, and the army is chiefly composed of Muggurs, Gurungs, and Krats. These tribes differ only in their religion, according as it combines in a greater or less degree the superstitions of the Hindoo worship with those of Bhuddism. But none of these races differed from one another more completely than did the Ghorka from them all; he was the only man among them born to be a soldier, and he looked with contempt upon the mongrel races that surrounded him.

The country from which he himself originally sprang is nevertheless a matter of speculation; he certainly is not of trans-Himalayan origin, but no doubt the comfortable life he leads in Nepaul prevents his caring to inquire whence he came. The Rajah claims descent from the Rajput princes. The capital town of the country from which they descended into the valley of Nepaul is Ghorka, situated about fifty miles westward of Katmandu. The Ghorkas had already possessed themselves of the whole territory to the westward for some hundred of miles until their border touched the kingdom of Runjeit Singh and the vale of Cashmere; they then turned their conquering arms eastward in 1716, and, overrunning the valleys of the Newars, their progress was only arrested on the Sikkim frontier.

The conquest of the valley of Katmandu was attended with circumstances of the greatest barbarity; thousands of the inhabitants were starved to death by the Ghorka King, Prithi Naraim. There were then in Nepaul a few Christians, converted by a Jesuit mission. These were all compelled to fly the country, some taking refuge in Thibet, others crossing our frontier and settling at Bettiah, where a Christian community at present exists. Not long after he had conquered Nepaul, the Ghorka monarch organized an expedition into Tartary, which was so signally successful that the H'Lassa Government was obliged to treat on humiliating conditions. This advantage was followed, in defiance of the treaty, by another invasion, which was only arrested by the forces of the Emperor, who, having heard of the violent proceedings in this distant part of his dominions, sent an army of 70,000 men to oppose the Ghorka invaders, who were completely overwhelmed and obliged to retreat. The Chinese followed the retiring force across their own frontier, and not until they had reached the valley of Noyakot, eighteen miles from Katmandu, did they consent to treat for peace, which was now humbly sued for by the Ghorka King.

Not satisfied with serving as soldiers in their own country, the Ghorkas have offered their services to the Indian Government, and two of its finest regiments are composed of soldiers of this race.

No European, as far as I could learn, has ever yet penetrated to their city, which however can contain no object of very great attraction, since it must want those Chinese peculiarities which render Katmandu and Patan so interesting, and must more nearly resemble the large cities of the plains. It has a large population, is well built and fortified, and is situated on a commanding eminence.

The Nepaul army is maintained partly by the state, the men being in some instances paid out of the treasury, but more frequently by an assignment of land to each man called a jaghire. They are thus remunerated at the expense of the Newars, who are the cultivators of the soil and were the original proprietors. Hence Nepaul is a warlike state, not merely from the natural disposition of its Ghorka conquerors, but from the inducements held out to them to become soldiers.

What would our grumbling agricultural population say to having soldiers billeted in each village, and living on the fat of the land? The Newars say, "Take away the army and give us free trade"; the farmers in England say, "Keep up the army and take away free trade."

The minister told us of out-stations at which different regiments were posted, and wanted us to believe that the standing army of Nepaul exceeded 25,000 men. Every male is obliged to serve in the army for a year, and it requires great interest to be allowed to remain above that period, so eagerly is the profession of arms sought after.

Immediately facing the parade-ground stands the famous monument built by Bheem Singh, one of the most eminent prime ministers that Nepaul has ever seen, and who has left behind him proofs of his greatness in the many works, both useful and ornamental, which he erected.

Two winged lions guard the chief bridge over the Bhagmutty, by which Katmandu is approached, and pronounce Bheem Singh its builder. Numerous temples and handsome palaces are adorned in like manner, but the monument above mentioned is the most remarkable memorial of his greatness, and is the chief ornament of the city. The people are deservedly proud of this its distinguishing mark, for, except as minarets, single columns are unknown in India, and in this respect their mountain capital can boldly challenge a comparison with the proudest city of the plains. The monument resembles in shape a portable telescope fully drawn out, and rears its head to a height of nearly 200 feet above the surrounding houses. The Minister Sahib contended that it was higher than the monument of London. This, as in duty bound, I patriotically denied; but which of us was led into error by partiality for our respective countries I am not prepared to say. The Mahila Sahib accompanied us to the summit, whence we had a most magnificent view. Looking down into the city beneath us, we could discern the turning of every narrow street, the palaces situated in the midst of gardens, the hovels in the midst of dunghills, though I am bound to say that the former preponderated in number, and the houses of the city were for the most part substantial and well built. Some of these streets were now crowded with a motley multitude, returning home from the review, the bright uniforms mixing amongst them as the soldiers joined their families after being dismissed parade, or here and there marched in companies back to the barracks. Officers were scampering down streets on ponies, dragging along the horse-boys, who were holding on by their tails. All this the Mahila Sahib pointed out with much affability. Had he been the man to seize a good opportunity, that was the moment to give Jung a push over the low parapet; but the Mahila Sahib is a man without decision of character; so we all descended, and he allowed the minister to reach the bottom his own way. We then proceeded with Jung to his residence, there to partake of a farewell feast. The carriage in which we were driving was one I had seen brought over the mountain passes on men's shoulders in detached portions; and this emanation from Long-Acre was to be trundled for the rest of its existence along the three or four miles of carriage-road which the valley of Nepaul can boast. Our way lay through narrow lanes, walled in by the enclosures of different rich men's suburban residences, and the prolific orange-trees drooped their luscious fruit over the garden walls for the benefit of anyone who chose to pick them, as they hung temptingly overhead. Jung showed us his horticultural arrangements with no little pride. His house is situated in the midst of gardens, adorned with fountains and reservoirs, and he informed us that upon one aqueduct alone he had expended £30,000. The garden was in its infancy, and, notwithstanding the great formality with which it was laid out, bid fair to do credit to Jung's taste and industry. In one direction the gardens extend to the river side, where he has built some handsome baths, not far distant from which, and at one corner of his grounds, stands a four-turreted building, inhabited by the Ranee of Lahore, who has taken refuge from the English under the hospitable roof of Jung Bahadoor. Here this extraordinary woman leads a secluded life, rarely venturing outside her doors, and never giving anyone a chance of judging for themselves of her rumoured beauty. She is, no doubt, meditating some bold design worthy of the heroism she has proved herself to possess, for she is said still to retain hope where hope is surely forlorn.

We had not on this occasion walked a whole day over Nepaul roads, as was the case when last we dined with Jung; consequently, when his feast was set before us, we did not do justice to it. Perhaps our appetites were spoiled by the parting which was about to take place, for we were not to see his Excellency any more, and to part from the prime minister of Nepaul is not like parting from any other man. Even were he only a casual acquaintance, it would cause a different feeling from that of bidding adieu to one who was to lead a peaceable life, and in all probability die in his bed; but when the chances are strongly against either of these suppositions, and when the friend whom you are leaving is a man of so interesting a character, the possessor of such great talents and of so many amiable qualities, one with whom you have journeyed and hunted and undergone all sorts of adventures and witnessed all sorts of scenes, and who has on all occasions proved himself a kind friend, an hospitable host, and an agreeable companion, it is anything but pleasant to look upon him for the last time. Doubtless, in the early years of his yet uncivilized life, Jung Bahadoor was guilty of great barbarities and crimes, but it was war to the knife, and self-defence no less than ambition prompted the acts of that bloody drama. Now he has proved himself a changed man, and his late generous and humane conduct might well read a useful lesson to many in the civilized societies in which he learnt to be what he now is, since he does not fear to change a line of conduct when its error is palpable.

The time at length arrived when we were compelled to bid adieu to this extraordinary man, whose future career is a matter of such vast importance to the country he rules with almost absolute power. Expressing the hope that the day might yet come when I should meet him in my own country, I took leave of my kind-hearted but perilously-situated entertainer as I would of a friend in a galloping consumption.

During my whole stay in Nepaul the weather had been unusually foggy, and the snowy range only displayed its wonders now and then. On the day following the review the sky was unclouded; I therefore resolved to ascend the Sheopoori, a mountain which rises to a height of 2000 feet above the valley, and from which it was said a most magnificent view of the snowy range is obtained. The ascent commenced at a distance of five miles from the Residency, and was very fatiguing from the total absence of any path, the steepness of some part of it, and the thick jungle through which we had to push our way. It occupied two hours' stiff climbing for one in pretty good mountain condition, but no fatigue seems too great if it is rewarded by a good view; and there is no prospect so cheering to the mountain traveller as that of an unclouded sky, with the summit of the hill he is ascending in clear relief against it.

At last we reached the shoulder, from whence I had a peep that made me long for more, but, determined not to spoil the effect, I pushed resolutely on after my guide through a low scrubby jungle, along a barely perceptible woodcutter's path, until the crisp snow crunching beneath our feet betokened our great elevation. I was glad to halt for a moment and cool my mouth with the snow, a luxury I had not experienced for years.

A few yards more and we gained the summit; a sort of shed, the residence of some departed holy man, marked the highest point, upwards of 6000 feet above the sea.

A keen sharp wind whistled about the ruin as I jumped on to a half broken-down wall in order to look over the low bushes which surrounded me. From this position a panorama, in every respect as magnificent as it was wonderful, stretched itself, if I may so speak, as well above as below me. Northward, and not thirty miles distant, the Himalayas reared their heaven-piercing summits, peak succeeding peak, and crag succeeding crag, far as the eye could reach, from east to west a glittering chain, while here and there the light clouds which hung upon its rocks and precipices became thinned, till they vanished altogether, or, rising in denser masses from some dark valley, obscured the lower portions of the range, only to give relief to the summits and elevate them in appearance—an aid they little needed, for the height of the lowest level of the chain is upwards of 15,000 feet. But it was not the actual height of the various peaks, nor the masses of glistening snow which clothed them, brightly reflecting the rays of an almost vertical sun, and tinted by the most brilliant hues, that was the chief cause of wonder and admiration. It was the sharpness of the horizon-line against the serene clear sky which displayed precipices and crags of inconceivable grandeur, the over-hanging peak looking down some thousands of feet upon the lower part of the range. Had it been possible to calculate upon such a stupendous scale, I felt I was gazing at sheer precipices 6000 or 8000 feet in depth, for the descent from 25,000 to 15,000 feet was not gradual, but the whole line was cragged and notched upon a scale of unsurpassable magnificence and grandeur.

The Dawalogiri, the highest mountain in the world, and 28,700 feet above the level of the sea, was as worthy a termination of the chain at one end as its rival, the Kinchin Jung, was at the other; while not ten leagues distant, and completely towering above me, the Gosain Than reared its gigantic head, the third highest in this mighty barrier.

Turning from this marvellous scene, I looked down upon the placid valley of Nepaul. Its four rivers appeared like silver threads, winding their way amidst rich cultivation to swell the waters of the parent Bhagmutty. Blooming and verdant, the populous plain lay embosomed in lofty mountains, shut out as it were from the cares of the world. It seemed a Paradise on earth, with an approach to heaven of its own along the summit of the Gosain Than.

I viewed with interest a country on which European foot had never trod, and my eye ranged over bleak hills enclosing fertile valleys, into which torrents first flung themselves wildly, then, flowing sedately through to the other end, dashed away again behind rocks and hills and jumbled masses of broken country, which must have afforded magnificent scenery as it gradually swelled into the towering mountains of the Emodus.

A distant hill was pointed out to me as that on which the city of Ghorka was perched, a fitting residence for the wild race to whom it gives birth. My guide also showed me the road to the mysterious capital of H'Lassa, winding through rocky glens, passable only for the droves of sheep that traverse those mountain defiles, a journey of twenty days in the Nepaul dominions; but how far from the frontier lay the city of the Grand Lama the guide did not know.

The valley of Noyakot is about eighteen miles distant from Katmandu, and was visited some years ago by Prince Waldemar of Prussia and his party. It does not offer much attraction to the traveller, and as I looked into it from the top of Sheopoori I thought it hardly worth the trip. Not so extensive as that in which Katmandu is situated, it lies lower and is very fertile. Its climate is much warmer and not so healthy. Looking up the valley of Nepaul, I could distinguish at its farther end, twelve miles distant from the present capital, the ancient Newar city of Bhatgong, the second in importance in the days when Patan was the first. It has now fallen into much the same dismantled state as its old rival, while it looked much more picturesque, standing as it does on a commanding eminence, terraced with rich rice-fields. The Durbar is a fine old building, characteristic of the architecture of the country, and the town contains many ancient Newar buildings of much interest.

But the valley of Nepaul, and the wild mountains of Ghorka, and the dashing rivers and the rocky glens, all sank into insignificance when I returned once more irresistibly fascinated by the wonders which the snowy chain seemed to exhibit anew every moment, as clouds cleared away from off the frightful precipices, or laid bare huge craggy peaks. For an hour did I gaze upon this incomparable scene, as upon one which the experience of a lifetime can seldom boast, for, though I was prepared by an alpine experience in Europe, and had stretched my imagination to the utmost in my anticipations of what would be the appearance of the highest mountains in the world, I could never have conceived—far less is it possible for me to describe—the scene I beheld from the summit of Sheopoori.

A visit to the Minister's brothers—Dexterity of Colonel Dhere Shum Shere—Scenes for lovers of the Fancy—Adieu to Nepaul—The view from the summit of the Chandernagiri pass—The scenery of Nepaul—The pass of Bhimphede—Night quarters

It was out of the question my leaving Katmandu without paying a farewell visit to the Minister's two younger brothers, Juggut and Colonel Dhere Shum Shere, so I hurried over in the afternoon to their house, which was situated in the centre of the town. On my road I met them driving in a buggy, the only one of which the town could boast, and, as it is not considered *infra dig.* in Katmandu to go three in a gig, I jumped in between them, and we were soon tearing along the narrow street at a most reckless pace, and finally pulled up in a small square, where a great crowd seemed to be waiting for something to take place. A Katmandu crowd doubtless possesses the same instinct in this respect that crowds in civilized parts of the world do, and, as it proved, they were quite right in their expectations, for the exhibition which almost immediately followed was well worth seeing. The Colonel said he had something to show us, but we could perceive nothing out of the common except a huge bull buffalo, whose head was firmly lashed to a stake fixed in the courtyard, so that it touched it from his forehead to his nose; he was then blindfolded, his legs were planted some distance apart, and he stood snorting at his confined position. Meantime we had jumped out of the buggy, the young Colonel, stripping himself of all superfluous clothing, had grasped a "korah," or native sword, and, first laying the keen edge of it gently upon the exposed neck of the buffalo, he drew himself to his full height, and raised his korah high above his head. Every muscle extended, every fibre strained, he seemed to concentrate his strength in a wonderful manner into that blow which was at one stroke to sever the extended neck of the buffalo. Down came the sword with sweeping force. I looked eagerly for the result; when suddenly his hand was arrested midway, and with a look of vexation the Colonel *let off the steam* he had got up for the occasion, as he pointed to one of the buffalo's legs; it had been moved an inch inwards, and that was sufficient to cause the failure of the operation. Three or four times did this occur, and it seemed essentially necessary to the success of the feat that the legs of the animal should be perfectly stationary in a particular position. How little was the buffalo aware that each movement he made prolonged his life some seconds! I could not help thinking that there was a strong resemblance between his position and that of Jung, for decidedly the only chance the Minister has of his life is to keep continually moving. At last down came the korah with crushing force, and passed right through the animal's neck: the headless trunk tottered for a second, and then fell heavily over.

I was horrified at seeing a second buffalo brought up for slaughter, and my horror was greatly increased when I understood that I was expected to exercise my skill upon it. This offer I declined as politely as I could, accepting from the young Colonel, as a remembrance of his dexterity and strength, the korah with which he had performed this extraordinary feat.

We next adjourned to another courtyard, which was surrounded with bulldogs and terriers of every description,—a collection worthy the most ardent votary of the Fancy. Two magnificent rams, which were tied up in the corners of the yard, soon after showed us that a sport existed in Nepaul unknown as yet to 'Bell's Life.' No sooner were these animals untied than they dashed at one another with the utmost fury; the violence of the shock caused the combatants to recoil, and it was a matter of astonishment to us that their brains were not dashed out.

The whole fight consisted in their being separated and then let go at one another again. This continued without any apparent advantage on either side until we thought that they had inflicted punishment enough on one another for our amusement, and then they were both tied up, and left to meditate upon their splitting headaches and to scowl at one another across the yard.

We walked through the Colonel's house, and found in his drawing-room the usual collection of theatrical prints and portraits of opera-dancers, mixed up with those of old statesmen, which he seemed to think perfectly natural, and no doubt he fancies he has good reason for so thinking. There were also a piano and some European luxuries strangely mingled with barbarous inventions.

In leaving these two excellent young men, I bade adieu to the last of my fellow-travellers from Ceylon. My especial favourite of them all was Colonel Dhere Shum Shere, whose thoroughly frank and amiable disposition endeared him to everyone, while his courage and daring commanded universal respect. I know of no one I would rather have by my side in a row than the young Colonel, and his brother Jung evidently thought so too when he chose him to assist in the capture of the conspirators in the attempt upon his life. Cheerful and lively, his merry laugh might be heard in the midst of a knot of his admirers, to whom he was relating some amusing anecdote, while his shrewd remarks were the result of keen observation, and proved his intellect to be by no means of a low order.

His elder brother Juggut was fat, lazy, and good tempered, but wanting the energy of his brothers. These two are the youngest members of the family, and are devotedly attached to Jung.

Mounting our ponies at an early hour on the following morning, we bade adieu to the Residency and its hospitable inmates, and cantered along narrow lanes bordered by hedges of prickly pear, and roughly paved with large stones: sometimes we passed between steep banks over gently swelling hills terraced to their summits, and reminding me strongly of a vine-growing country.

Soon the road became more broken, and, on gaining the top of a steep hill, we took our last view of the valley of Katmandu before commencing the ascent of the precipitous Chandernagiri. From this point we gazed with indescribable delight on the valley so peculiar if not unrivalled in its beauty: its compact red-brick villages or straggling houses, which, with their quaintly-carved gables, clustered up the hillsides; its sacred groves containing numerous venerated shrines in picturesque proximity to the clear streams that gushed down from the neighbouring hills; its ancient cities, whose dismantled walls enclosed the ruined tenements of a departed race; the richly-cultivated knolls, the Chinese pagodas, the Bhuddist dagobas on the banks of the sacred Bhagmutty, the narrow but substantially-built brick bridges by which it was spanned, continually traversed by an industrious population;— all these objects formed a picture, "with all the freshness and glory of a dream," to which the towering monument of Bheem Singh in the far distance, while it indicated the position of the capital of this favoured vale, was a fitting centre.

At Thankote, eight miles from Katmandu, we dismounted, and commenced in earnest the ascent of the Chandernagiri. It is the steepest pass on either of the roads by which the valley of Nepaul is entered, and for that reason seems generally chosen by the natives, who would not for the world miss the pleasure of toiling up an almost inaccessible mountain. They certainly cannot be accused of neglecting the opportunities their country affords them for strengthening the muscles of their legs. The traveller had need to have his shins cased if he intends to climb a hill with a Newar mountaineer, for the path is so steep that the hillmen, as they clamber up, frequently dislodge stones, which come tumbling down upon those behind. However, I should have despised the blows from the stones, and should not have cared for the fatigue of the rugged ascent, if, on reaching the summit of the Chandernagiri, I had been rewarded with the view which it commands in clear weather.

Colonel Kirkpatrick thus describes this glorious scene as it burst upon him in all its magnificence:—"From hence the eye not only expatiates on the waving valley of Nepaul, beautifully and thickly dotted with villages and abundantly checquered with rich fields fertilized by numerous meandering streams, but also embraces on every side a wide expanse of charming and diversified country. It is the landscape in front, however, that most powerfully attracts the attention—the scenery in this direction rising to an amphitheatre, and exhibiting to the delighted view the cities and numberless temples of the valley below, the stupendous mountain of Sheopoori, the still supertowering Jib Jibia, clothed to its snow-capped peak with pendulous forests, and finally the gigantic Himaleh, forming the majestic background to this wonderful and sublime picture."

This majestic background was now concealed behind a dense bank of clouds, and the prospect was bounded by Sheopoori.

The snowy range is the most striking feature in Nepaul scenery, and the most important element in its composition, since the effect produced by the grandeur of its stupendous summits is probably unequalled.

It would be hardly fair to compare the valley in which Katmandu is situated with any other part of the world, since it is so peculiar in its characteristics and totally unlike the rest of the Nepaul dominions; but, standing on the summit of Chandernagiri, and looking over the mountainous district which stretched away to the south, and across which our road lay, we could not but be struck by the bleak appearance of the mountains, neither desolate nor rugged enough to possess the majesty of a bold and sublime solitude, nor sufficiently wooded and populous to exhibit that softer and more animating character which in the scenery of Switzerland is no less charming than its grandeur is imposing. Of course this does not apply to all Nepaul; the lower ranges are more woody, the valleys more sunny and fertile, but there is a lamentable want of water throughout. I do not remember ever to have seen so much as a horse-pond in Nepaul, or a single waterfall of any magnitude: the traveller will therefore probably be disappointed in the scenery, until he reaches the

Chandernagiri, when indeed he must be difficult to please if he is not fascinated by the view of the valley at his feet, unsurpassed in the singular character of its beauty, and of the mountains beyond it, unparalleled by any in the whole world.

We followed the course of the stream down the mountain and along the valley of Chitlong, until we reached the foot of the Bhimphede pass, when, striking into the path by which we had entered Nepaul, we toiled up it, reaching the summit just before sunset, when we were delighted by the farewell view of the snowy mountains which we obtained at this point. The upper edge of the curtain of clouds had now become slightly lower, allowing a single peak to show itself. Gilded by the rays of the declining sun, it shone out in strong relief, like some unusual phenomenon; and as we gazed upon it high in the heavens we found it difficult to believe that it was part of the earth we stood on, and felt almost inclined to agree with the faithful, who throughout India regard this heaven-piercing summit as the centre of the universe, around which the sun, moon, and stars perform their courses, the sacred and mysterious Mount Menou.

Gradually the bright crimson rays of the setting sun began to fade, and reminded us that we had to make a long descent ere we could reach the tent pitched at the bottom for our reception; and our former experience had taught us that the Bhimphede pass was not the most pleasant road in the world on which to be benighted. So we hurried on at the risk of our necks, the loose stones rolling down before us, and rendering our footing anything but safe in the growing darkness.

When we reached the foot of the mountain our servants met us with torches and guided us to the tent; and as we spread our dinner upon a rickety old bedstead, which, wonderful to relate, this out-of-the-way village supplied, we came to the conclusion that there were many worse lodgings in the world than the snug little single-poled tent at the old Newar village of Bhimphede.

CHAPTER XV

A dilemma at Bisoleah—Ignominious exit from the Nepaul dominions—The resources and capabilities of Nepaul—Articles of import from Thibet and Chinese Tartary—A vision of the future

At Bhimphede we remounted our elephant, following, as before, the valley of the Rapti to Hetowra, thence through the great saul forest to Bisoleah, where we expected to find our palanquins. In this we were not disappointed; but unfortunately our bearers, tired of waiting for us at so uninteresting a spot, had thought themselves justified in absconding; which proceeding, while it was a considerable saving to us in a pecuniary point of view, was particularly annoying under existing circumstances, the day being far advanced and Segowly still thirty miles distant. However, by dint of a great deal of threatening, and coaxing, and bribing, and a very frequent use of the magic name of the Minister Sahib, who, we assured them, would take into his especial favour every coolie that volunteered for our service, and would visit with his heavy displeasure all those who refused, we induced a sufficient number of men to agree to bear our empty palanquins. Unloading two ponies, which were carrying cotton, we put our luggage on one, riding the other by turns, and so, one of us sitting on a rough sack without bridle or stirrups, the other walking by his side, we marched out of the village and across the open plain of the Terai. We were soon after left in darkness, and, becoming separated from our palanquins, as was to be expected, we lost our way, and wandered for some time disconsolately over the grassy plain, until at length, stumbling upon a village, we procured a guide and overtook the bearers a little beyond the Nepaul frontier. Ere we reached it, however, we were obliged to traverse numerous streams, which we crossed riding double on our pony. Altogether we made our exit from Nepaul in very different style from that in which we had entered it, and were not a little glad to arrive at Segowly shortly before dawn.

The journey from Katmandu to Segowly can scarcely be accomplished in less than three days and three nights, not on account of the distance, but of the frightfully bad roads, which quite preclude the possibility of travelling faster than at the rate of two miles an hour.

There is scarcely a country in the world in which the state of the roads is so much to be lamented, since, apart from the benefit which would accrue to Nepaul itself, we too should be gainers, by having not only the valuable productions of Nepaul brought to our markets, but also those of the more distant Thibet, which are always precious from their intrinsic value, and the cost of which is at present greatly increased by reason of the expensive journey across the Nepaulese hills in addition to the transit of the Himalayas.

The Terai is at present the only part of the Nepaul dominions which is profitable from the revenue yielded by its productions. Valuable timber and turpentine, ivory and hides, are shipped down the Boori Gundak, on which river Segowly is situated, to Calcutta; still the cost of a government licence for cutting timber is so heavy as in a great measure to deter speculators from engaging in an undertaking in which so considerable an outlay is demanded, exclusive of the expenses attendant on the felling and transport of the timber. Besides the saul the Terai contains ebony, mimosa, and other useful trees.

The trade in hides is not, as I have already remarked, carried out to the extent it is capable of. But in spite of all these drawbacks, the Terai alone, of all the Nepaul dominions, can be looked upon by the British as offering a profitable field for trade and commercial speculations.

Nevertheless, the interior of Nepaul contains productions far more valuable than those of the Terai. Its mineral resources are such as would in all probability, if properly developed, render their mountainous, and in some parts barren country, one of the richest in the world. Iron, lead, copper, and zinc mines abound, and are in fact worked, but, from all I could learn, so very badly, that, even did their roads allow of the export of the metals, it is to be questioned whether, without the application of a better system, enough metal could be obtained to do more than supply the home demand.

However that may be, there is no doubt of the existence of these mines, and, if ever there were tolerable roads, the necessary skill for working them would doubtless follow. So backward are the Nepaulese in their treatment of minerals, that they cannot smelt lead: the fact of their *beating* cannonballs into shape proves their incapacity to cast iron, unless it results from a peculiarity of the ore, so frequent in India, which, instead of yielding cast-iron at once when reduced in the usual way, gives wootz—a condition of iron closely allied to steel, ductile but not fusible. Of this I had no opportunity of judging.

Nepaul also possesses mines of sulphur, and, it is said, of antimony; whether this latter is found in the country does not seem certain; it is, however, an article of import from Thibet. Amongst other minerals are corundum, figure-stone, and talc; and amongst the present exports from the interior of Nepaul may be noticed turmeric, wax, honey, resin, pepper, cardamums: all these, however, are exported in but small quantities, owing partly to the difficulty of transport, and partly to the want of enterprise and capital in a nation thoroughly ignorant of all mercantile transactions.

It is much to be regretted that no European is now allowed to settle in Nepaul; for its many latent resources must remain undiscovered, or at least undeveloped, until the present blind policy of its government is changed, when British enterprise and British capital introduces a new era in its commercial existence, which will doubtless prove no less profitable to the country itself than to the capitalist.

Of the immense expanse of country lying in a north-westerly direction towards Cashmere we know nothing, save by report, and that is not always to be trusted. The Minister told me that, in a province three days' journey from the capital in that direction, sufficient horses were bred to supply the wants of the whole country. That seemed perfectly possible, considering how limited is the demand in this respect; but, on our homeward journey, we passed a drove of upwards of two hundred long-backed, spindle-legged colts, going up to Katmandu, and that did not seem exactly corroborative of the Minister's assertion.

But, whatever may be its capabilities as regards horses, it doubtless possesses many resources; but it is not on the productions of Nepaul alone that the European speculator would calculate, but on the rare and precious merchandise of Thibet and the northern provinces of China—such as the miledo, or exquisitely soft material fabricated from the wool of the celebrated shawl-goat, itself a rare and valuable animal; and the chowries or tails of a peculiar species of bullock inhabiting the snowy regions, at present an article of export from the hill states in the north-west provinces of India, and extensively used throughout the continent as fly-flappers.

Musk, procured from the musk-deer, is a most valuable article of commerce, and the present trade is exceedingly lucrative; of very inconsiderable bulk, and of great intrinsic worth, it is one of the few things that can be imported into India with a profit. It there fetches enormous prices; a small musk necklace, which I saw in the possession of the Minister, and which certainly was not a foot long, was valued at £25. It is very seldom, however, that musk can be procured un-adulterated. It is not, however, so much as an ornament, as a medicine, that we should use this now costly substance.

But the most valuable productions at present imported from Thibet are mineral. Immense quantities of salt are brought over the Himalayas on sheep's backs; gold-dust, borax, sulphur, antimony, arsenic, orpiment, and medicinal drugs are also imported into Nepaul.

The animals which abound in these cold regions, and which might be worth importing, are musk-deer, sheep, shawl-goats, chowrie bullocks, falcons, pheasants—in fact, it would be hopeless to attempt to enumerate all those productions, animal, vegetable, and mineral, which are now scarcely known except by name, but which will doubtless some day be objects of traffic and commercial enterprise. For instance, there are various medicinal drugs and dyes (among which may be mentioned madder and spikenard) which are said to exist, but are now almost totally unknown.

Among the present articles of import are embroideries, taffetas, chintz, silk, cotton, cloth, carpets, cutlery, sandalwood, tobacco, conch-shells, soap, &c.

Surely it is no very extravagant flight of imagination to suppose that the day may yet come when the unattainable and almost unknown productions of the trans-Himalayan regions will be transported across that mighty range, in well-appointed carriages, over macadamised mountain-passes; and the noble work of the scientific engineer will thus supersede the flocks of heavily-laden sheep, driven by uncivilized and ill-clothed Bootyas, who, "impelled by the force of circumstances over which they have no control," will don their smockfrocks and turn draymen; when the traveller, going to the coach-office, Durbar-square, Katmandu, may book himself in the royal mail through to H'Lassa, where, after a short residence at the Grand Lama Hotel, strongly recommended in Murray's 'Handbook for the Himalayas,' he may wrap himself in his fur bukkoo, and, taking his seat in a first-class carriage on the Asiatic Central Railway, whisk away to Pekin, having previously telegraphed home, *viâ* St. Petersburg, that he proposes returning through North America, and will, therefore, probably be detained a few hours longer than he had anticipated.

Such a state of things *we* may not live to see, but it is by no means unlikely that ere long a railway may run from Calcutta to the northern frontier of British India; so that, when Nepaul is thrown open to European enterprise, its costly productions will be easily and cheaply transported to the nearest port, while the now almost uncivilized Nepaulese would obtain

European luxuries unknown to any of them except Jung Bahadoor and his travelled suite.

Nor will the idea of a direct communication between Nepaul and Pekin seem either so improbable or impossible when we consider that an embassy now makes the journey once every five years. It occupies no less than two years, including a residence of less than two months in the capital of the Celestial Empire. I met two or three Nepaulese who had accomplished the enterprise, and who spoke in glowing terms of Pekin, and of the magnificence displayed throughout those portions of the Chinese Empire which they traversed, as well as of the great city of Lassa, and the terrible mountains to be crossed and the incredible dangers to be overcome.

The mission is composed of twenty-seven persons, and would not be admitted across the frontier of China if it consisted of one more or less than the stated number. It must arrive on the frontier on a certain day, and is subject to various rules and regulations: at the same time every provision is made by the Chinese for the comfort of the members of the embassy while on their journey. The journey from Pekin to Lassa has lately been made by Messrs. Huc and Gabet, two French missionaries, and has been graphically described by them.

The Nepaulese look with the greatest awe upon their wealthy and highly-civilized neighbours; but the Minister, having now lived amongst people more warlike and accomplished than even the Chinese, regards them with great contempt; and I should not be surprised if, before long, accounts reach us of the invasion, by the Nepaulese, of the northern provinces of China, when the Minister would bring to bear his recently acquired knowledge, and would doubtless prove more than a match for the rudely-equipped forces of his Celestial Majesty.

The Tartar race, however, who would oppose the progress of a Nepaul army, are a very different set from their tea-drinking countrymen on the southern coast.

But to return from Chinese Tartars to the country we had just quitted. The kingdom of Nepaul extends for upwards of three hundred miles along the southern slopes of the Himalayas, and is said to contain a population of about five millions. Of these four hundred thousand inhabit the valley of Nepaul proper. The lands are divided into four classes of tenures—first, crown lands; secondly, Kroos or Soona Birtha, belonging to Brahmins or Newars; thirdly, Kohriya or Bari, barren lands granted for cultivation; and, lastly (and this is the most extensive class of the four), Kaith, in which the proprietor is at all charges of tillage, dividing the produce with the cultivator.

The silver coinage of Nepaul is somewhat similar to that in use throughout British India; in all the northern provinces of which, adjoining Nepaul, it passes current: the copper coinage is most extensive, and consists of shapeless lumps of copper, eighteen or twenty of which go to a halfpenny; they are used by the natives of India in preference to their own pice.

But it is time to take leave of this interesting country, with its snowy mountains and sunny valleys—its ignorant people and enlightened Minister—its bloodstained past and hopeful future. I had already mentally whispered my adieu, as, riding behind my companion on the rawboned pony, I crossed the boundary stream; and pleased and interested as we had been with our short stay in Nepaul, still we could not help regretting that it had not fallen to our lot to discover new wonders—to encamp on the shores of the great lake situated in the distant province of Malebum, the existence of which was vaguely hinted at by my friend Colonel Dhere Shum Shere—to explore unvisited mountains, and to luxuriate in the magnificent scenery which they must contain; the enjoyment heightened by the feeling that we were the first Europeans who had penetrated their inhospitable recesses.

CHAPTER XVI

Journey to Lucknow—Nocturnal disasters—View of the Himalayas—Wild-beast fights—Banquet given by the King of Oudh—Grand display of fireworks—Our return to cantonments

Unquestionably the pleasures of travelling cannot be said to be altogether unalloyed—a consideration which the journey from Segowly to Lucknow irresistibly forced upon our minds, how determined soever we might be to adhere to the traveller's first principle of making the best of everything. We left the station about dusk, upon a night in which the elements seemed to have combined to cause us as much discomfort as possible, and the violence of the storm about midnight compelled us to take shelter in every tope of trees we came to, or, as it appeared to me, wherever the bearers thought we stood a good chance of being struck by the lightning which was vividly flashing in most unpleasant proximity. The deluge of rain soon made the path so slippery that our progress was much retarded, which would not have signified had it not happened that every now and then my slumbers were most disagreeably disturbed by a crash which flattened my nose against the side of the palanquin, or produced a violent shock to every part of my body, the effect of a slip of some unhappy bearer who was himself on the broad of his back, and had brought down the palanquin, bearers and all, in his tumble.

This occurred to me no less than five times in one night, and the consequence was that my palanquin was in even a worse condition than my body; it did not possess a single uncracked panel, nor were there any means of keeping the doors in, far less closed, and the cooling influence of the rain which pelted upon me was only counteracted by the feverish anxiety I experienced from the momentary expectation of feeling the bottom give way, which would have inevitably landed me in the mud in a most deplorable condition—as had been the case with every book or other loose article about me.

Daylight, however, revealed a prospect which banished at once the remembrance of our nocturnal annoyances. The whole of the Himalayan range, tinged by the glowing rays of the rising sun, displayed to our delighted and astonished gaze its long and majestic line of snowy peaks, while the atmosphere, cleared by the night's heavy rain, brought out in bold relief the sharp outline of every point and angle from the clear horizon-line of the various summits down to where the light morning haze still shrouded their base.

Unobscured by intervening mountains, and towering high above a sea of mist, well may they impress with wonder and admiration the traveller journeying over the plains of India, as he beholds them for the first time; nor could I, familiar as they were to me, withdraw my gaze until the increasing power of the sun rendered the atmosphere more hazy, and gradually veiled this glorious picture from my view, as if it were too precious to be exhibited for any length of time.

The journey to Goruckpore occupied us two nights and a day of incessant travelling over a flat but cheerful-looking wheat country. It is a pretty little station, containing a regiment and a few civilians, and is situated on the banks of the Rapti, our old Nepaulese acquaintance under a very different face.

The Gograh, which we crossed the following morning, is the boundary that divides the British territory from that of his Majesty of Oudh; and Fyzabad was the first town in his dominions at which we halted. Situate about six miles from the river, it is approached by a narrow muddy lane which winds among numbers of squalid huts, while a considerable sprinkling of handsome mosques and minarets showed the predominance of Mahomedanism in the country in which we were now travelling; but they all seemed falling to decay, and were inhabited chiefly by Hindoo monkeys, who lazily inspected one another on the sunny corners of some ruined temple, or chased each other irreverently through the sacred groves.

Fyzabad was formerly the capital; but the seat of government was changed to Lucknow at the accession of Azof-up Dowlah in 1775.

We were not sorry, after spending another twenty-four hours in our rickety palanquins, to see the massive mosques and lofty minarets of Lucknow looming in the distance, while handsome buildings in varied styles of architecture gave to this city a handsome and more imposing appearance than any I had yet visited in the provinces of India.

We had been so much delayed by the weather, that we missed seeing the wild-beast fight, which was just concluded as we entered the town. This was not so much to be regretted however, since, from all we heard, it had on this occasion proved a tame affair, though it is often most exciting. The fight between the buffalo and tiger seemed to have caused most interest, but the unfair practice of blunting the horns of the buffalo was not congenial to the fair-play feelings of the British portion of the community. Those who have witnessed a combat between a hyæna and a donkey, however, say that it exceeds in its ludicrous interest any other of these animal encounters; the donkey (as is natural) possesses the sympathies of the spectators, and usually comes off victorious.

His Majesty had prepared a grand entertainment for the evening, whither, in company with my kind host, the Assistant Resident, I was by no means sorry to repair—for the King of Oudh is necessarily associated in one's mind with exquisite sauces and viands, and we promised ourselves a first-rate dinner after our tedious journey.

The street leading to the palace was brilliantly illuminated, as was also the palace itself, while the view from the reception-rooms was most unique. The glare of lamps lighted up a square, in which was a garden fitted with the grotesque frames of the various fireworks of the evening. Birds and beasts of all descriptions were there, waiting to be let off. Meantime, extraordinary equipages came driving up in rapid succession; the magnificent coach-and-six of the King was followed by the unpretending buggy of the bold subaltern, while natives of high degree descended from gorgeously attired elephants, or sprang lightly off their prancing Arabs: the varied costumes of the different guests as they passed under a blaze of lamps added not a little to the brilliancy and novelty of the scene.

The courtyard behind contained a large tank, in which the reflection of hundreds of lamps glittered brightly. Servitors, soldiers, and officers of his *Condimental* Majesty's household, filled every available portion of the yard. The spacious reception and banqueting rooms were crowded to excess, and smelt like a perfumer's shop in which, by some accident, all the bottles had been left uncorked; while brilliantly-attired natives scratched past you, glittering with jewels, and *chevaux de frise* of sharp gold tinsel.

At last the King made his appearance, and the guests all jostled into chairs as best they might. My position, almost immediately opposite his Majesty, afforded me ample opportunity of inspecting the quantity and quality of the jewels with which his person was absolutely loaded, and which I had never seen equalled in magnificence: a rope of pearls, passing over one shoulder, was tied in a knot at his waist, from which the costly ends negligently depended; his turban and breast were covered with diamonds and other precious stones; and it was a matter of wonder that he did not sink under the heat of the room, combined with the extent of mineral productions he carried on his person. But the jewels, though worthy of great attention, did not possess nearly so much interest in my eyes as did the mode by which he renovated the burly form that they adorned. On one side of him stood the bearer of his magnificently-jewelled hookah, on the other the bearer of the royal spoon, the contents of which he was already wistfully surveying as it was mixed up by the skilful feeder into the form and consistency that his Majesty loved, and put, as a nurse would put pap, into his Majesty's mouth, which was then carefully wiped by another man, who, I presume, is called the "wiper," and who was succeeded in his turn of duty by the hookah-bearer, who gently inserted the mouthpiece between the royal lips, in order that his Majesty might fill up, by a puff of the fragrant weed, the time required for the preparation of another spoonful. This routine of feeding, wiping, and smoking was only varied when the King slowly licked his lips, which he did in a dignified manner, and with a reproachful look at the wiper, whereat the wiper might be observed to tremble: poor wiper! I dare say that, if his Majesty finds it necessary to lick his lips thrice in one meal, it is equivalent to signing poor wiper's death-warrant. But his Majesty was not the only person that licked his lips; I found myself repeatedly doing the same, but it was with the feelings of a hungry hound as he envies a more fortunate member of the pack the possession of a juicy bone. Though the royal table groaned with viands, and though I was famishing, there was nothing but sponge-cake that any but a madly imprudent person could have ventured on. The cold cutlets, fried in rancid lard, rise up before me now, an unpleasant vision of the past; and I distinctly remember the mingled disgust and horror which I felt while breaking the crust of yellowish tallow to help a gallant young officer near me, who must have endured the privations of a Sutlej campaign to enable him to eat it.

At last we discovered some drinkable champagne, and drank her Majesty's health with all the honours; after which we paid a similar compliment to his Majesty of Oudh, while all the grandees of the realm—who, sitting on chairs like ourselves, lined one side of the long range of tables, and seemed enveloped in a blaze of glistening jewels—looked as if they thought it all a very disrespectful proceeding.

There was a very loud band that played "God save the Queen," and two or three very discordant singing women, who sang what I suppose was an Ode upon Sauce, as being the Oudh national anthem. At length dinner was over, and immediately there was a rush to the windows to see the fireworks, which seemed to be all let off at once, so that it was impossible to distinguish anything but a universal twisting and whirling, and fizzing and cracking; and an elephant looked very brilliant for a moment, and then went off through his eyes with a bang, and was no more;—sham men exploded; and real men jumped into sparkling, crackling flames; and rockets and fire-balloons went up; so that, if the lessee of Vauxhall or Cremorne could let off or send up half as many things as were let off and went up on this occasion in the courtyard of the Lucknow Durbar, he would make a fortune. At last everything that had not gone in some other direction went out; the King stood at the top of the stairs, and those who were presented, after receiving tinsel necklaces from the hands of royalty, passed downstairs, and the guests went away by whatever means of conveyance they might possess—a very motley and somewhat noisy party. The mode which we made use of to return to cantonments, a distance of four miles, was rather singular, not to be recommended except on an emergency: the carriages seemed to have decreased in proportion as the number of guests had multiplied, and in some unaccountable manner many of us were left to accomplish our return as best we could. It was in vain that we attempted to persuade the seven occupants of a buggy to receive us among them—we met with a stern refusal. It was useless to supplicate a number of rich Baboos, on a handsome elephant, to help us in our difficulties; the rich Baboos laughed, and told us we might get up behind, if we liked. And so all that brilliant throng went whirling back to cantonments, and we were left disconsolately standing in the courtyard, with the probability of having to trudge home. This was not to be thought of for a moment, and we had just arrived at a pitch of desperation when a handsome carriage, with the blinds all up, and drawn by a pair of high-stepping horses, came rattling toward us. Not a moment was to be lost; we rushed frantically forward and ordered an immediate halt. In vain did the venerable coachman and determined-looking servant intimate to us that the carriage was his Majesty's; his Majesty, we assured them, was still carousing in his palace: so, depositing them both in the interior, without loss of time we mounted the box, and a moment after the high-stepping horses were dashing along the road to cantonments in brilliant style. We looked contemptuously down into the buggy, still clung to by its seven occupants, and galloped at a startling pace past the jocose Baboos, very much to the annoyance of their sedate elephant. On arriving at the cantonments we liberated his Majesty's domestics, and, ordering them to be careful how they heated his high-caste Arabs on their way back, we adjourned to a repast, to which the King's dinner had not incapacitated us from doing ample justice.

CHAPTER XVII

A Lucknow Derby-day—Sights of the city—Grand Trunk Road
to Delhi—Delhi—The Coutub—Agra—The fort and Taj—
The ruins of Futtehpore Secreh—A loquacious cicerone—
A visit to the fort of Gwalior—The Mahratta Durbar—
Tiger-shooting on foot

On the following morning, in spite of all this dissipation, we, as
well as the greater part of the population of Lucknow, were
perfectly ready to go to the races, which took place at an early
hour. After seeing the first race, which was a well-contested
one, and in which the natives seemed to take particular
interest, I went towards the town, and was amused on the way
by comparing the various conveyances used at Lucknow with
those that may be seen on the road to Epsom on the Derby-
day.

Here came dashing along a coach and six, the four leading
horses ridden by postilions, while a sporting Baboo drove the
wheelers, and two more sporting friends sat inside, and
outriders vociferously cleared the way. Here two of the King's
eunuchs jogged along in great style on camels with gaudy
trappings; after them came prancing steeds bearing some
gorgeously-dressed young princes, and then innumerable
elephants bearing all sorts of disreputable-looking characters,
the gents and blacklegs of the Lucknow community. In fact, I
recognised specimens of nearly all the various classes of
society which are to be met with at races in England, except
that none of the fair sex were to be seen on this occasion.

There can be no doubt that Lucknow is a fast place, and
contains a very sporting population; and, if I remember right,
the winning horse was the property of the turbaned owner of
a four-in-hand.

As in duty bound, we explored the whole city, but a correct
idea of the edifices with which it abounds is only to be gained
from the drawings, which are executed by the natives with the

most delicate minuteness, and convey a very correct notion of the exterior of the handsome mosques, minarets, tombs, and palaces, which render Lucknow a most interesting locality.

The Imaum Bara is said to contain the largest arched room in the world, a fact which we very much doubted. The "Gate of Constantinople" is handsome; not so La Martinère, an attempt at an Italian villa, the figures on the roof of which look as much out of keeping with the rest of the edifice as the building itself looks out of place planted in the midst of paddy-fields; it was erected by General Claude Martine, originally a French grenadier, and it is now, according to his express intentions, devoted to educational purposes.

One cannot but be struck by the singular taste of eastern potentates, who are so much more careful to provide a handsome place for their reception when dead than they are for their residence while alive. Were I the King of Oudh I should immediately move into the handsome tomb at present vacant, and leave directions to be buried in my palace.

A night's journey took us to Cawnpore, one of the largest and most disagreeable-looking stations in India. Here I resumed my acquaintance with the great trunk road under more favourable circumstances, and was not a little pleased to find how rapidly I was approaching Delhi. The carriage in which I travelled was a small palanquin on wheels, which one horse dragged along with ease; and as the stages were short, and the road very good, he was generally put into a hand-gallop at starting, and kept his pace up for the five or six miles allotted to him.

The great number of carts we passed confirmed me in thinking that this was the proper line for an experimental railway. The country is here well cultivated throughout; there is no water-carriage to contend against, and the present means of conveying goods is lamentably slow and expensive. The formation of the country affords every facility for the construction of a railway, being perfectly level throughout; whereas between Calcutta and Benares, the Rajmahal hills have

442

to be traversed: besides these many advantages, this line would be attended with a pecuniary saving to the Government, as the two or three military stations now on this road might be abolished.

The sights at Delhi are worth a visit, but are too well known to need description. In the centre of the town stands the Jumma Musjid, the St. Peter's of Mahomedans; its handsome domes and tapering minarets are built of red sandstone and white marble, a combination which is common in the edifices of this city, and which produces a most agreeable effect. From the summit of one of the minarets an extensive view is obtained.

The large and well-built city, containing 156,000 inhabitants, is enclosed by a wall, beyond which the country stretches away in appearance much like the Campagna at Rome. It is covered with ruins, which, with a few modern tombs scattered amongst prostrate slabs, give it a picturesque aspect. Through this Campagna we drove one day to see the Coutub. We passed the handsome tomb of Suftur Jung, and the mausoleums of many other worthies, the splendour of whose present resting-places betokened their former greatness. The Coutub is a tall column that is said to have been originally intended for a minaret, though the Hindoos claim it as having been erected before the Mahomedan invasion; however that may be, it is a singularly beautiful monument, and rises to a height of 260 feet. It was worth toiling up its narrow circular staircase to enjoy the view which the summit afforded of the country I had just traversed: the Jumma Musjid at Delhi was discernible in the distance, while immediately below lay the large camp of the Commander-in-Chief, the tents of which were pitched with great regularity, and looked dazzling white in the bright sun. After descending the column, I wandered awhile amidst the ruins at its foot, some of which looked very much as if they were of *Jain* origin,—and then returned to a desirable tomb, which the hospitable commissioner has converted into a delightful retreat from the noisy city.

I left Delhi with no little regret after an agreeable sojourn of a week, and rolled rapidly over the excellent road to Agra, so smooth that it was *irresistible* to the laziest horse, and 130 miles were easily accomplished in eighteen hours including stoppages.

Of Agra the passing traveller can say little, because its wonders are so inexhaustible and so interesting. The magnificent tomb at Secundra of that greatest of Mahomedan princes, Ackbar, must be left to the description already given by travellers of more leisure; so must the fort and the white marble palace which it contains, where dwelt the powerful Aurungzebe when he made Agra his capital. It was an endless source of interest to me to wander through the paved courts and under the marble columns of that glistening palace,—to look down upon the river, winding at the base of the lofty walls,—to descend into dark vaults in which were fountains and baths with water ever cool,—to creep yet lower, with a dim flickering light, into the execution chamber, and stand under the beam which had sustained the fair form of many a frail and faithless beauty,—to retreat from the stifling influence of its confined air, and return to inspect delicate little mosques, in which the Queen and her maidens used to perform their devotions, and which were as pure and chaste as the ladies were supposed to be.

The only other interesting relics in the fort are the renowned gates of Somnath, which are placed in the arsenal, and which need no description from my pen. But the greatest sight which Agra affords is the far-famed Taj Mahal: situated on the banks of the river, it is a conspicuous object from every quarter, and is as beautiful in its proportions when seen from a distance as in its details when more closely and minutely inspected: an unfailing source of gratification to the beholder, it well merits repeated visits. In its vastness, in its costly material, in its beautiful proportion, and in its delicacy of detail, it stands a noble monument of the talent which devised, and of the skill which executed it. It is said to have incessantly occupied 20,000 men for 22 years, and three million pounds sterling were expended upon it.

The intention of Shah Jehan, whose ashes it covers, was to have connected it by a marble bridge with a tomb exactly similar on the opposite side of the river, in which were to be interred the remains of his wife. This vast design he never lived to accomplish, and his son, who was of an economical turn of mind, did not consider the maternal ashes worth a further expenditure of three millions, and so Shah Jehan and his wife lie buried in one tomb, which may safely be pronounced the most magnificent in the world.

I like the Indian system of starting on a journey after dinner. When other people are going to bed, you get into your comfortable palanquin, and wake up 30 miles from your companions of the previous evening, who are only beginning to rub their eyes, when you have already actively commenced the work of exploring the sights at your destination. Thus did I inspect the old city of Futtehpore Secreh under the guidance of Busreet Alee, a garrulous old man, and a perfect specimen of a cicerone, with whom I at once plunged into the most extensive ruins I had seen in India: cloisters, colonnades, domes, walls, kiosks, and turrets, heaped together in the utmost confusion, a mass of red sandstone, except when some white marble denoted a more sacred or interesting spot as it glistened in the beams of the rising sun.

Ackbar, the founder of the spacious palaces here situated, was an exception to the general rule of Eastern potentates, and his residence must have been even more magnificent than the handsome tomb of Secundra, in which his ashes repose. The legend regarding the reason for which Futtehpore Secreh was pitched upon by the monarch as his seat of government is somewhat singular. It seems that he had long desired a successor to perpetuate his great name, and rule over his vast dominions, the possession of most of which he owed to his own strong arm and fertile genius: it was therefore a great disappointment to him that the wished-for prince did not make his appearance. Ackbar accordingly consulted Shah Selim Shurstre upon this important subject, and Shah Selim Shurstre, who lived at Futtehpore Secreh, recommended a pilgrimage to Ajmeer, which was no sooner accomplished than Ackbar became the happy father of Jehan Giri. In gratitude for so eminent a service, and in order to have the benefit of such sage advice in future cases of emergency, Ackbar left Delhi, and fixed his residence at Futtehpore Secreh, which place possessed the further advantage of being more in the centre of his recent conquests. Notwithstanding his devotion to the holy man, Ackbar was a most unorthodox Mahomedan, as the figures of animals carved upon the pillars of the palace plainly testify. These figures were sadly mutilated by his undutiful grandson, the bigoted Aurungzebe, who held all such representations in much the same horror that a Presbyterian would a picture of the Virgin.

Busreet and I went over the ladies' apartments, which must have been very cheerless, since they are entirely composed of immense slabs of red sandstone and look hard and uncomfortable. Descending from them to the level of the courtyard, Busreet took me into a narrow sort of corridor, and jabbered incessantly for some minutes. I thought I could distinguish the words "hide and seek;" but it was so very unnatural to suppose that the only words of English Busreet knew were "hide and seek," that I imagined he was repeating some Hindostanee phrase, until he dodged round corners and behind pillars, crying out as he did so, "Hide and seek! Hide and seek!"—from which I at last understood that he meant to inform me that the ladies used to play that Occidental game in Ackbar's harem; so, after a short game to show the old man that I understood him, we strolled on to a singular kiosk-like little building, my guide every now and then renewing the game and hobbling round corners despite of my remonstrances to the contrary. The little temple was the residence of the holy man, and near it a room of most extraordinary construction astonished me not a little, since I could not divine its use, and Busreet afforded no information on the subject, as he pulled my head down and whispered something in my ear, which left me in doubt whether what he told me was a secret, or whether he meant to intimate that it was a whispering gallery: its real use I afterwards discovered.

In the centre of a square room was a pillar 15 or 16 feet in height, the circular top of which was six or eight feet in diameter and had been surrounded by a stone parapet; communicating with this singular pulpit-like seat were four narrow stone passages or bridges, one from each corner of the room. In each corner a minister of the realm used to sit, only one of whom might approach their royal master at a time. Seated on this centre point high above the heads of his subjects, who crowded the room below, and approached only by the four narrow causeways, the King deemed himself secure from assassination.

It was an original idea, and, after inventing so novel a method for guarding against treachery, he deserved to die in his bed, as in fact he did.

Emerging from this singular apartment, we crossed a square, in the midst of which was placed an immense slab of stone, raised a little off the ground; on each of the four sides of this slab there were 16 squares marked on the ground like those on a chessboard.

Four ladies used to stand on the squares on each division, making sixteen in all, each party of four dressed in garments of different colour from those worn by the others. The King and his ministers sat on the slab in the middle, and the game, which was something like chess, commenced. It must have been a glorious game: the prizes were numerous and worth playing for, and one can easily imagine the crafty old King moving his Queen so as to take the lovely slave of one of his ministers, or a handsome and fashionable young noble giving check to Queen and concubine; probably the Queen could not be taken, but it must have added immensely to the interest of the game to be playing with pieces that were interested in the result.

We ascended a handsome gateway of the mosque, 120 feet in height, whence I looked over a wide expanse of level country, while the intricate maze of ruins through which we had been wandering lay spread at our feet like a map; the wall of the city is still entire, and encloses a space of six miles in circumference, the extent of this once famous place.

The courtyard of the mosque, which was at least 150 yards square, contains the white marble tomb of the holy man. It is, without exception, the most perfect little bijou imaginable. The walls are composed of immense slabs, or rather screens of marble, delicately carved and perforated, so that, while they allow a dim light to penetrate, the effect of the tracery, when viewed from the interior, is exquisite. While I was admiring this beautiful structure Busreet suddenly assured me that he was very fond of tea. As he had already made many other observations equally unconnected with the matter in hand, I merely assured him of my sympathy; when the more home-question of whether I had any tea at once enlightened me as to his meaning. I accordingly invited him to take tea with me, and we sat on the steps of the good man's tomb, and had a sociable cup together; after which I entered my palanquin, and, travelling through the heat of the day, returned to Agra in a semi-grilled condition.

Having seen most of the sights of Agra (and it has a goodly share of its own), and having made the necessary preparations for the conveyance to Bombay of our party, now four in number, we took our departure from the handsome and hospitable residence of the Lieutenant-Governor, on the evening of the 9th of March, and drove in our buggies by moonlight over rather a wild country, in rather a wild manner, arriving at the station, where our palanquins were to meet us, a little before midnight.

An Indian coolie's powers of endurance are marvellous. Our

cortège consisted of 112; and they were to carry ourselves, servant, baggage, and provisions, at the rate of thirty-five miles a night, for as many consecutive nights as we should choose to require their services.

We arrived at Dholpoor next day—looked down a magnificent well, about sixty feet in diameter, with corridors round it, and a handsome flight of stairs leading down to them—and then pushed on for Gwalior, crossing the battlefield of Maharajpore, and paying a visit to the fort perched upon the scarped rock. Some portions of the fort walls were covered with various devices in green and yellow porcelain, which added to their singular and characteristic appearance.

We visited the young Rajah in Durbar, and the difference between the Mahratta and Nepaulese Courts was most striking. The waving plumes, hussar jackets, and gold-laced pantaloons of the latter were exchanged for the simple white turban and flowing robe of the Indian senator; but though the character of their costume may have been more in accordance with our ideas of Oriental habits, there was a lamentable deficiency of intellect in their faces, and the fire and intelligence which flashed from the eye of the Highland noble were wanting in that of the Mahratta chief. After two days' agreeable sojourn at the Residency we proceeded for two or three consecutive nights over flat dreary country, spending the days in the miserable little resthouses provided for the accommodation of the traveller, and generally picking up a few partridges for breakfast.

At Goonah we had a prospect of more important game. We here fell in with a most ardent sportsman: the numerous trophies of bears and tigers with which his bungalow was adorned proved his success as well as his skill.

With him we sallied forth at about 10 a.m., some on horseback and some on an elephant, all equally indifferent to the sun, fiercely blazing in an unclouded sky, and reached a dell, the sides of which were covered with a low scrubby jungle, where sport was to be expected.

As tiger-shooting on foot is almost unheard of in the northern part of India, and is practised in the southern only, because the tiger there is a much less formidable animal than his majesty of Bengal, we were told to proceed with considerable caution by the veteran, who posted us in the most likely places, saying to one of our party, as he stationed him in the most *favourable* locality, "I put you here because the tiger is nearly sure to charge down this hill; and if he does, there will be very little chance of escape for you, as you see he has so much the advantage of you, that if you do not kill him with either barrel—and the skull of a tiger is so narrow that it is exceedingly improbable you will be able to do so—he must kill you; but I would not for the world that you should miss the sport."

Thus did this self-denying Nimrod debar himself the pleasure of being charged by a tiger, reserving it, in the kindest manner, for his guests, who but half appreciated the sacrifice he was making on their account, from their dread of themselves becoming a sacrifice to the tiger. And as they crouched behind their respective bushes they had time to brood over the appalling stories of hairbreadth escapes just recounted to them by the gallant captain, who had been particular in describing the requisites for the successful tiger-shot—the steady hand and steady nerve—admitting that these were not always efficacious, as the last tiger he had encountered had struck him on the leg, and his torn inexpressibles existed to this day to testify to it. The thoughts of this and sundry other escapes he had experienced made the blood run cold, as one imagined every rustle of the leaves to be a bristling tiger, preparing for his fatal spring.

Gradually the beaters approached nearer and nearer, and, as the circle became smaller, pea-fowl innumerable flew over our heads with a loud whirr, their brilliant plumage glancing in the sunshine like shot-silk. A few moments more, and I perceived stripes gliding rapidly behind a bush, and a shot from L—— made me suspect that our *worst* anticipations had been realised, and that we had really found a tiger—a suspicion which soon disappeared, however, as a grisly hyæna bounded away, having received a ball in his hind-quarters, which unfortunately did not prevent his retreat.

The beaters soon after appeared over the brow of the hill, and relieved us for the present from further apprehension of that charge which was to seal our fate, for the monarch of the Indian jungle had changed his location. We beat some more jungles, in the hope of finding other game, but only succeeded in bagging a deer. I had a long shot at a four-horned buck, but the smooth bore of my piece was not equal to the distance.

On our way home we came upon a cave, which, from marks in the neighbourhood, bore evident signs of containing a panther; we accordingly attempted to smoke him out by lighting quantities of straw at the mouth, but he was not to be forced out of his secure retreat, and preferred bearing an amount of smoke that would have stifled a German student.

On the following day we renewed our attempt to find a tiger, and were to a certain extent successful, as at one time we were within a few yards of him, and could see the bushes move, but he succeeded in breaking through the line of beaters; and some deer and a neelgye were all the game we could boast of, notwithstanding a perseverance and endurance of heat worthy of greater success.

The carnival at Indore—Extraordinary scene in the palace of the Holkar—A night at the caves of Ajunta—The caves of Ellora and fortress of Doulatabad—The merits of a palkee—Reflections on the journey from Agra to Bombay—Adieu to India

After a few days' more travelling over the hot dry plains of Malwa we reached its capital, Indore, where we spent some days at the hospitable mansion of the Resident, and paid a visit to the Rajah, whose palace is situated in the centre of that large and populous town. During our visit a most extraordinary scene occurred. It happened that a sort of carnival was going on; but the bonbons and bouquets of Italy are here represented by little balls containing red, purple, or yellow dust, which burst the moment they strike the object at which they are thrown, and very soon after the *row* commences two-thirds of the population are so covered with red dust that they present the most extraordinary appearance; but it is not the dust-balls which contribute so much to the dyeing of the population as the squirts full of similar coloured liquids, which are to be seen playing in every direction. Woe to the luckless individual who incautiously exhibits himself in the streets of Indore during the "Hoolie;" not that we ran any risk upon the occasion of our visit to the Rajah, as we were on that account tabooed, and could laugh at our ease at the rest of the claret-coloured world. Here a woman passed spotted like a coach-dog: she had just come in for a spent discharge, and had escaped the deluge, which her puce-coloured little boy had received so fully that his whole face and person seemed to partake of the prevailing tint; while yonder old greybeard is dusting his moustache from the red powder which tinges it in strong contrast to the rest of his sallow countenance.

After going through the ceremony of squatting on the floor of the Durbar—our seven pair of unruly legs all converging to a common centre, from our inability to double them under us, as his Majesty did—we adjourned to the hall below to witness the "Hoolie" in safety. On each side of the courtyard was a sort of garden-engine, one filled with a purple and the other with a light-red fluid. The King's body-guard were now marched in and divided into two parties, each sitting under one of the garden-engines. At the main gateway of the courtyard stood two elephants, with tubs of coloured liquid before them. At a given signal the gallant troops were exposed to a most murderous cross-fire, which they were not allowed to return: both garden-engines began playing upon them furiously, and the elephants, filling their trunks, sent the contents far and wide over the victims, who crouched down and bore in patience the blood-red storm. At the same moment that a dexterously-applied squirt whisked off some individual's turban, a fountain from the other side playing into his eyes and mouth prevented him from recovering it until some more fortunate neighbour, suffering perhaps from ear-ache, received the claret-coloured salvo with such violence that, if it failed to drive away the pain altogether, it must have rendered him a martyr to that complaint for the rest of his life.

After getting a thorough soaking they were sprinkled all over with a fine red powder, which, caking upon them, completed the ceremony by rendering them the most muddy, sticky-looking objects imaginable, as they withdrew from the presence of the young Rajah, after receiving pawn.

We were now offered balls of powder: had we thrown one at his Majesty, which some of his household seemed very anxious we should do, nothing could have saved us from a deluge. To commence the game upon the royal platform is the signal of indiscriminate warfare throughout the whole palace; the now passive troops would then have been allowed to retaliate, the garden-engines would have been stormed and captured by opposing squadrons, and the battle would have raged furiously until dark: whereas now, company of soldiers after company were ordered in to be shot down like sheep. We, however, were contented with seeing each party come in white and go out red, without wishing to go out red ourselves; besides which, we should have been outnumbered, and Britons, for the first time, would have been obliged to beat a retreat with tarnished honour as well as tarnished jackets.

The usual ceremony of presenting scents, spices, and garlands, having terminated, we left the young King, much pleased with his intelligence and good-nature: though only seventeen, he is a stranger to those vices which are generally inherent in natives, and inseparable from their courts.

We were ten days on our journey to the caves of Ajunta, having spent two or three at the hill fort of Aseerghur, a characteristic Mahratta stronghold; it is perched 700 feet above the plain, and just capacious enough to contain a regiment, who must find some difficulty in climbing its rocky steep approach, up which, however, the ponies of the garrison scramble nimbly enough.

We galloped over one afternoon from Furdapore to the caves of Ajunta, and were delighted with their romantic situation high up the rocky glen terminating in a waterfall, and so narrow, gloomy, and silent that it harmonized well with these mysterious caverns, in one of which, more free than the rest from bats, we determined to pass the night; and here, surrounded by staring Bhuddas and rampant elephants, and gods and goddesses making vehement love, according to the custom of such gentry, we had a most comfortable tea preparatory to turning in: spreading my blanket under the nose of a huge seated figure of Bhood, and guarded by two very tall individuals in faded painting, which, as they had watched over Bhood for twenty centuries, must have been well competent to perform the same kind office for me, I was soon comfortably asleep, my head pillowed on a prostrate little goddess, whom I was very reluctant to leave when daylight warned us to proceed upon the work of examining the wonders of the Rock Temples of Ajunta.

So much has already been written on the interesting subject of the caves of Ajunta, that they are more or less familiar to everyone, or, if not already familiar, are destined soon to become so, thanks to the skill and energy of Captain Gill, who is at present engaged in making copies of all the paintings. These will form a splendid collection, and some of them have already been sent to England, and placed in the collection at the East India House. It was doubly delightful to us, who had just previously examined the originals, to look over the portfolios of this talented draftsman.

Ere we left the village of Ajunta we visited its neat whitewashed mosque: the association connected with it must be replete with interest to the Englishman, when he calls to mind that in it the Duke of Wellington—then Sir Arthur Wellesley—wrote his despatches immediately previous and subsequent to the victory of Assaye.

The caves of Ellora are two days' journey from those of Ajunta, and are much more cheerfully situated on the face of a hill commanding an extensive view over a more smiling country than is usually to be met with in the Deccan.

It is difficult to say which set of caves are most worth seeing; differing in many respects, they may be said to afford equal attraction to the traveller. Ellora can boast of the wonderful "Kylas;" Ajunta of those most interesting frescoes which carry the art of painting back to an unknown period, but which at Ellora have been almost totally obliterated by the ruthless and fanatical zeal of Aurungzebe.

A few miles from the caves of Ellora frowns the rock fortress of Doulatabad, a conspicuous object from every side, and we soon discovered its interior to be as singularly interesting as its exterior was formidable and imposing. The rock itself is a pyramid rising abruptly to a height of 700 feet above the village which nestles at its base, while it is scarped all round to the broad moat by which it is encircled, forming a sheer precipice of 100 or 150 feet in depth.

Passing through a massive gateway which led into the town,

we entered the fort by a similar approach, and crossing the moat by a narrow bridge we plunged into a dark hole directly opposite; then passing by torchlight through some small caves which were entered by very low portals, we began to ascend the inclined plane which wound up the interior of the rock, and which gradually became steeper till it ended in a flight of steps, our guides lighting us on our uncertain path, until we emerged into daylight by a large iron trap-door, pierced with innumerable small holes, the object of which, as well as of a groove in the rock communicating with the subterranean passage, was to enable the garrison, by filling the passage with smoke and flame, to suffocate and blind the besiegers should they ever succeed by any accident in penetrating thus far—in itself, as it seemed to me, a very improbable contingency. We clambered up the face of the rock to its summit, whence we had an extensive view of the arid plains of the Deccan.

Arungabad is the first station which we had visited in the dominions of the Nizam. We were now approaching the confines of civilization, and it became necessary to part with our palkees and the bearers, who had accompanied us from Agra. A separation from the latter was easily borne, and they, on their part, were no doubt glad to get rid of the burdens they had been carrying for the last month. But to bid adieu for ever to one's palkee is a severe trial; and no wonder, for to a man not in a hurry it is the most luxurious and independent means of travelling conceivable.

If judiciously arranged it contains everything the traveller can want—a library, a cellar, a soda-water range, a wardrobe, a kitchen; in fact, there is no limit to the elasticity of a palkee. My plan was, surreptitiously, to add a new comfort every day, and the unsuspecting coolies carried me along as briskly as if my palkee contained nothing but myself, and never seemed to feel the additional weight, upon the principle of the man who could lift an ox by dint of doing so every morning from the time when it was a calf.

Then the delightful feeling of security, and the certainty that your bearers won't shy, or come into collision, or go off the rails, or otherwise injure your nerves or bones. You are independent of hotels and hospitality. If the traveller in India depended upon the former, he would pass many a night with the kerbstone for his pillow, if he had not courage to claim the latter—which, be it remembered, he is certain to receive abundantly at the hands of the Burra Sahib. A modest man has his palkee; and for lack of courage on the one hand, and a resthouse on the other, he orders himself to be set down for the night by the wayside, and, shutting the doors towards the road, after boiling the water and making tea with the apparatus contained in his pantry, he lights his lamp, reads for an hour, pulls a light shawl over him, turns round, and goes to sleep as soundly as if he were sumptuously couched in Belgravia.

If the palkee be a good one, it defies weather; but I admit it is not pleasant, on a dark night, to be carried along a slippery road with a careless set of bearers.

During the whole period of our journey since we had left Agra, with one or two breaks in its ordinary routine, we seemed to have been passing a monotonous existence at the same small and uncomfortable bungalow. It consists of two rooms; in front is a tope of trees; behind are a few low sandstone or trap hills, some scrubby bushes climbing up the sides, out of which a partridge may easily be flushed: for the rest, the view extends over a boundless plain, assuming during the heat of the day a light yellow colour, at which period the coolies are all asleep in the verandah, snoring in an infinite and interesting variety of notes and keys.

At sunset we take a constitutional, followed by our portable residences, into which, after a romantic tea-drinking by the roadside, we turn in for the night, awaking at daylight to find ourselves thirty miles nearer to our journey's end, in a bungalow precisely similar to the one we had lately quitted, and containing the same rickety table, greasy with the unwiped remains of the last traveller's meal, which the book will inform you was eaten a month ago—the same treacherous

457

chairs, which look sound until you inadvertently sit upon them—the same doubtful-looking couch, from which the same interesting round little specimens emerge, much to the discomfort of the occupant—the same filthy bathroom, which it is evident the traveller a month ago did not use—the identical old kitmutgar or bungalow-keeper, who looks as uncivilized as the bungalow itself, and seems to partake of its rickety and dirty nature—the same clump of trees before, and the same desert plain behind;—all tend to induce the belief either that you have never left the bungalow in which you spent the previous day, or that some evil genius has transported the said bungalow thirty miles for the express purpose of persecuting you with its horrors and miserable accommodation.

Thus are 700 miles insensibly accomplished in a month by the traveller, who only passes a dreamy existence in dâk bungalows, to be roused into violent action on his arrival at some sporting vicinity, a large cantonment, a native Court, rock temples, or other excitements, which must occur in the experiences of the Indian traveller.

I went seventy miles in a bullock hackery, the most unpleasant mode of travelling I conceive that can exist; then one hundred miles in a rickety phaëton with a pair of horses, which was in a slight degree less intolerable; and after visiting Mahabuleshwa, the hill station of Bombay, I reached that mercantile emporium itself, not a little pleased at seeing the sea on the English side of India. I was disappointed with the far-famed Bay; but perhaps it is difficult to do justice to scenery after so much wandering, when the most interesting view is the sight of home. Certainly one's impressions of a place are regulated in a great degree by the circumstances under which it is visited. Had Bombay been the port of debarkation instead of embarkation, the bay would have been lovely and the various points of view enchanting; as it was, the prettiest object to my perverted vision was the "Malta" getting up her steam to paddle me away from that land, whose marble tombs and rock-cut temples will continue to afford attractions to the traveller when its Princes no longer exist sumptuously to entertain them, and whose towering mountains will still disclose fresh wonders when that last independent state which now extends along their base shall have been absorbed into one vast empire.

EDITOR'S NOTE

Laurence Oliphant was one of the most extraordinary characters of that most extraordinary of periods, the Victorian age. The familiar of Palmerston and Bismarck, on occasion companion to Garibaldi and to Omar Pasha, he led a life of restless spirit and bright event. His travels took him to India and Nepal, to Russia, China and Japan, to the USA and Canada, throughout Europe, and to Palestine, where the side of him that craved rest attempted to settle. Travel writer, novelist, diplomat, agent, reporter extraordinary, sexual mystic, society lion, Oliphant was a phenomenon.

He was born in South Africa, in the Cape Colony, in 1829, and following his father's appointment as Chief Justice in Ceylon he was raised partly in England, with visits to France, Germany and Switzerland, and partly in Ceylon, where in 1848 he became his father's private secretary. He was called to the bar there, but appears to have been temperamentally ill cut out for a humdrum professional life, and when Jung Bahadoor invited him to Nepal he did not hesitate to accept. That journey, made (1850–51) when he was in his early twenties, produced his first travel book, *A Journey to Katmandu*. Published by John Murray in May 1852, it sold two thousand copies in the first ten days, and proved a substantial success.

The Russian journey, undertaken with Oswald Smith, the scion of a prominent banking family, followed shortly. It was originally conceived as a fishing and shooting trip to Russian Lapland, but complications with Russian customs led to a change of plan and, fortunately for travel literature, a substantial change of route. His travels down the Volga and the Don to the Black Sea not only provided Oliphant with the material for *The Russian Shores of the Black Sea* (1853), a wry, colourful and sharply-observed narrative in the new mould of Kinglake's *Eothen*, but also made him a man of the moment. Tensions were mounting between Britain and Russia; and by the time Oliphant's book had gone into its fourth impression (within nine months) the Crimean War had been declared, on 28 March 1854. "One morning early in 1854," writes Oliphant's biographer Philip Henderson, "Laurence was startled by the clattering of a mounted orderly, who reined his mount at the door of his lodging in Half Moon Street. The orderly carried a despatch from Lord Raglan's chief of staff requesting his immediate presence at the Horse Guards—that is, the old War Office. The Crimean War had just broken out, and [...] Laurence had become something of an authority on that area." The young man did not hesitate to map out an entire plan of campaign to the general staff, emphasizing what he had already written in *The Russian Shores* concerning Sebastopol's undefended state on the landward side; and later, in the Crimea as a war correspondent, he had the mixed satisfaction of being told by Sir John Burgoyne, who had been present at the Horse Guards meeting, that his information concerning the defences had indeed been correct, but that the British forces, failing to act on it quickly enough, had allowed the Russians time to fortify the town, with the result that Sebastopol had to be subjected to a protracted and gruelling siege.

By his mid-twenties, then, Laurence Oliphant was not only the author of two travel books that have effortlessly stood the test of time, but was also a man with a reputation for scenting out trouble. He had acquired a taste for travel, for challenges, for danger; and was satisfied in every respect when James Bruce, 8th Earl of Elgin took him on his mission to China and Japan in the late 1850s. This mission (after detouring to the Mutiny-torn India of 1857) saw the bombardment and capture of Canton and displays of gunboat diplomacy on the Peiho river, and sealed the Treaty of Tientsin of June 1858, which enforced Anglo-French aims to open up China more fully to a European presence. From there the mission proceeded to Japan, recently "opened" by the USA after a centuries-old tradition of tolerating no greater contact with the West than token presences by missionaries and traders. Might it not be, wondered Oliphant in his *Narrative of the Earl of Elgin's Mission to China and Japan* (1859), that being "opened" would prove a mixed blessing? Into the mouth of a Japanese aristocrat he put this arresting argument: "'We desire nothing which we have not got. It has not been proved to us that railroads and electric telegraph make people happier. We tried the Christian religion, and it led to the destruction of thousands of our countrymen. We do not think our civilization would be increased by a knowledge of the latest improvements in gunnery, or the latest invention for the destruction of our fellow creatures. [...] At present our subjects are peaceable and well-conducted, of an honest and simple nature, not given to brawling and quarrelling; but from what we have seen of the Europeans who man the ships coming to our country, we do not think this simplicity and tranquillity in our seaports would be likely to continue.'" It was ironic, no doubt, that on 5 July 1861, when the man who tried so hard to sympathize with the Japanese point of view had finally achieved an official diplomatic posting and was first secretary at the British legation in Yeddo (as Tokyo was then called), Oliphant should narrowly escape death in an attack by Japanese swordsmen on the British diplomats.

His taste for troubleshooting remained. He went to the Prussian war with Denmark in 1864, and to the Franco-Prussian War of 1870-71. But he also increasingly found time, in his thirties and forties, for steadier, quieter pursuits. In the latter half of the 1860s he served for three years as a Liberal Member of Parliament. He published a well-received satirical novel, *Piccadilly*, in 1870. And on 8 June 1872 he married. With his bride, Alice le Strange, he lived (in the words of his second wife Rosamond Dale Owen, though he made similar assertions to others) "without claiming the rights of a husband"; and indeed a notion of sexual purity that admitted auto-eroticism but not intercourse gained an extraordinary hold on Oliphant's mind, which increasingly tended to mysticism in his middle years. In the latter half of the 1860s he had spent an experimental period in the US under the guidance of the English-born American spiritualist Thomas Lake Harris (1823–1906), founder of the Brotherhood of the New Life, and it was to Harris's community at Brocton that he returned with his wife shortly after their marriage. When Harris moved to Santa Rosa (in that favourite playground of the sectarian and peculiar, California), Alice but not Laurence was summoned to go with him, in 1876; and there she experienced the "deep spiritual experiences" that could be afforded by a man who declared himself to be the incarnation of Christ's Second Coming. There, on that lunatic fringe of life, going out to California in 1878 to discover what was becoming of his wife, we find Laurence Oliphant once more, approaching fifty—the man who could write in his twenties books of such robust sense, wit and discernment.

One substantial adventure still lay before Oliphant. While his ideas on Jews were tainted by the widely-shared prejudices of his times, he nonetheless had thoughts of enabling the oppressed Jews of Europe to settle Palestine that have long assured him a deserved place among the pioneers of Zionism. For his views on the subject, his campaigns and efforts, the reader is referred to the biographies mentioned below. What is worth stressing here is that he had a very real and personal sense of Palestine. Both Laurence and Alice Oliphant developed a profound affection for the region, choosing to build a home in the Carmel range inland from Haifa. "With the assistance of the Druses," writes Henderson, "the Oliphants built their house and laid out a terrace. Digging the foundations, they came upon massive cut blocks of stone, cornices, a coin of one of the Constantines, tesseræ, pottery and glass. They were able to make use of an antique cistern on the site as well as a tomb near the house as a wine cellar. On the roof they erected leaf huts for their guests, and though they aspired to nothing more than a summer cottage, to the people of Dalieh it appeared palatial. In fact, the Oliphants' house soon became one of the sights of Carmel." And so, indeed, it remained, with memorabilia of the eccentric couple, who were held in respectful memory, until the modern troubles that began in the late 1940s swept away this evidence of early English support.

Laurence Oliphant, who remarried in 1888 following the death of Alice and died of lung cancer on 23 December of the same year, surely led one of the most curious of 19th century lives. The tributes to his personality were legion. "He seemed exceptionally sane," wrote the American Henry Adams in his *Autobiography*, "and peculiarly suited for country houses, where every man would enjoy his company, and every woman would adore him." Alexander Kinglake, impressed by Oliphant but alarmed by his susceptibility to the charlatan of the Brotherhood, wrote to John Blackwood: "He has a real genius for alighting upon the spots where the interests of the world's drama gather, and I trust with you that his charm and his cleverness will somehow deliver him from the redoubtable Harris." The finest of Oliphant is in the two travel books collected in the present volume, but those who wish to know more about this remarkable man are referred to Philip Henderson: *The Life of Laurence Oliphant* (London, 1956), a lively and colourfully-written biography, and the more soberly academic *Laurence Oliphant 1829–1888* by Anne Taylor (Oxford, 1982).

Michael Hulse